# WALKABOUT EUROPE

Cliff Roles

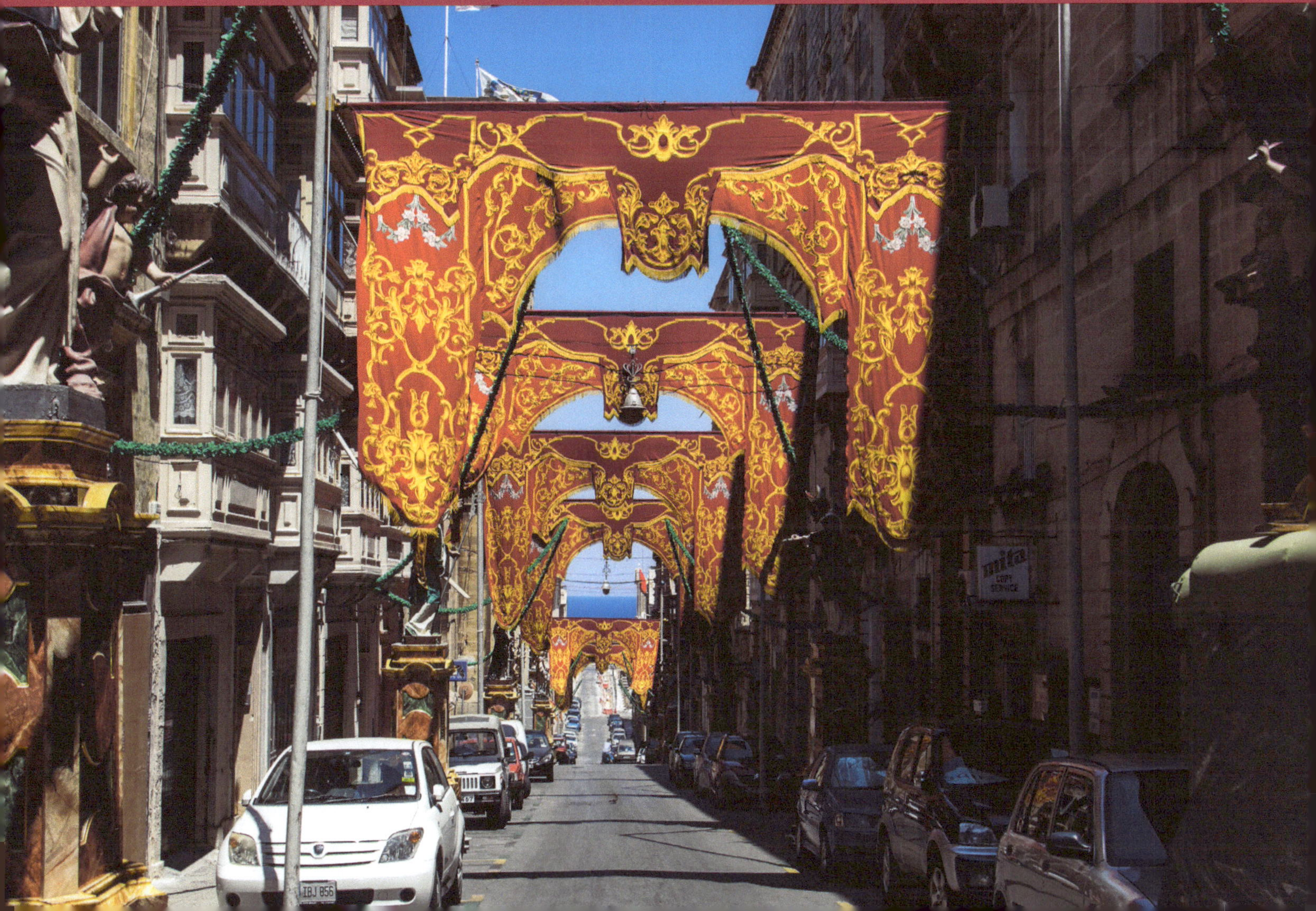

Published by Bardolf & Company

*Walkabout Europe*

ISBN 978-1-938842-21-4


Bardolf & Company
5430 Colewood Pl
Sarasota, FL 34232
tel. 941-232-0112
www.bardolfandcompany.com

Printed in the United States of America

*Front Cover: Warsaw at night*
*First page: Malta*
*Opposite: Malta*
*Contents pages: Crete*

*Back-cover photo credit: Brian David Braun, who sadly left us in September 2014 and will be sorely missed.*

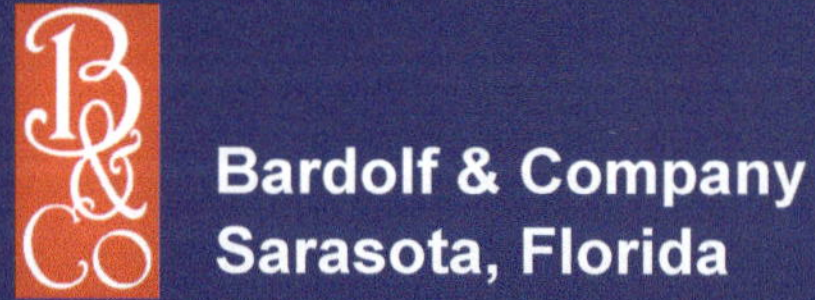

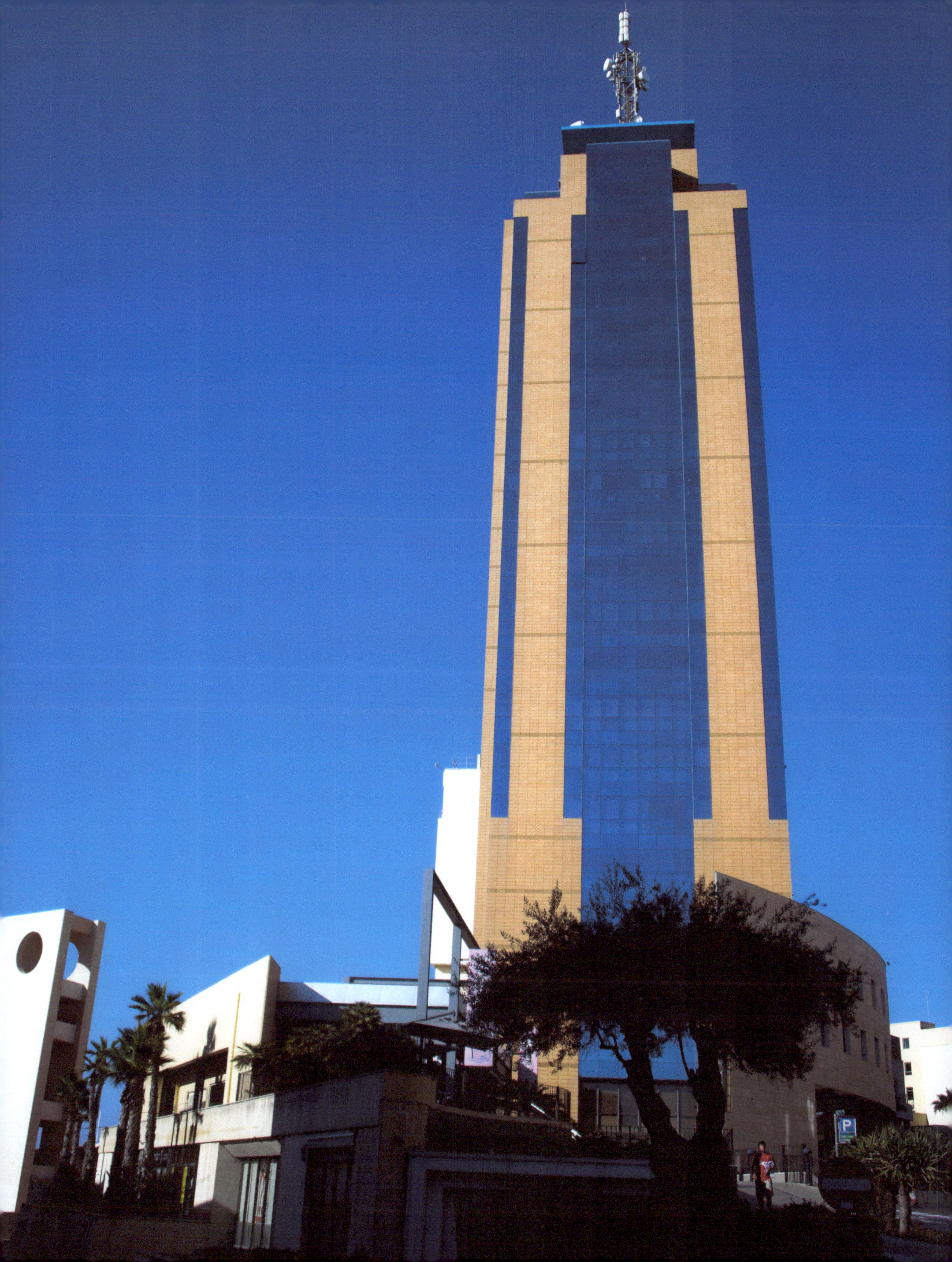

# CONTENTS


INTRODUCTION.....7

1 MALTA.....10

2 CATANIA.....16

3 CRETE.....20

Street Hustlers.....28

4 SANTORINI.....30

5 TEL AVIV.....38

Transportation.....44

6 JERUSALEM.....46

7 THE DEAD SEA.....54

8 BUCHAREST.....58

Arcades.....64

9 BRASOV.....66

10 ISTANBUL.....72

11 SOFIA.....80

Churches and Cathedrals.....86

12 KRAKOW.....88

13 THE JEWISH GHETTO.....94

Love Locks.....98

14 WARSAW.....100

15 VILNIUS.....106

16 RIGA ..... 110
17 TALLINN ..... 118
Old and New ..... 124
18 HELSINKI ..... 126
19 BERLIN ..... 132
Kitch ..... 138
20 HAMBURG ..... 140
21 COLOGNE ..... 144
22 FRANKFURT ..... 148
Old and New Friends ..... 150
Acknowledgments ..... 152
Final Tally ..... 153
Postscript ..... 154

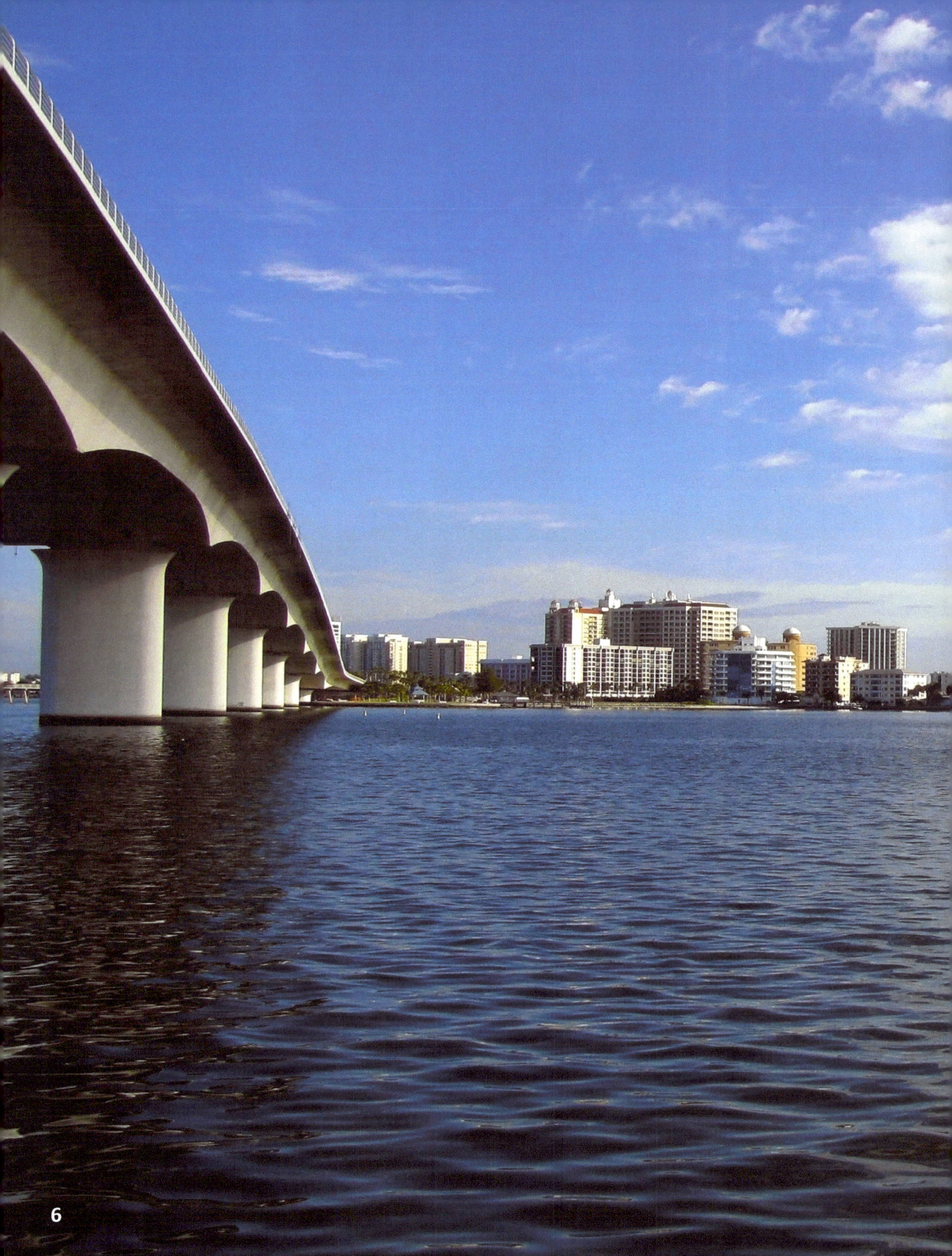

# INTRODUCTION

I've had a lot of careers in my life: rock and roll promoter, actor, circus ringmaster, to name just a few. I became a professional photographer in 2009, and discovered that I could make a living with it in Sarasota, where I've lived for the last twelve years, shooting all types of events, from galas and stage plays to concerts and nonprofit fundraisers.

I knew I wasn't the best photographer in the world, but I have the ability to shoot from the hip, so to speak. As an event photographer, you don't have time to prepare a picture for an hour; you have to do it on the fly and get the best shot of people in fractions of a second—unposed, unstaged—spontaneously.

Another thing that helped me was that my becoming a professional photograper coincided with the expansion of social media, in particular Facebook. Facebook and I have come up together and I have really profited from the fact that people have fallen in love with our social media. People hire me in part because I've got almost 5,000 FB friends, and they want to benefit from the exposure they receive when I post my photos on my gallery.

There is one drawback. With Sarasota being a tourist town with a big winter season, you can work nine months of the year like crazy and really earn money, but it all stops in June. The place empties until October, and like a teacher, you're essentially unemployed for a good three months.

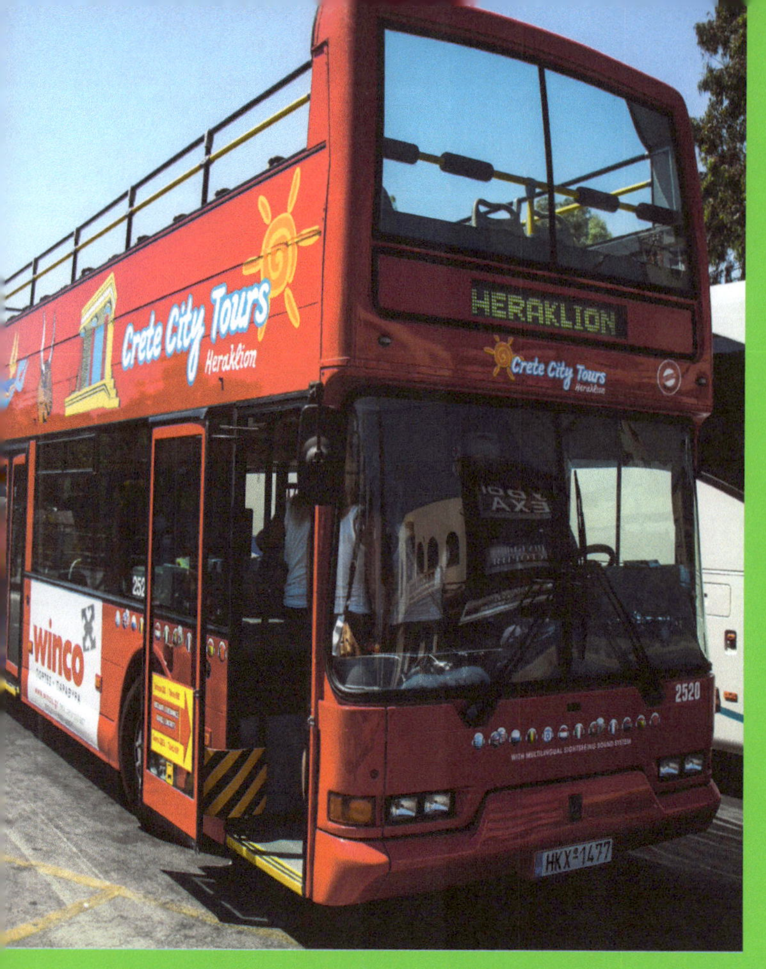


I sat around in the off season of 2012 and missed the opportunity to go to London and photograph the Olympic Games. After that I decided I wouldn't let it happen again and started to prepare to go to Europe the next summer. Coincidentally, my nephew was getting married on the island of Malta in early July, and I figured it would be a good jumping-off point.

So I challenged myself to go wherever the camera would take me. The only stipulation was that I wouldn't visit any places I had seen before. I had lived in Germany for 28 years, promoting music acts, and I had traveled extensively during that time on a company expense account. Now I was going to do it on limited funds and in the rough. I knew I wanted to go to the Greek island of Santorini on the recommendation of my friend David Breitbarth, and I also wanted to see Israel. Beyond that I had no definite plans about which cities to visit. I planned to involve my Facebook friends in the trip by posting photos as I went along. They'd tell me which ones they liked, and I would try to capture what I learned from them on the next leg of my journey.

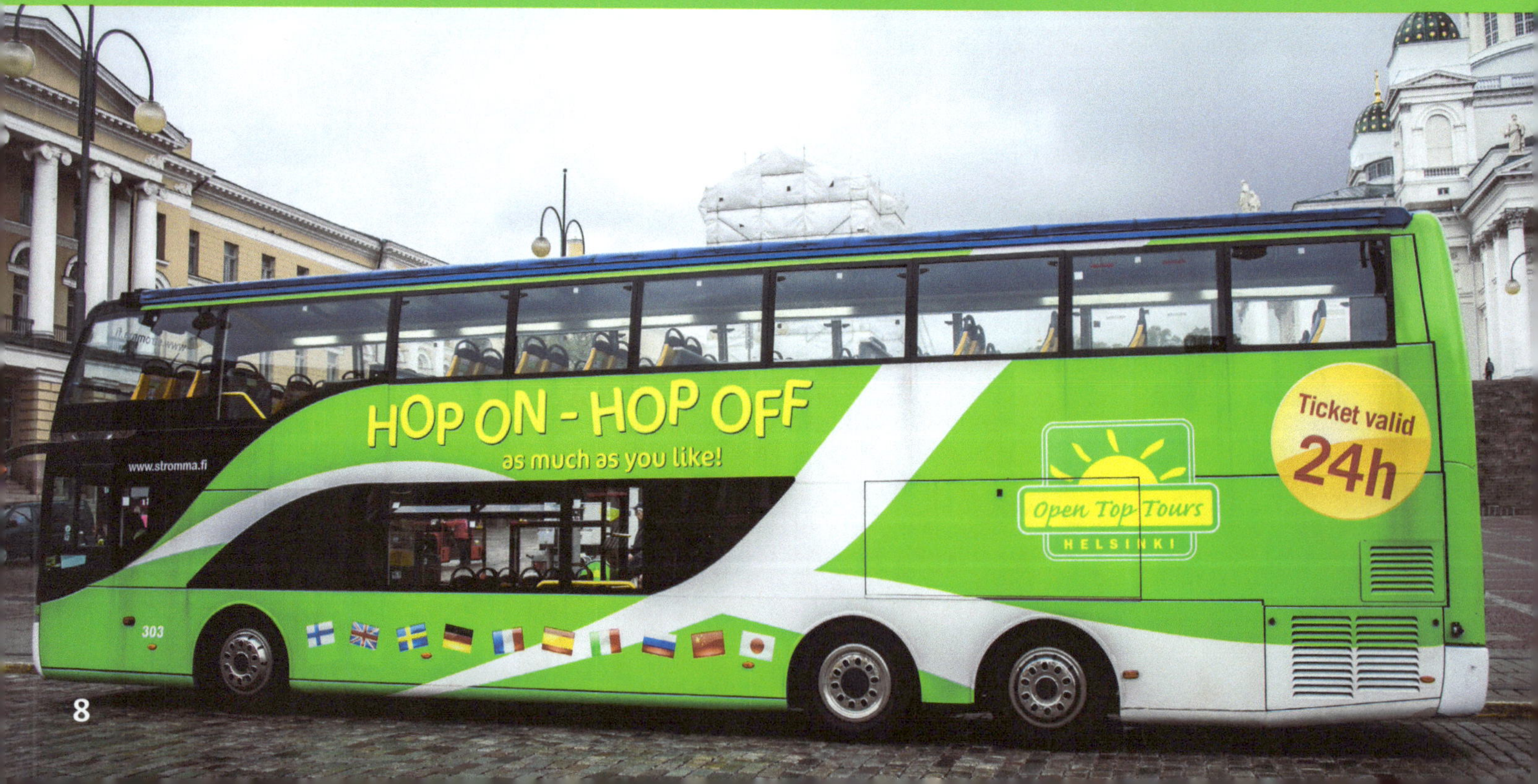

So I went walkabout, as they say in Australia. I was on the road for seven weeks—53 days to be exact—and visited 22 cities in 15 countries. Fortunately, getting around as a tourist

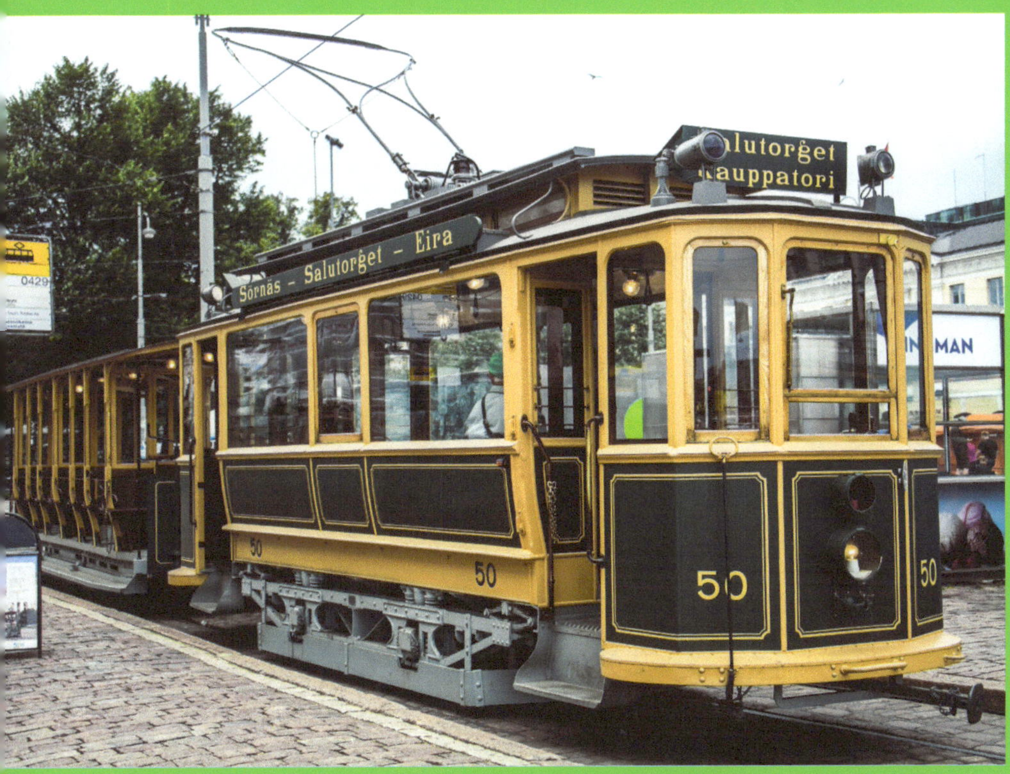


in Europe is not that difficult, and I had plenty of help. Every city has excellent public transportation. My favorite were the Hop On – Hop Off buses, which follow predetermined routes. You can use them any time they come by. You buy a 24-hour ticket for about 35 Euros. In some cities, the ticket comes with a river cruise, which is another great way to see a town.

Another mode of transportation was the little pedicabs manned by enterprising students who need some extra spending money. For 10 Euro, they'll take you around town and describe it all.

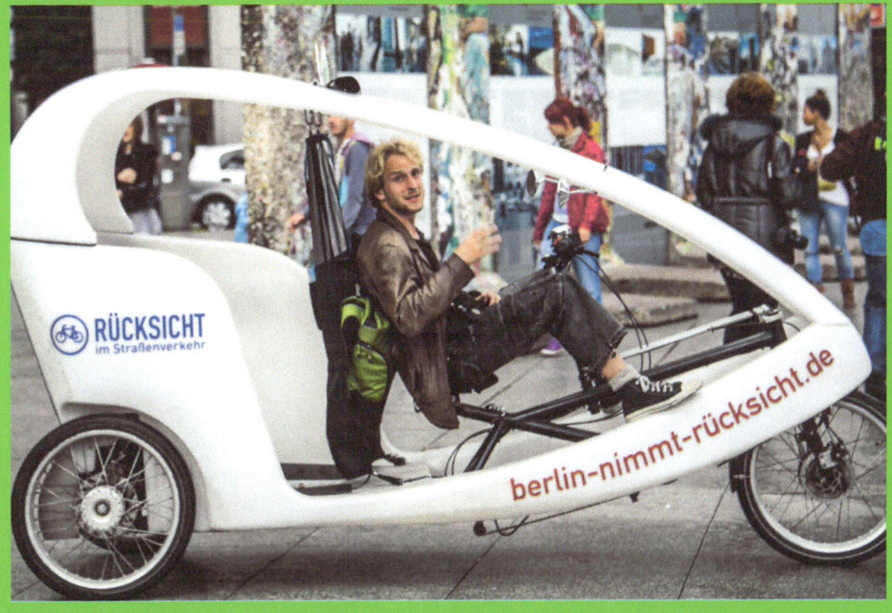


I didn't count the miles I walked, although my feet did get sore from time to time. I enjoyed some aspect of every city I visited. I aimed my camera at people and places that captured my interest and took my pictures as the spirit moved me. To my surprise, I felt safe everywhere I went, even at night. Maybe I was just lucky, or maybe I avoided the dangerous parts of town with some second sense of what was good for me. But I think European cities are perhaps safer than many American towns. At any rate, I had such a wonderful experience that I decided to do the same thing the following summer and go walkabout in Australia and New Zealand.

In the meantime, here's a sampling of my European adventure. If looking at these pictures gives you just a fraction of the pleasure and fun I had shooting them, putting this book together will have been more than worth it.

Cliff Roles
Sarasota, December 2014

# 1
# MALTA

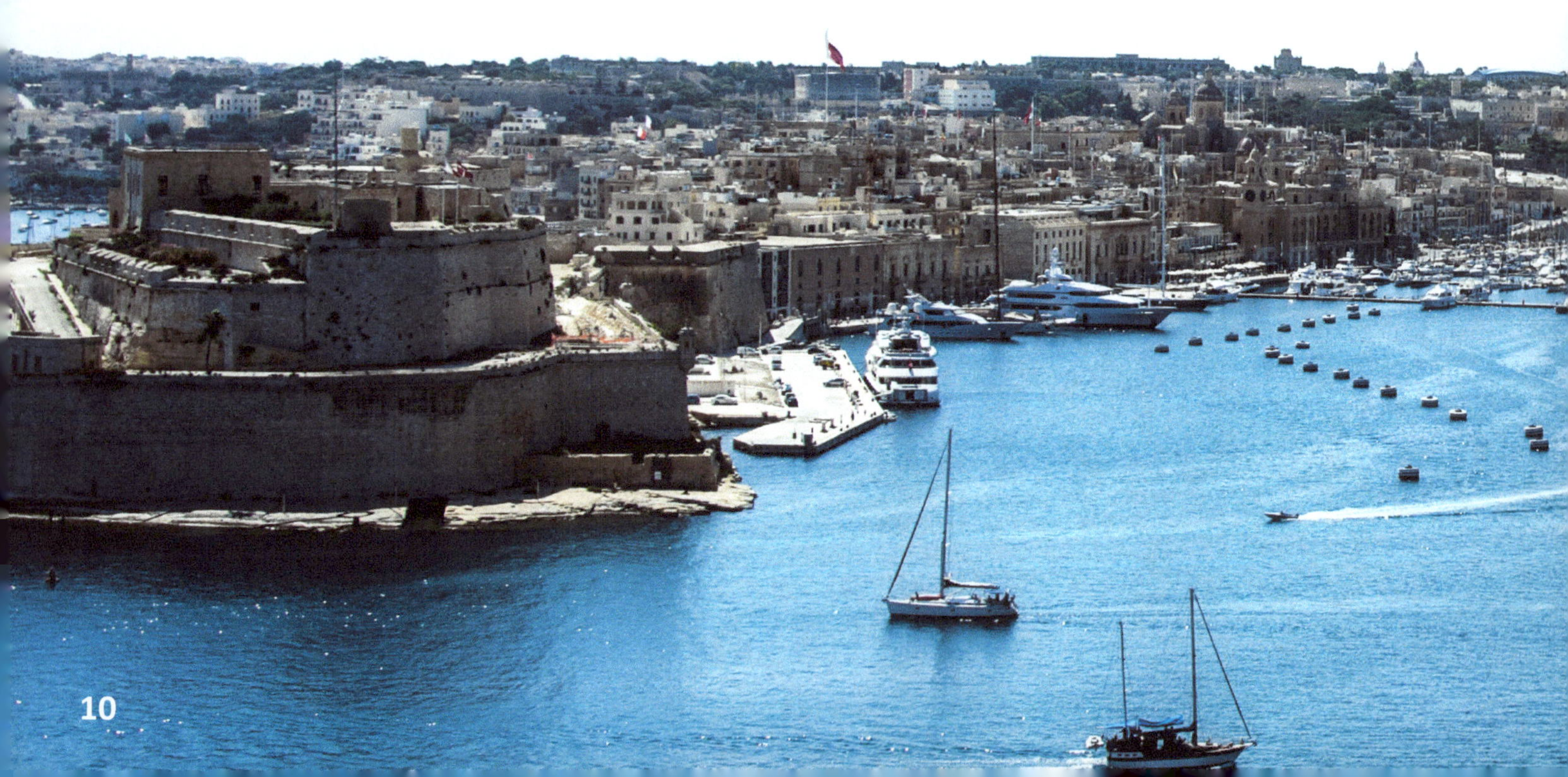

The island of Malta was the beginning of my walkabout. My brother's son had decided to get married there, and we all flew there from London.

The Republic of Malta is actually an archipelago of seven islands about 50 miles south of Sicily and 176 miles east of Tunesia. Because of its strategic location in the Mediterranean Sea, it has been an important naval base since antiquity, seen a lot of wars and changed hands many times. It has been ruled by the Phoenicians, Romans, Moors, Normans, the Knights of St. John, the Spanish, French and most recently, the British. England administered from 1814 until 1964 when Malta finally gained its independence. It became a republic ten years later and joined the European Union in 2004.

We flew Jet Blue into Malta's capital, Valetta, and stayed in the nearby suburb of St. Julian. I had fun touring the city. Valetta has monuments everywhere. I didn't know where I was going or what I was doing—I just wanted to get to know the island.

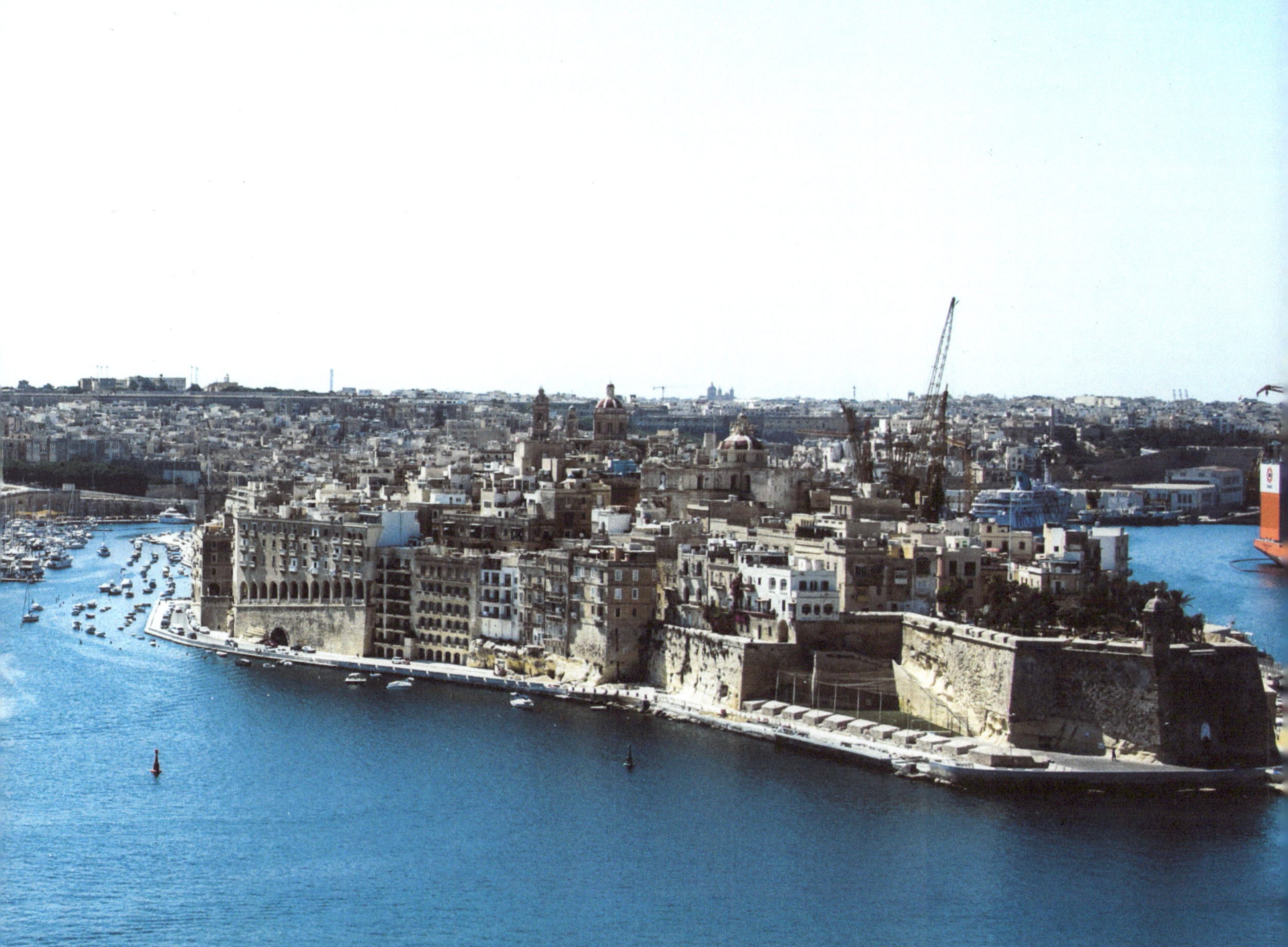

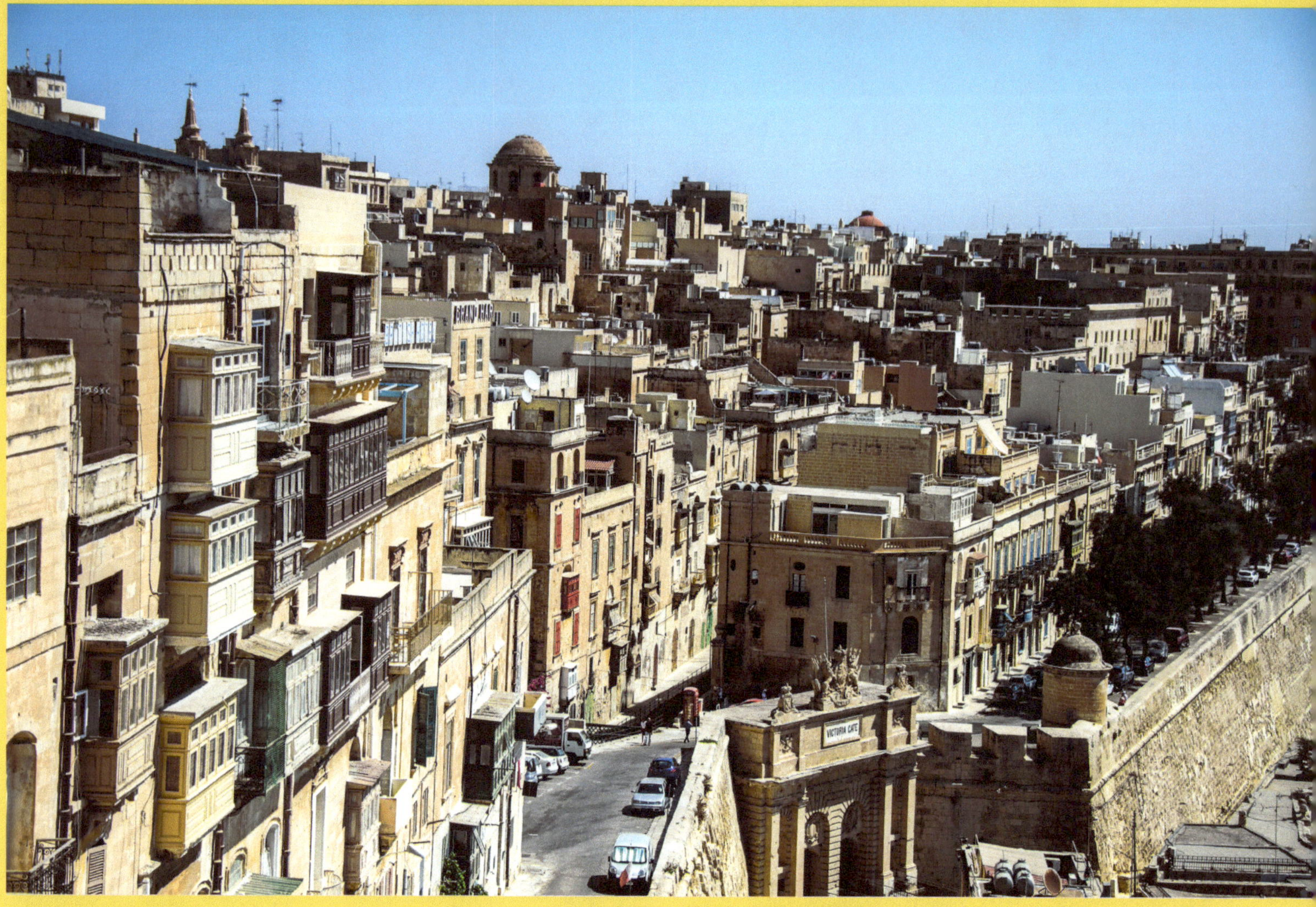

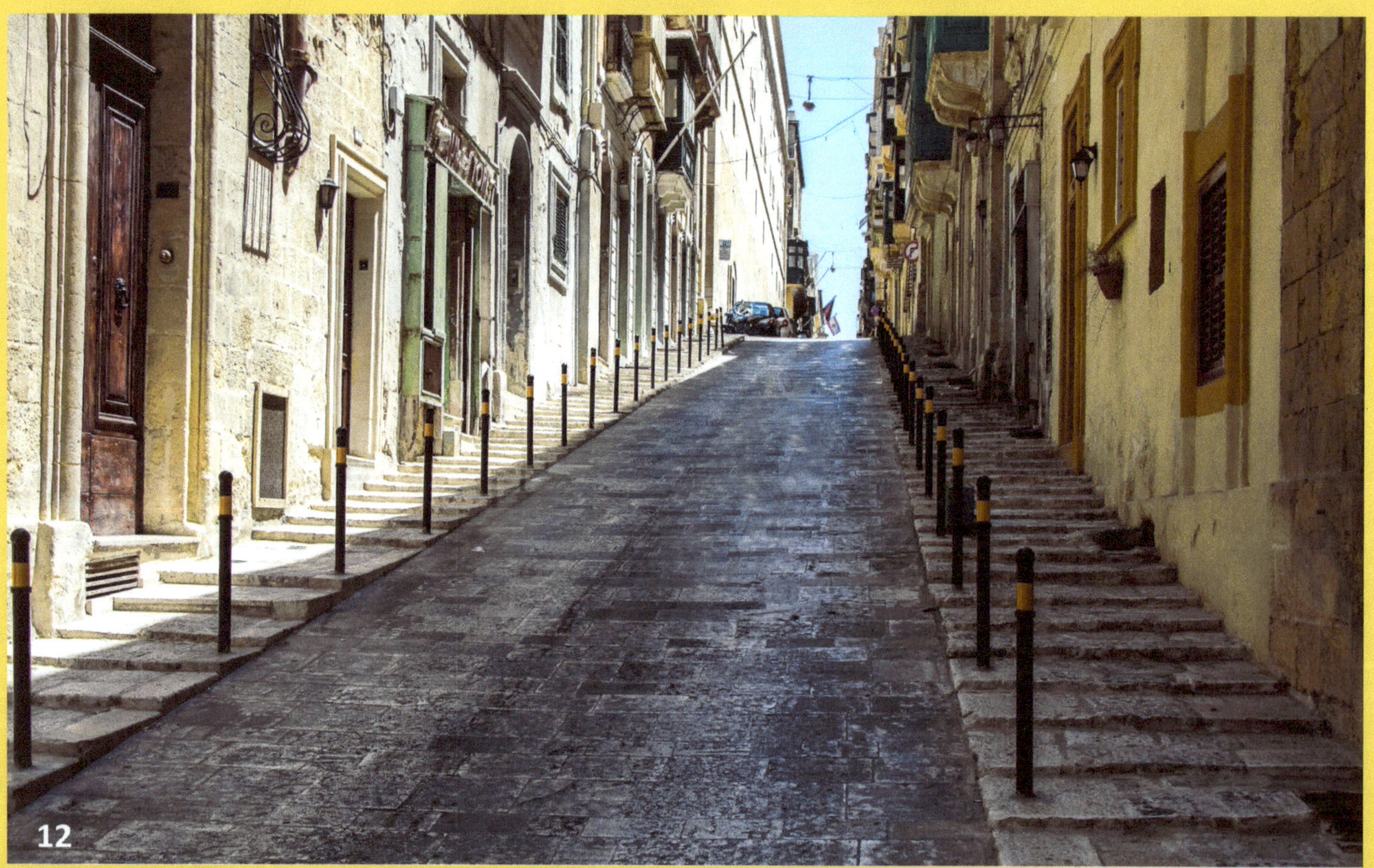

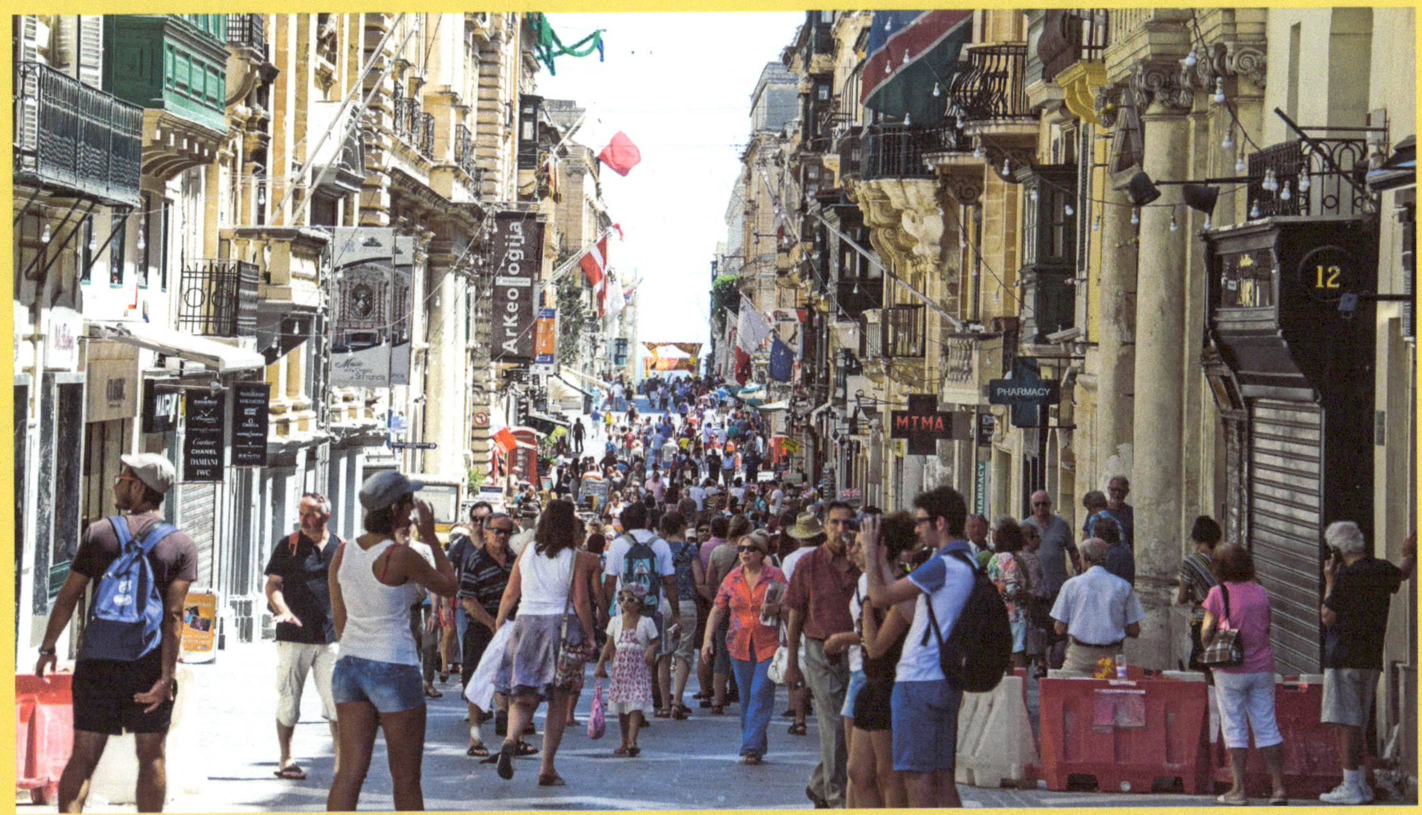


The architecture shows both African and Ottoman influences. The Turkish balconies on the sandstone buildings in the photo on the opposite page are a good example. I took the picture beneath it because I loved the straight lines. I think it may have been early on a Sunday afternoon, and the streets were empty. There was nothing going on. Maybe it was siesta time.

What struck me most about Malta was how British it felt. Cars drive on the left side of the road. I suppose because it has been part of the British Empire for so long and is easily accessible from the United Kingdom by air, it caters to a northern clientele. A lot of UK men's clubs fly out for boozing and bachelor weekends. There are British sitcoms and sports on every TV

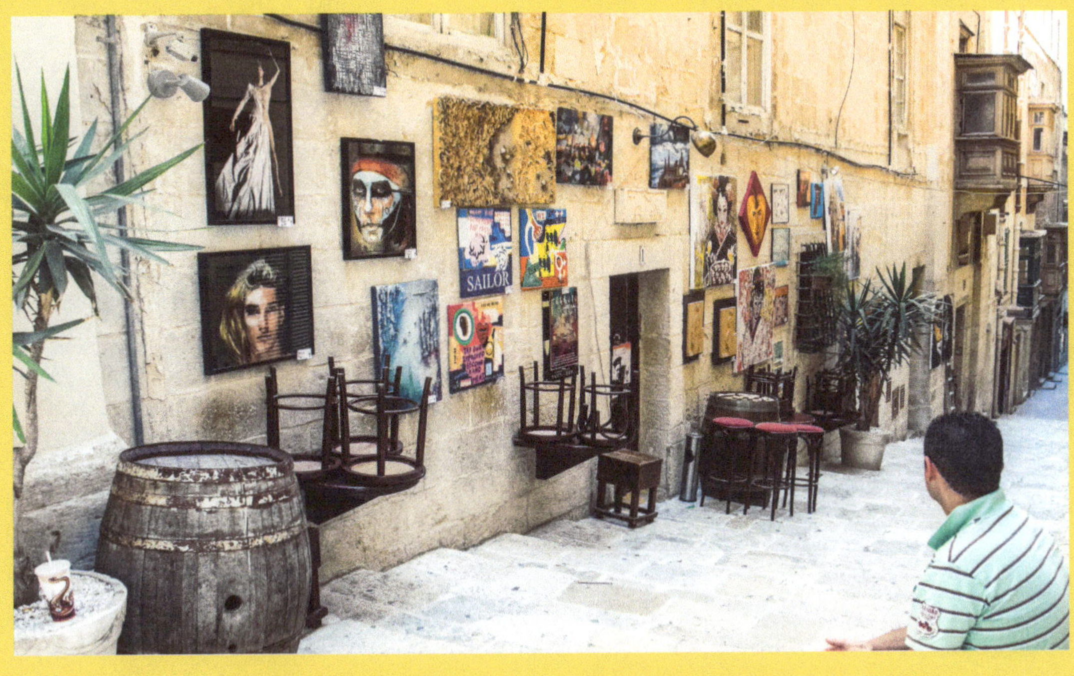

in the multitude of English and Irish pubs, and "fish-and-chips" is available all over the island. It's basically the UK with sun. The locals have different public and religious holidays and make it as pleasant and agreeable as possible for visitors both during the day and at night.

Being close to Africa, it gets quite hot. You can see in the photo on the opposite page that the sky was a perfect blue. Walking down the steps to the water, I passed four restaurants. No way was I going to dine there—they were way too expensive.

Malta was perfectly located for me to begin my journey, because I could go nearly anywhere from there.

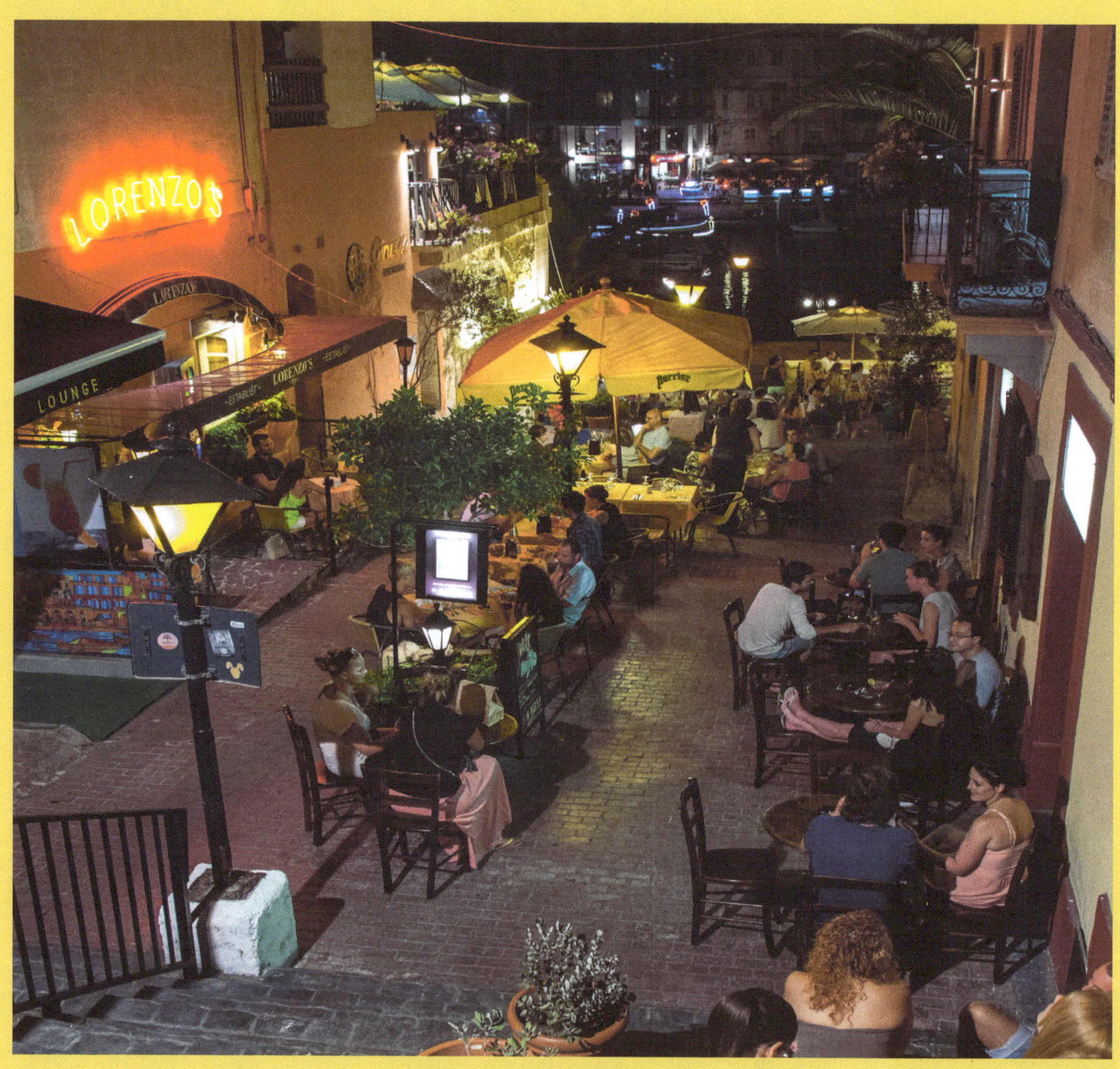

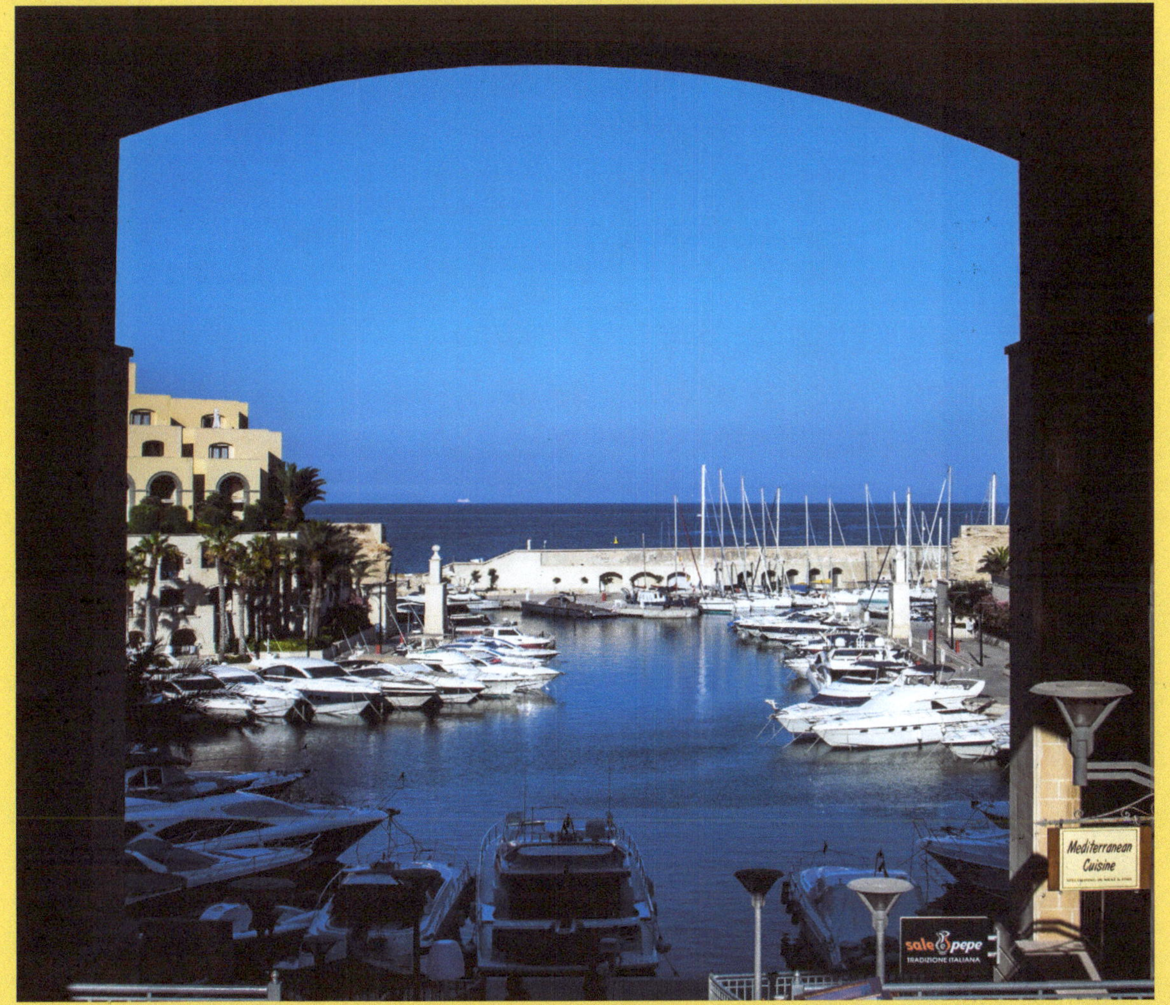
Mediterranean
Cuisine
sale e pepe
TRADIZIONE ITALIANA

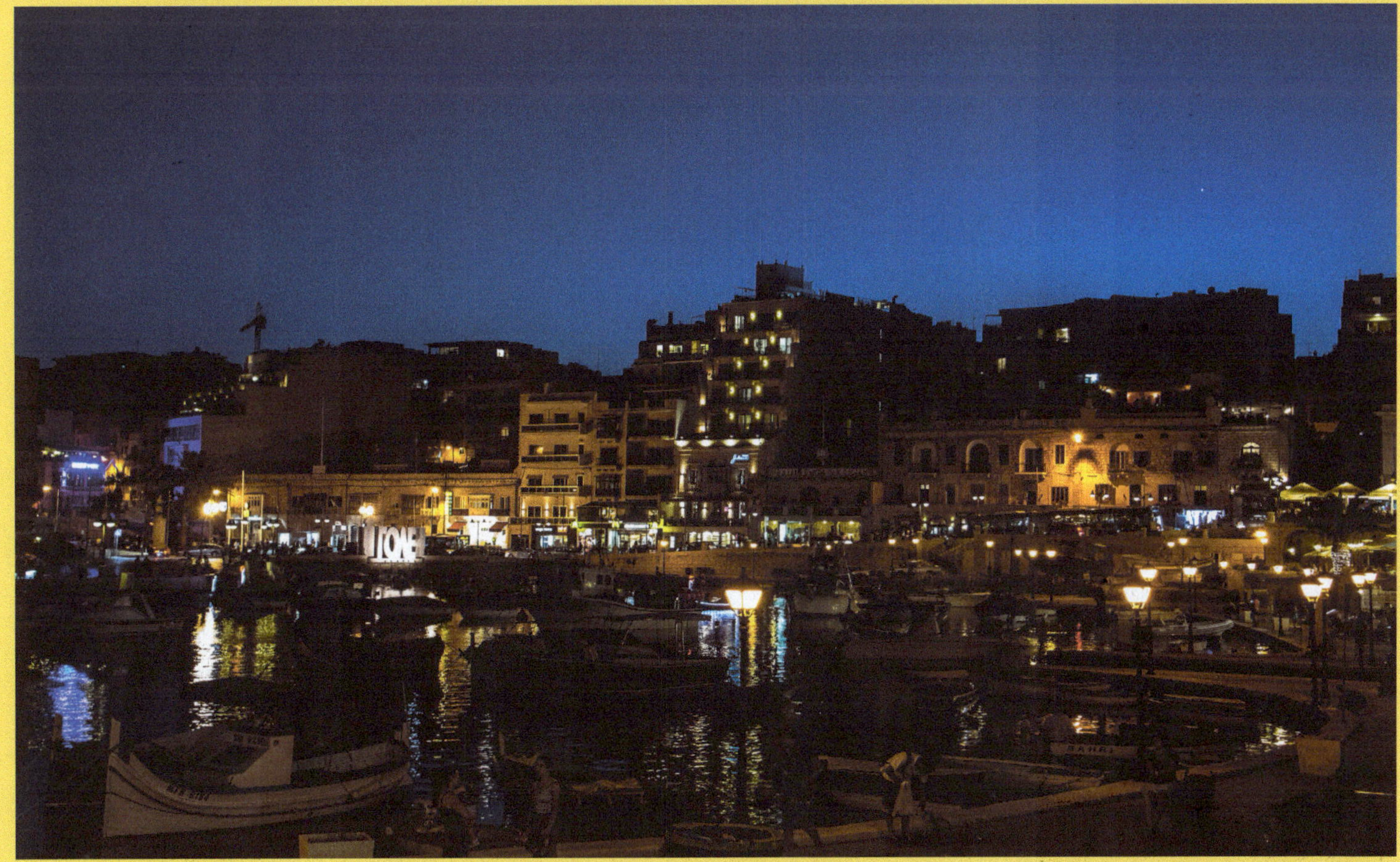

# 2

# CATANIA

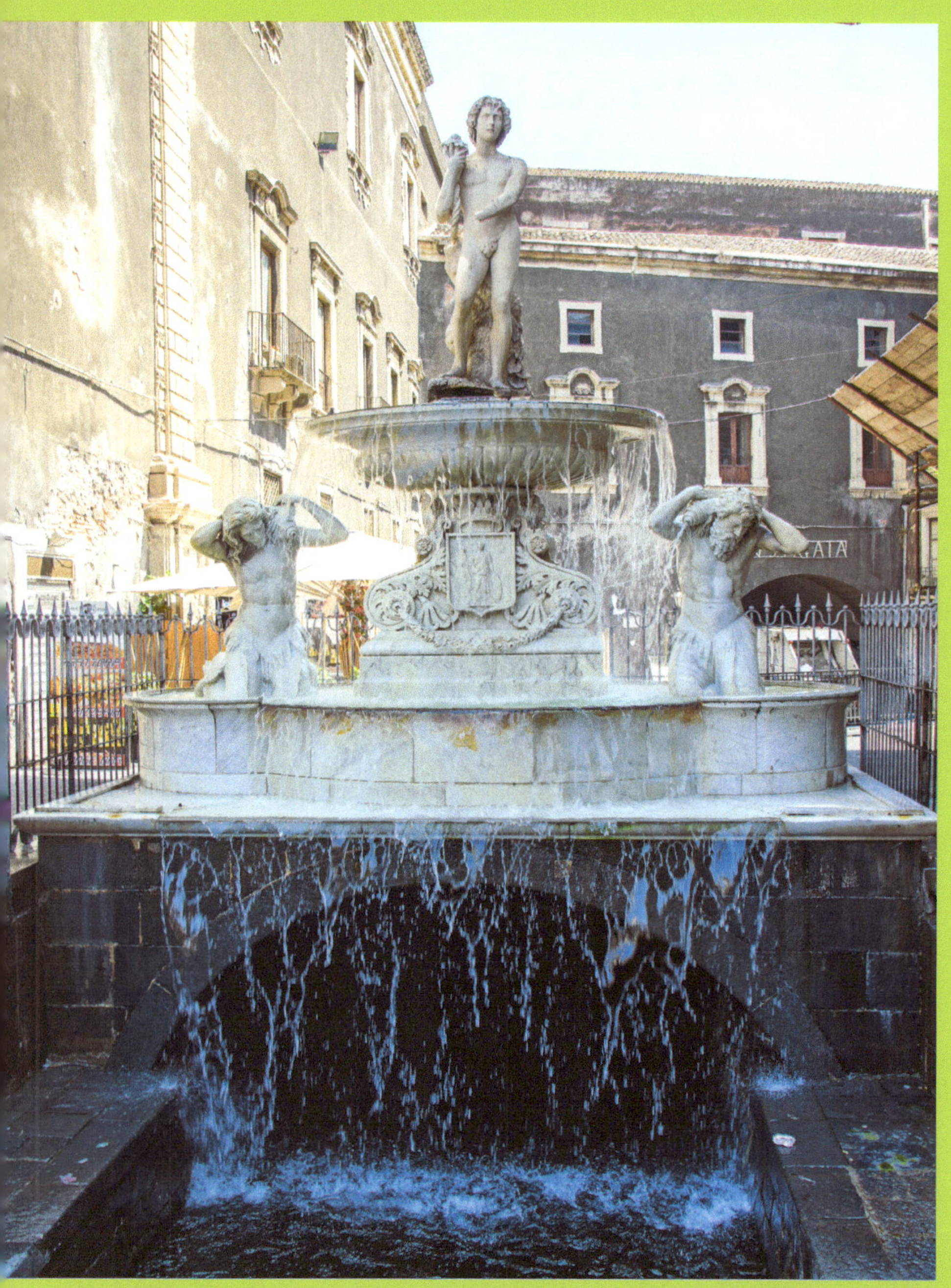


I took a ferry very early on a Monday morning from Malta to Catania, the second largest city on the island of Sicily, on the east side at the foot of Mount Etna. When you arrive you may think you've docked in Catania, but the ferry actually moors about an hour and a half drive to the south. From there you have to take a bus, which deposits you in Catania's harbor. As the bus door opened, a horde of shady types stood around offering the descending passengers various travel services. Looking at all the flattened noses, I thought I'd landed in a episode of *The Sopranos*. I managed to walk around them and get a taxi to my hotel.

It pays to take as little luggage as possible when making this kind of journey. I was carrying a heavy backpack, and there was no elevator in the hotel, so I had to walk up narrow stairs to get to my little room. After the luxury of Malta in the hotel with my brother, I figured this was how life would be for the next two months. After I freshened up I got on a Hop On-Hop Off and walked around. Catania is a beautiful city, although it has fountains in the oddest

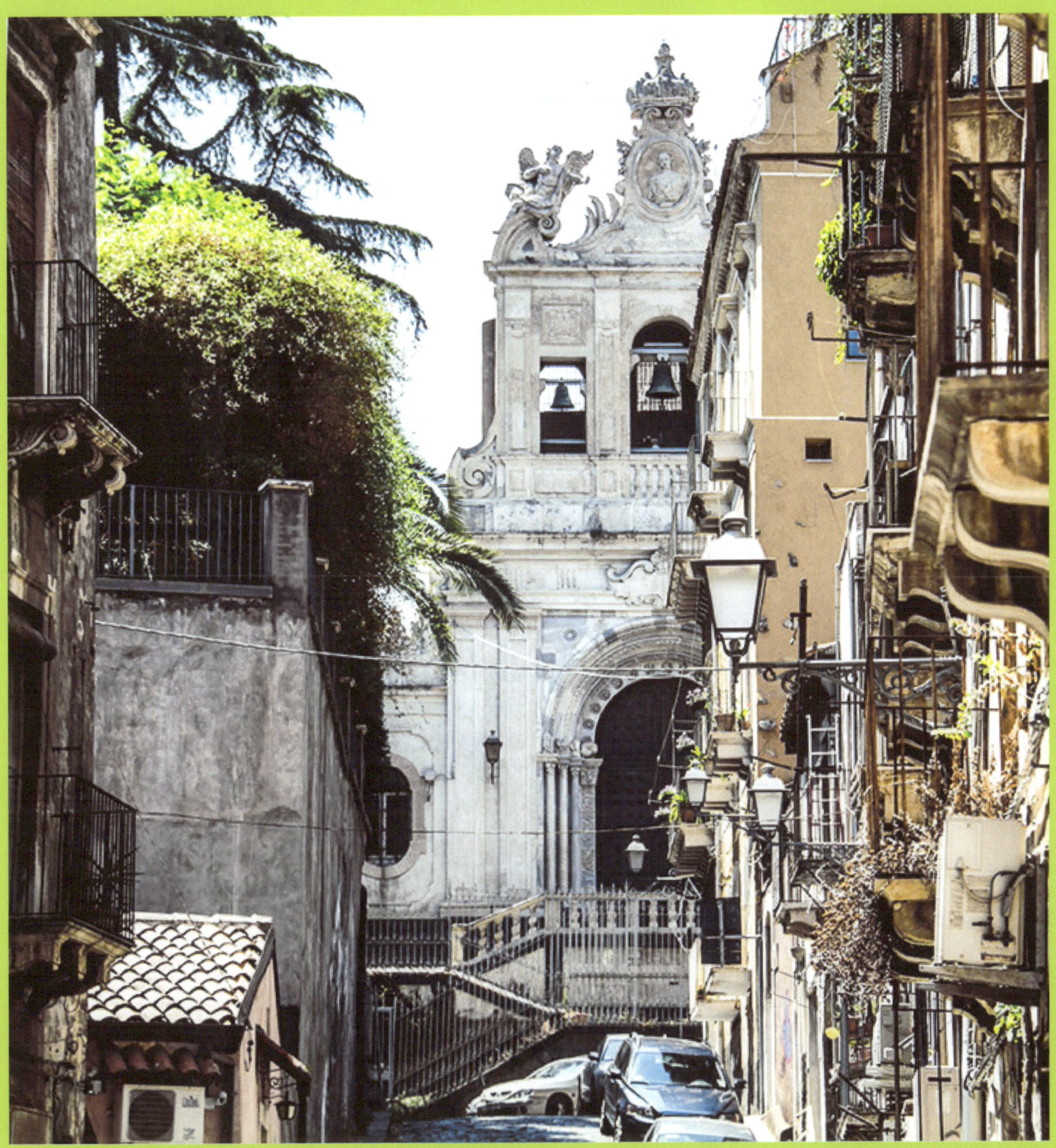

places. It dates back as far as the 8th century BC. The name comes from Latin and means either a bay or bowl, both appropriate for the location of the city.

As I ambled down a road, I looked to the right and saw that view. Catania has lots of confined spaces—residential, retail and religious architecture all jumbled together—that's how Sicily is. This one appealed to me and I managed to catch it just right.

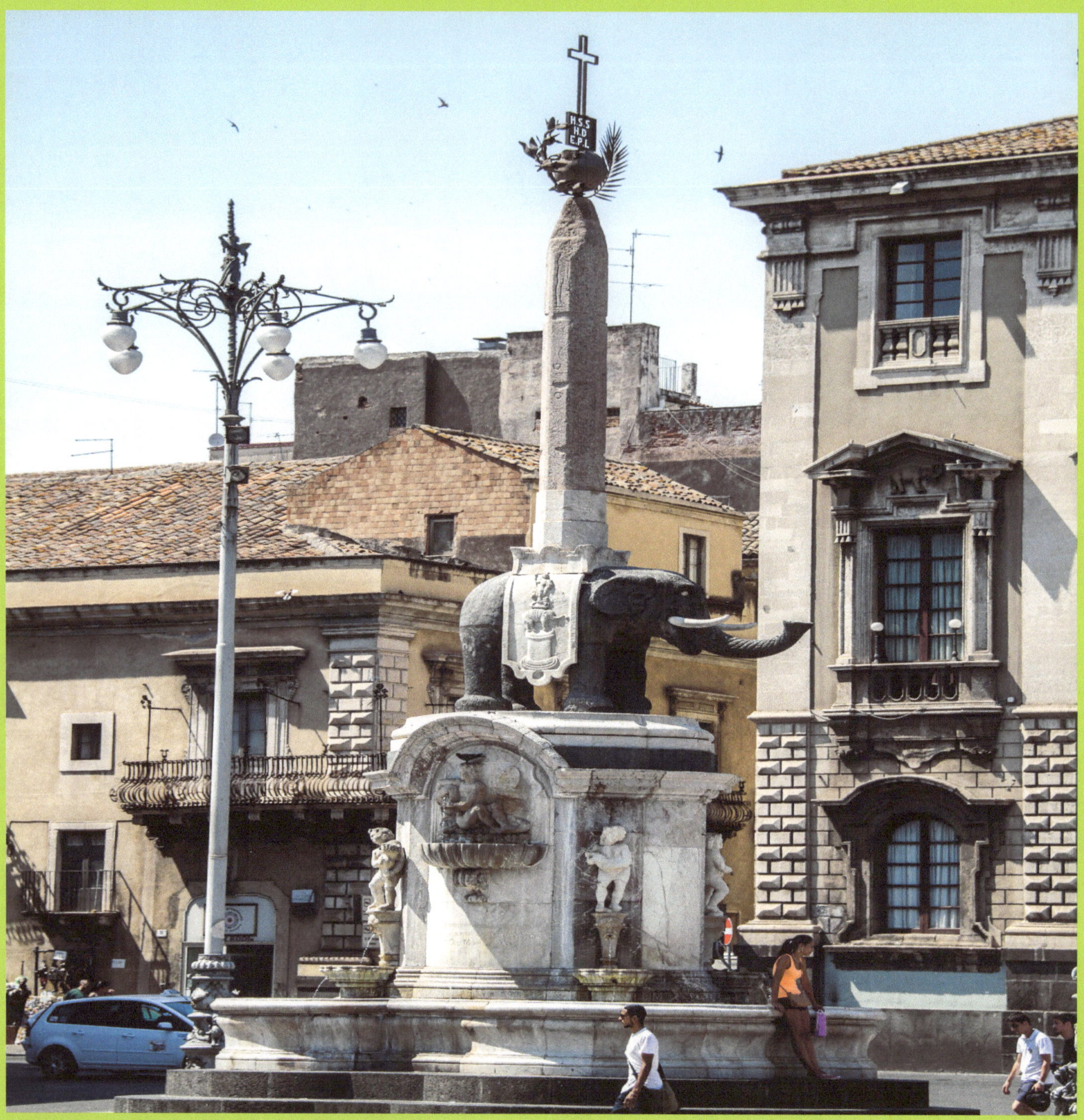

The elephant fountain—*u Liotru*, or the *Fontana dell'Elefante*—is the symbol of the city. It was assembled with the obelisk on top by Giovanni Battista Vaccarini in 1736. According to legend, the original lava stone elephant going back to Byzantine times was neuter, which the men of Catania took as an insult to their virility, so Vaccarini added testicles to the statue. The monument's nickname, u Liotru is a reference in the Sicilian language to Helidoros, an eighth century heretic and wizard who claimed he could make the elephant walk by magic. Apparently he didn't succeed, but the local bishop was not amused and had the magician burned at the stake.

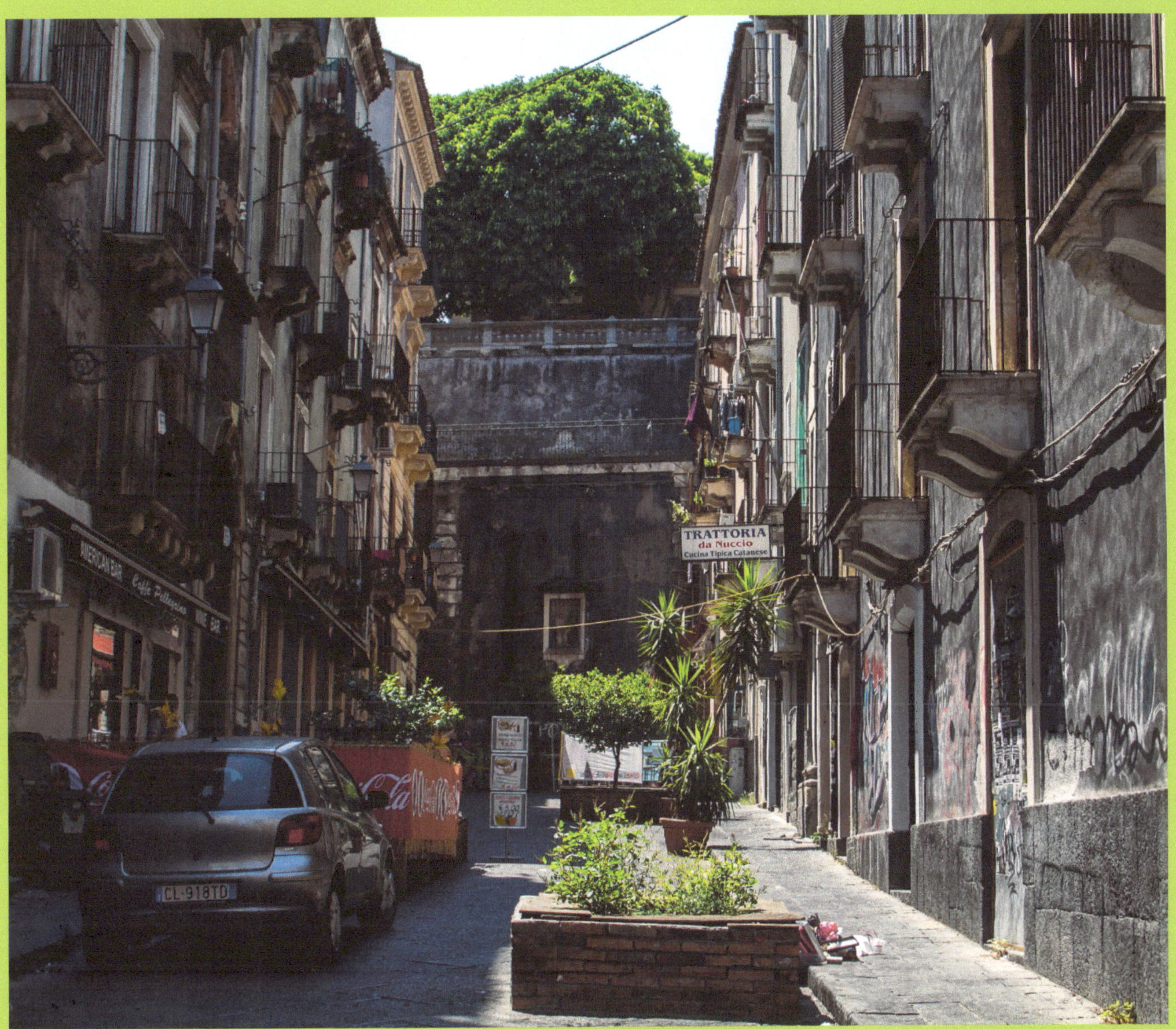


When I saw this confined space of apartment buildings with sprigs of greenery, it looked very Italian to me. That's why I took the photo.

I liked Catania. Italy's tenth-largest city, it is heavily populated. You have to dodge cars all the time because the Italians drive like maniacs. I'm pretty sure my city tour driver was under some kind of influence. When he wasn't slurring around the roads, he was merrily talking to himself while a loud, incomprehensible soundtrack blurted out something I wouldn't have understood even if I'd been able to speak Italian.

After spending the whole day taking photos, I crawled into bed early enough to get a good night's sleep before my early flight the next morning.

Although the town was attractive, I can't say Catania was one of my favorites. The reasons may have been because it was about 102 degrees outside and I sweated through two shirts in no time. I don't think I did it justice. After Malta, it was the first city where I was on my own, and I was probably a little daunted. I hope I can go back to Sicily sometime in the future and give it another chance.

# 3

# CRETE

I took a flight from Catania to Crete, the largest of the Greek Islands, and arrived in the early afternoon. I'd been to Athens and the Greek mainland before, but never to that island. Not knowing where I was going, I got off the plane in Heraklion thinking that my hotel would be just across the street. Instead, I had to take a taxi, which cost 50 Euros (about 60 U.S. dollars). I was irritated having to pay that much, but it took me along the coastal road which runs up to a cliff, and all of a sudden, after the confines of Malta and Catania, it opened up onto this beautiful view. It was absolute gorgeous. My hotel was located in Agia Pelagia, about a 25 minute drive from Heraklion. I asked the driver to stop so I could get out and breathe it all in. When you have to take an expensive ride, being able to shoot a picture like that makes it worth every cent of the ride.

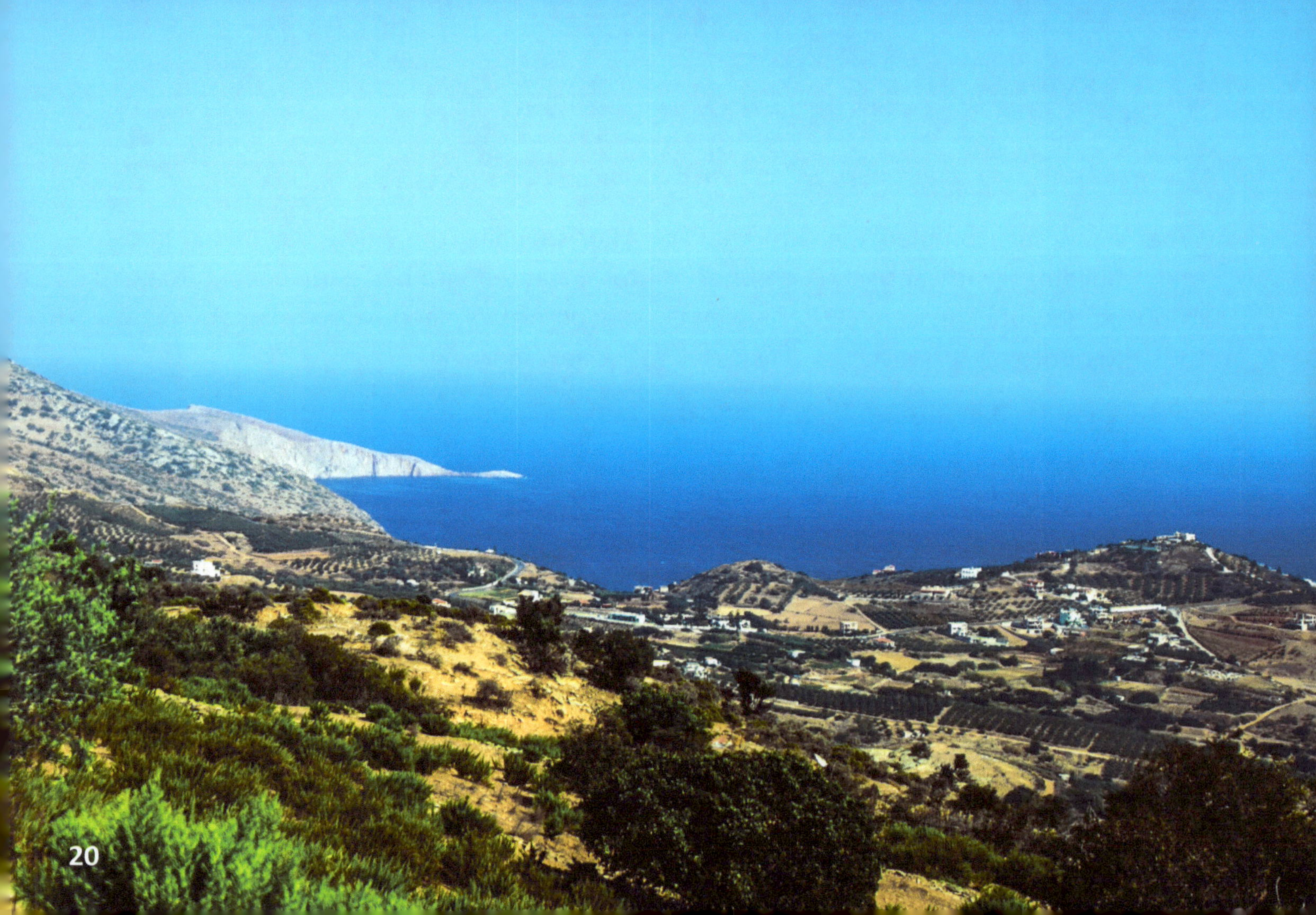

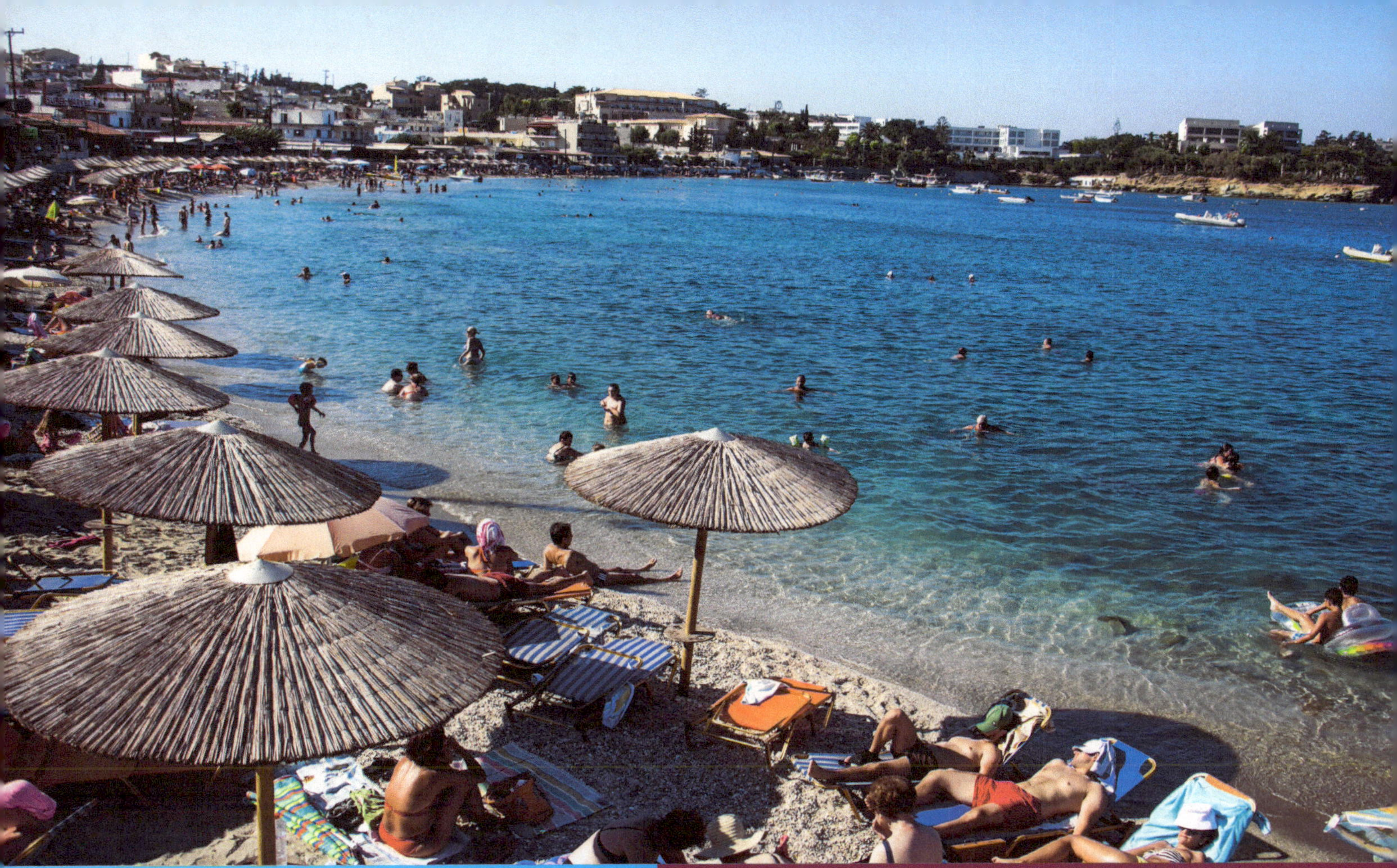

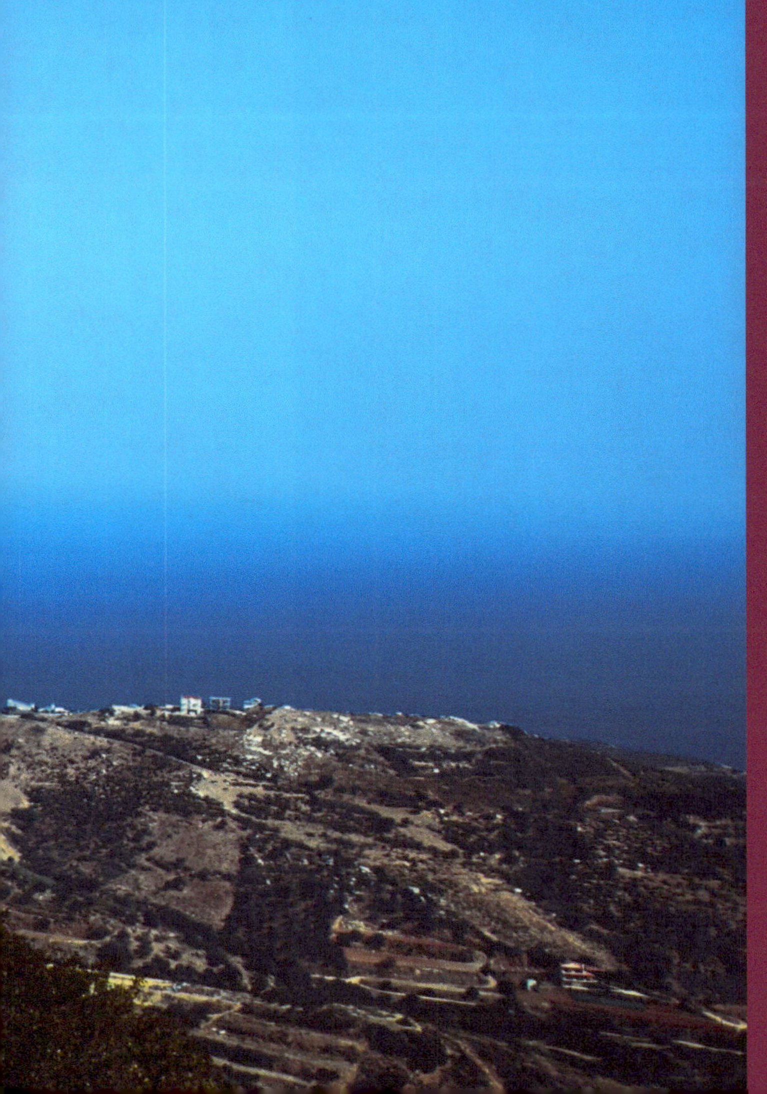

I feel very much at home in Greece and love the easy-going mentality. I had booked the hotel online, and the people running it were pleasant, but I didn't like the building. When I mentioned it, they said, "If you like, we've got a beach-front apartment as well." Even though it had no A/C, it made up for it in location. When I stepped outside in the morning, the sea was right there in front of me.

Every night I would visit a different tavern. All it had to have was free wi-fi and good Tsaziki, a Greek appetizer of cucumbers and garlic yogurt, and you dip bread in it—I love Greek food. I could sit, drink a beer, and look out at the people walking and enjoying the sunsets.

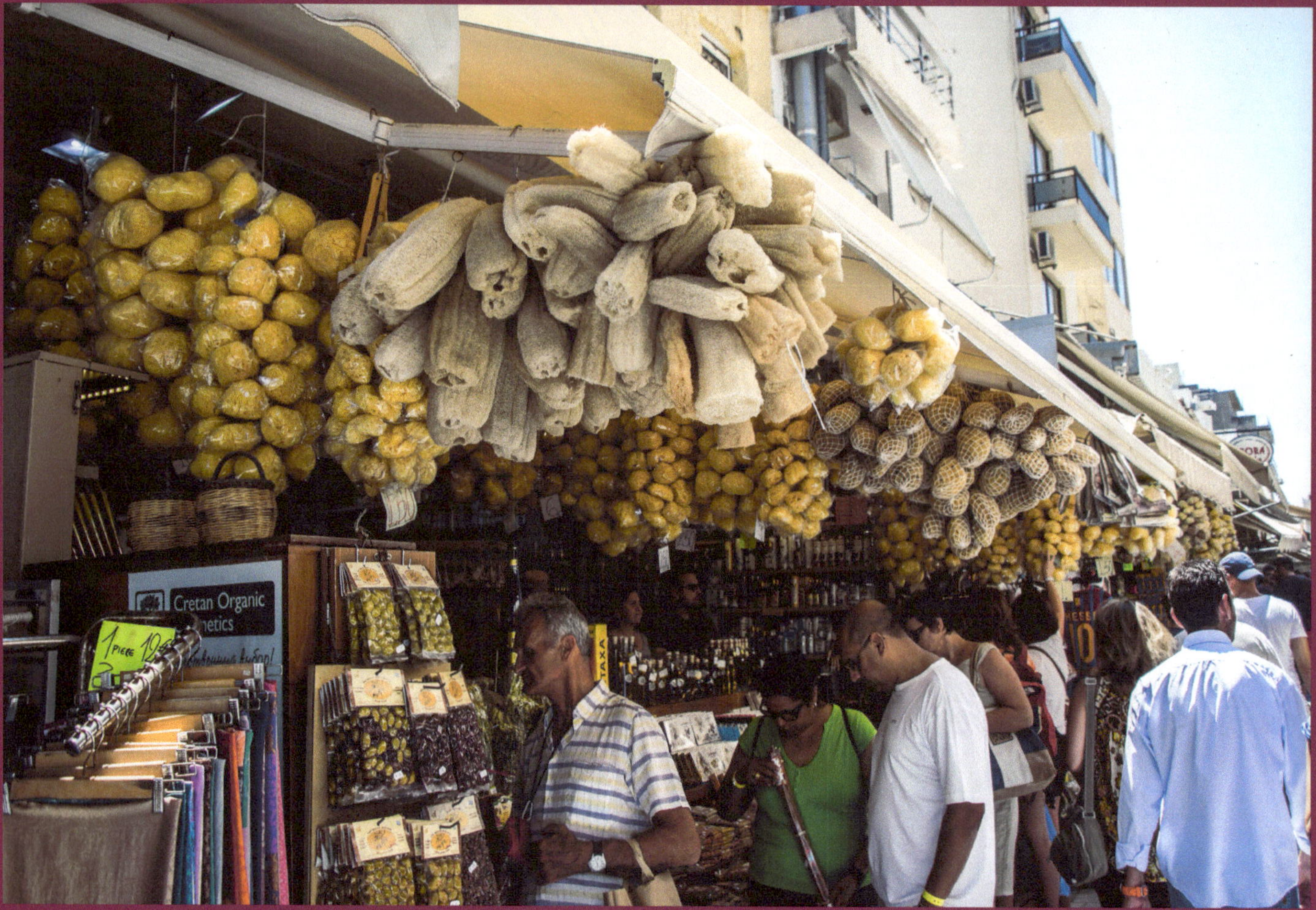

Just about every second person in Crete was a Russian tourist. Every brochure you opened up was in Russian, created by enterprising local agents to advertise things to do on the island for their Eastern Eropean visitors. Russians don't speak any language but their own—like the Brits in the Age of Imperialism—but they head in droves to where it's warm, enjoy it and in the process spend lots of money. The locals like that.

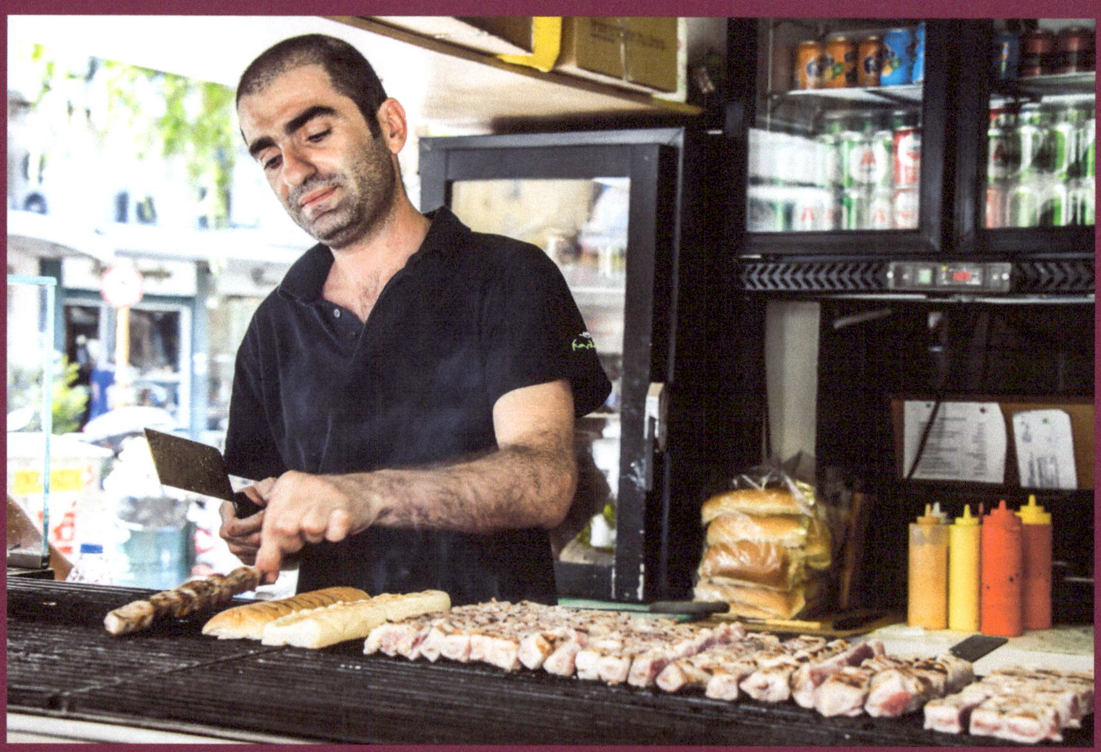

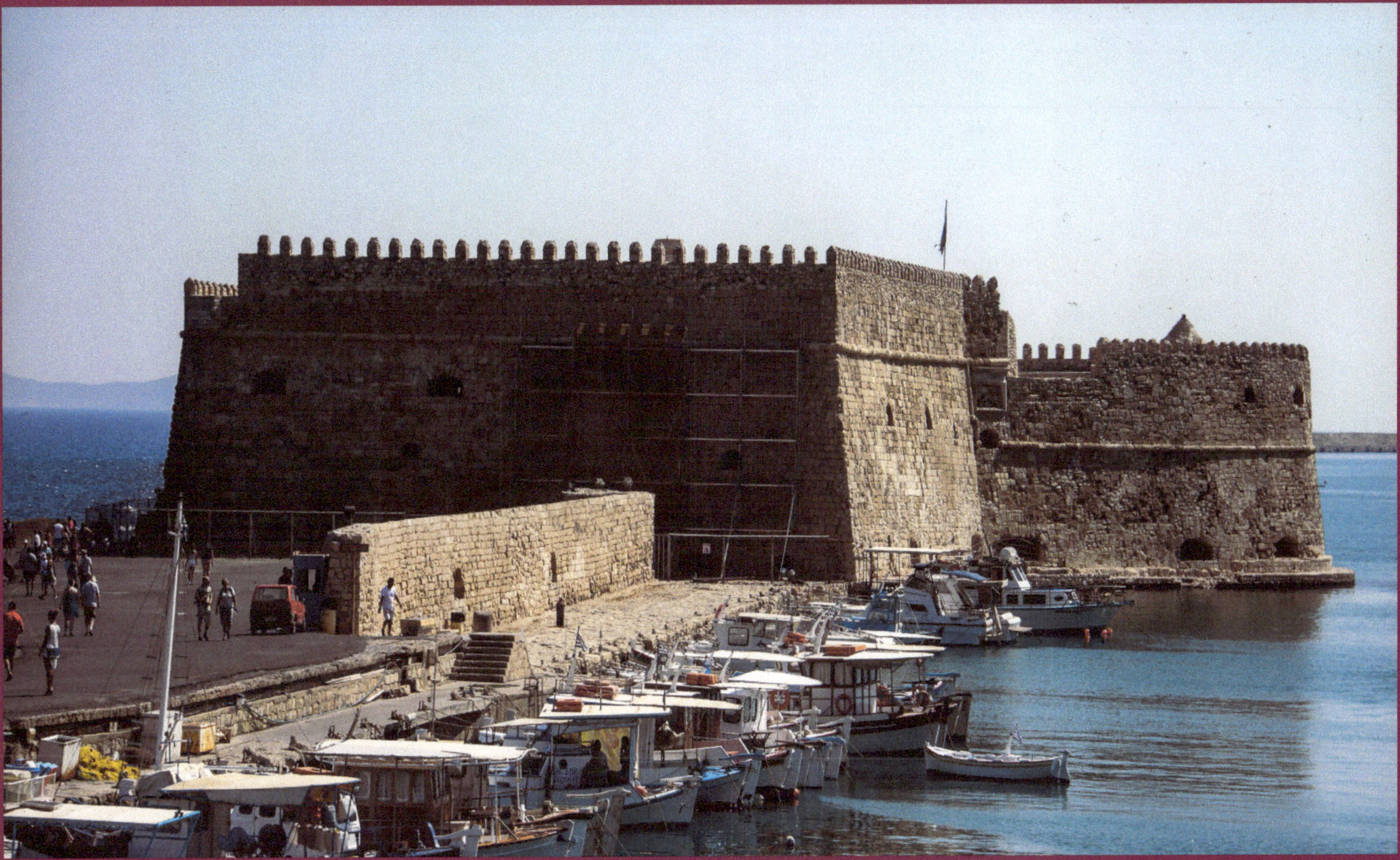

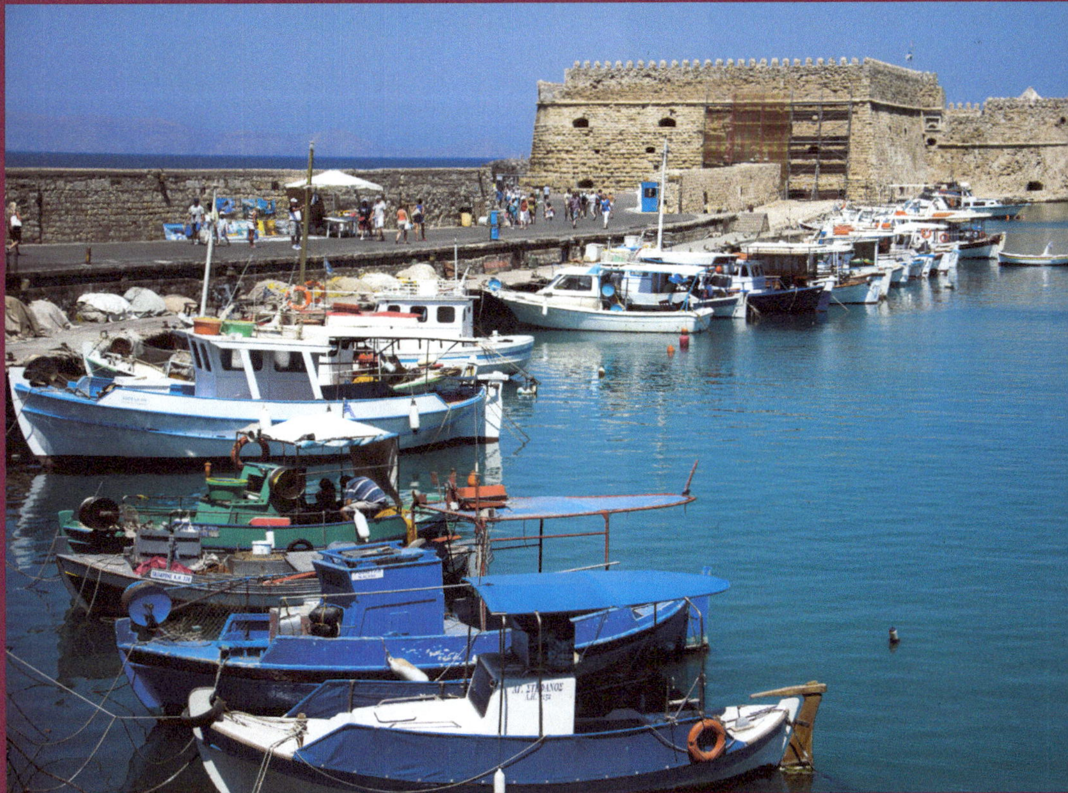

The scenic Harbor in Heraklion, was built between 1320 and 1356 by the Venetian occupation forces. In those days Venice was not only a great maritime trade city, but also a military power that fielded its own armies. The soldiers constructed the lighthouse, the fortress at the harbor entrance and the St. Nicholas bastion in the middle of the breakwater to defend against marauding pirates. The Venetians, and later the Turks, used the small chapel as a place of execution for condemned prisoners.

One day I took a busride to Heraklion, which lasted over an hour, but was worth the time. Heraklion is a beautiful place, and people treated me with great friendliness.

Every European city has its beggars and street hustlers, but these two old ladies were the most unusual I encountered on the trip. I met the one on the right when I got off the Hop On – Hop Off, and walked into the enclosed pedestrian zone of the central market. She was being pushed out into the street to beg by her pimp who looked like he was 85 years old. I took her picture with my telephoto lens from a long way off. She was 4 ft. 2, crippled by arthritis and hunched over. When I gave her a little money, she bent over even further to thank me.

Thinking nothing of it, I walked on. About two hours later in Lions Square—a big square in Heraklion—there was the same old pimp pushing the woman in the photo below out into the street. Apparently, he had a nice little ring of old lady beggars!

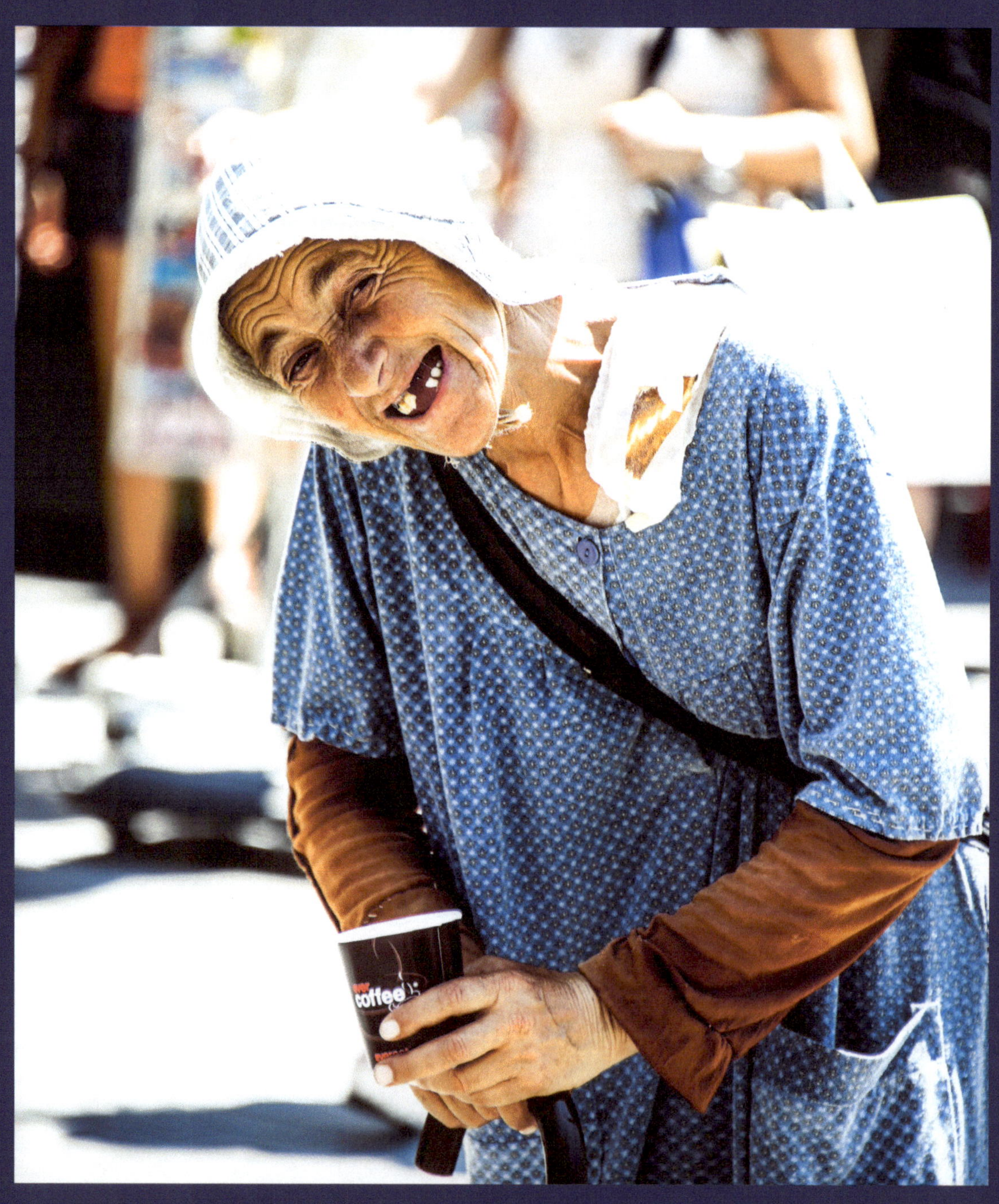

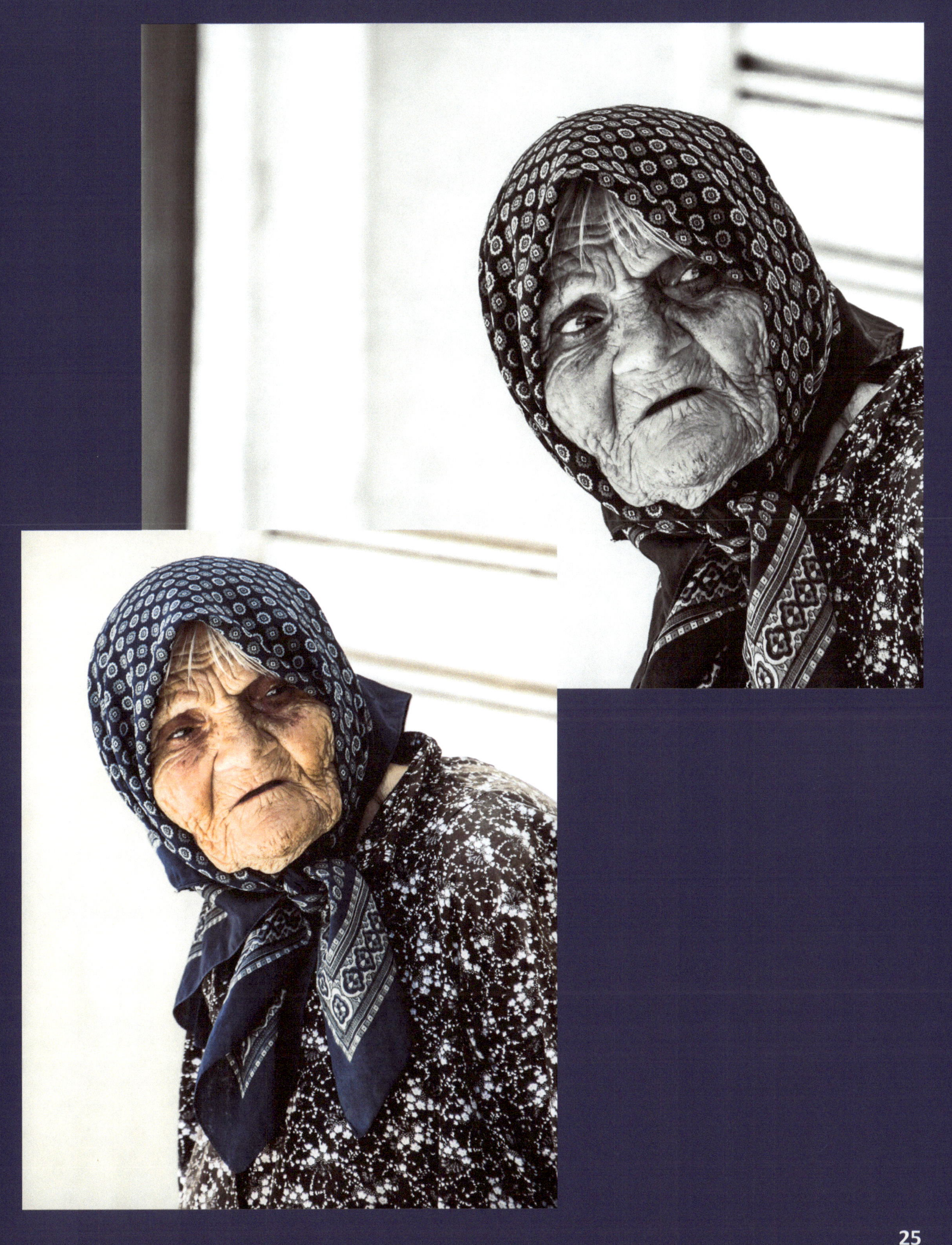

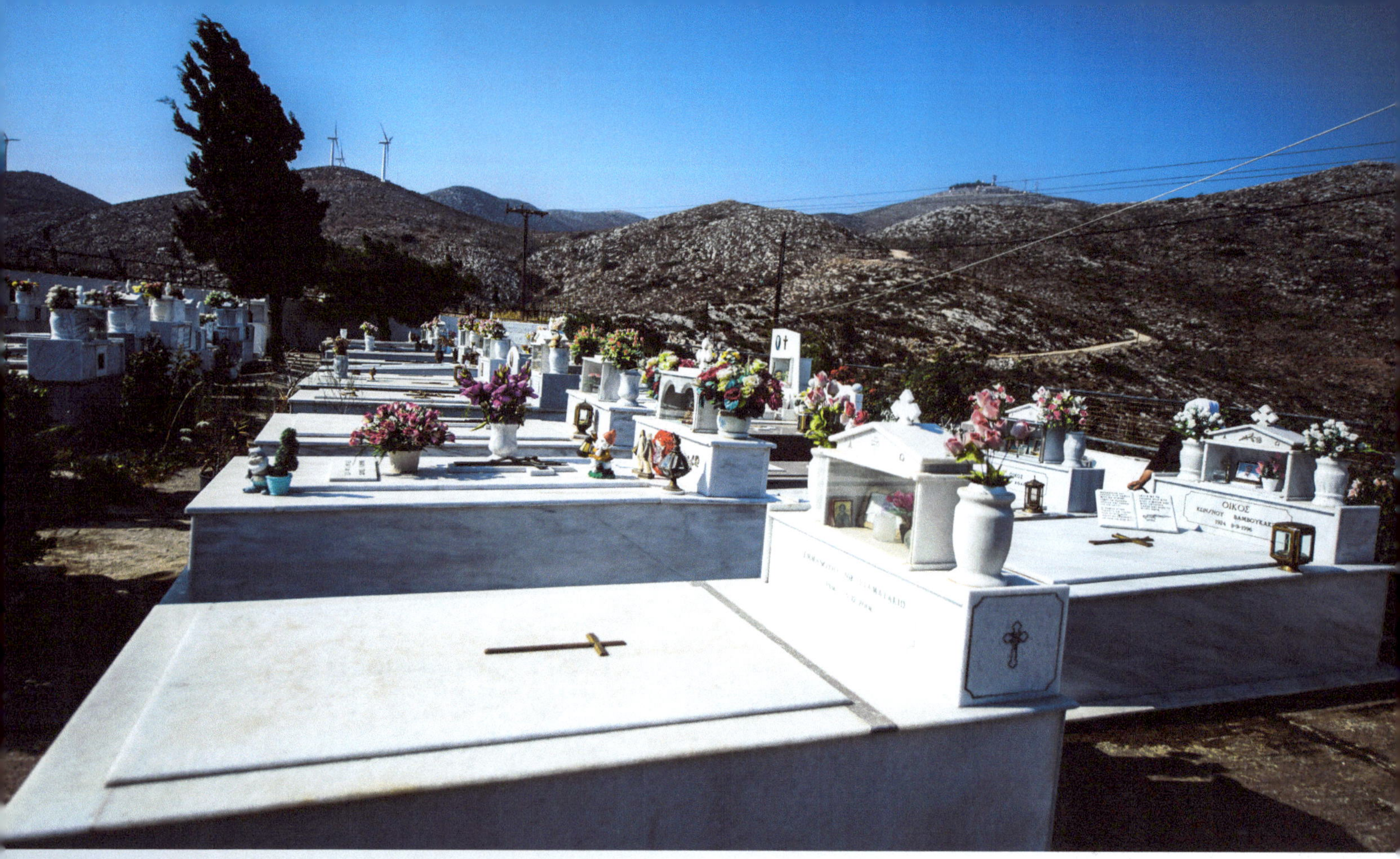

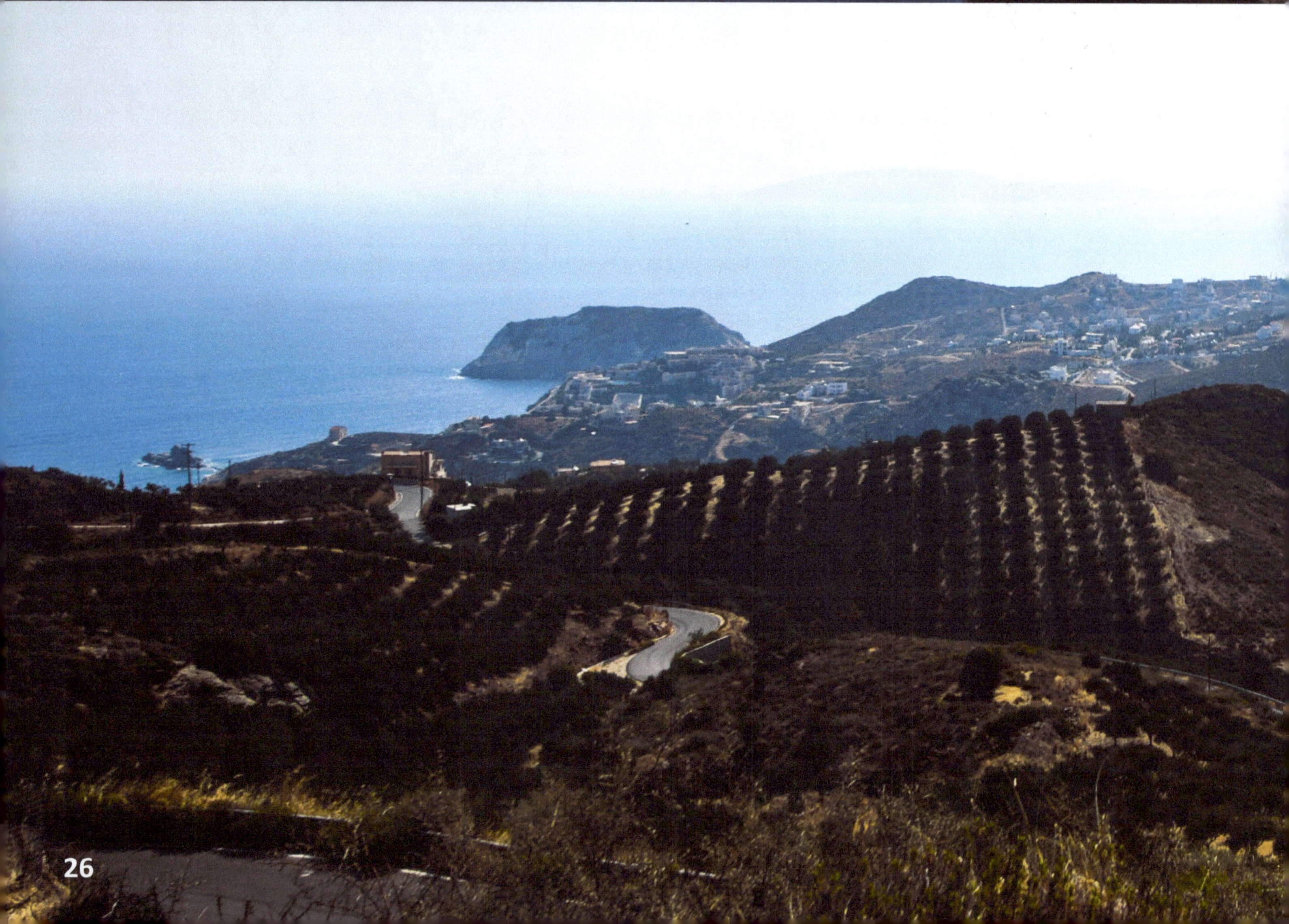

One day I rented a scooter and rode up into the mountains above Heraklion. At some point, I came upon a cemetery. This woman was in charge of the place. She was gardening and putting flowers on the graves. Another woman with her ducked behind one of the gravestones—she didn't want to be photographed. But the cemetery keeper was happy to pose for me.

I'd go back to Crete tomorrow, and when I return to the Greek islands, it will definitely be among my first ports of call. After four days there, however, it was time for me to move on and head to Santorini, where I knew another slice of heaven was waiting for me.

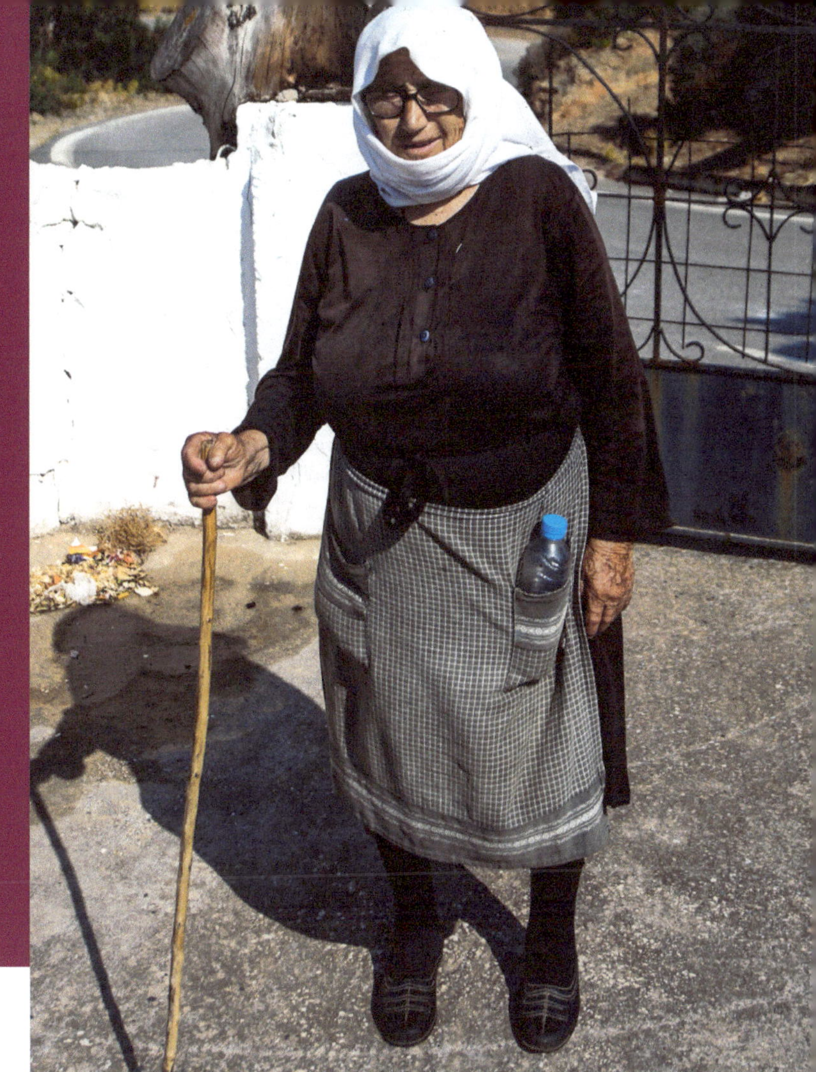

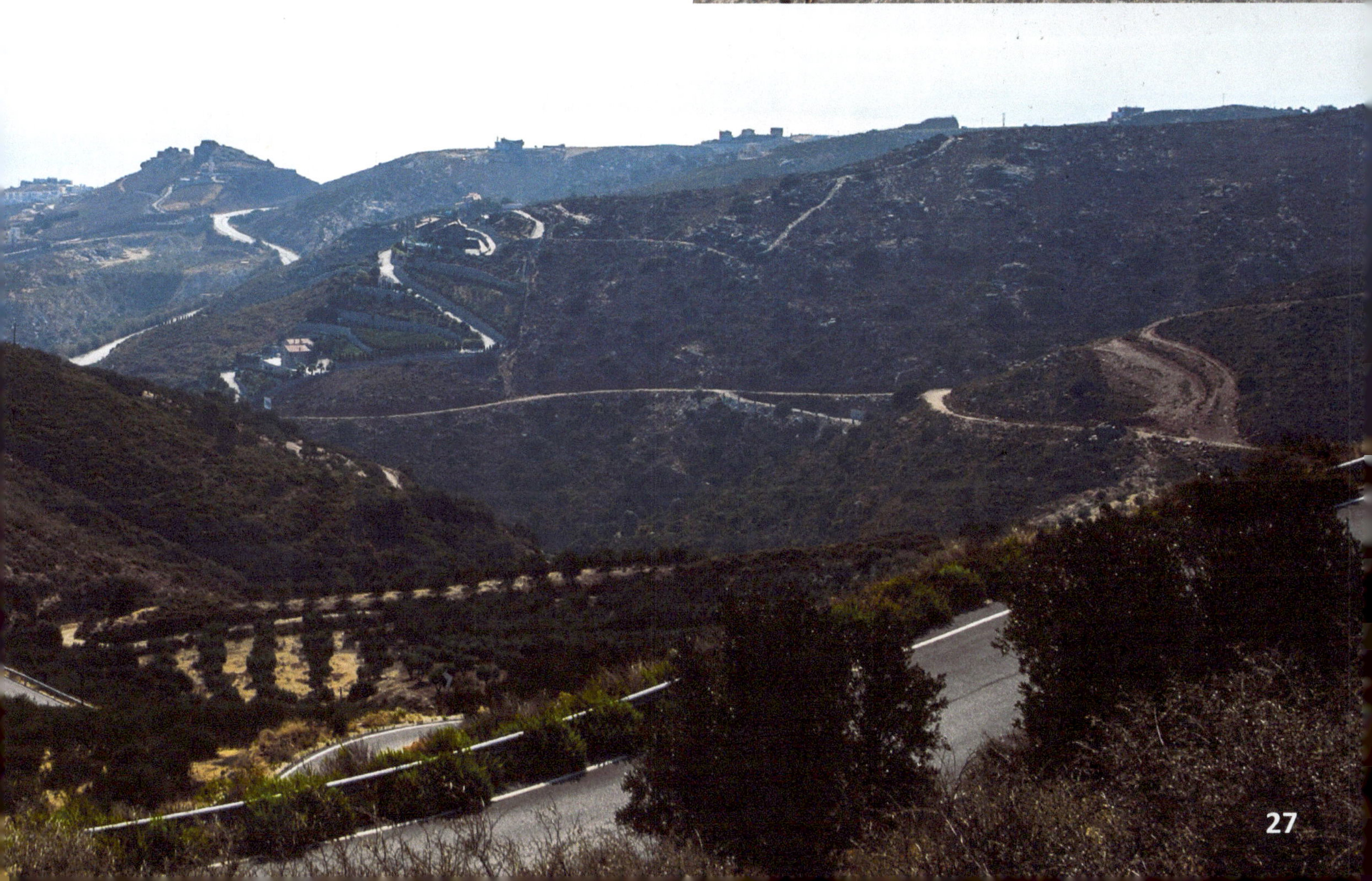

# STREET HUSTLERS

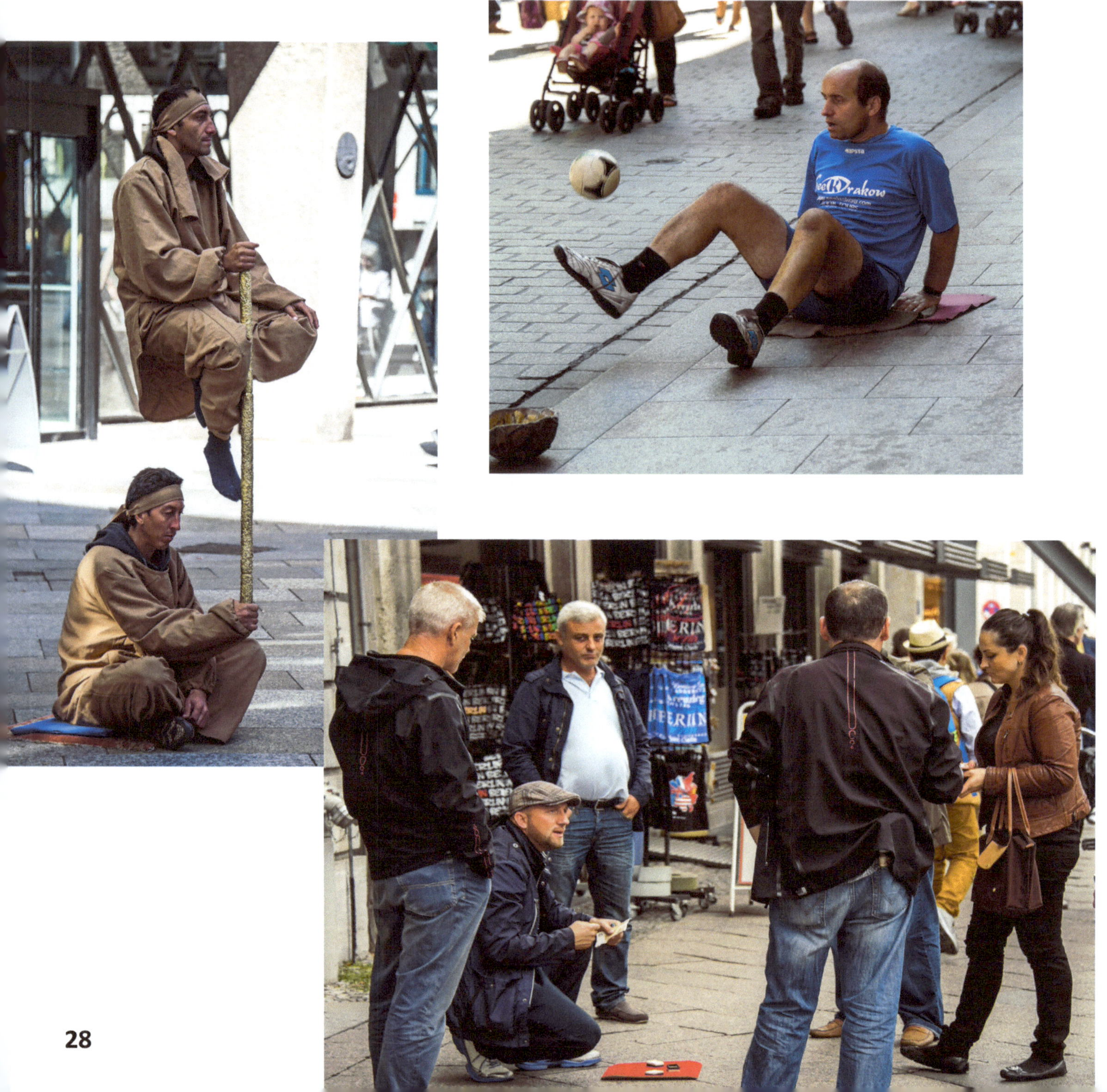

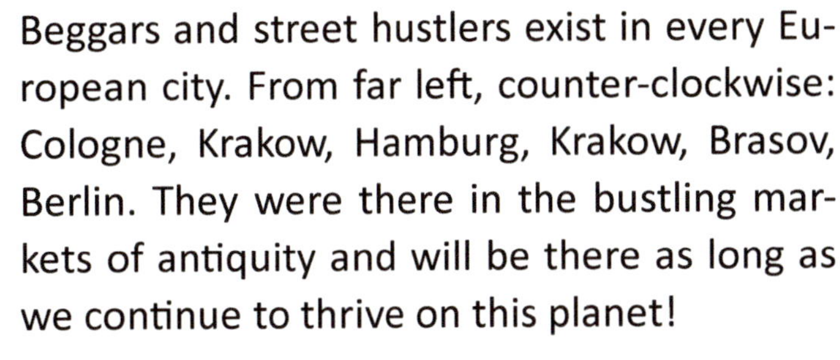

Beggars and street hustlers exist in every European city. From far left, counter-clockwise: Cologne, Krakow, Hamburg, Krakow, Brasov, Berlin. They were there in the bustling markets of antiquity and will be there as long as we continue to thrive on this planet!

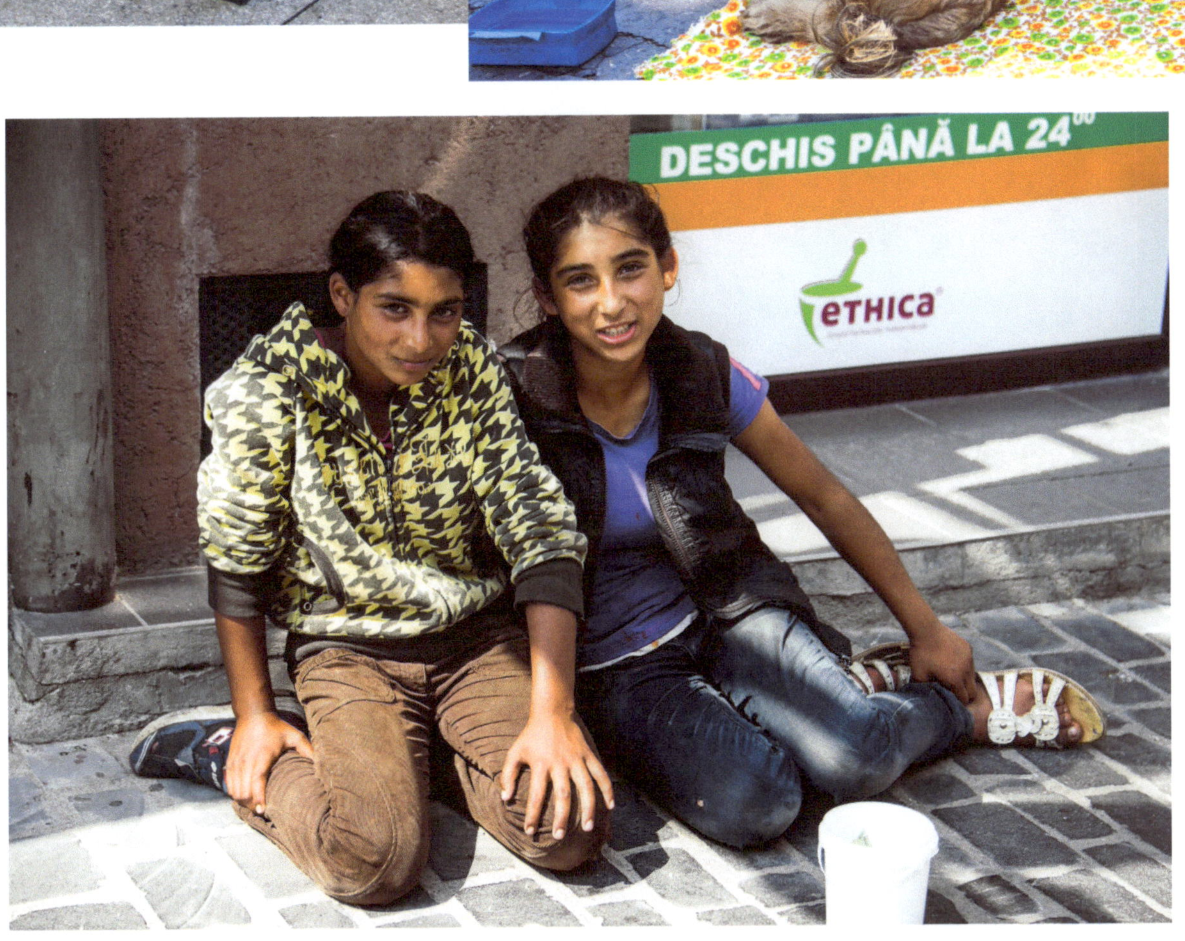

# 4
# SANTORINI

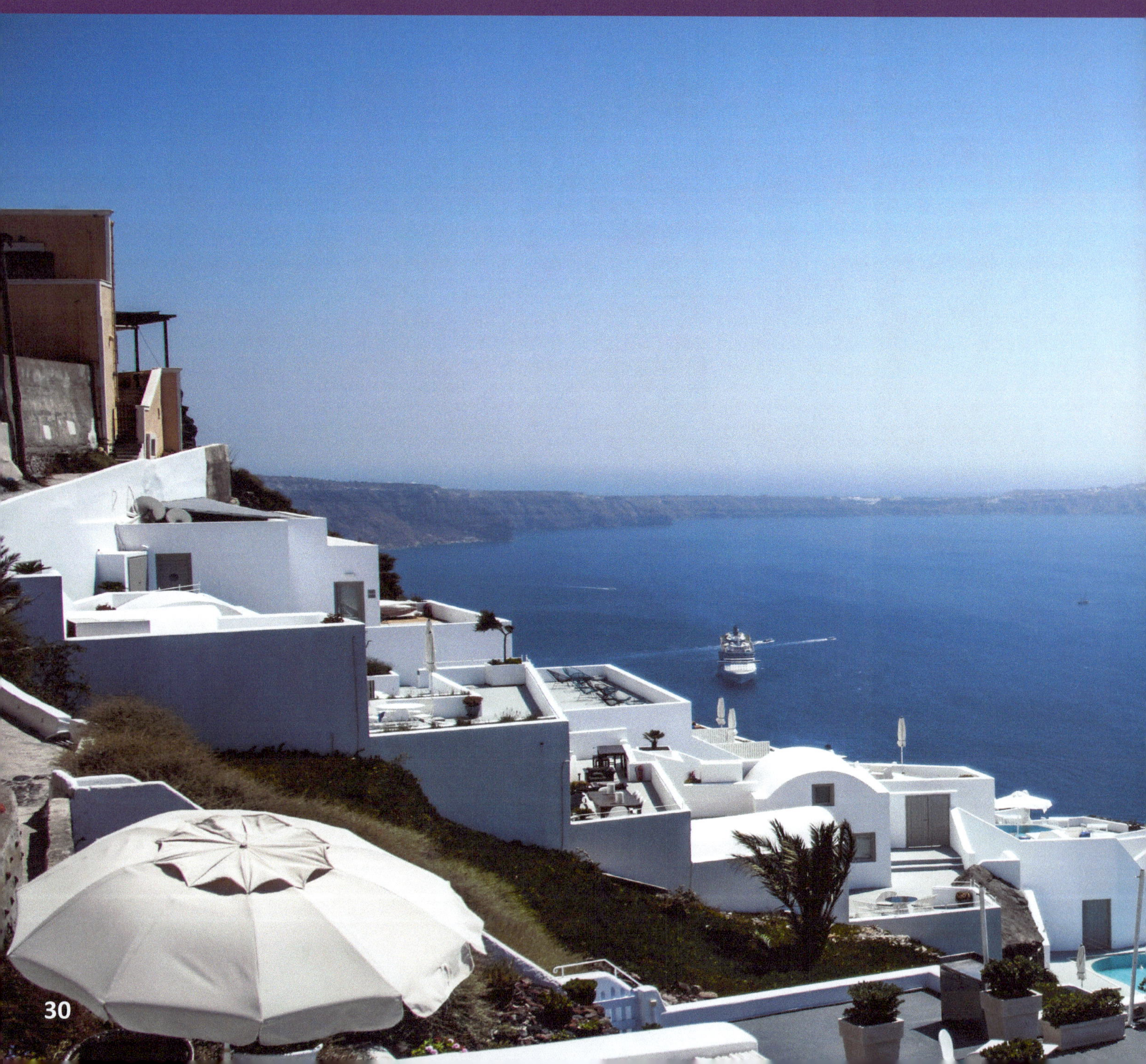

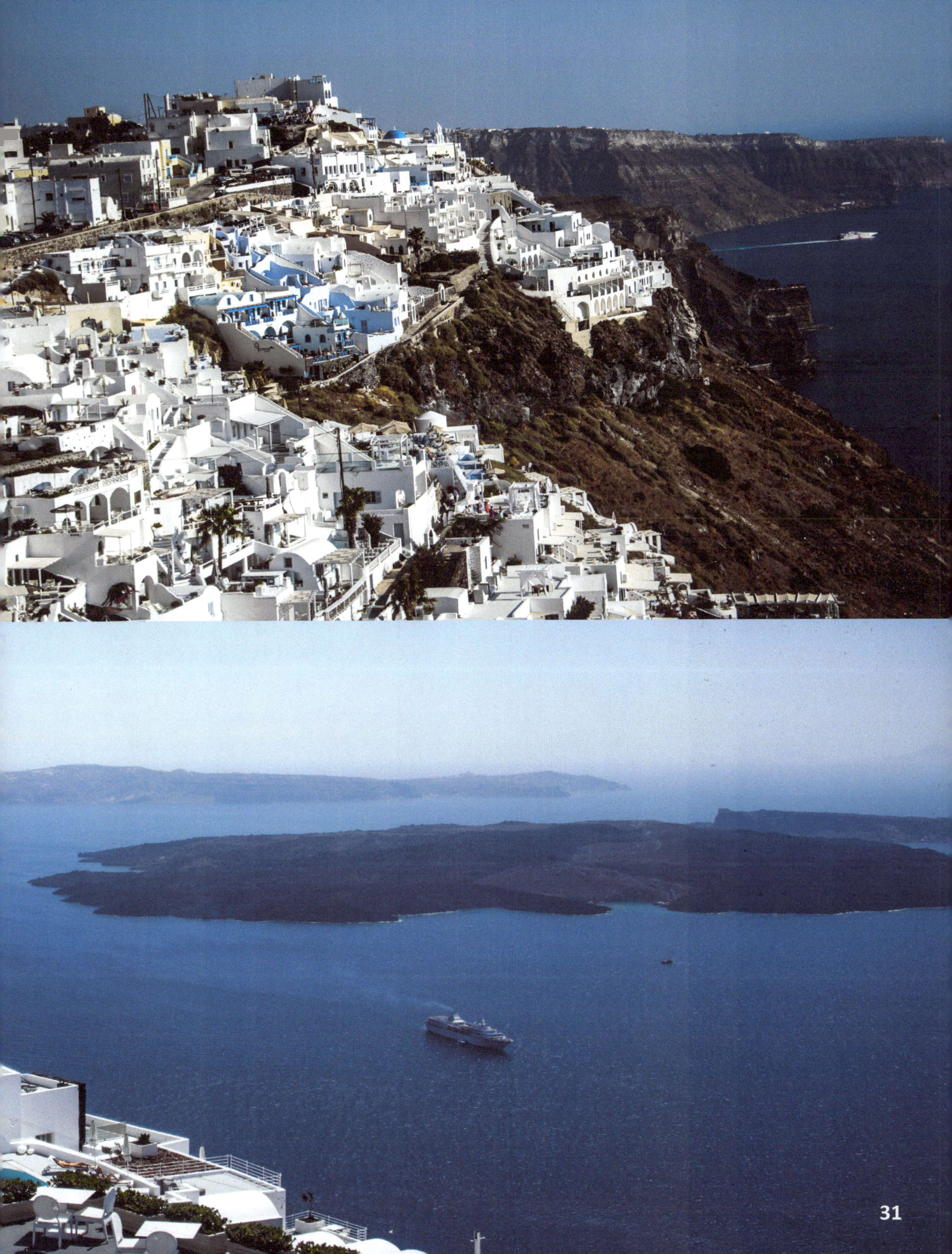

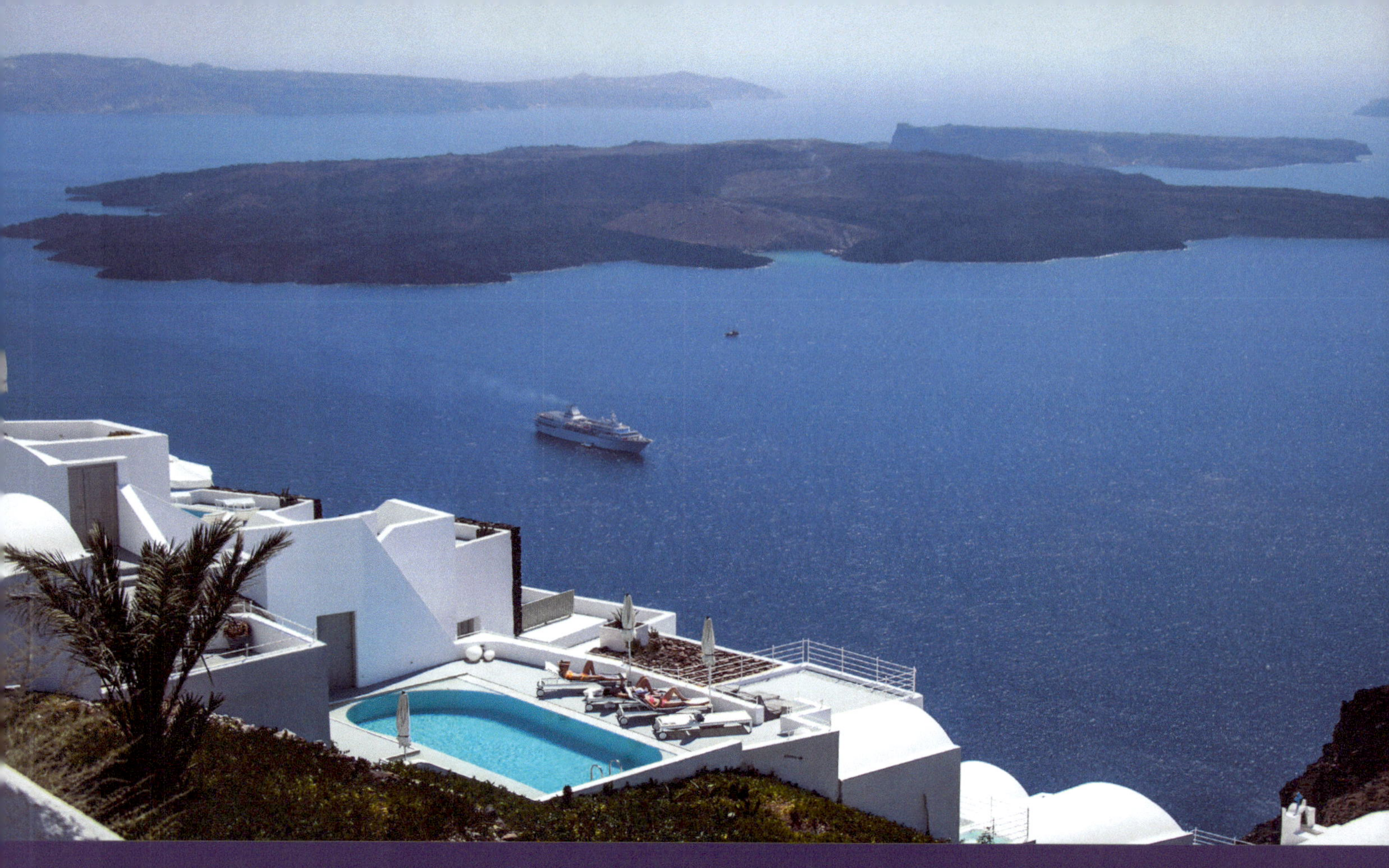

From Crete I took the ferry to Santorini, about 68 miles to the north. I went there because of a tip I got from David Breitbarth, my actor friend at Sarasota's Asolo Repertory Theatre. He and his wife Kate had traveled to Santorini for part of their honeymoon, and he kept raving about how beautiful the island is. So I thought, "Right, I want to see it!" I'm glad I did.

It's the most beautiful island I have ever visited. I fell in love with it the moment I arrived. Of all the places I saw on this walkabout, it is on its own pedestal. I'd seen the pictures, but nothing prepares you for that view, because the water is a million shades of blue and looks like a painting. Nothing's moving—it's all still because you're so far up on the cliff that you don't notice the people below.

More than 3,600 years ago, Santorini had one of the largest volcanic eruptions in recorded history. It created a giant tsunami and caused devastation throughout the Aegean Sea, and it may have been the downfall of the Minoan civilization in Crete. Some consider that catastrophe the source of the legend of Atlantis. Although as old as antiquity, Santorini got the name by which we know it today in the 13th century—it is a contraction of "Santa Irini," a reference to Saint Irene.

I booked the same hotel where David and Kate had stayed—Remezzo Villas. Vasili, who owns it with his sister Cassandra, personally welcomed me. I'd walk out of my room, and the view above is what I'd see—this amazing expanse of blue sea.

Below: the outside eating area at the hotel, which was great for me. When you're on your own, you don't eat out much in restaurants and have three-course meals. Instead, I'd go to a bar for a beer and an appetizer. Or I'd head to a supermarket to buy crackers, cheese and pate, and take them back to the the hotel room and edit my photos while snacking. The photo at the bottom shows the sun-lounging interior of the hotel. My room is the door in the shadowed area, just behind the two lounge chairs.

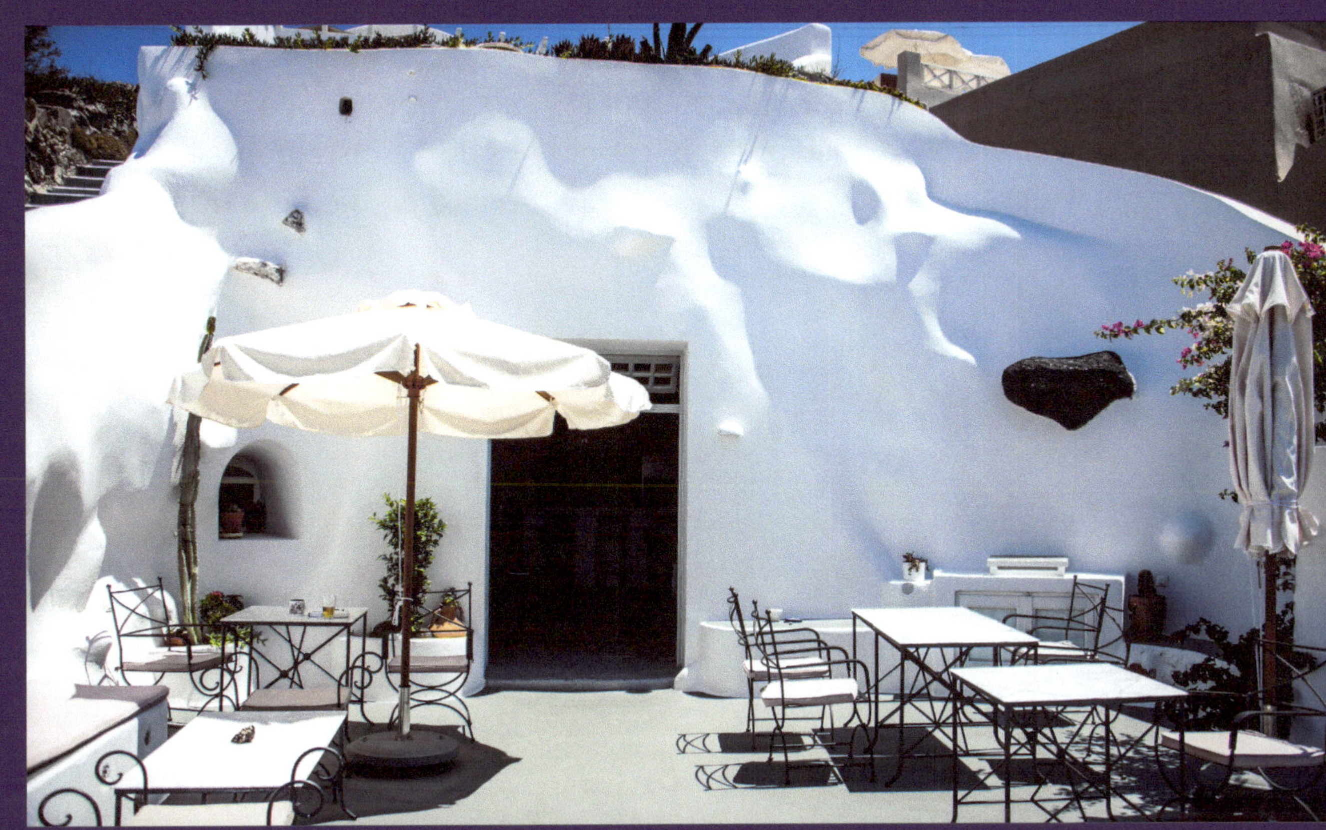

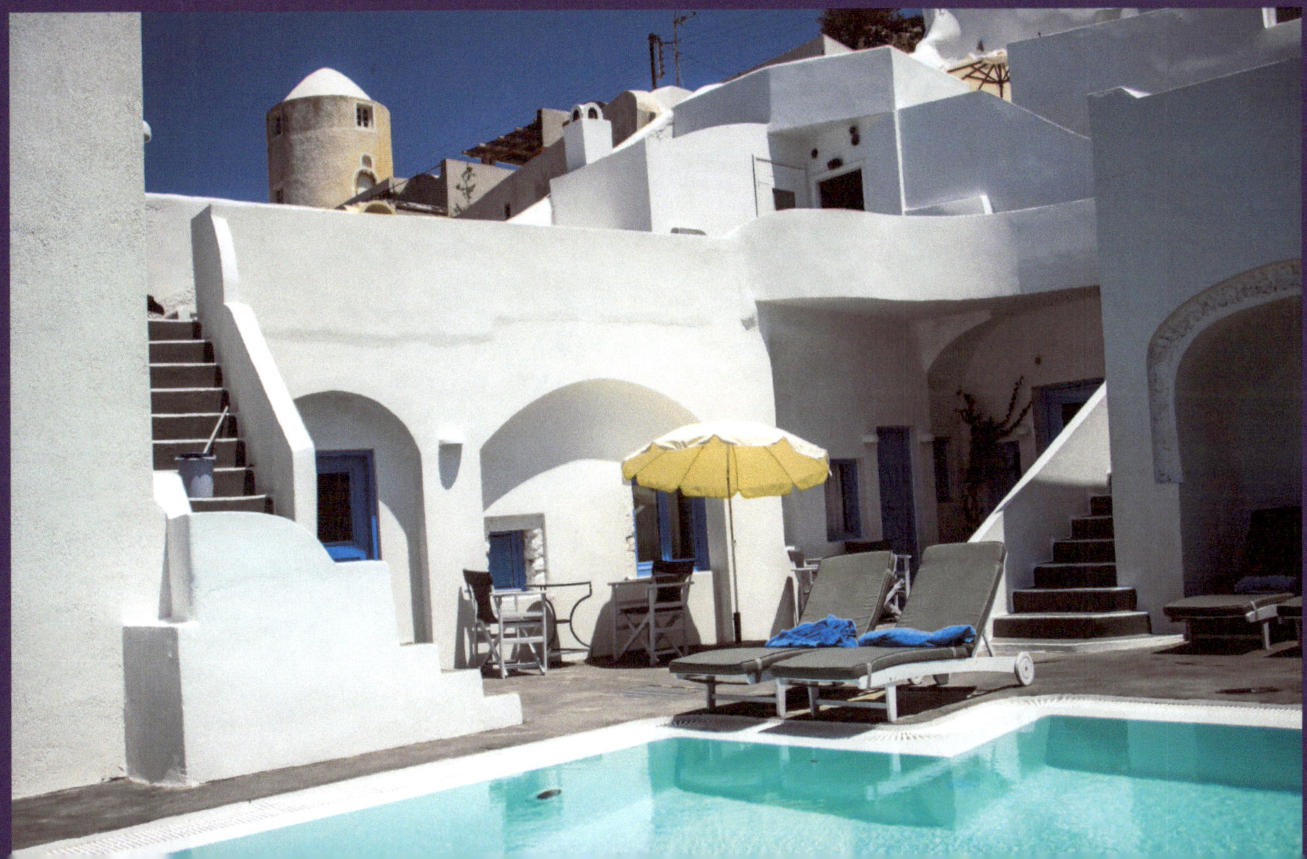

I rented a scooter again and rode it to the northern tip of the island. There's one small town named Oia, which is the tourist trap on Santorini where everbody goes to buy souveniers. Below is what you'll see from the shopping zone—remnants of buildings and lots of stone steps.

At sunset, people take their coolers, cameras and iPhones, and compete for the best places on the rocks from which they can watch the sun going down. We have the most beautiful sunsets in Sarasota, but this one is beyond comparison. I sat in a restaurant and shot the sunset photo on the right from there.

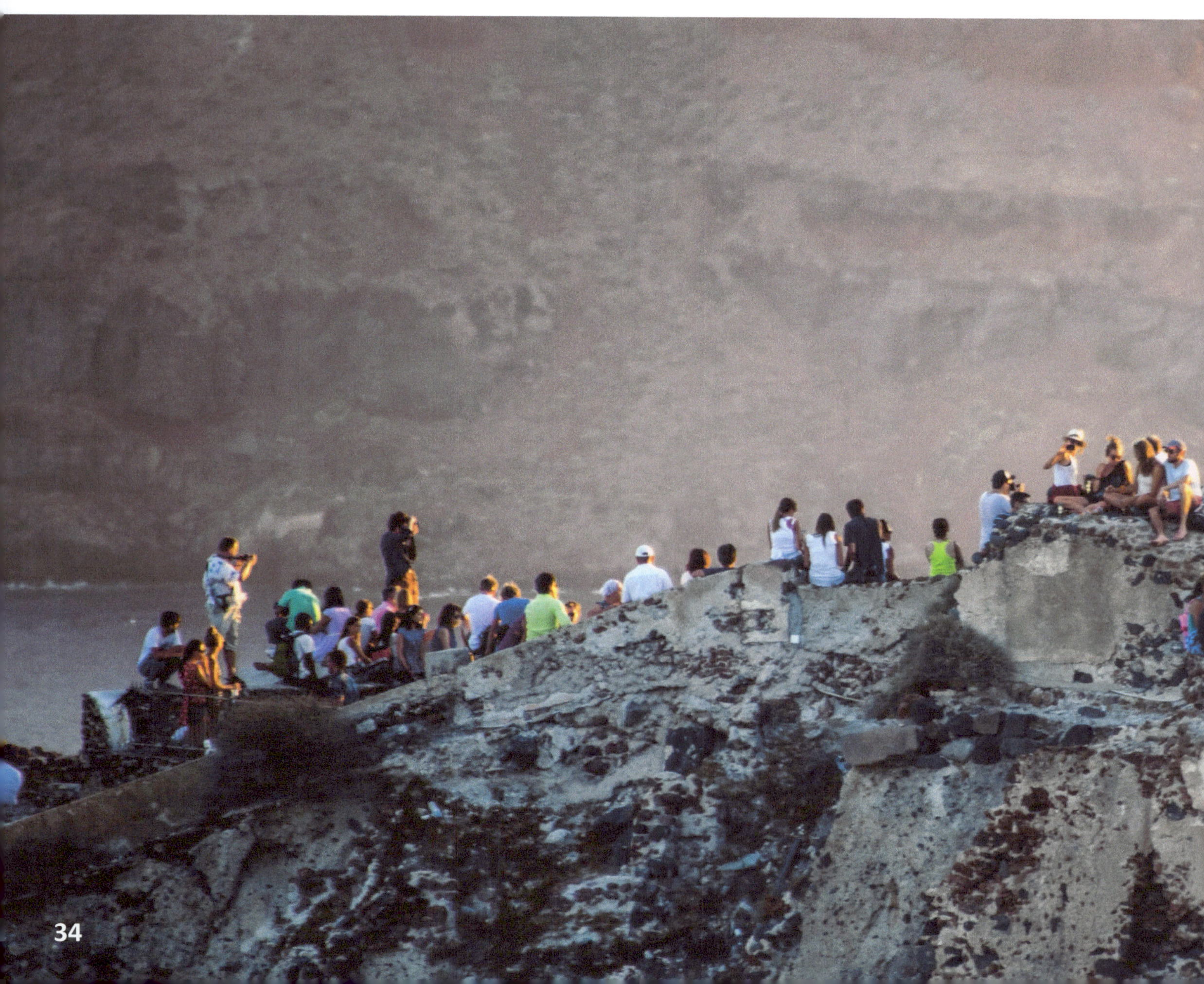

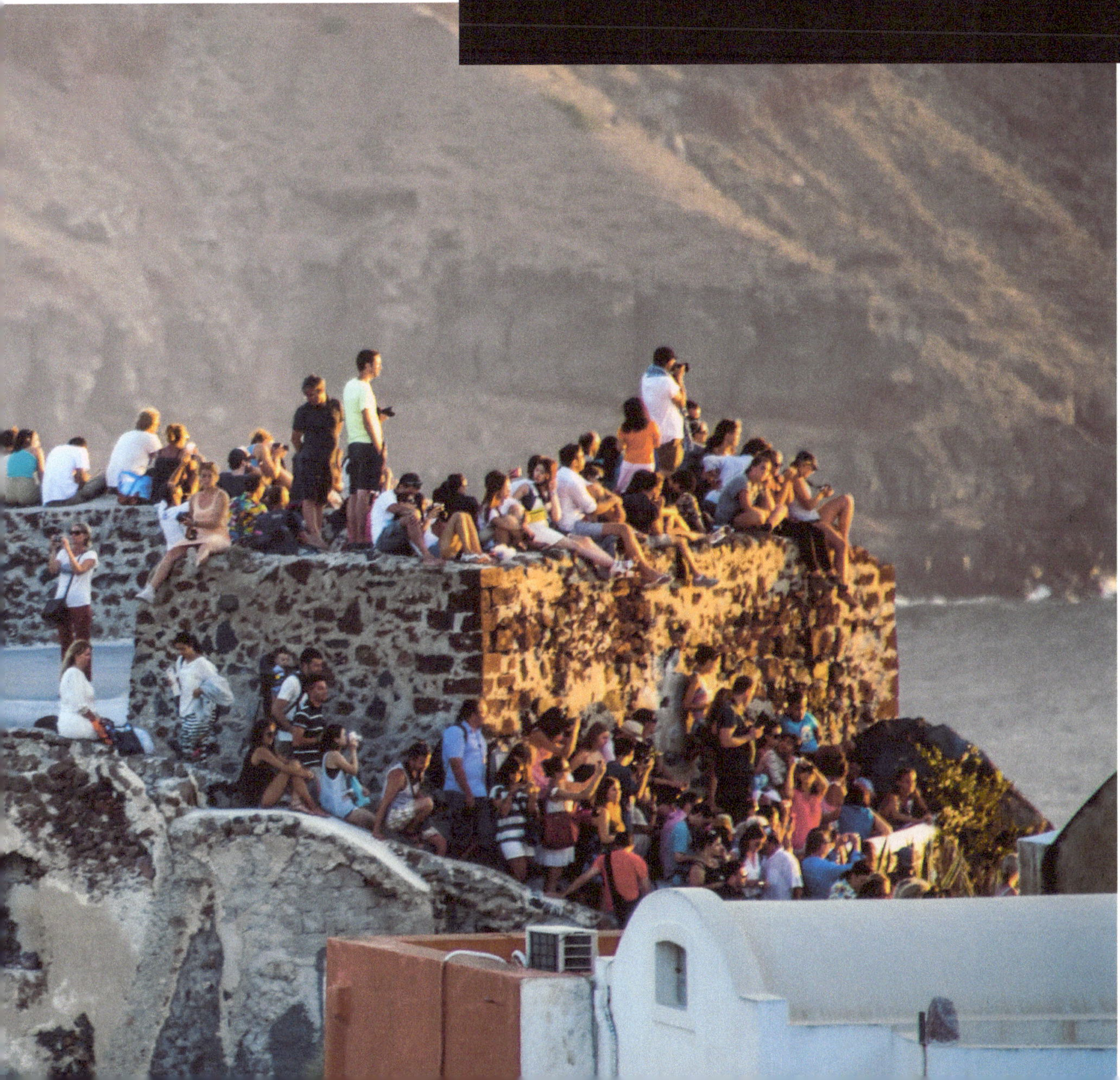

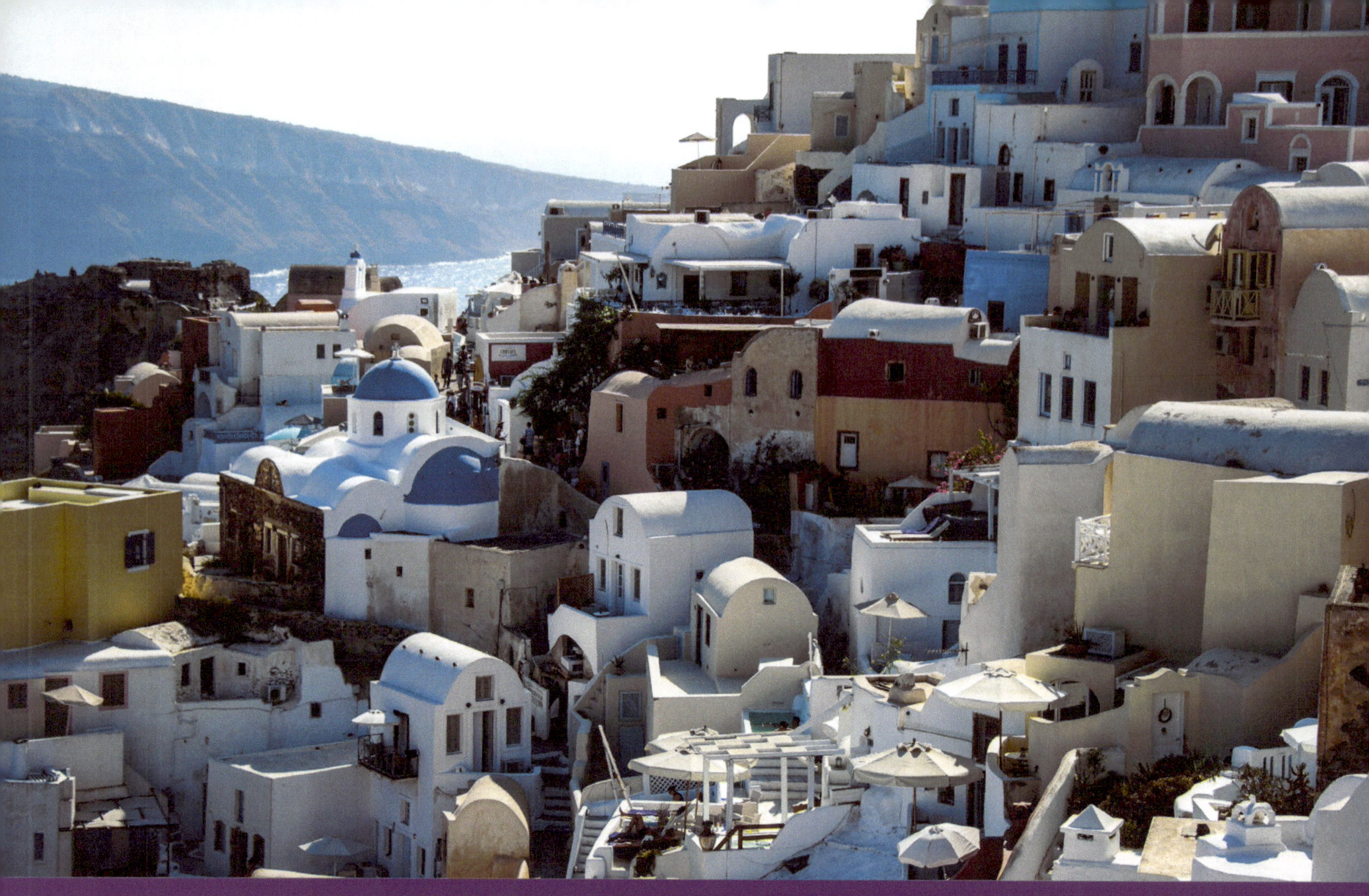

I shot these photos looking down the cliff from the promontory at Oia. When the houses start lighting up for the evening and night, it's magical.

These are the typical Santorini pictures you see on walls in apartments and in restaurants, and I was able to shoot them live. What you don't see in the photos are the little walkways you have to take to get from place to another. Although they're paved, you feel as though you're trekking through someone's living room.

The sad thing is that the cliff wall of Santorini is gradually falling apart. Unless we figure out a way to shore it up and save it, at some point it will plunge into the sea, and with it, all these beautiful buildings.

That catastrophe may be hundreds of years away, but when you hear about the island's ultimate fate, surrounded by such beauty, you can't help feeling a bit melancholic. You become aware of your own mortality, and it leaves you with a bitter-sweet taste.

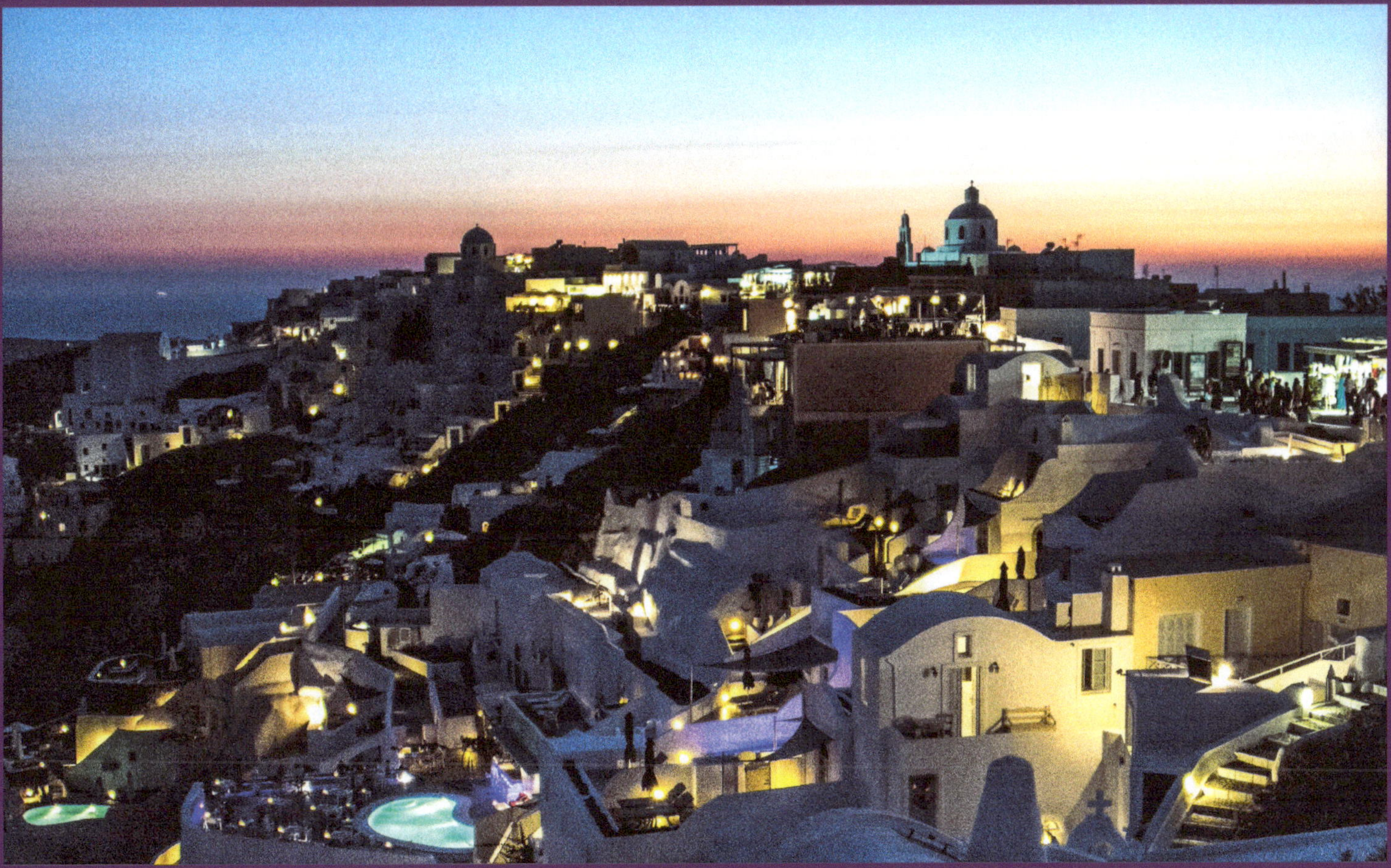

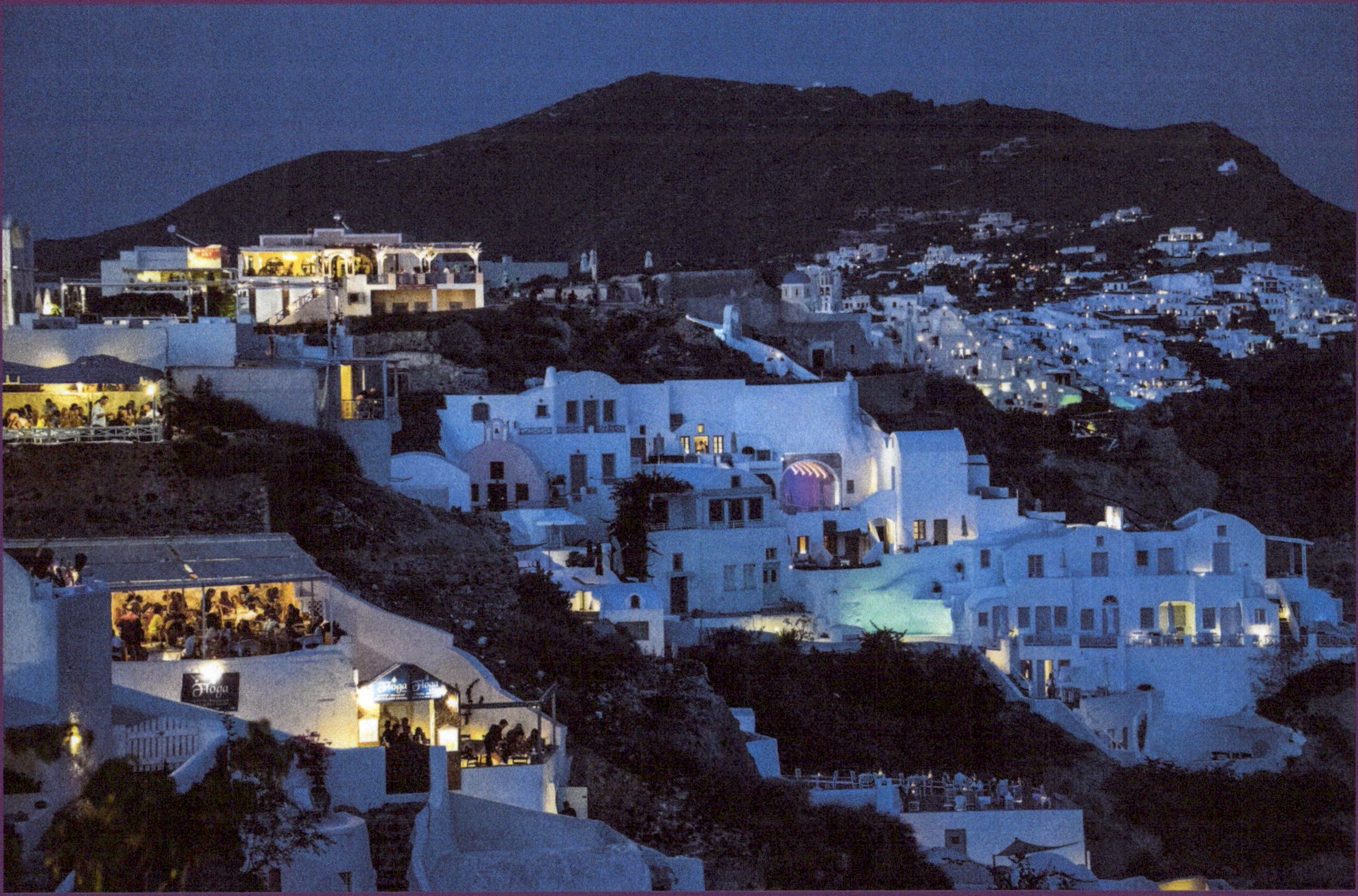

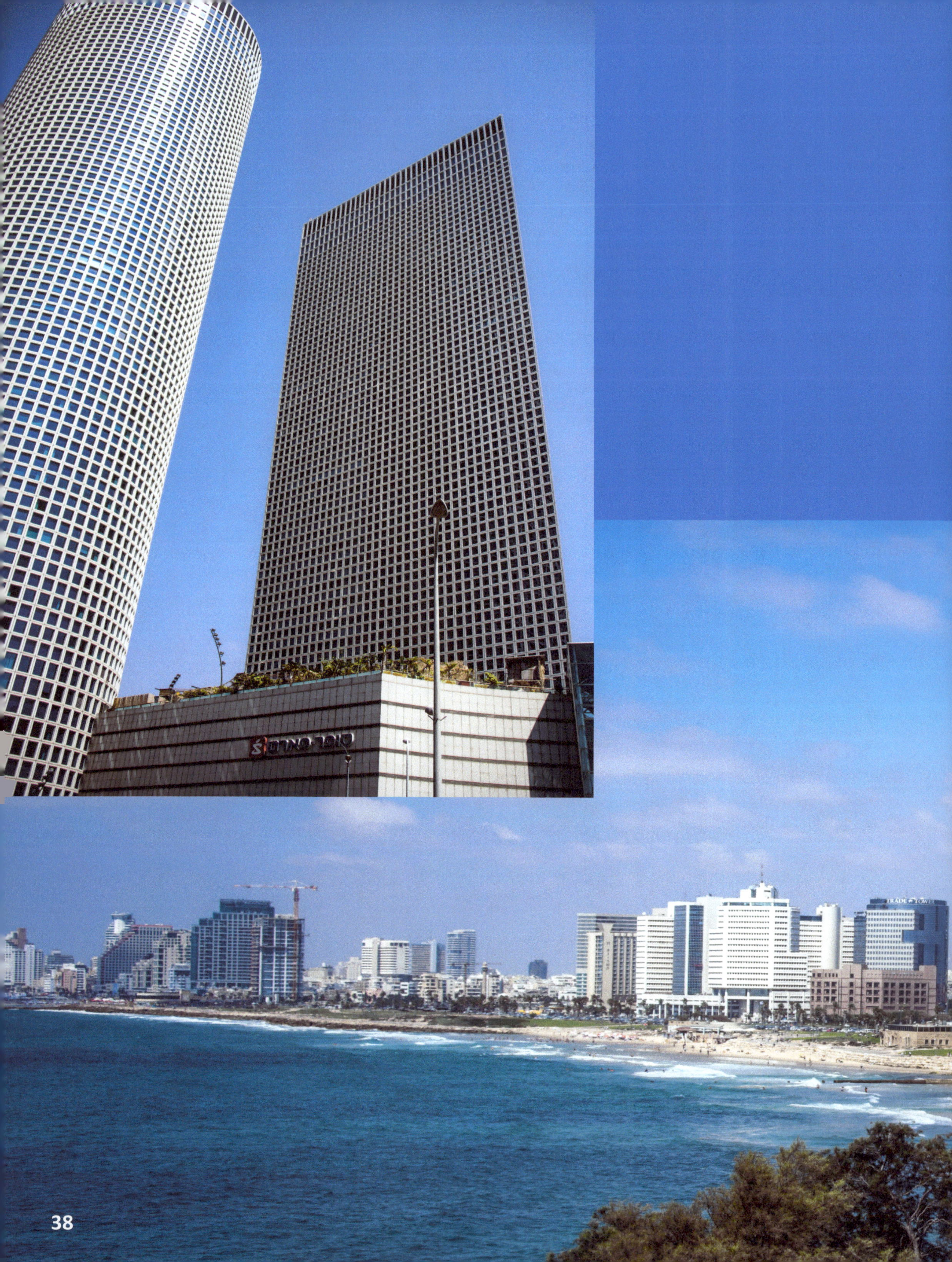
סופר-פארם
TRADE TOWER

# 5

# TEL AVIV

I left Santorini on a late Sunday afternoon and flew to Athens. Athens International Airport, *Eleftherios Venizelos*, is like Hartsfield in Atlanta and O'Hare in Chicago—you have to go there to fly anywhere. I had a four-hour layover and eventually arrived in Tel Aviv at 2:30 in the morning. You go through a rigorous custom control, and everyone's in uniform wearing an AK rifle. It was very daunting, but somehow reassuring.

I had never been to Israel before and didn't know what to expect. I had no idea where my hotel was. Fortunately, the taxi driver knew, but when I got there, it was shut for the night because it was very small. I had booked it online and received a code to get in—when you're on the road on your own, you hope it works, because otherwise you may end up spending the night sitting in front of your hotel with your backpack for company.

The code worked, but when I got to my room, it wasn't big enough to swing a cat. I felt like I was trapped in a cage. I made the decision right then and there never to skimp on a decent hotel room again.

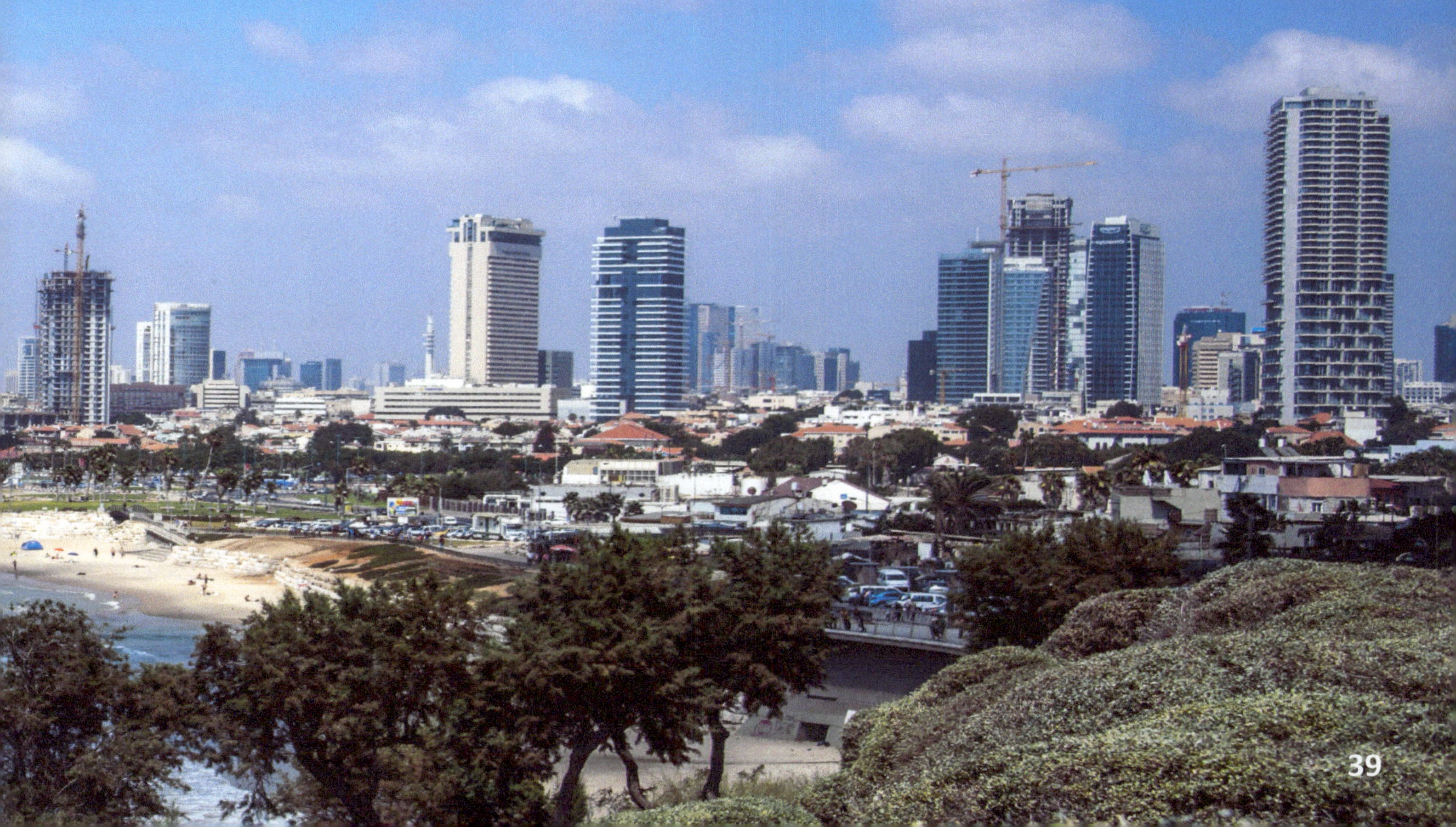

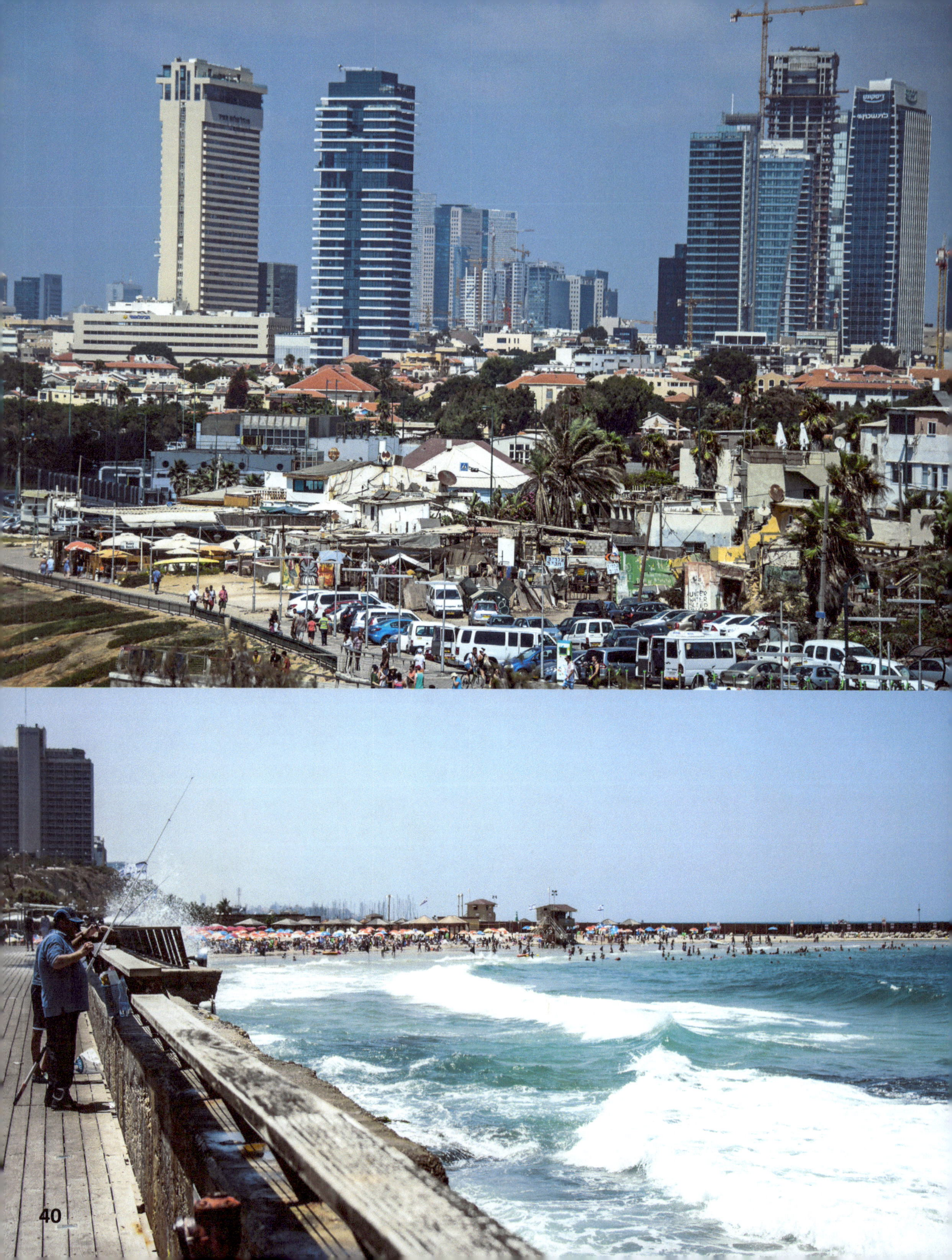

I walked round Tel Aviv for two days taking photos and enjoying the city. I also hired myself a taxi driver and had him take me on a more extensive tour. Tel Aviv is like any modern European city. Modern architecture, modern conveniences, lots of restaurants and public beaches on the Mediterranean Sea.

It was my first time seeing Hebrew signs everywhere. When I told the concierge that I was looking for an ATM, he pointed in a certain direction. I walked over to a machine that had Visa and MasterCard icons on it and a slit—it looked very official—and all the writing was in Hebrew.

I looked for a place to slide or insert my card in for at least five minutes until a security card walked up and said, "What are you doing?"

I told him, "I want to get money out of the machine."

He smiled and said, "This is where you redeem your parking ticket."

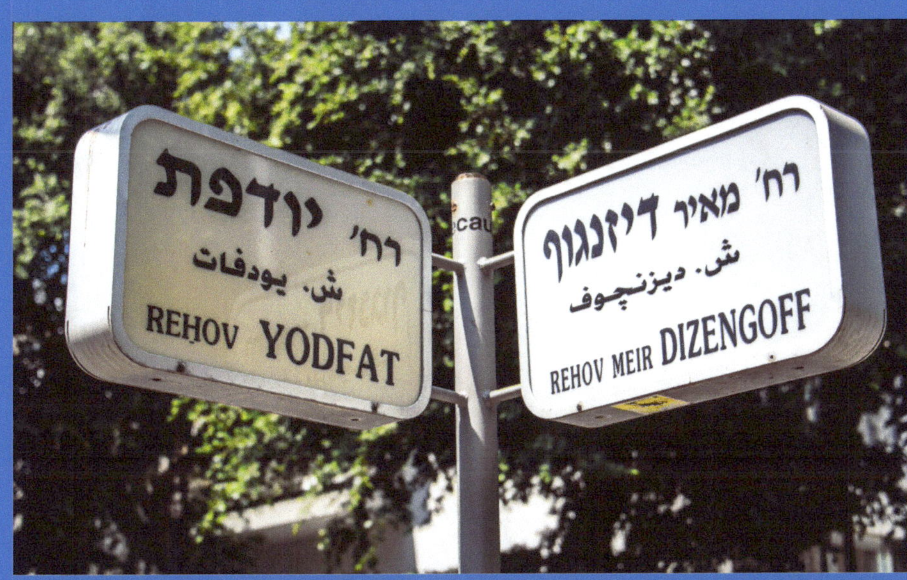


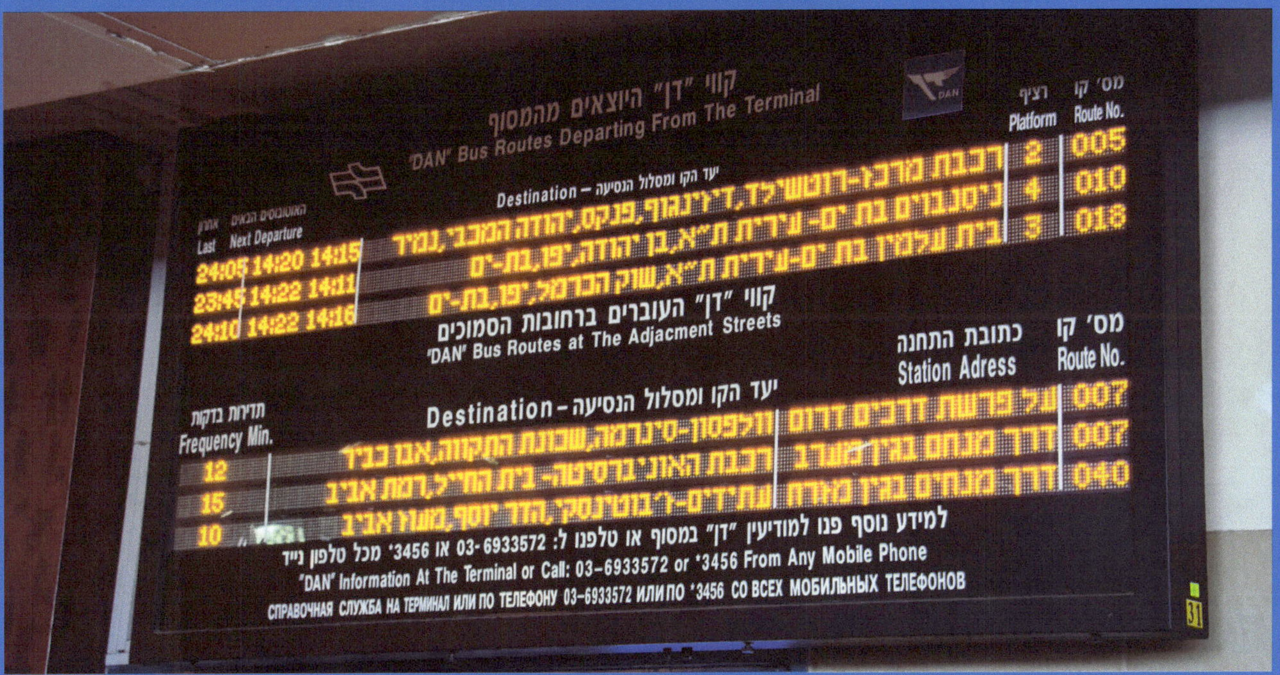

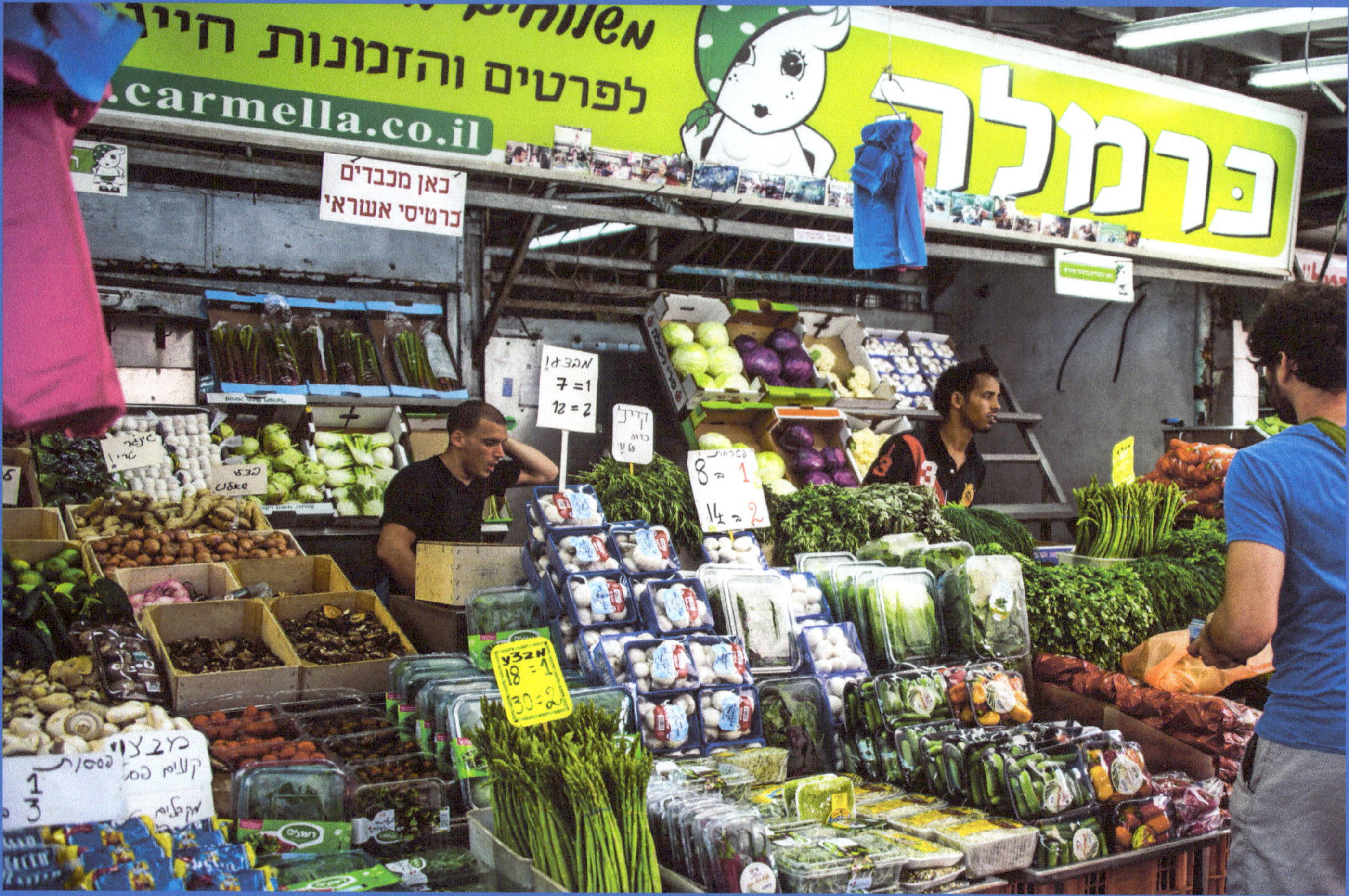

לפרטים והזמנות
carmella.co.il
כרמלה
כאן מכבדים
כרטיסי אשראי


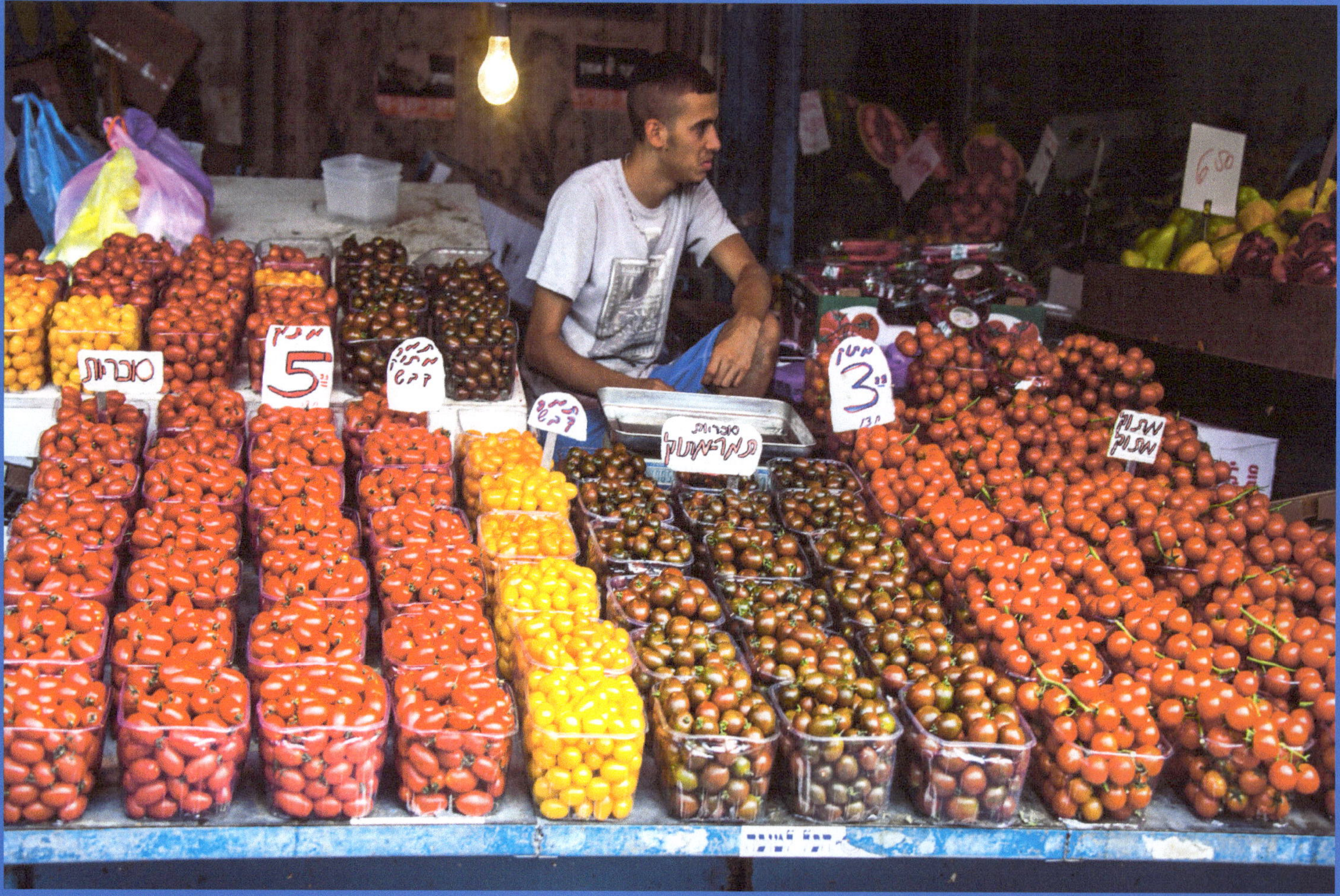

סוכריות

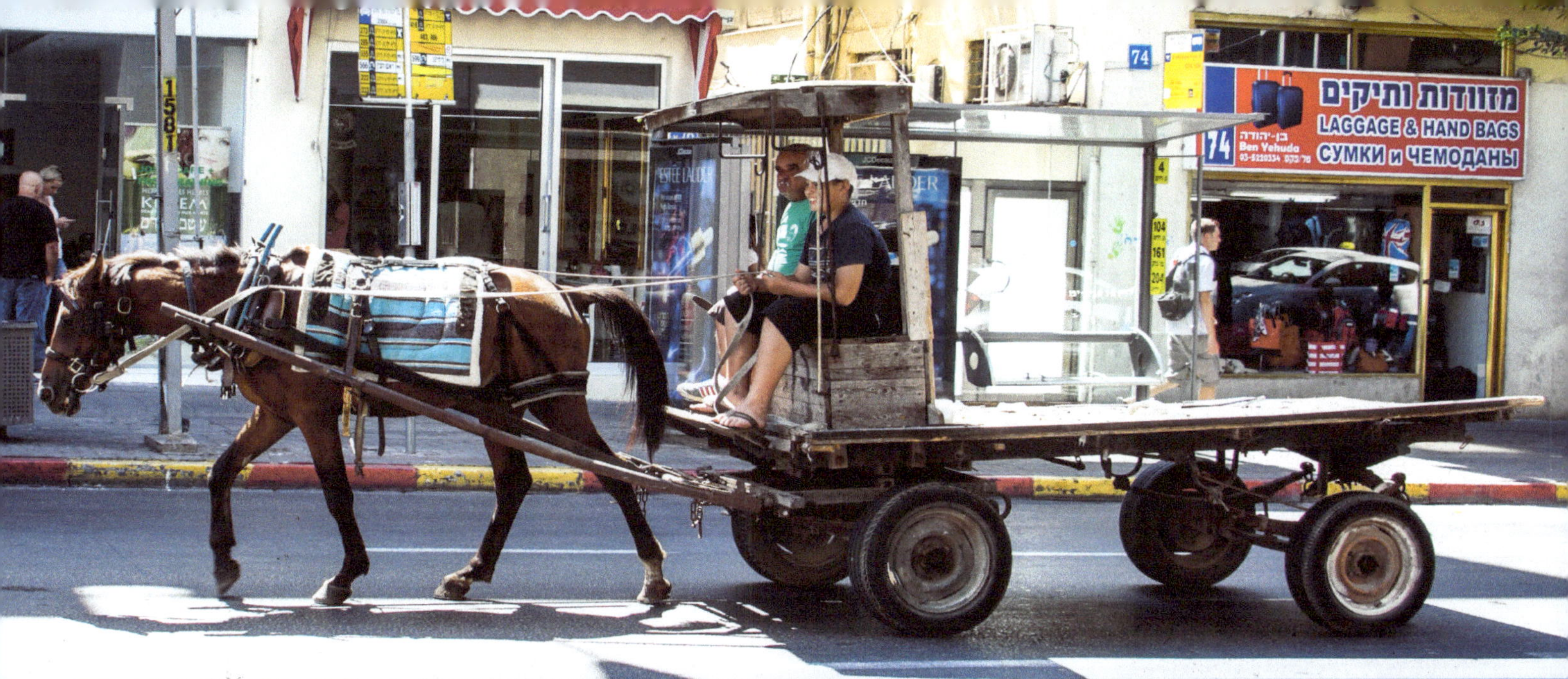


This is in a market in Tel Aviv. I love market places. The way the sellers present their goods with so much pride—dates, figs, olives, tomatoes, yellow peppers, and more. Many of the vendors speak English. Most of the people you meet in Tel Aviv and Jerusalem have spent some time in the United States; in fact they can speak 15 different languages because they have to.

Not all ways of getting around are modern. There are times when you think you're still in the 1940s and 50s. Another form of transport that I'd never seen before: I was walking from my hotel and this man rides by with this contraption and a gaggle of kids on it. Everybody was happy.

That was the same morning I decided to catch a bus to Jerusalem. In Israel, everyone uses little mini buses. Passengers stand around the depot and haggle. The buses have signs on them to every village and town in the country. Mine cost 25 shekels.

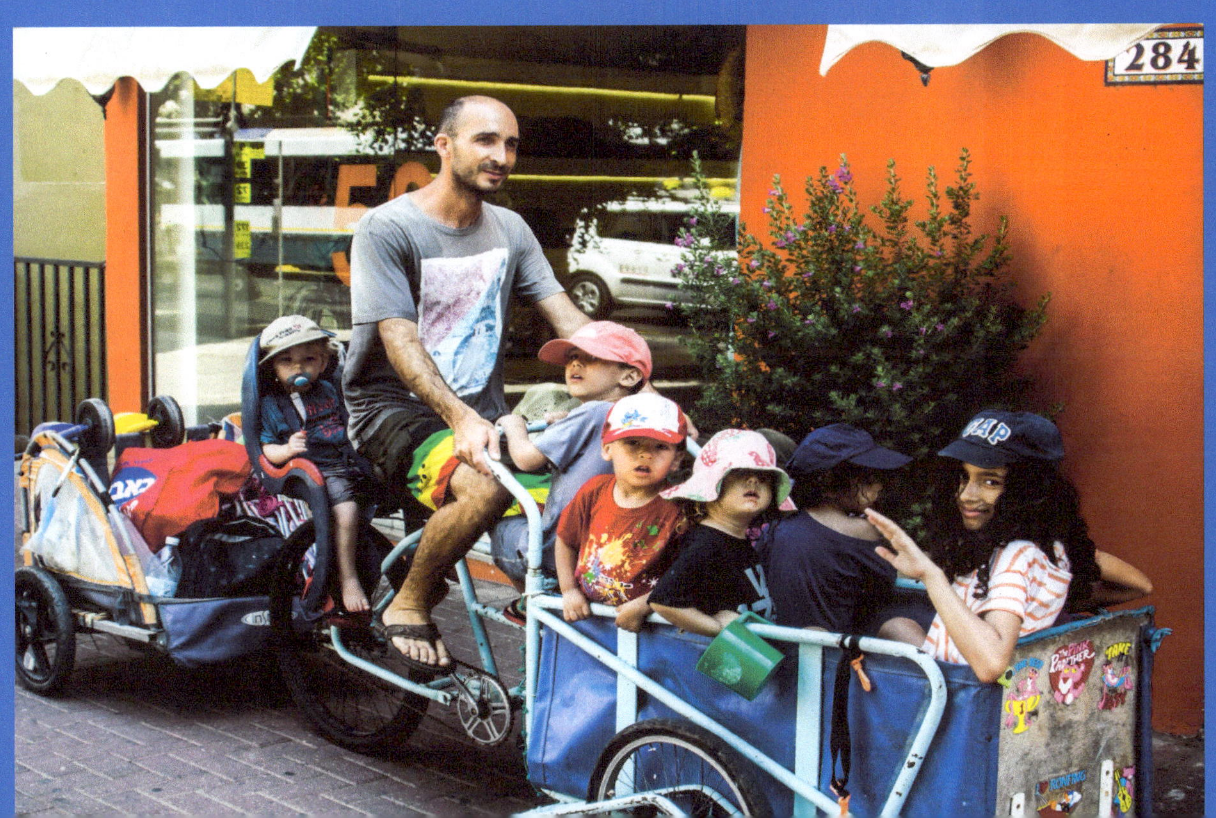

# TRANSPORTATION

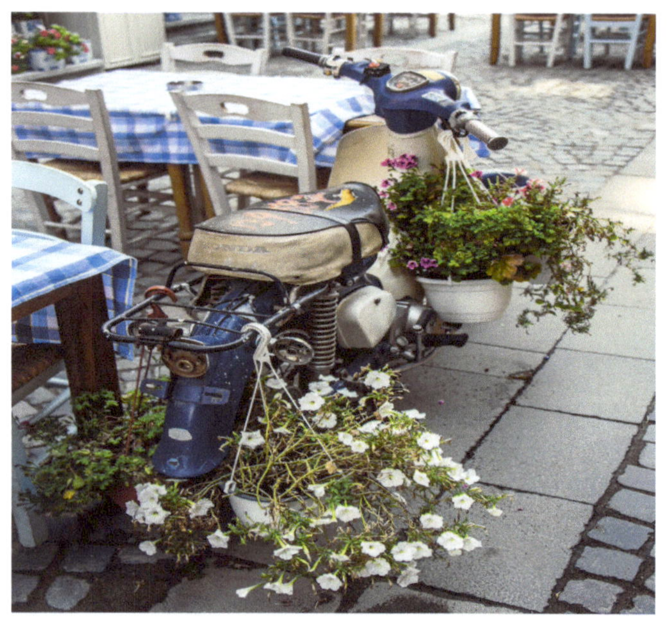

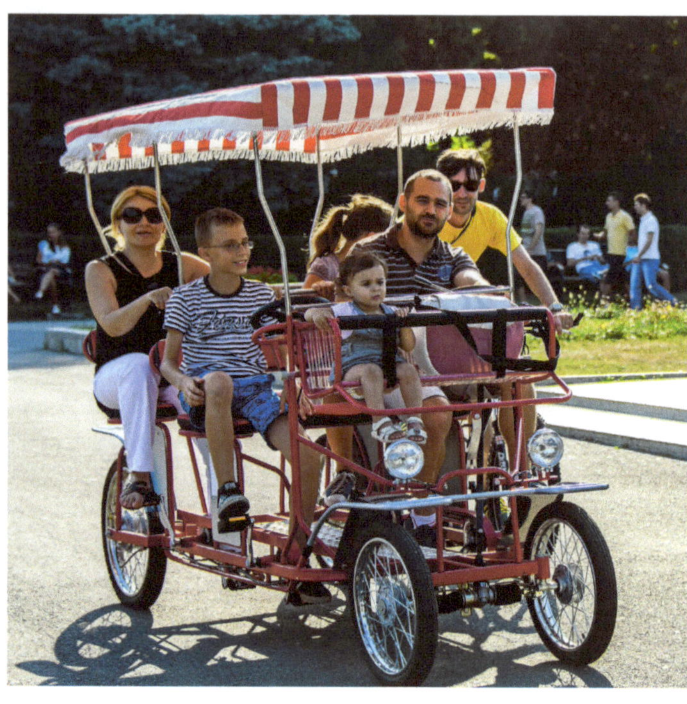

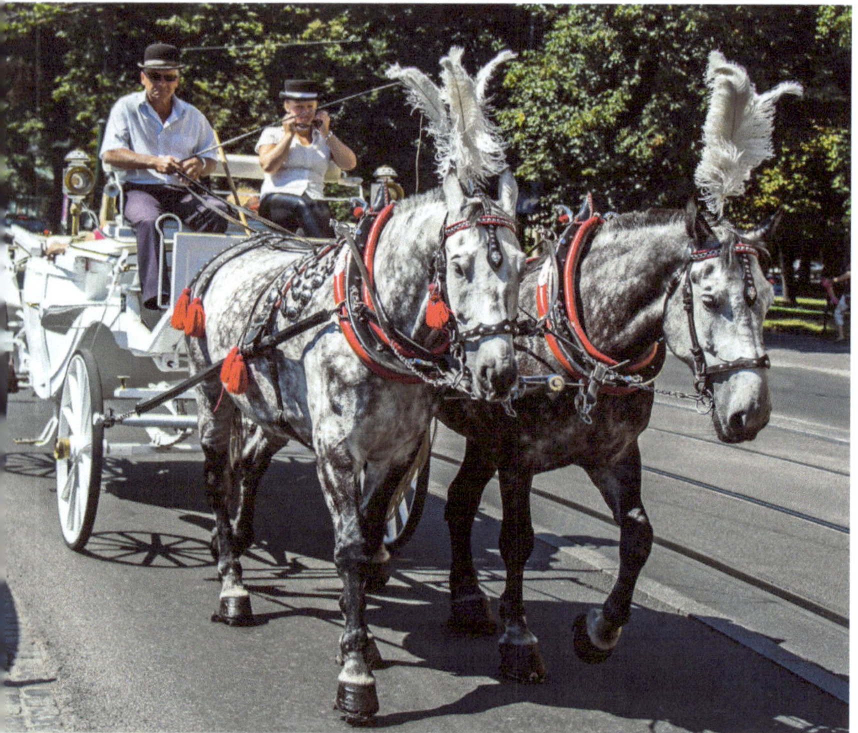

Speaking of transporation, I found everywhere I went that people were really creative when it came to getting around.

From traditional horsedrawn carriages (Krakow) to decorative motorcycles to all kinds of pedal bikes, there is more variety among conveyances than in American cities.

The flower motorcyle and four-wheel family "taxi" are from Bucharest.

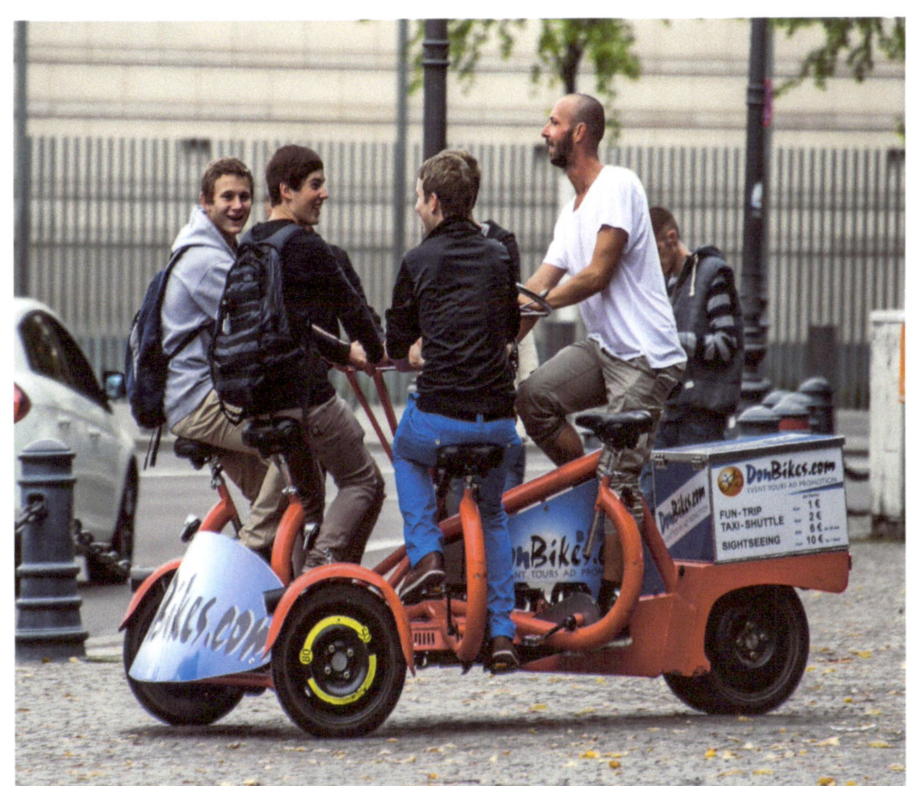


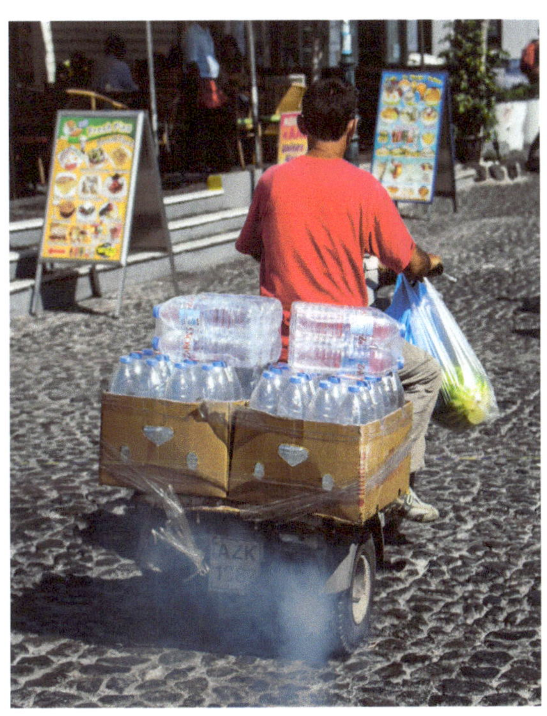

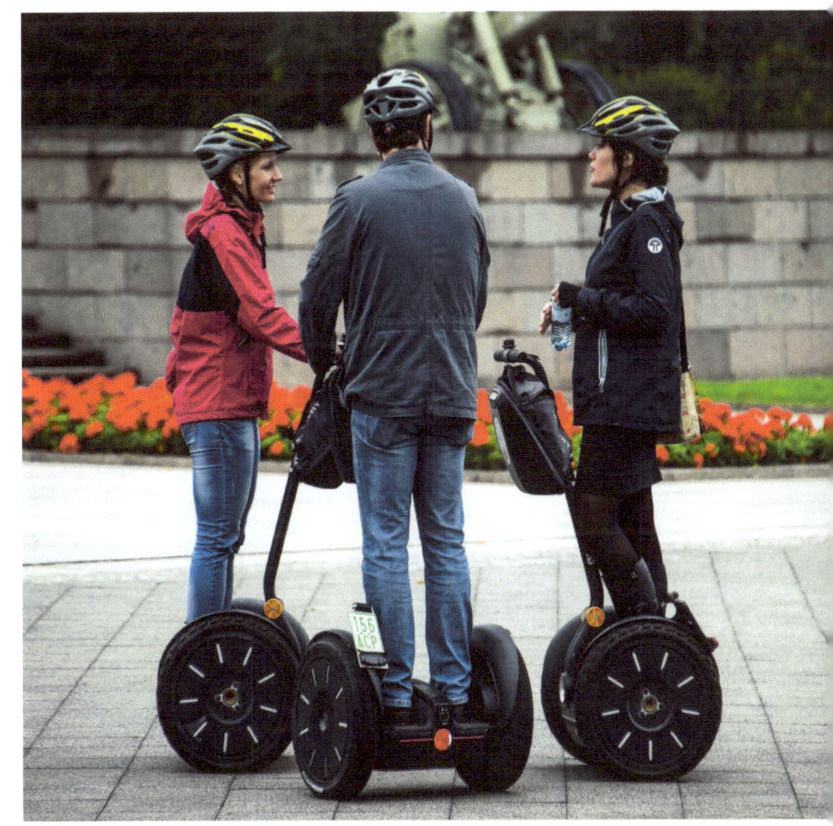

You can rent the above bike contraption in Berlin, and everyone gets to pedal—incredible.

The putt-putt, three-wheel moped is from Santorini.

Segways have become more popular everywhere in Europe. A lot of towns offer tours and rent them. They use them with a guide that goes round the city with you. These three are in Berlin.

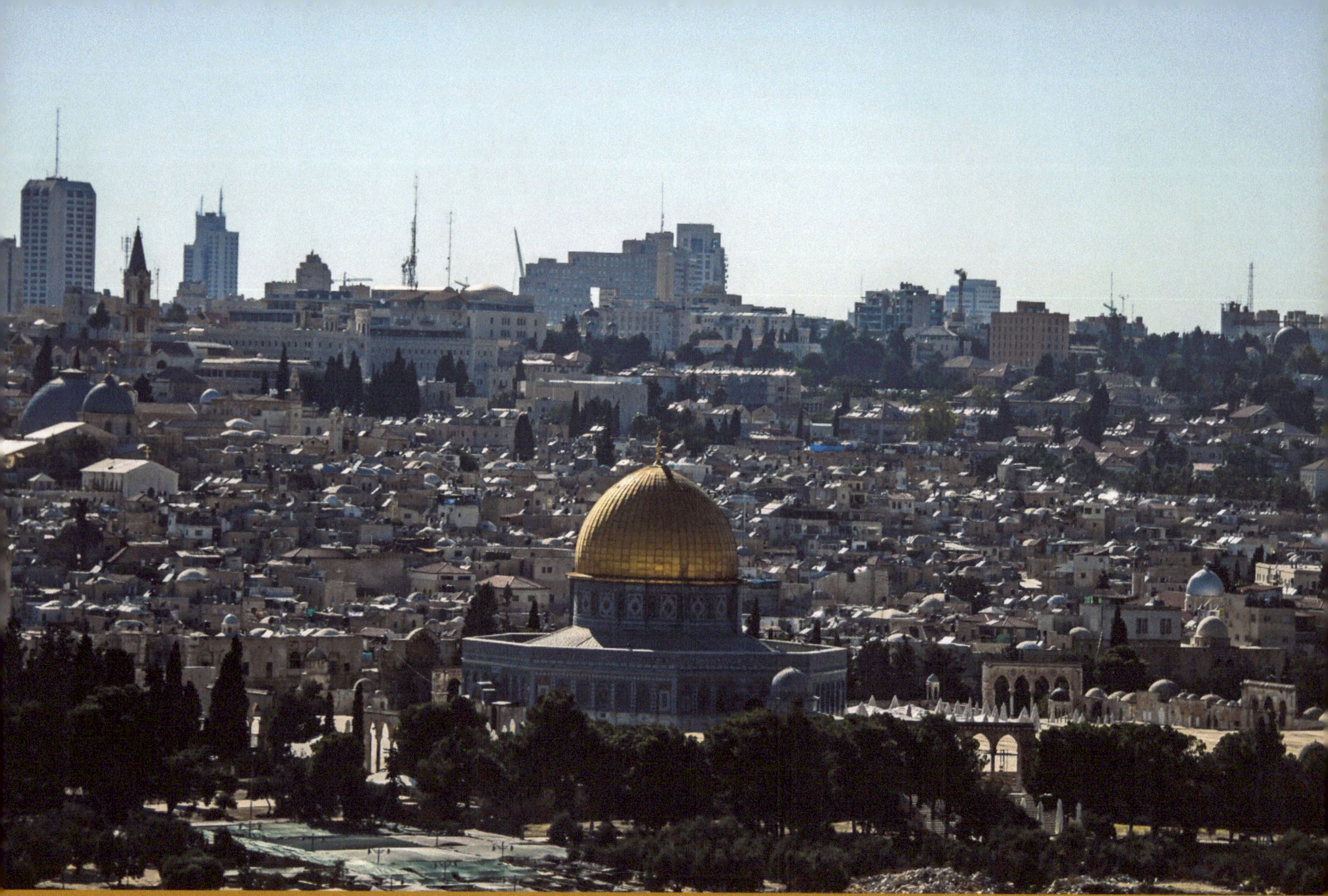

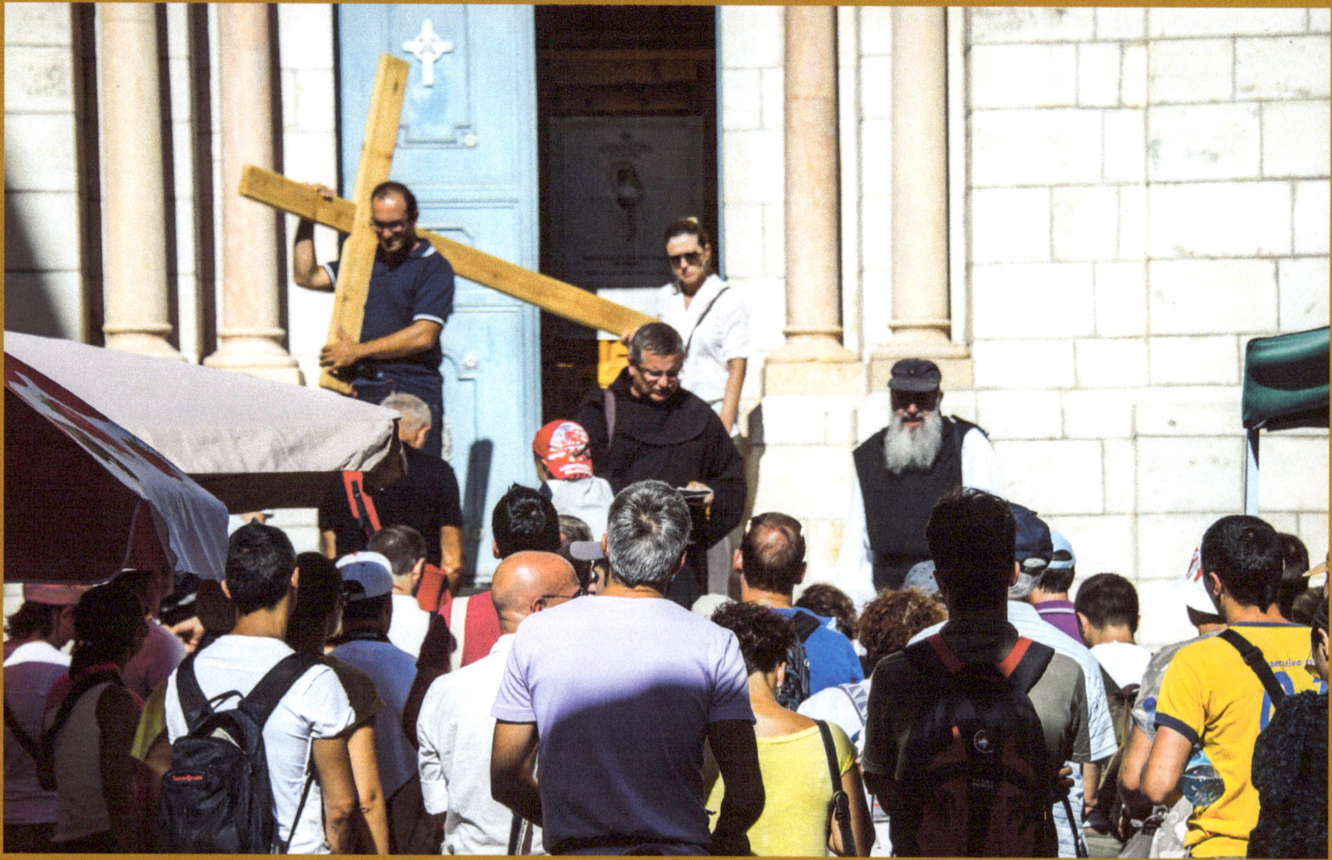

# 6

# JERUSALEM

You cannot go to Israel without going to Jerusalem. It's an incredible city—my Number 1 favorite place of the whole trip. I want to return and take people back with me and experience it again. I never was in a city before where three major religions bounce off one another—Islam, Christianity and Judaism.

This is the view of old Jerusalem from the Mount of Olives. Anyone who travels to Jerusalem must go there. Take a taxi or whatever because you have to get that view—preferably early morning when the sun is behind you and you'll get a better picture. It's a wonderful site—you're mesmerized, you really are, just to be there.

I got a great hotel on the outskirts of town—it had restaurants and a clean bed. It was called the Jerusalem Gate, and I used it as my base. Just started walking, got on the hop on/hop off, and rented a taxi guide. There is also a lovely tram system, brand-new and wonderfully clean, that runs around the whole of the city. You can't get lost. At some point, everything lands you in the old part of the city.

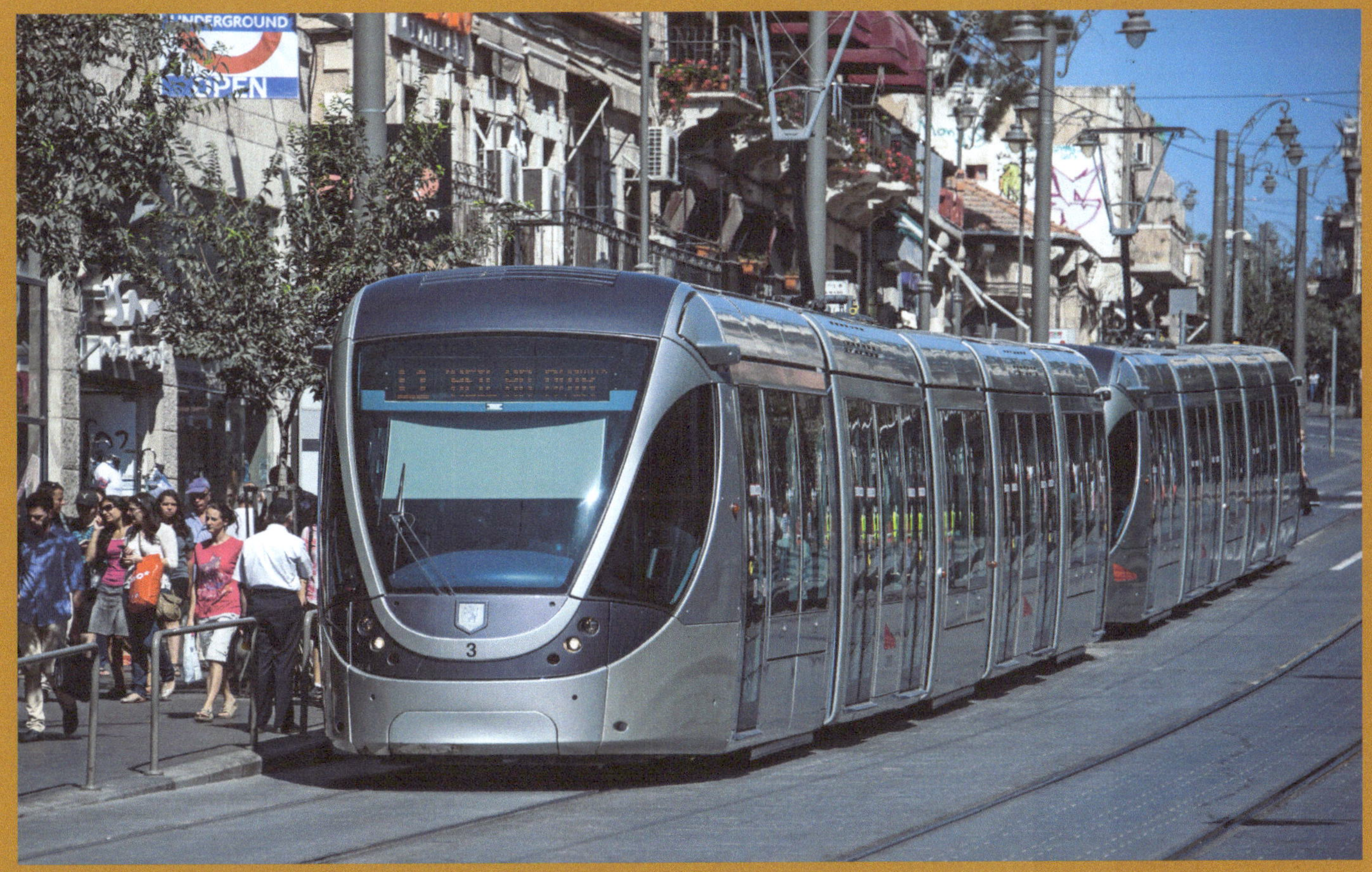

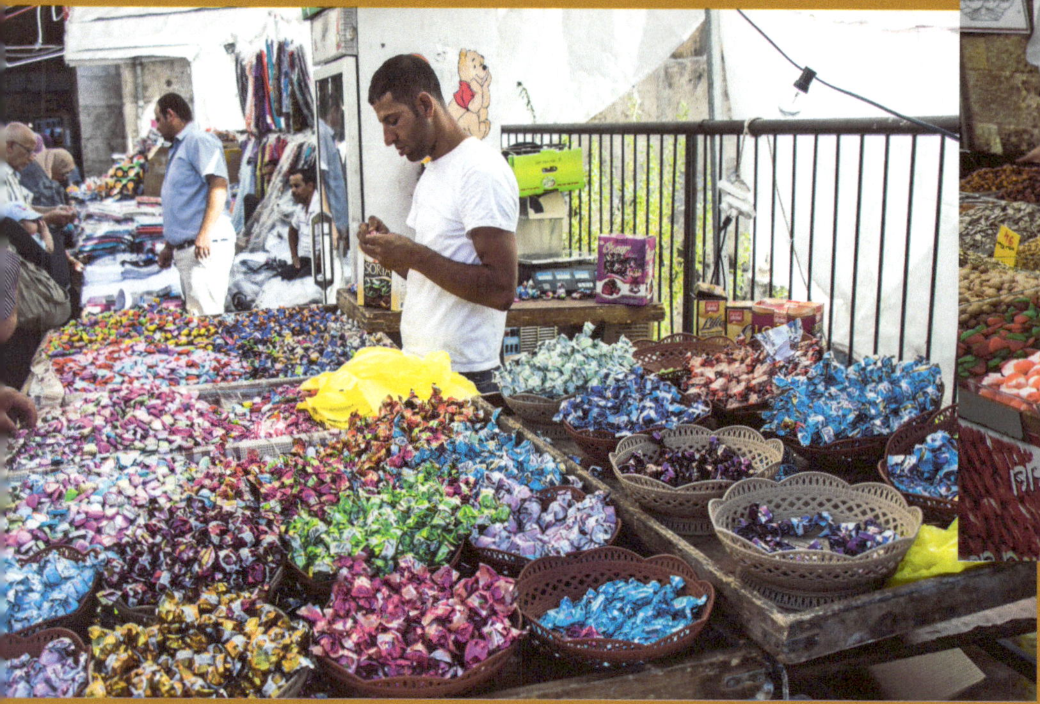

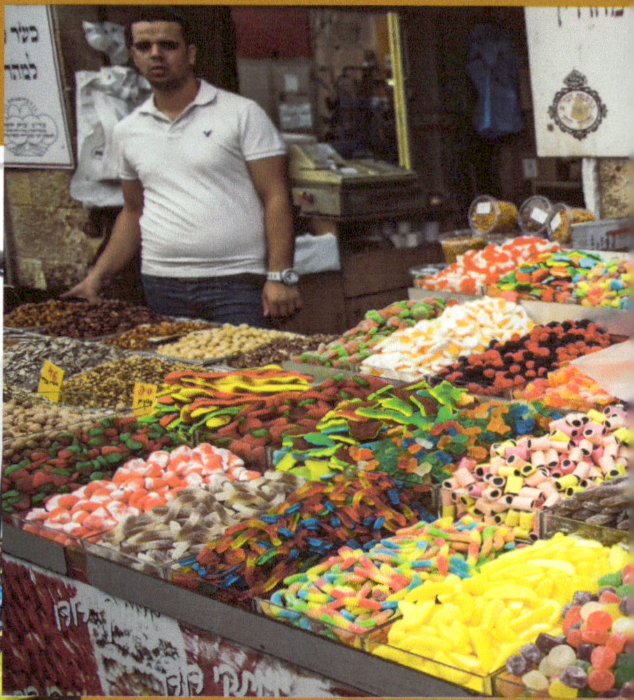

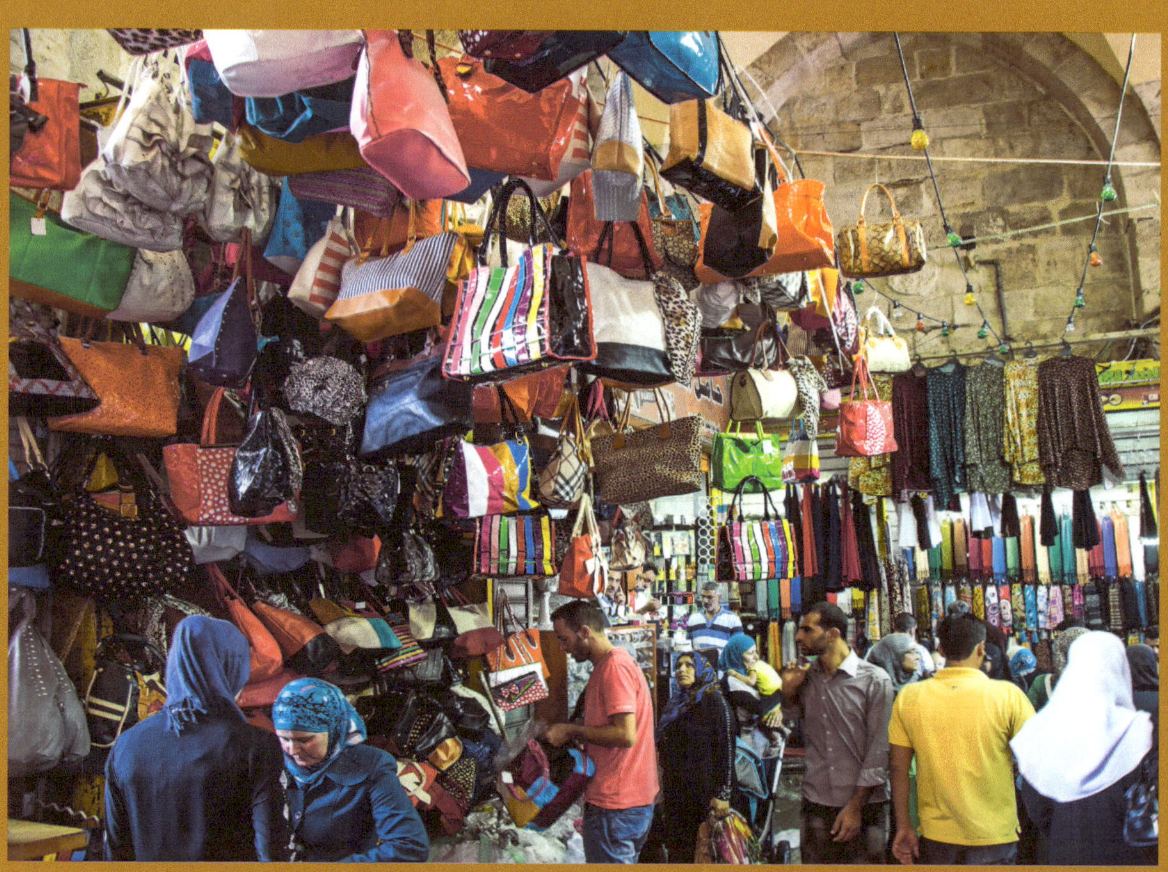

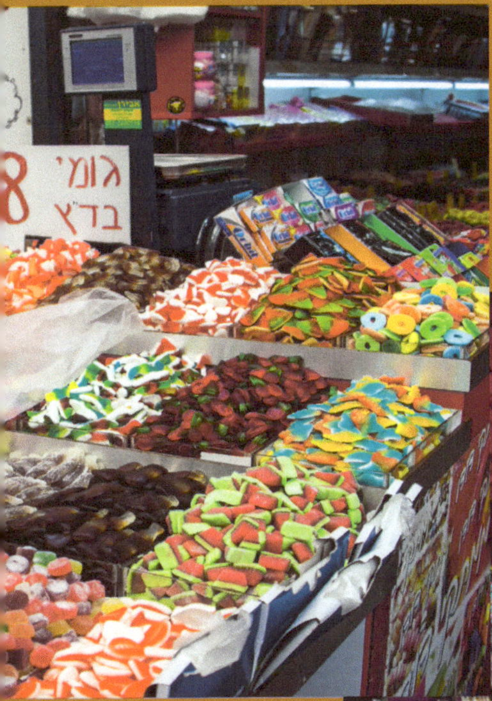

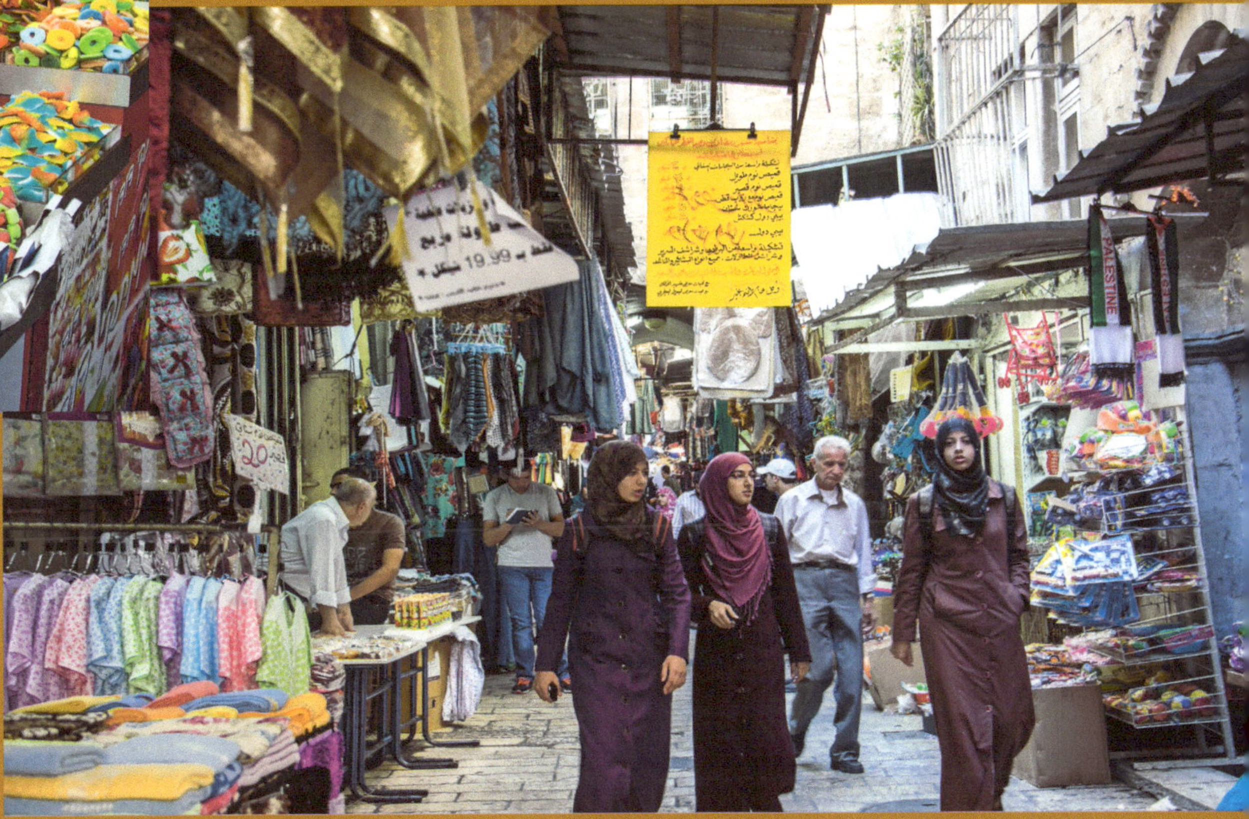

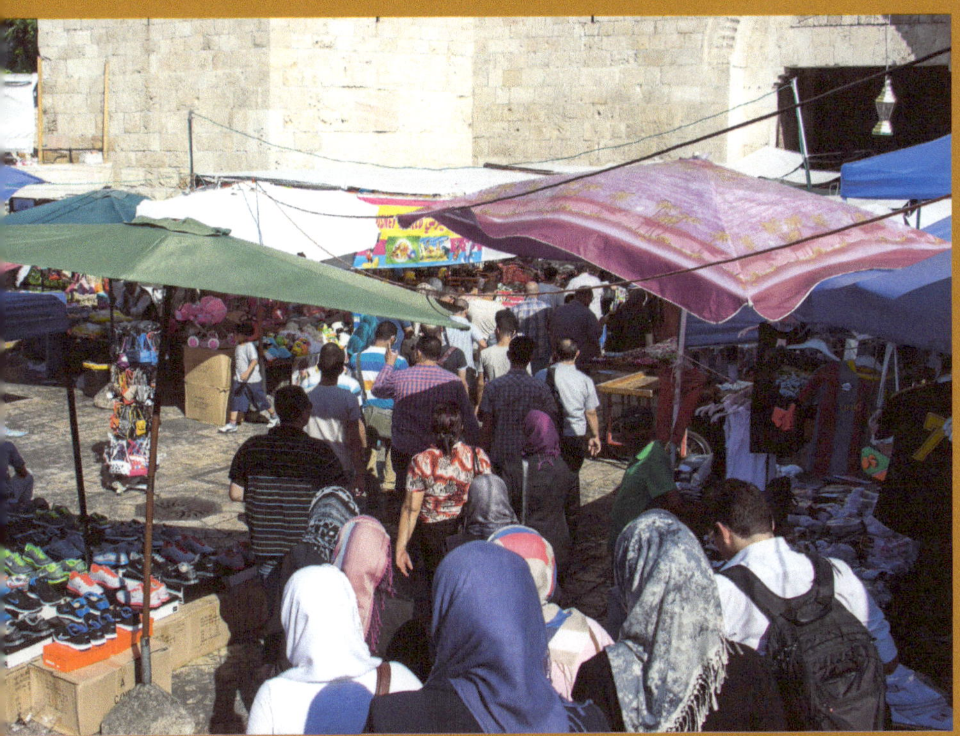

To reach the Jewish Wailing Wall you have to walk through the Arab market. Everyone's shouting and trying to sell you their wares. It's a bit unnerving at first, if you're on your own and not familiar with the noisy bartering and competing vendors. Once I got used to it, I felt okay, and even enjoyed it. Being surrounded by such energy is an incredible feeling—the sounds, smells and amazing colors...

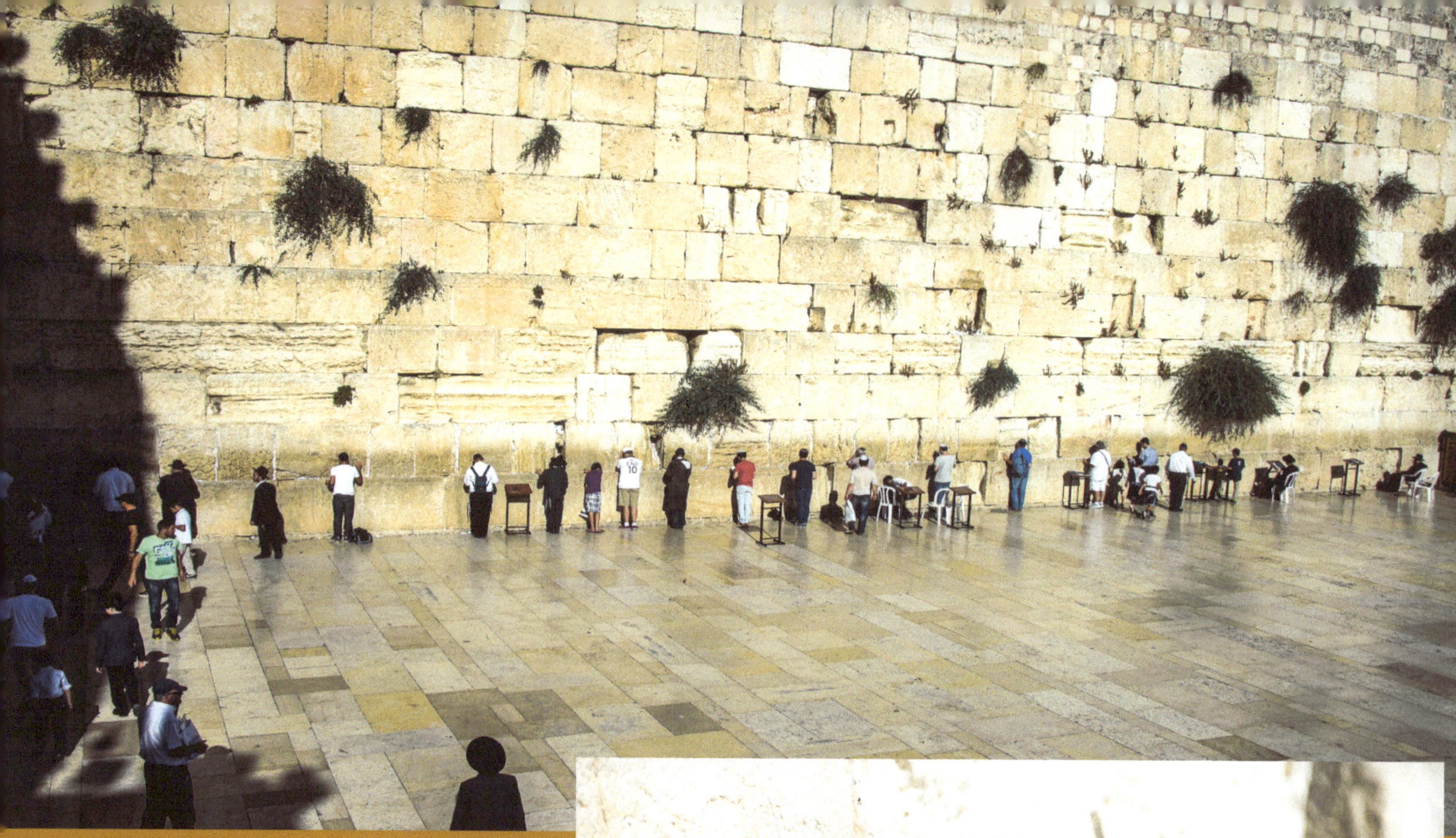

...and then, all of a sudden, you emerge onto the big plaza and there is the Wailing Wall, located at the foot of the Temple Mount, the holiest place in Judaism where Jews can go to pray. One side has men only, and a primitive fence separates them from the women and children on the other side.

There are people standing with their head against the wall, putting paper into the cracks and rocking from side to side, reciting the Torah. It's as if they are in a trance. I could have lifted their wallets from their back pockets and they wouldn't have noticed. You can go up to them, stick your camera right next to them and start clicking, and they don't mind.

If you go to the left of the wall inside the covered part, clerics, teachers and tourist are sitting, reading, studying and rocking, all in their own worlds. Ancient books and plastic chairs. When you visit the Wailing Wall, you have to wear a yamulka or they'll run after you and make you put one on.

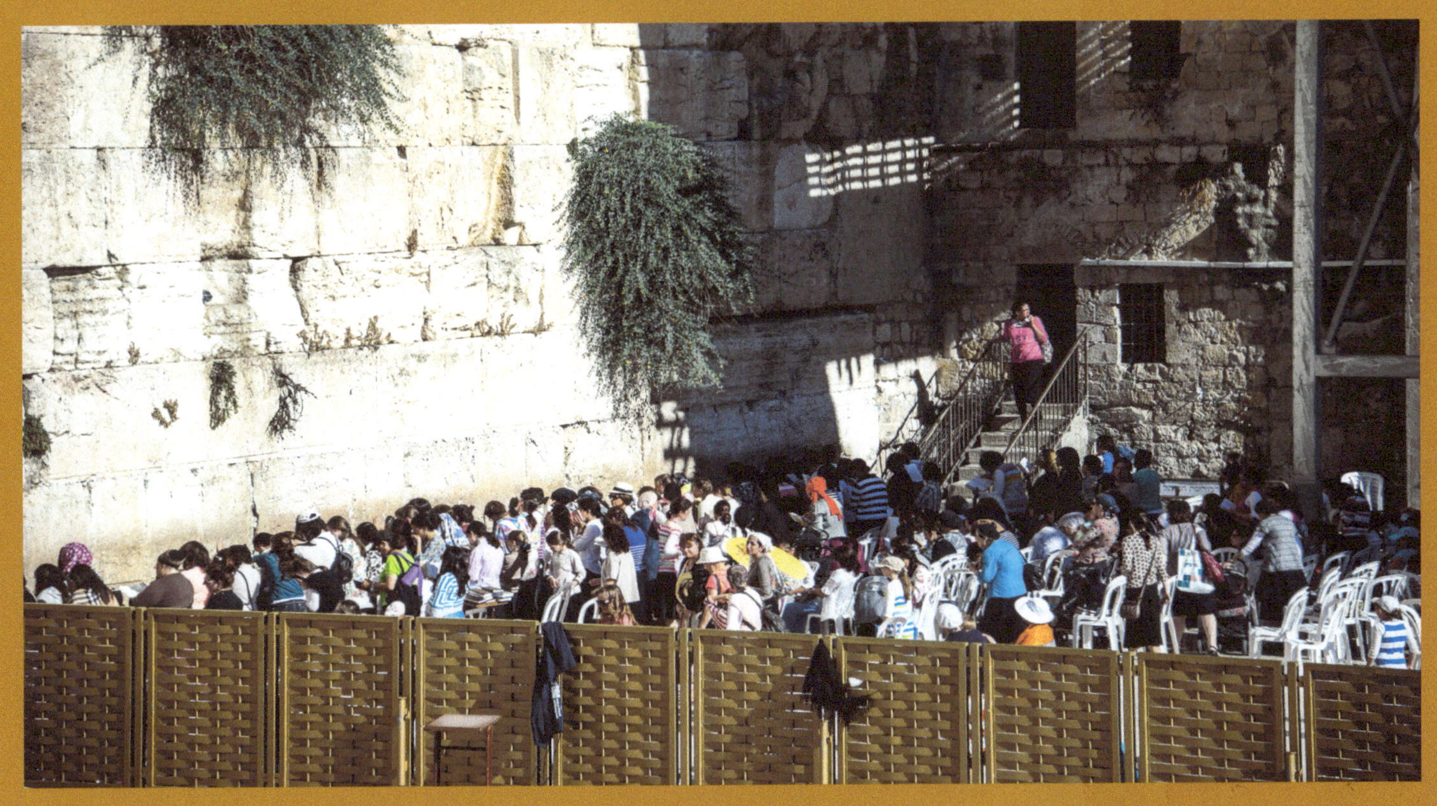

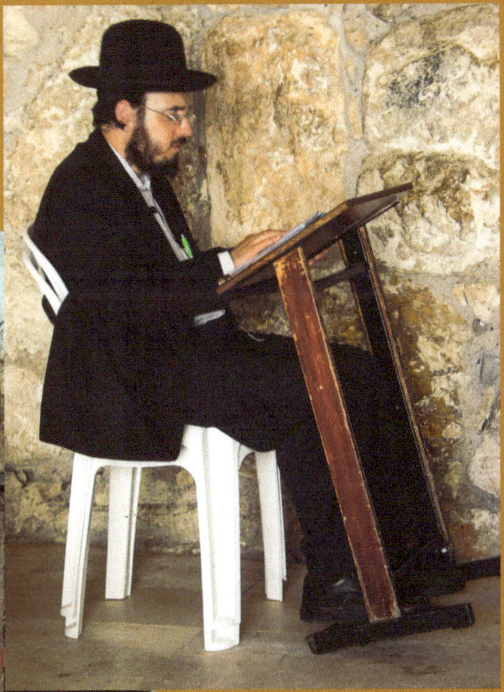

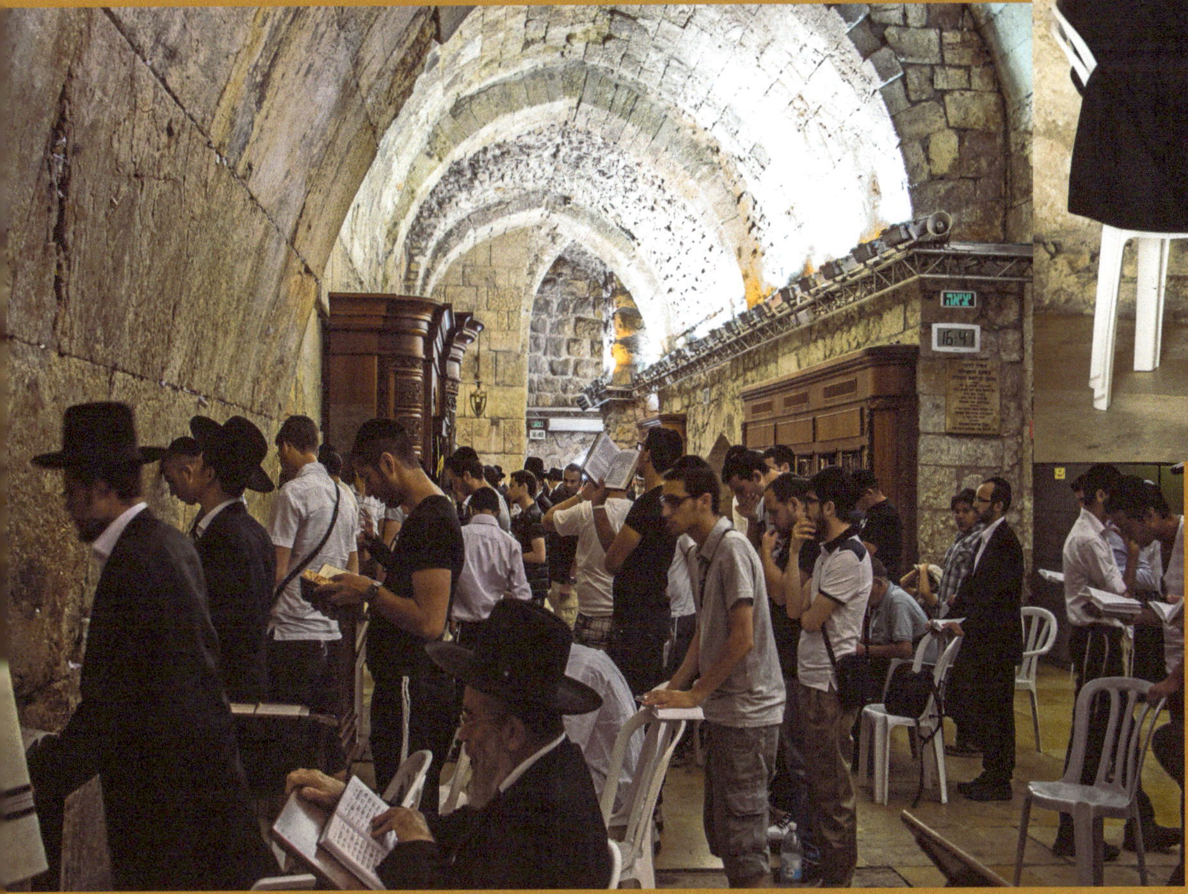

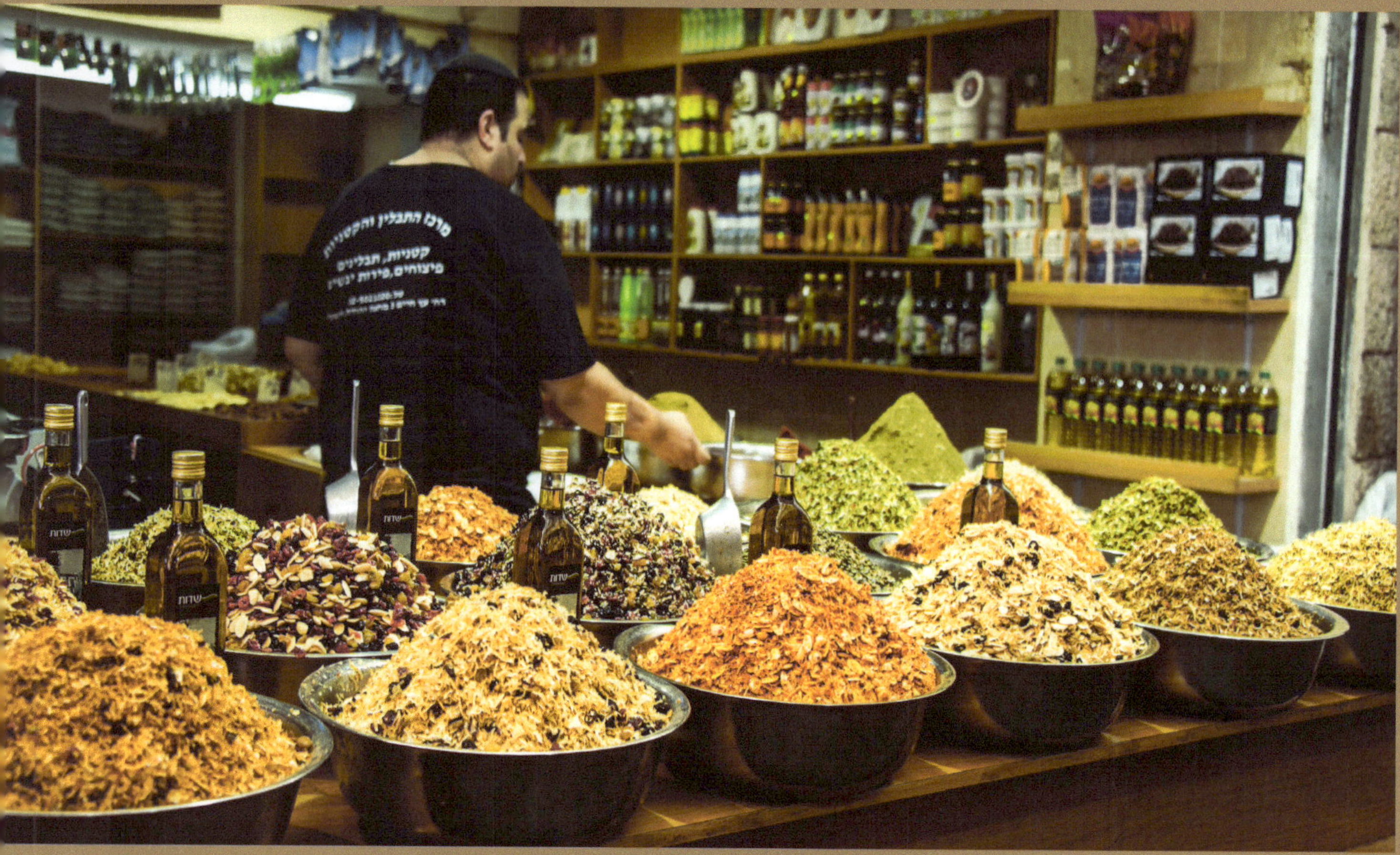

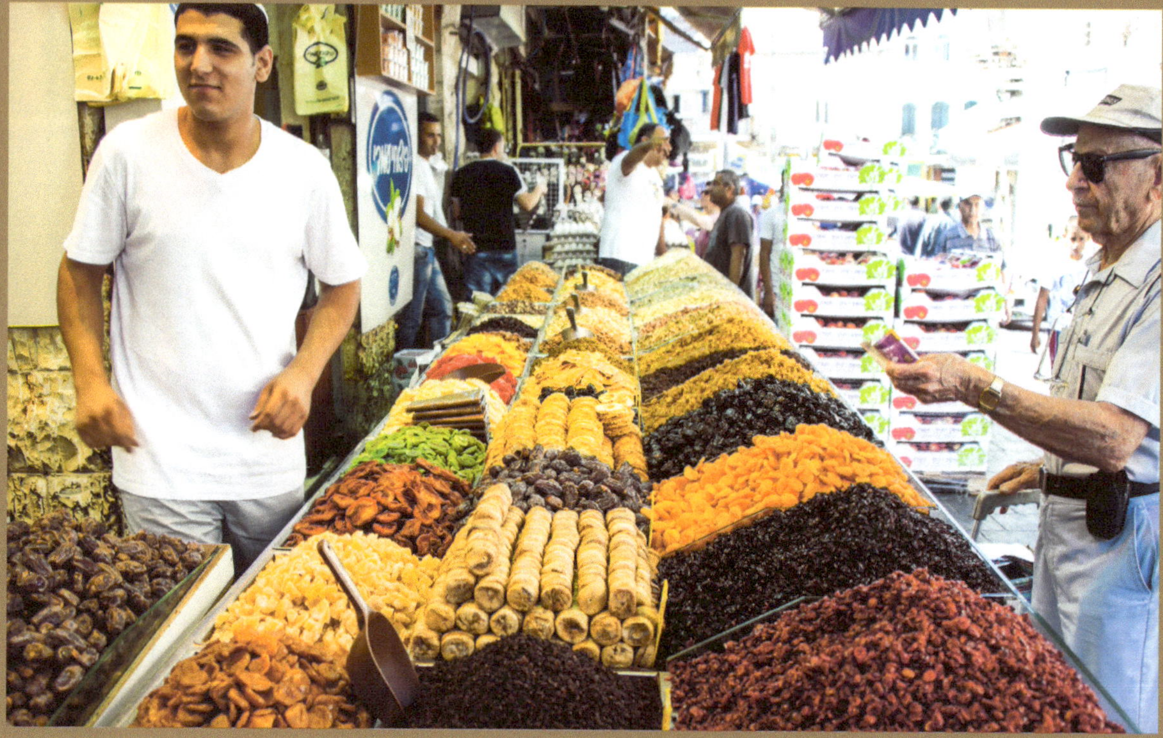

You could you tell the difference between Jewish and Arab parts by the distinct difference in wares and products, sights, sounds and smells. I went to the most fantastic Jewish indoor market. I could've spent all day photographing, it was so fascinating. The beautiful selections of herbs, spices, fruit, figs, nuts, bananas, soaps, cheeses, breads, all so appetizing. The Israelis love their confectionery, too.

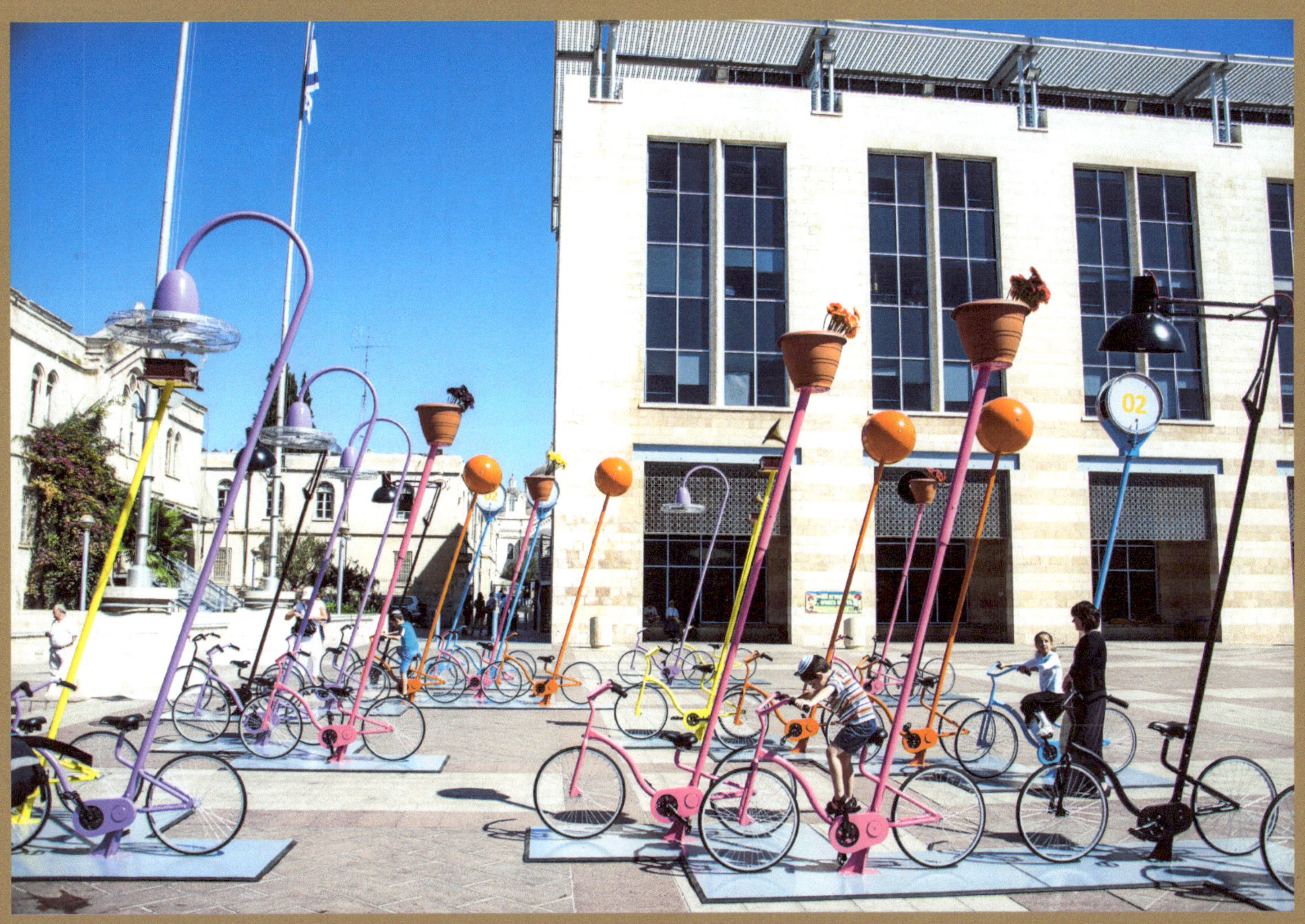


On the edge of Safra Square, which is surrounded by city hall buildings, I saw this art installation of colorful bicycles, which had just opened. It was created by Anat and Ilan Berman to liven up the somewhat sterile surroundings. They called it "Full Gas in Neutral," a local expression that refers to doing something futile.

Every one of the 30 bicycles has a post attached to it with a different mechanism or instrument perched up top. Some have drums, which pound when the rider pedals; others play music. Still others have lamps that light up, or fans that circulate air.

The bike seats are mounted at different heights so that people of all ages can participate and pedal. Apparently, most of the people taking the opportunity to ride the bikes are visitors, tourists and school children, rather than the local residents.

# 7

# THE DEAD SEA

I went on an excursion to the Dead Sea. It was an hour-and-a-half bus ride, and by far the hottest day of the whole trip—close to 120 degrees in the sun. On the way we stopped at Ein Gedi, an oasis that has a waterfall and shallow pool partway up the mountain. Everyone wants to get there to go bathing.

Then you have to walk about another mile or so down the road to the Dead Sea, which is more than 1,400 feet below sea level. People lie in the water for hours on end and enjoy drifting about. You couldn't sink in it even if you weren't very good at floating.

It looked inviting, and I wish I could have gone in to cool off, but I had my camera equipment with me and didn't want to leave it unattended. I did put a hand into the water so I could say I'd been there.

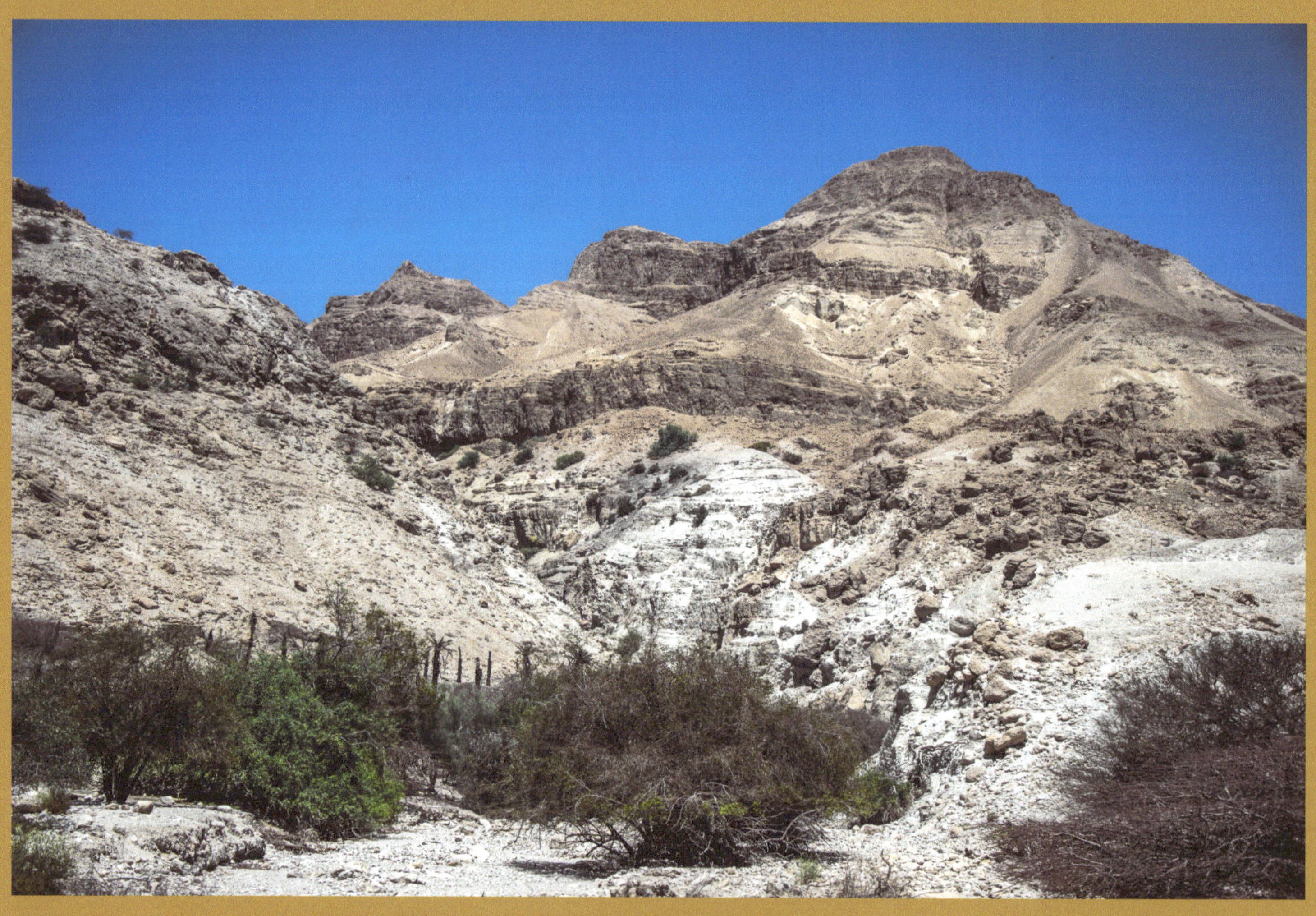

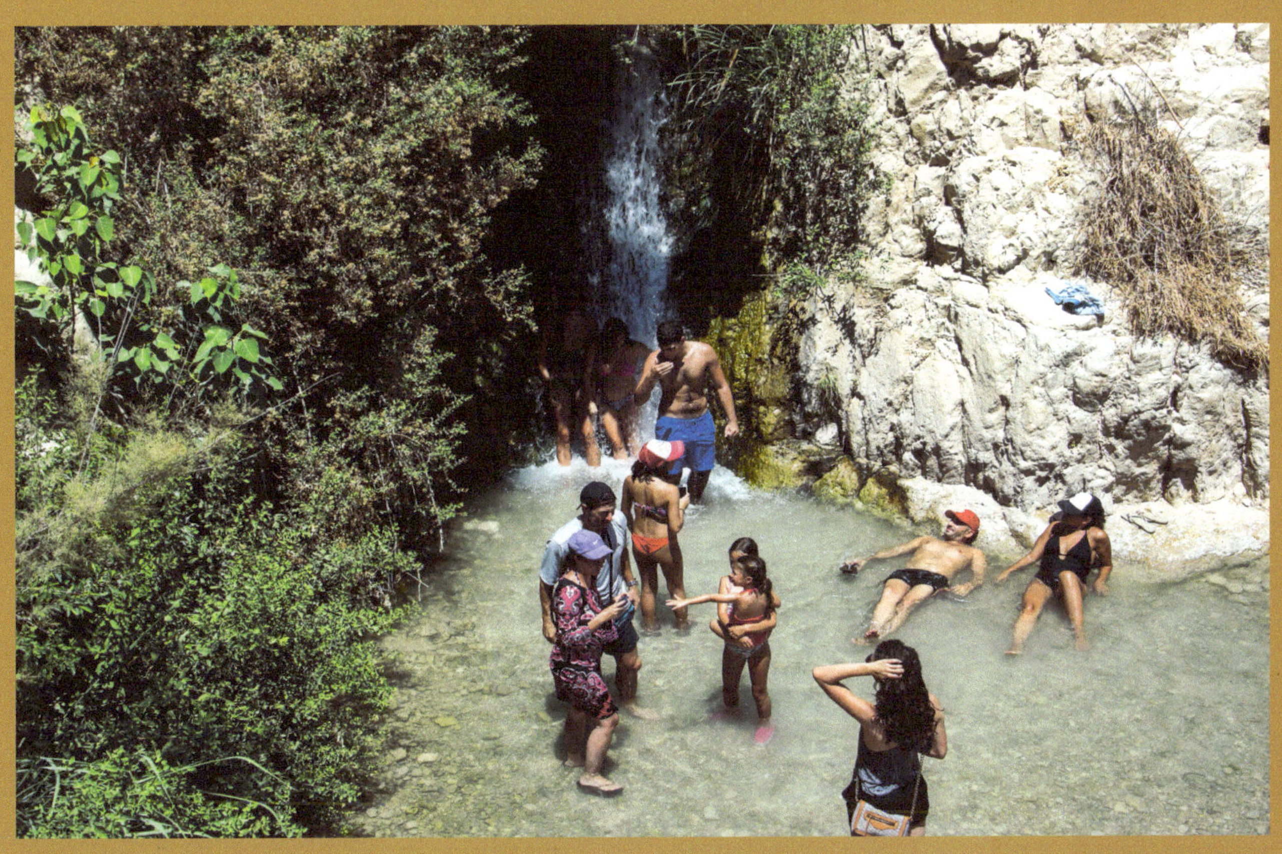

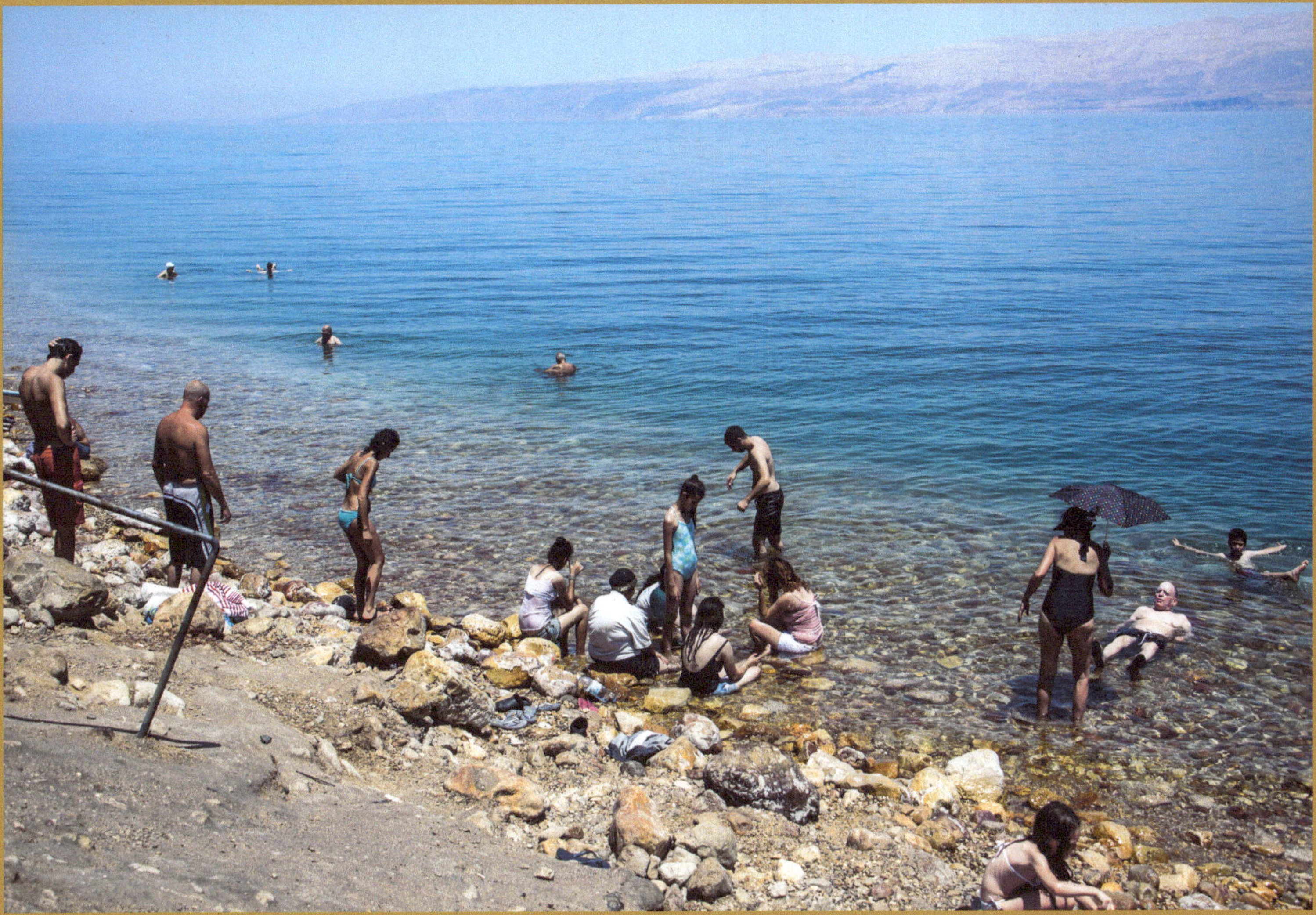

Everywhere you'd see white patches encrusting the rocks: it was salt. The Dead Sea is the world's saltiest body of water, containing 9.6 times more salt than any of the oceans. The mineral content is so high that they warn you not to splash water on yourself or others, drink it—not even a sip—and not to immerse your head, or you could get sick and die.

The sea and surrounding landscape is such a harsh, unforgiving environment that no animals can live there—that's why it's called the Dead Sea—although there are a few hearty plants that cling to the hillsides. Still, it looked as barren as the moon.

A lot of people went mud bathing. For some it was just a fun thing to do, but many visitors claim that the black mud, which contains nearly twenty minerals from the sea, has cleansing and healing qualities.

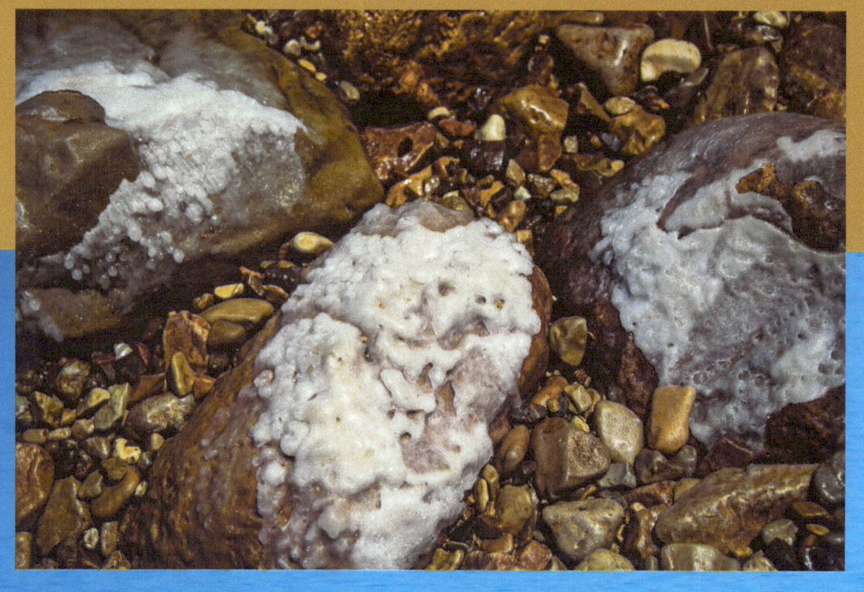

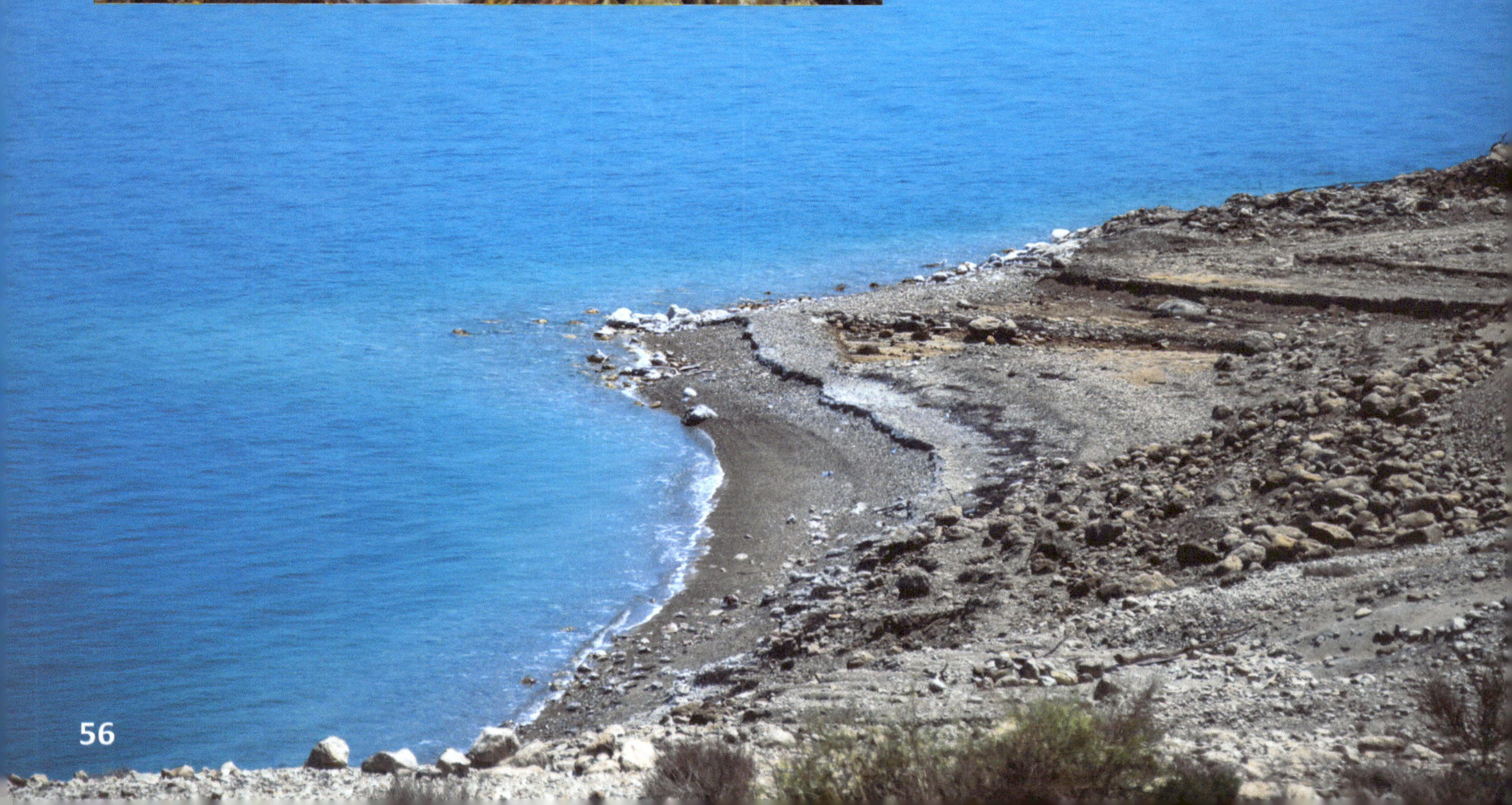

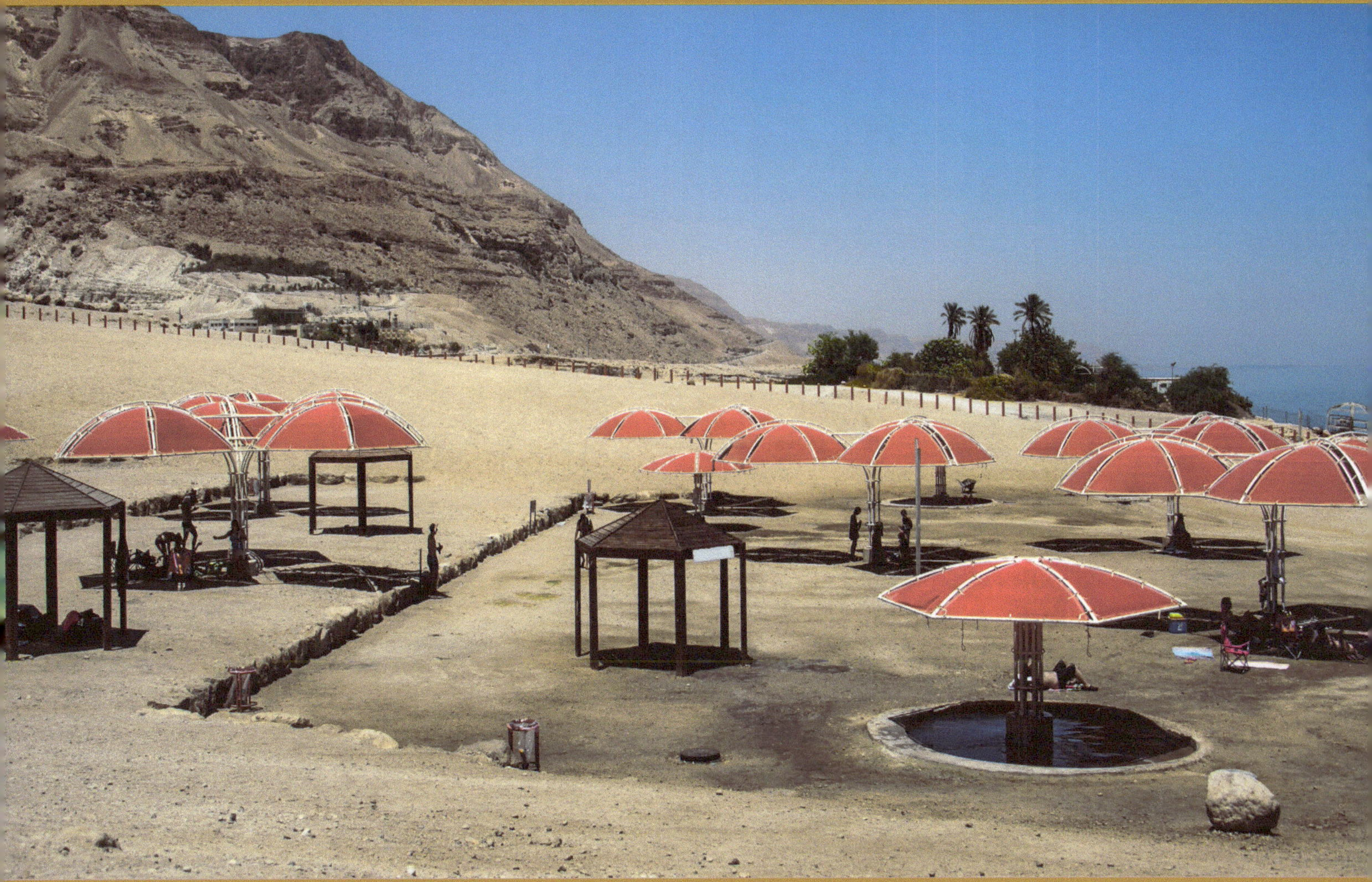

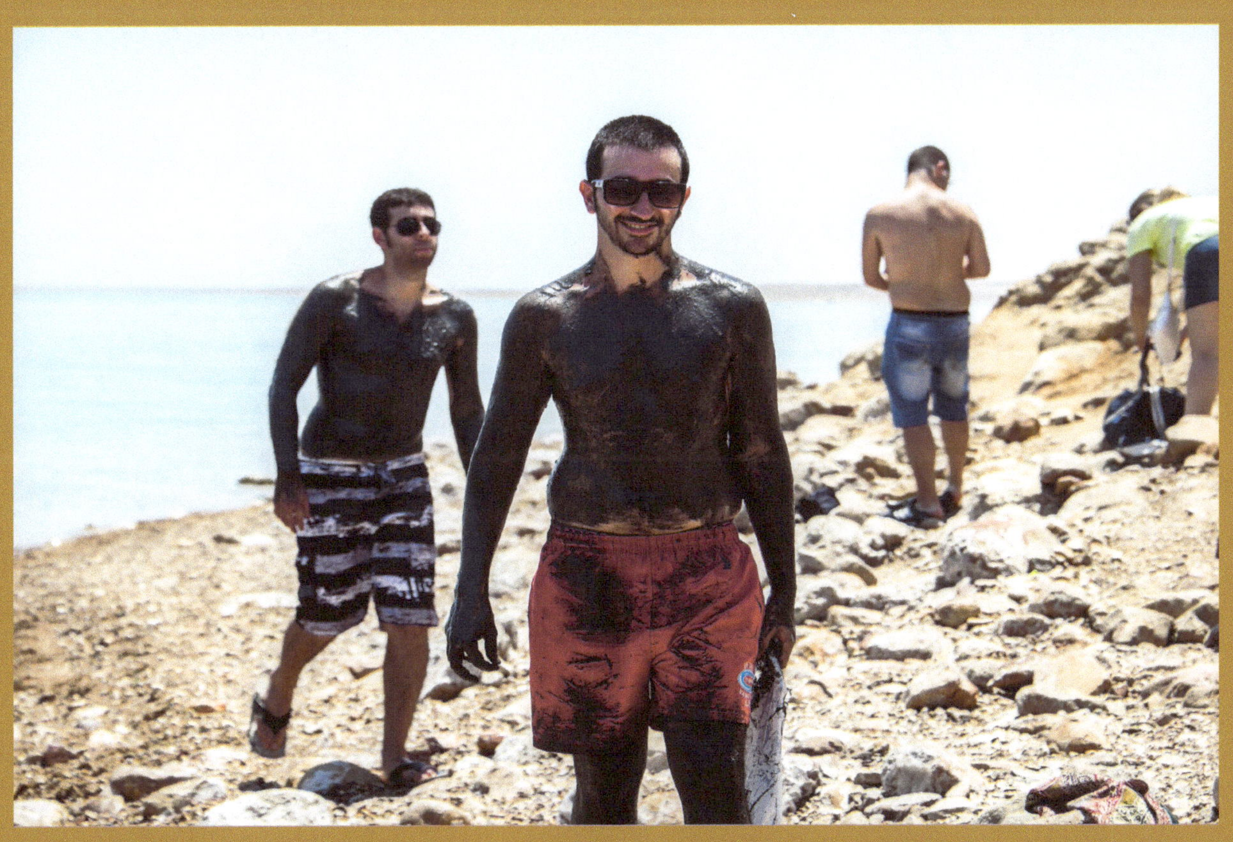

# 8

# BUCHAREST

I very much wanted to go to Istanbul but I couldn't find a convenient connection or a cheap flight that didn't involve going back to Greece, so I decided to fly first to Romania. I flew from Ben Gurion, Tel Aviv's airport, to Bucharest, the capital of Romania. Talk about culture shock.

The first thing that strikes you is how depressing it all looks. Going from the vibrancy, colors and smells of Jerusalem to the sterile atmosphere of a city struggling to get out from under years of Communism and the legacy of being a USSR satellite wasn't a pleasant experience.

On the streets, you meet a lot of shady looking characters, homeless people and beggars. Everybody smokes and you feel like you're in a cancer cloud everywhere you go. At some point, I sat eating pizza outside a restaurant and felt as though I was mainlining nicotine the whole time.

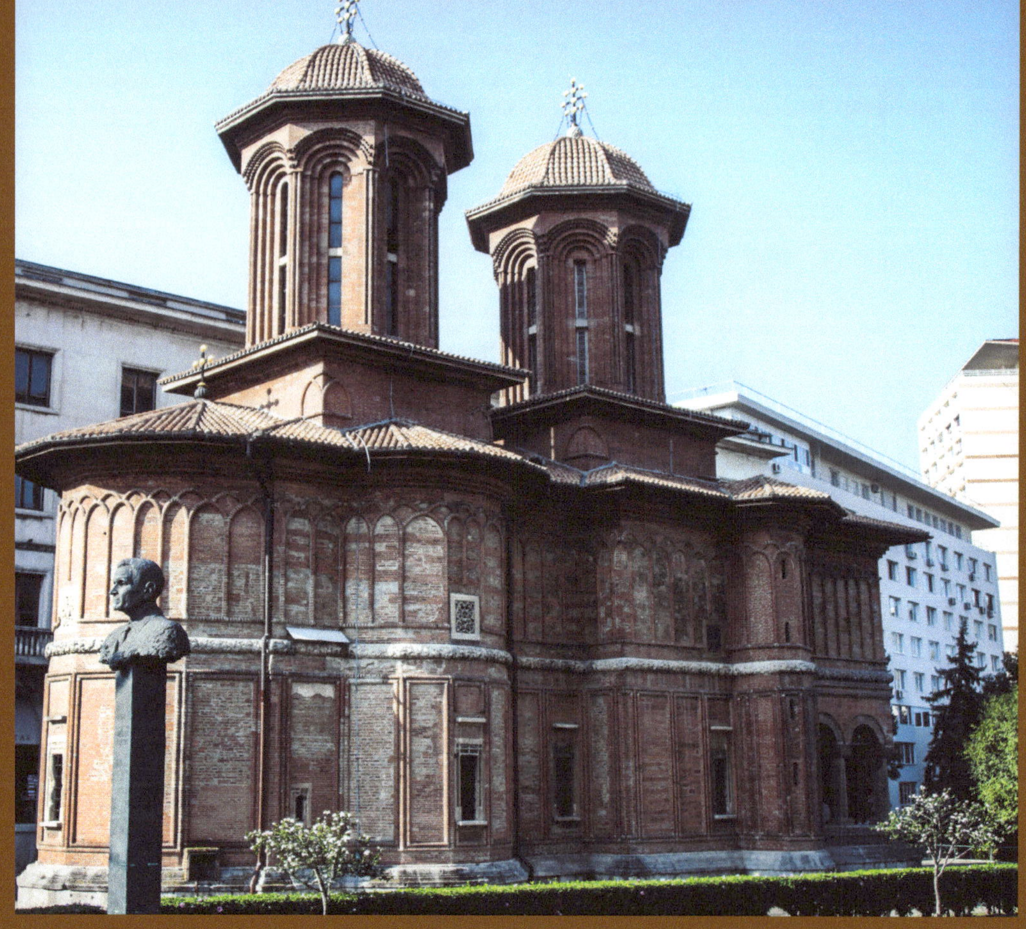

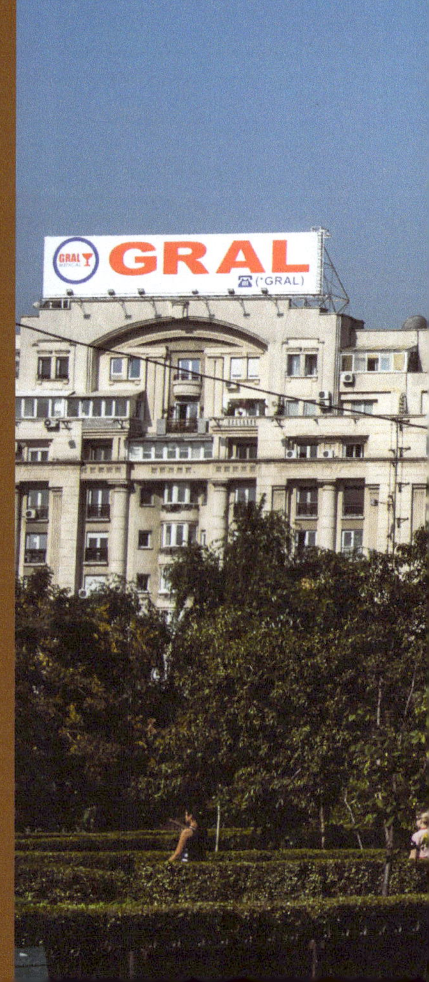

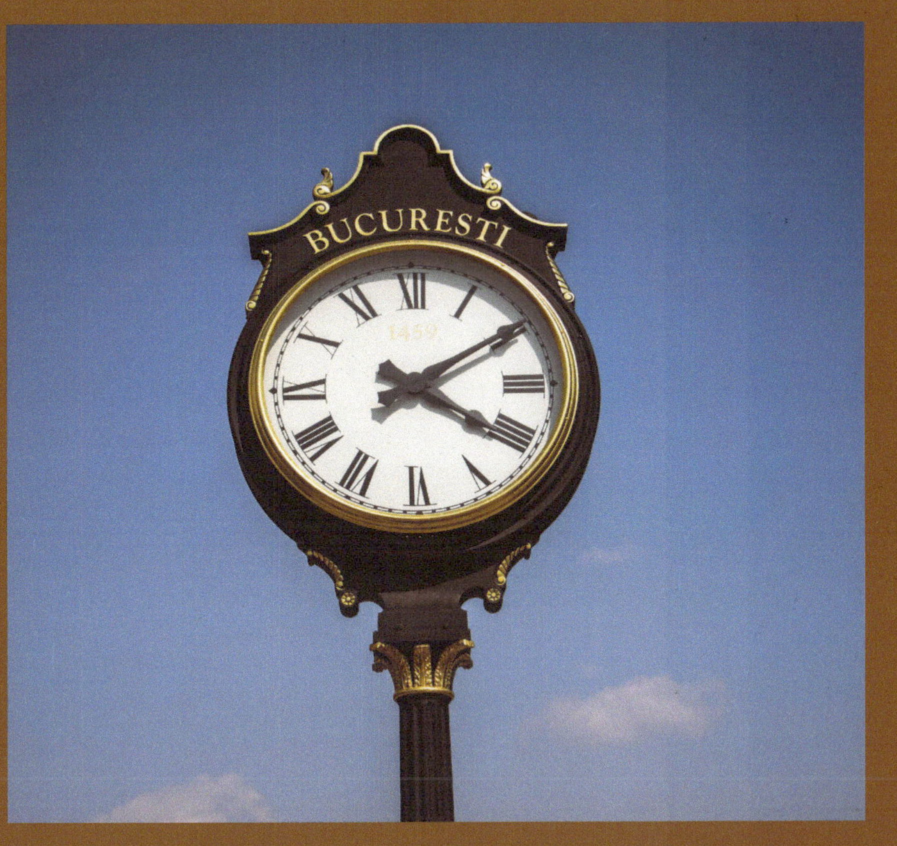
BUCURESTI

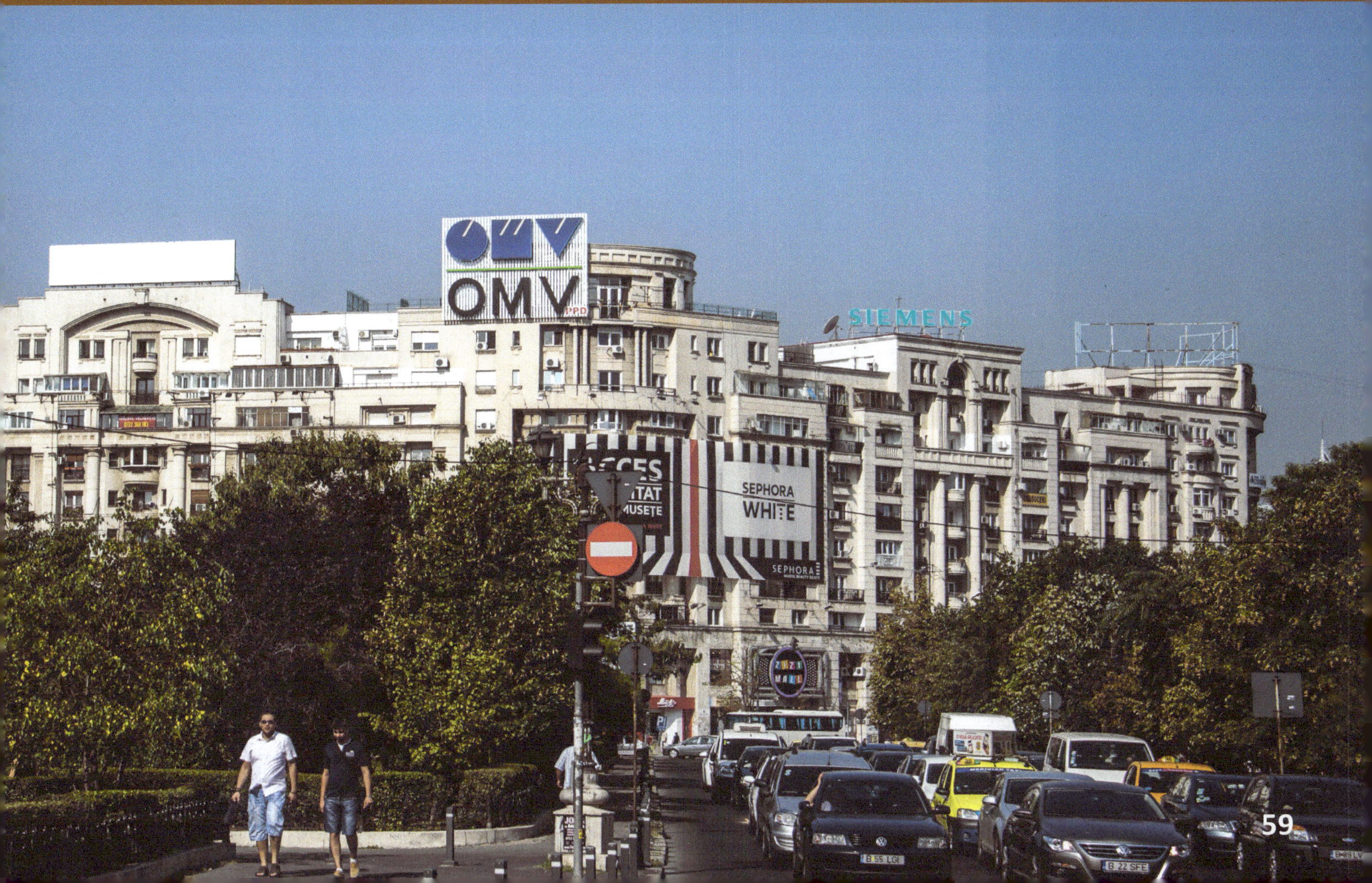

As I walked around the city, I came upon this monstrosity. The Palace of Parliament or People's Palace was built by Nicolae Ceaușescu, the country's Communist dictator from 1967 until 1989—his regime collapsed after he ordered his security forces to fire on anti-government demonstrators, leading to the Romanian Revolution.

With 6,000 rooms, it's the second biggest building in the world, after the Pentagon. It is one massive, ugly building in the middle of Bucharest, but I managed to get it all in one picture.

*Top Gear*, a popular British television series about cars, did a show on Romania. It included a race in the tunnels under the palace to determine which of their cars, an Astin Martin, a Ferrari and a Lamborghini, was the loudest. Apparently, the basement is quite an echo chamber. The outcome? All three cars were deemed equally loud.

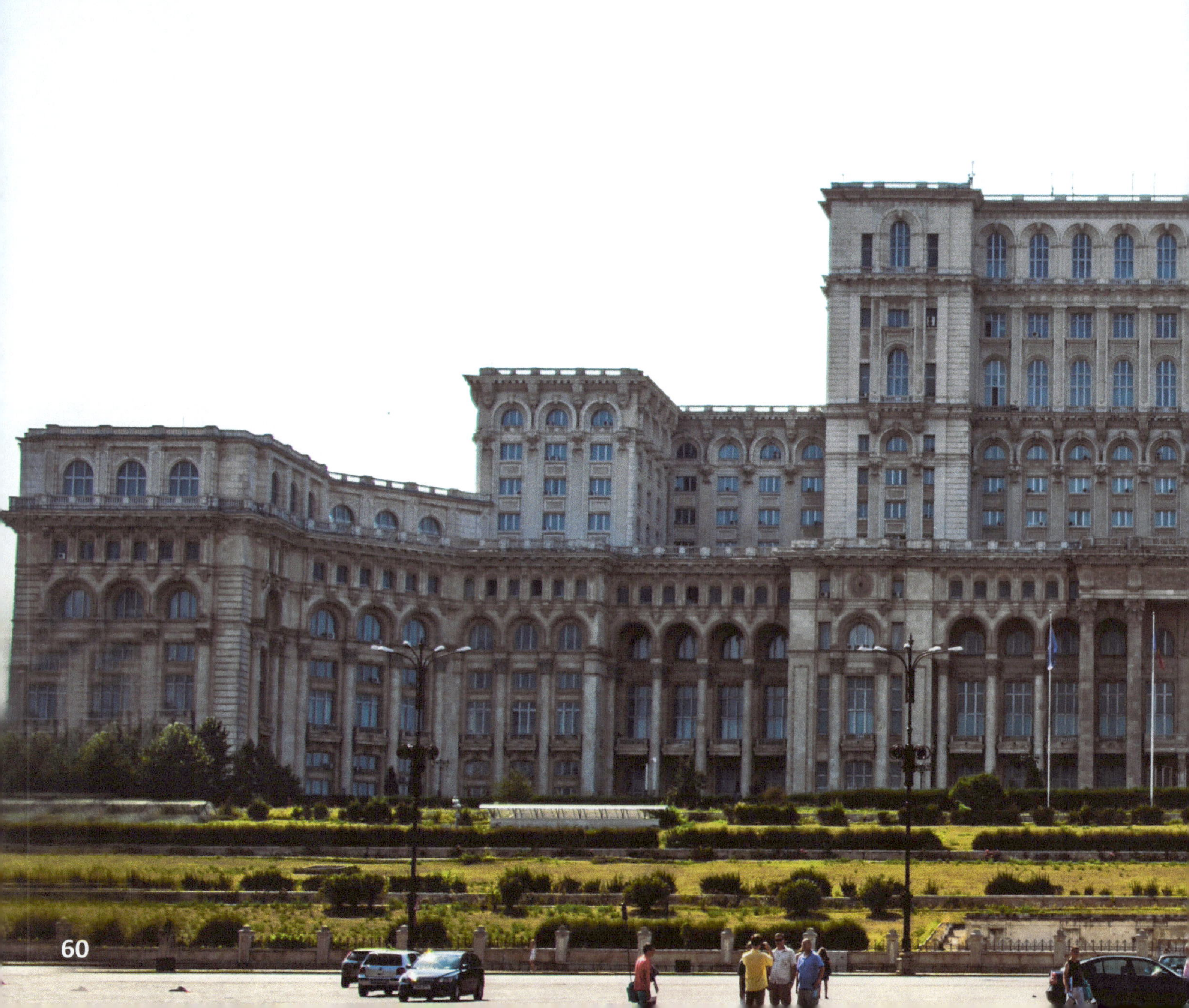

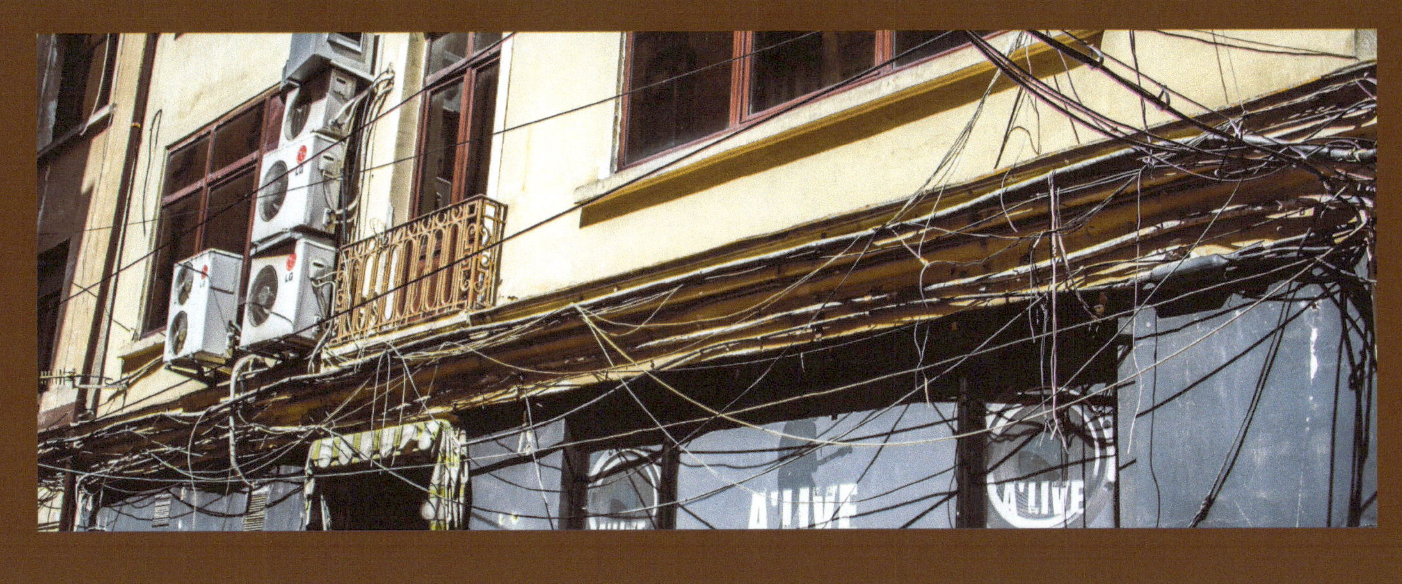
A'LIVE
A'LIVE

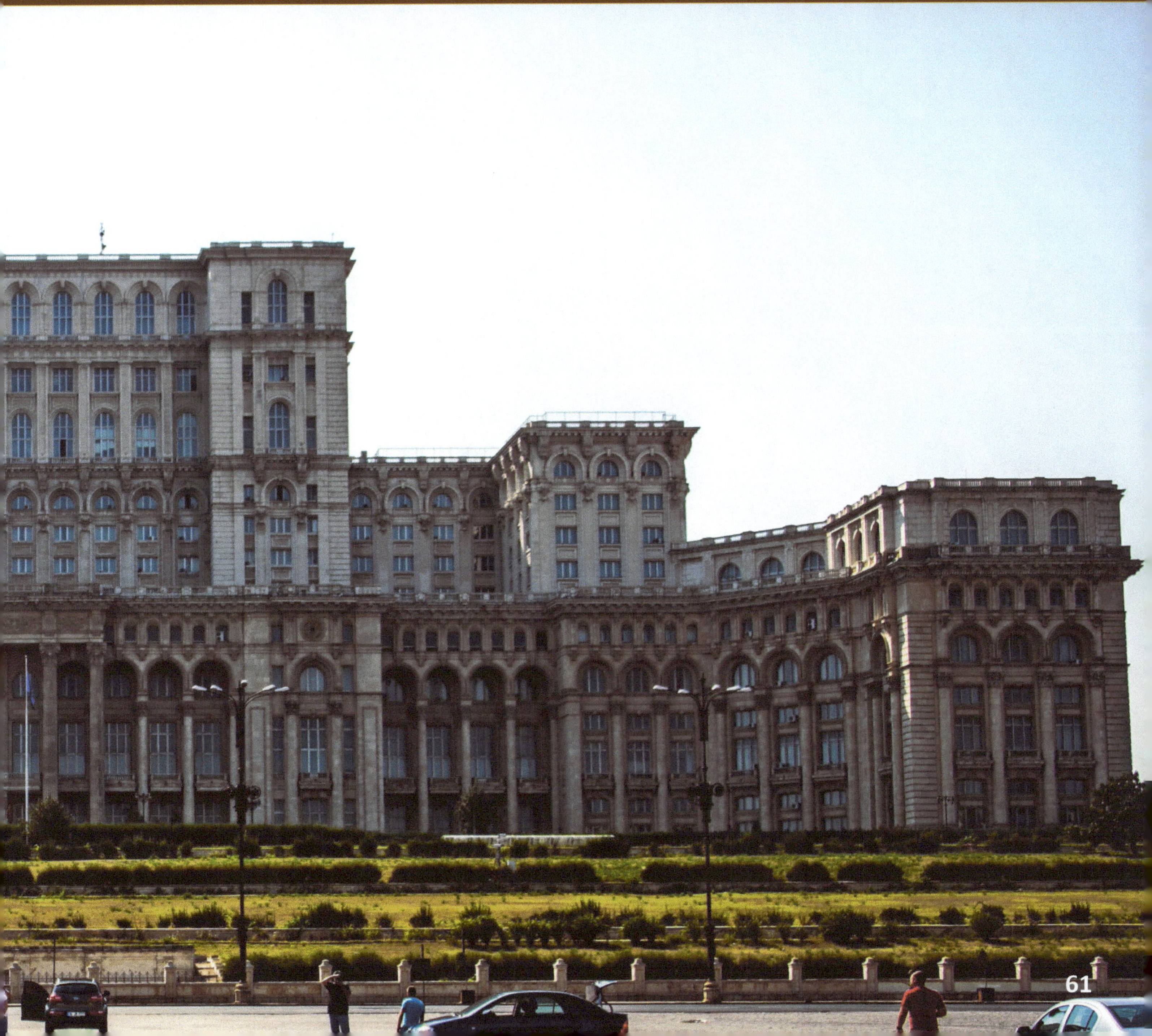

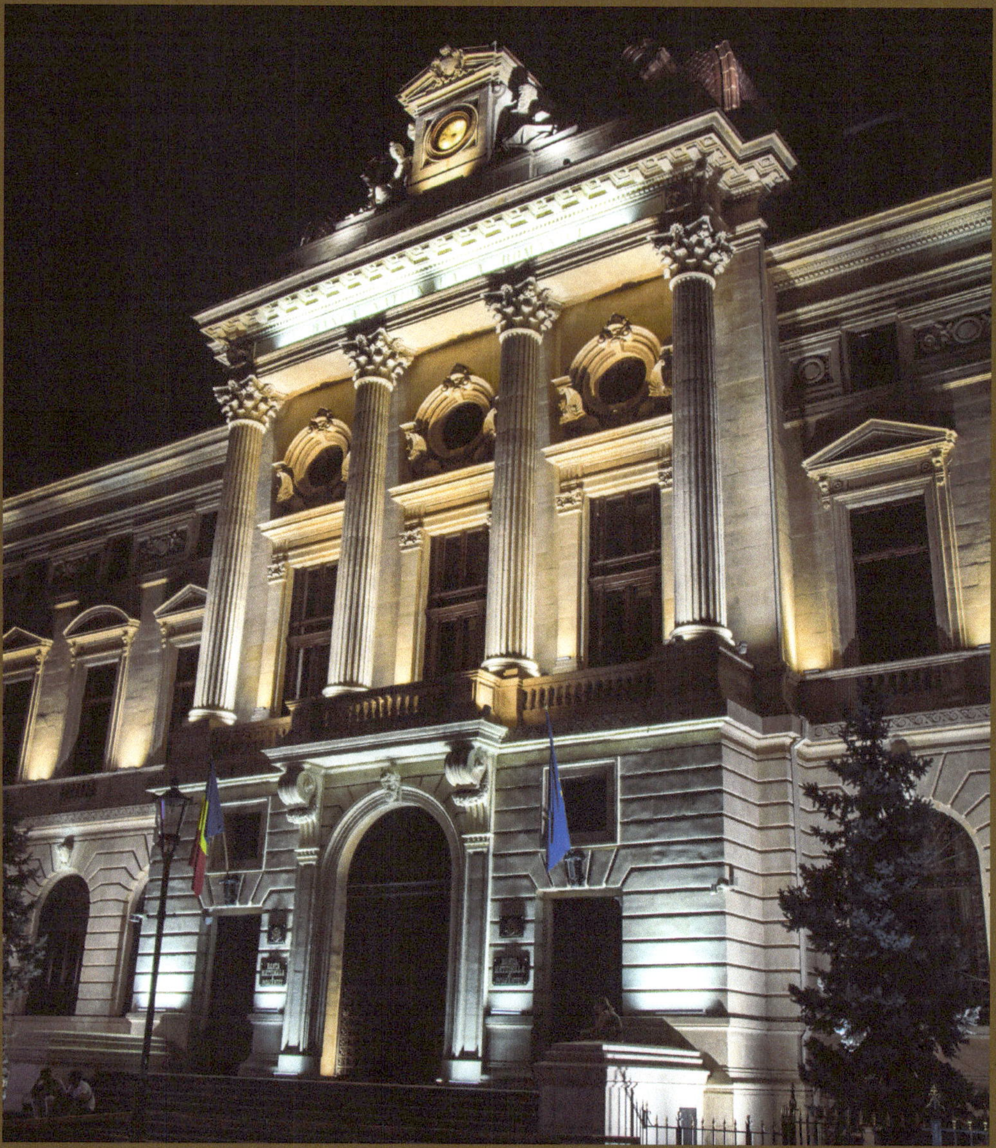

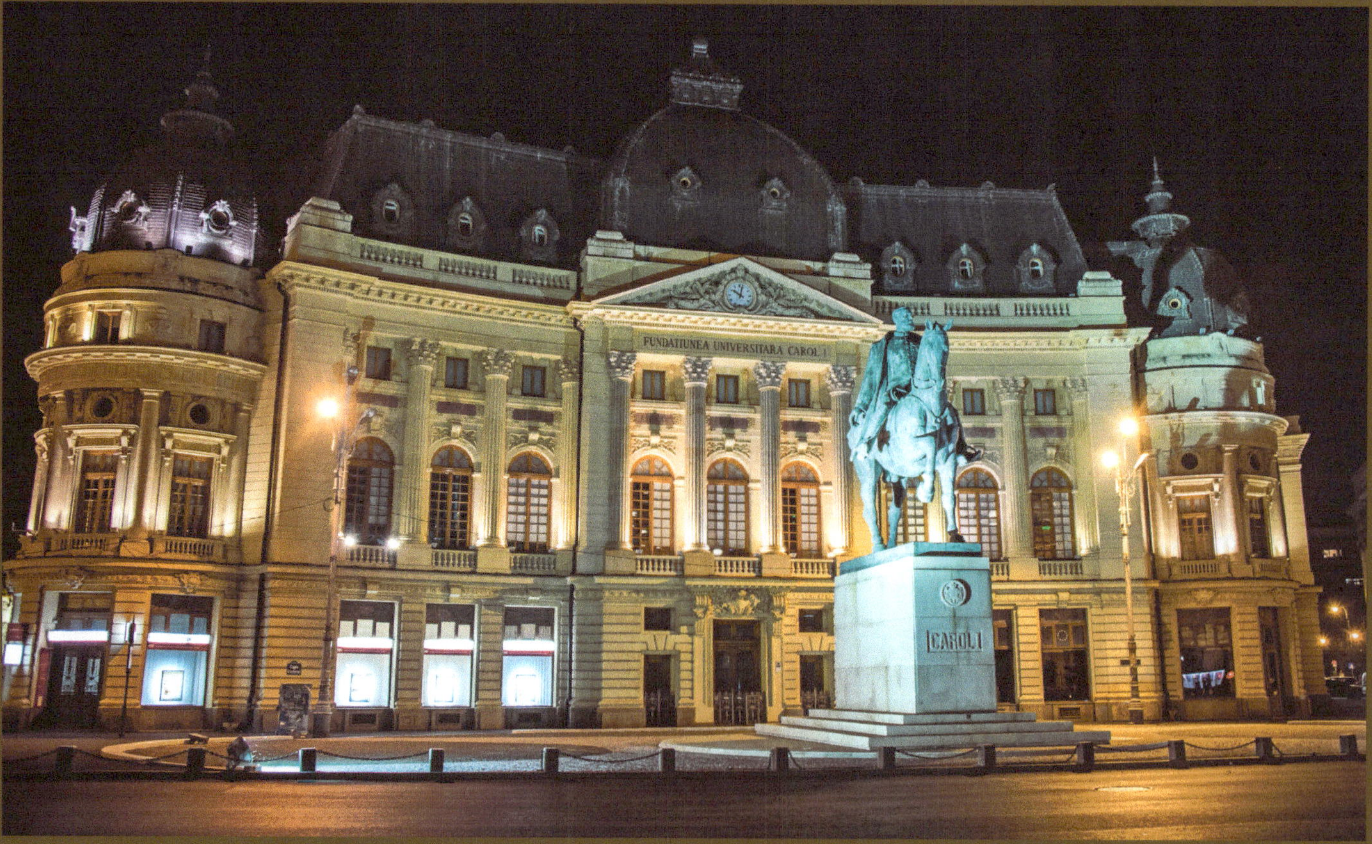
FUNDATIUNEA UNIVERSITARA CAROL I
CAROL I

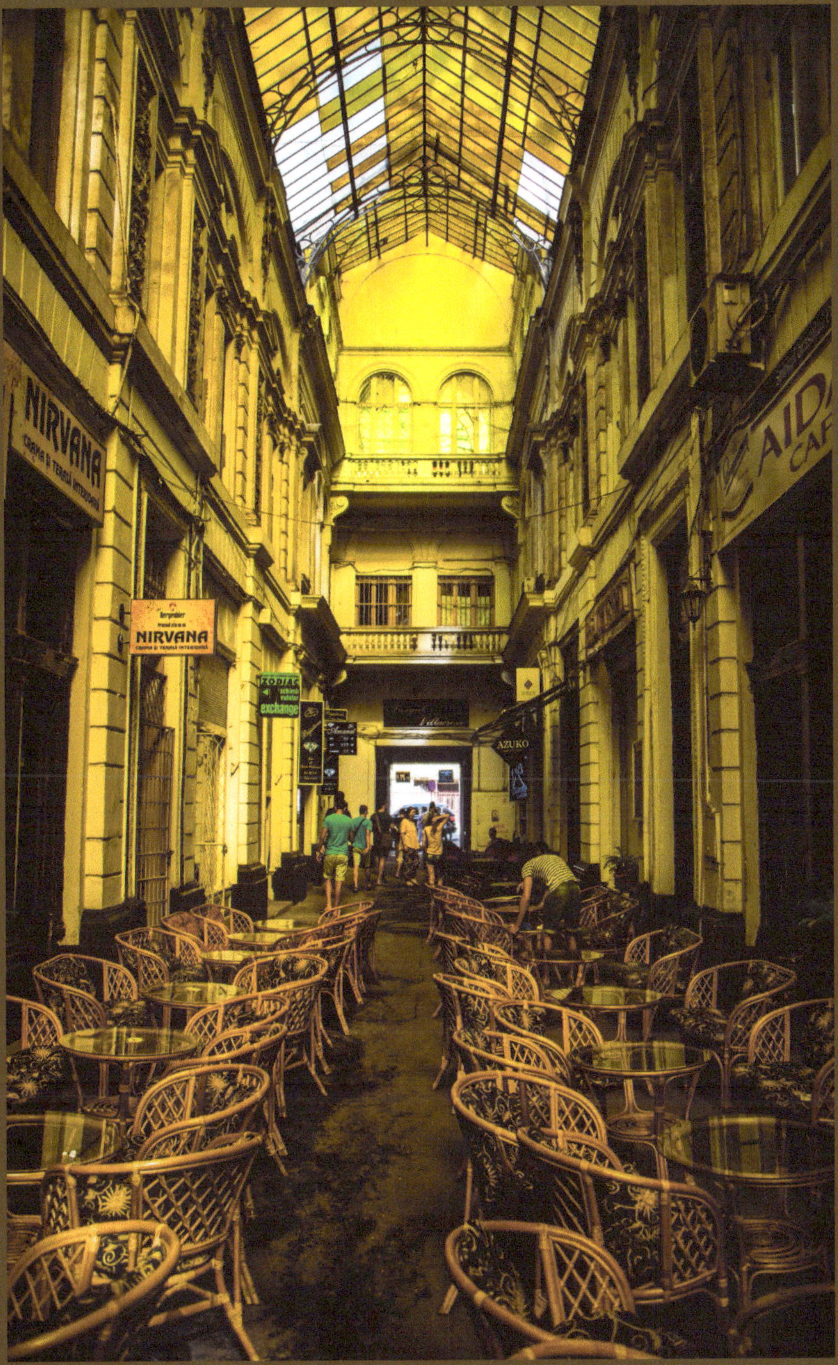

The best thing about Bucharest was the Old Town at night, because the illuminations of the buildings were spectacular. Note the way the statue of the horseman is lit up. Wherever I went, I saw statues honoring some politician or other, invariably covered in pigeon droppings.

These covered arcades have shops and little places where you can sit and have a coffee "outside." When I took these photos, it was very early in the morning, and the Bucharesters hadn't come out yet for their breakfast.

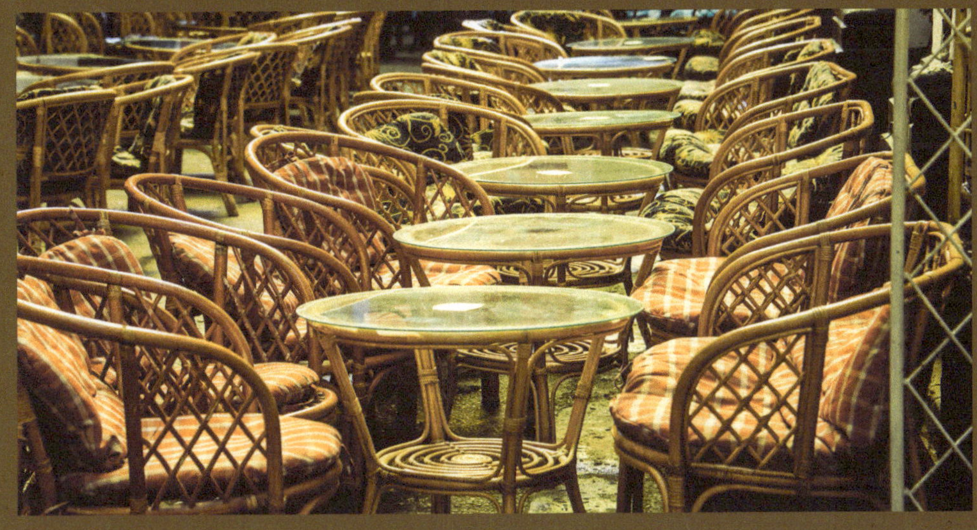

# ARCADES

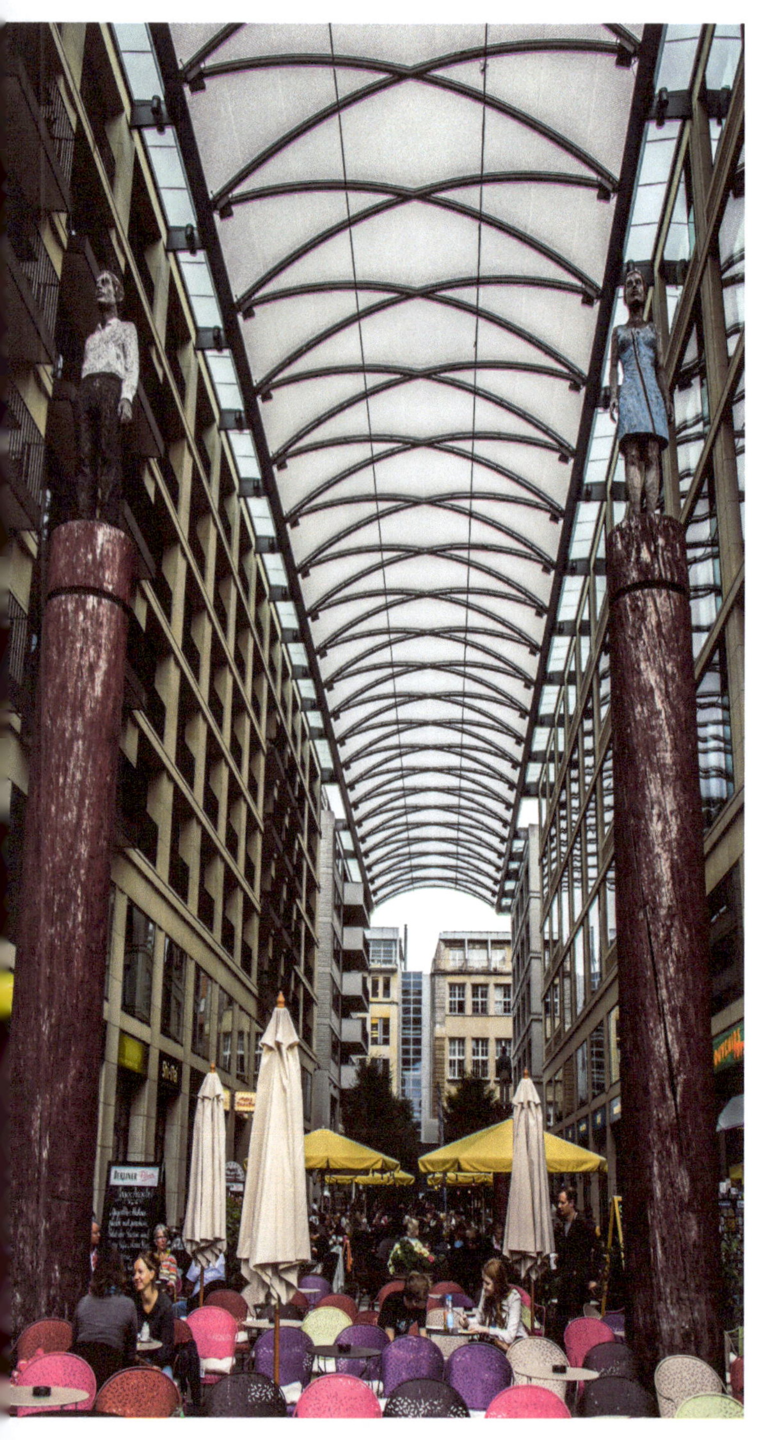

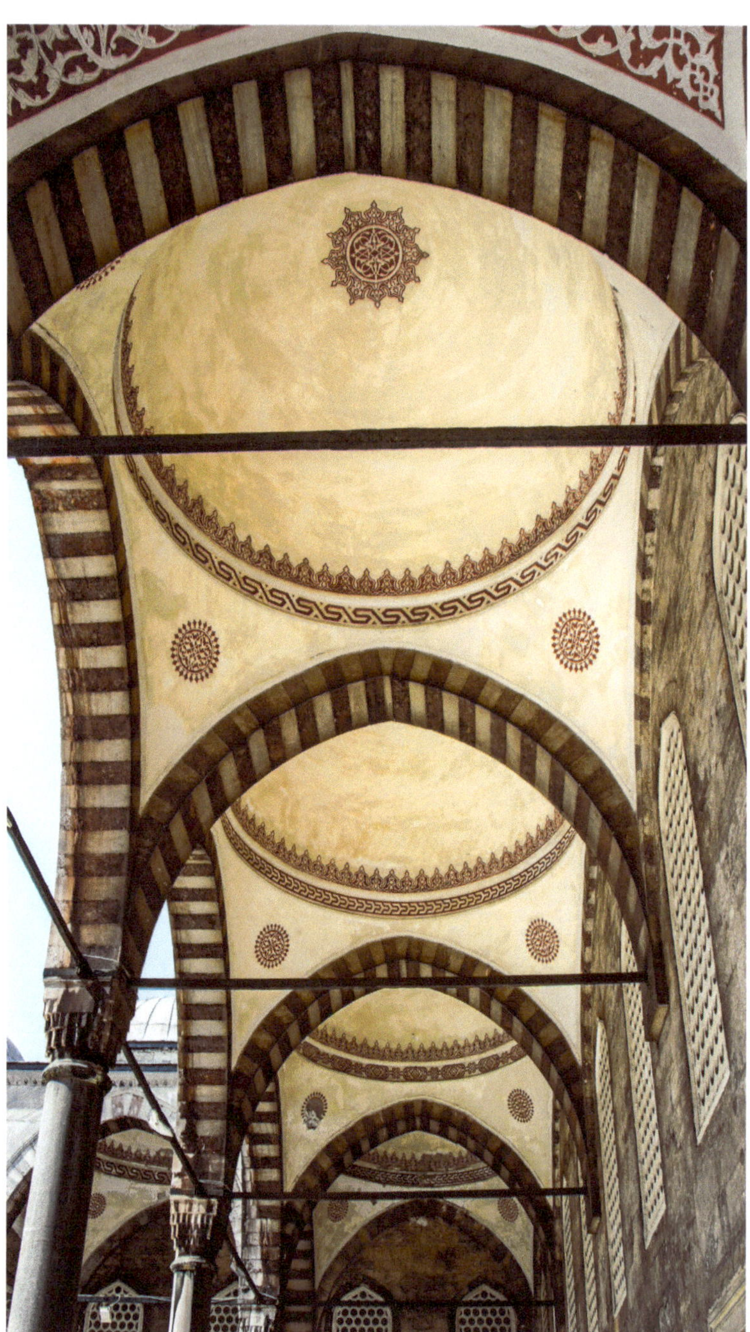

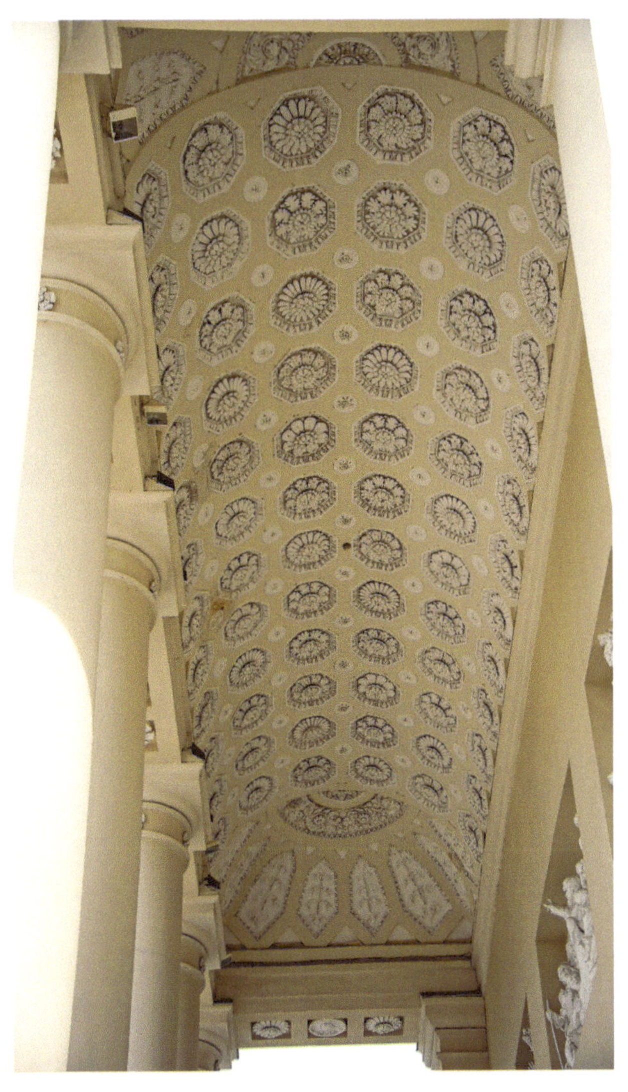

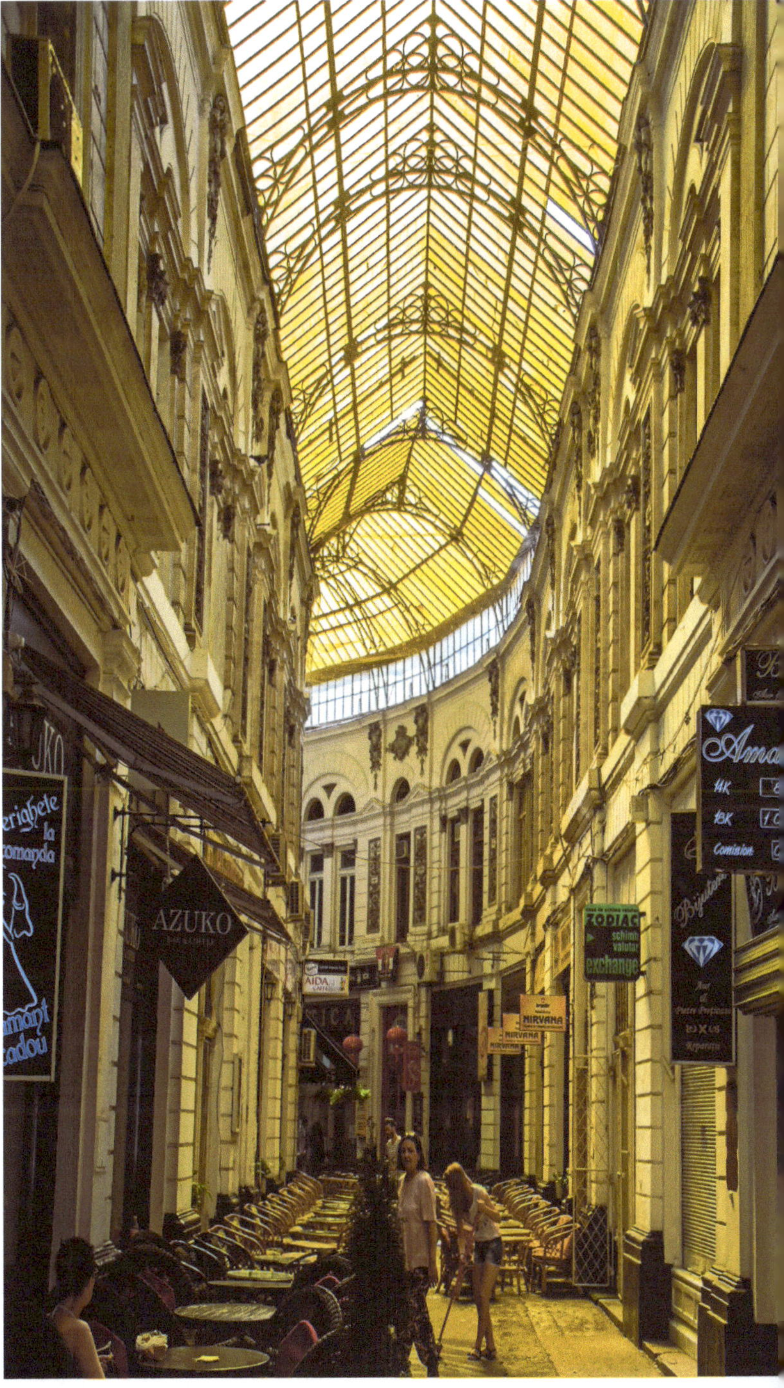


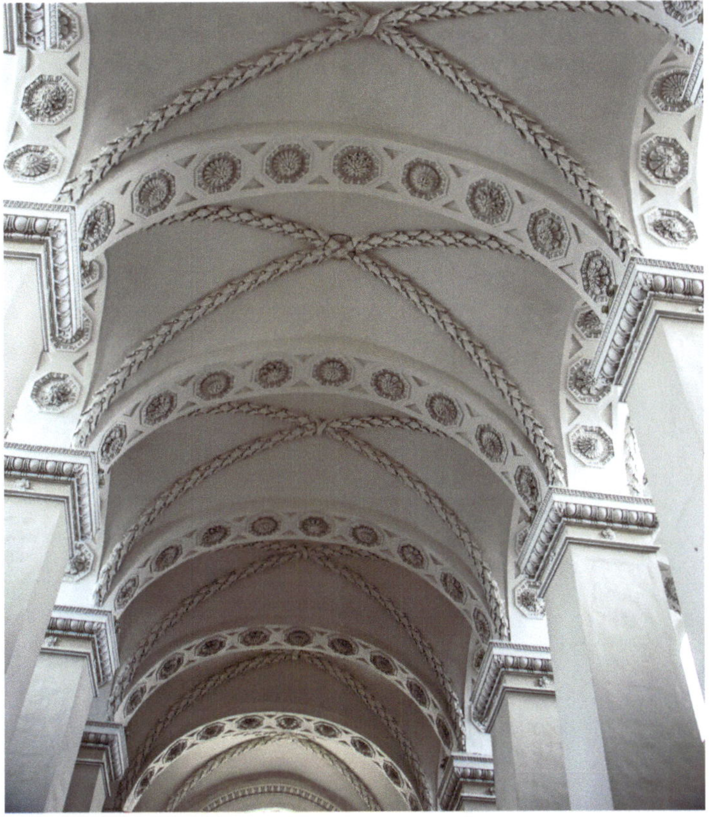

Arcades, covered passages or walkways between arches supported by columns or piers go back to ancient Roman times and I saw them in every major city in Europe. These examples, from left to right are from Istanbul, Berlin, Vilnius and Bucharest.

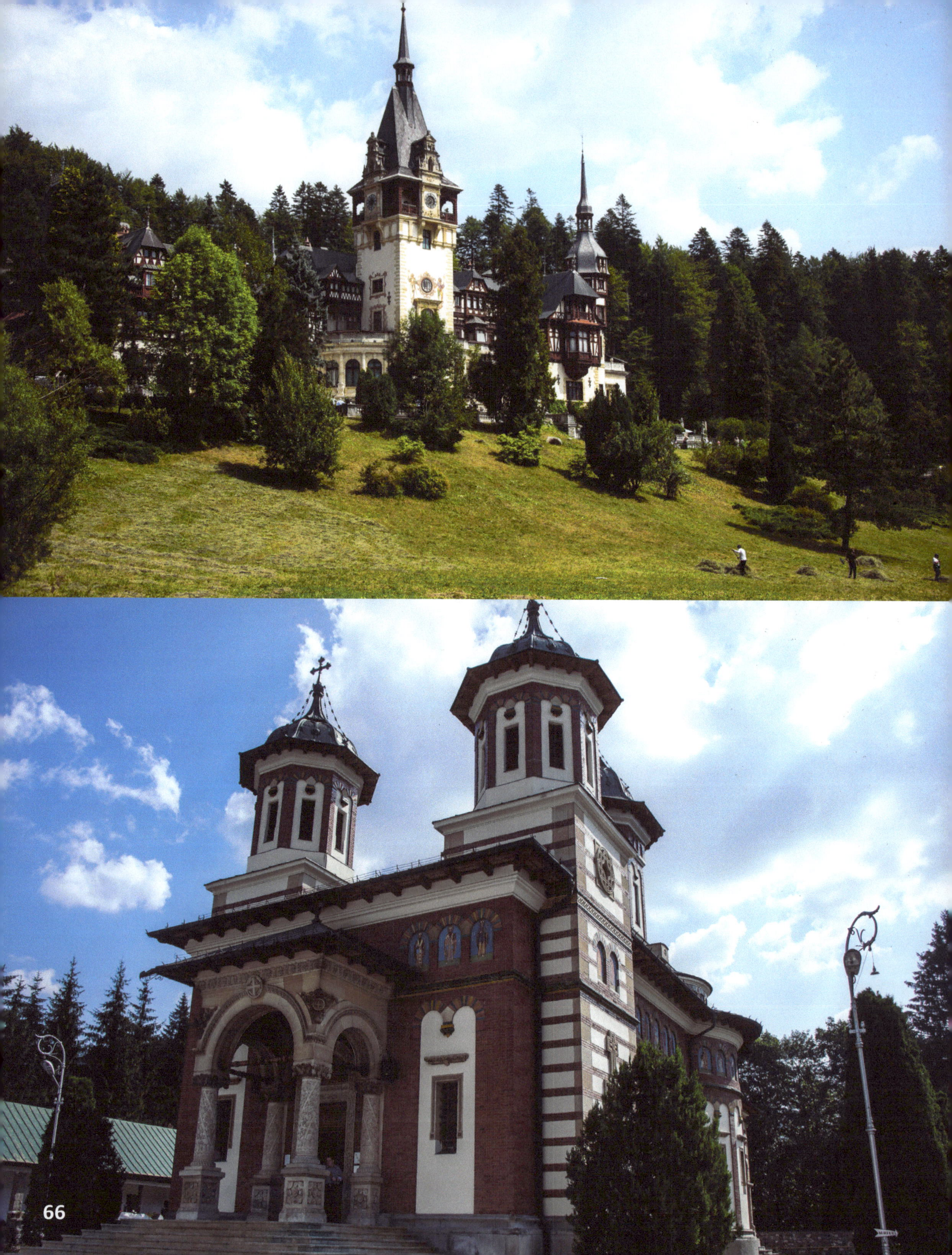

# 9

# BRASOV

One of the main reasons I went to Romania was that I wanted to go to the Carpathian Mountains and see Transylvania—Dracula country!

I got on the bus early in the morning with a group of five other people for a day excursion beause it's a good 4-hour drive from Bucharest. It was one of those holidays when everyone was on the road at the same time. With the roads still underdeveloped—mostly one-lane—if you get stuck behind a slow car or another tour bus, it takes forever to get there.

Along the way, they let you visit an old monastery, then a new one, and then a castle. Eventually you reach Brasov for lunch—it's all pre-planned. This amazing ceiling fresco is from the church at the Sinaia Monastery (opposite page, lower left) built from 1690 to 1695.

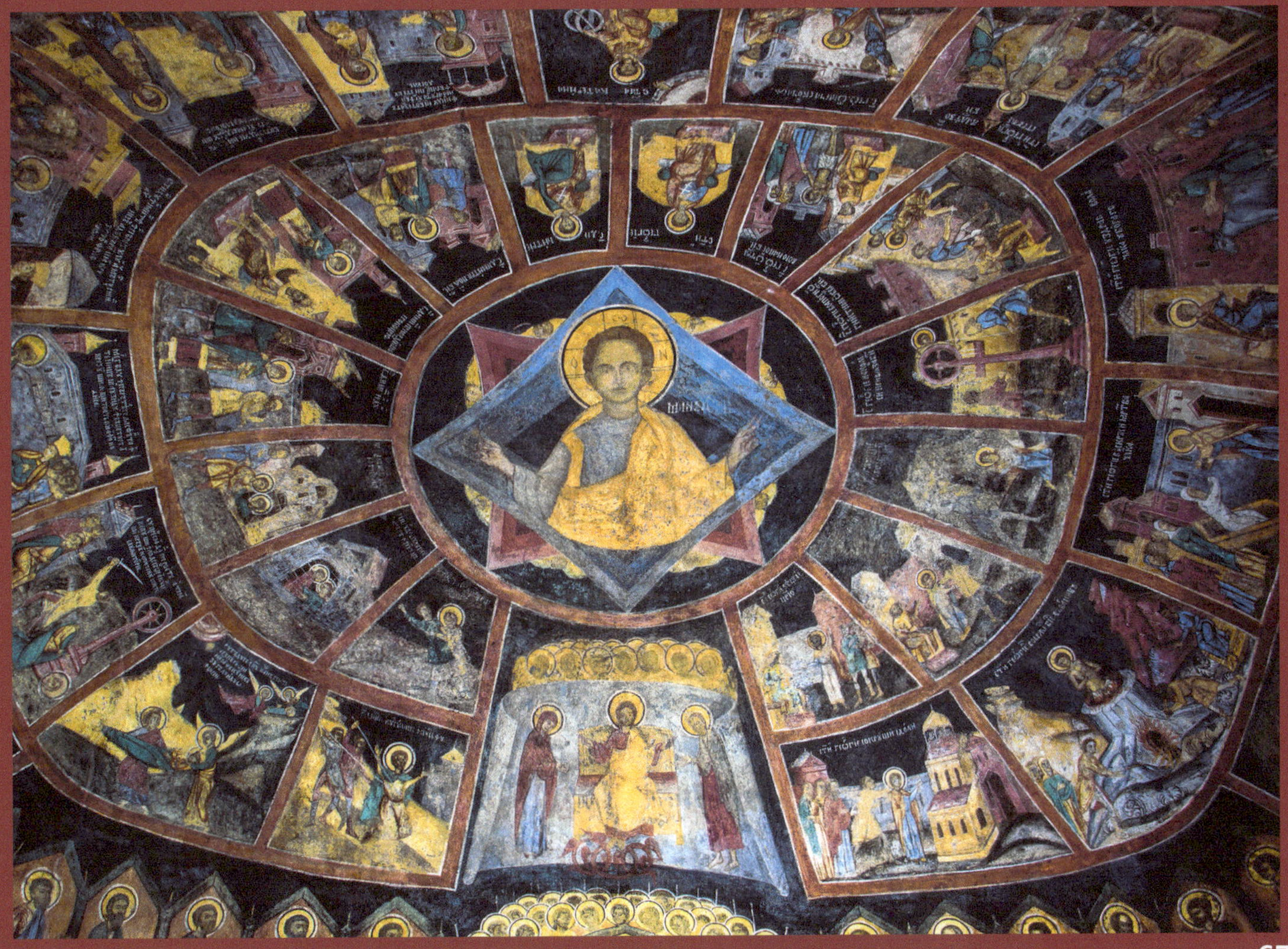

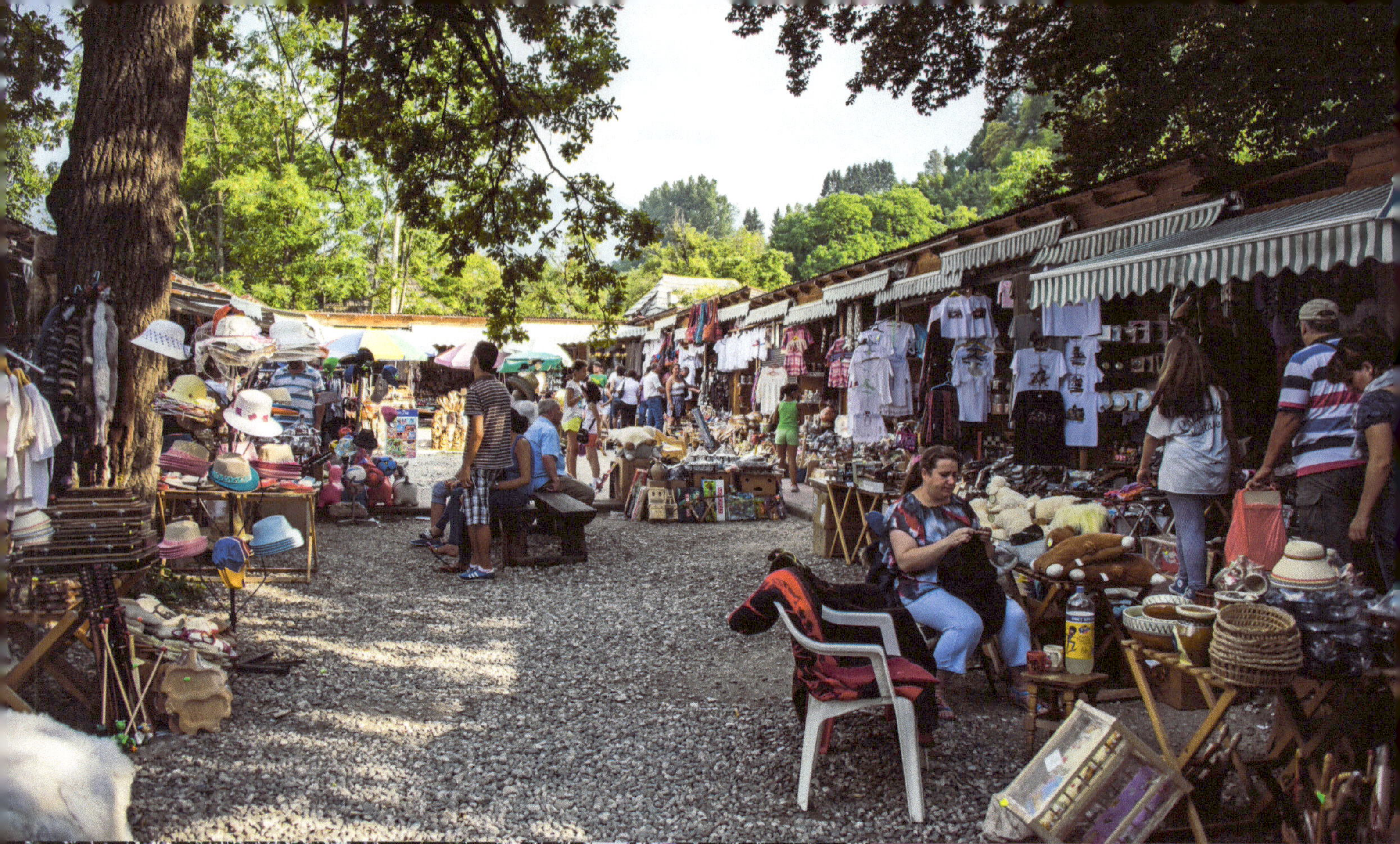

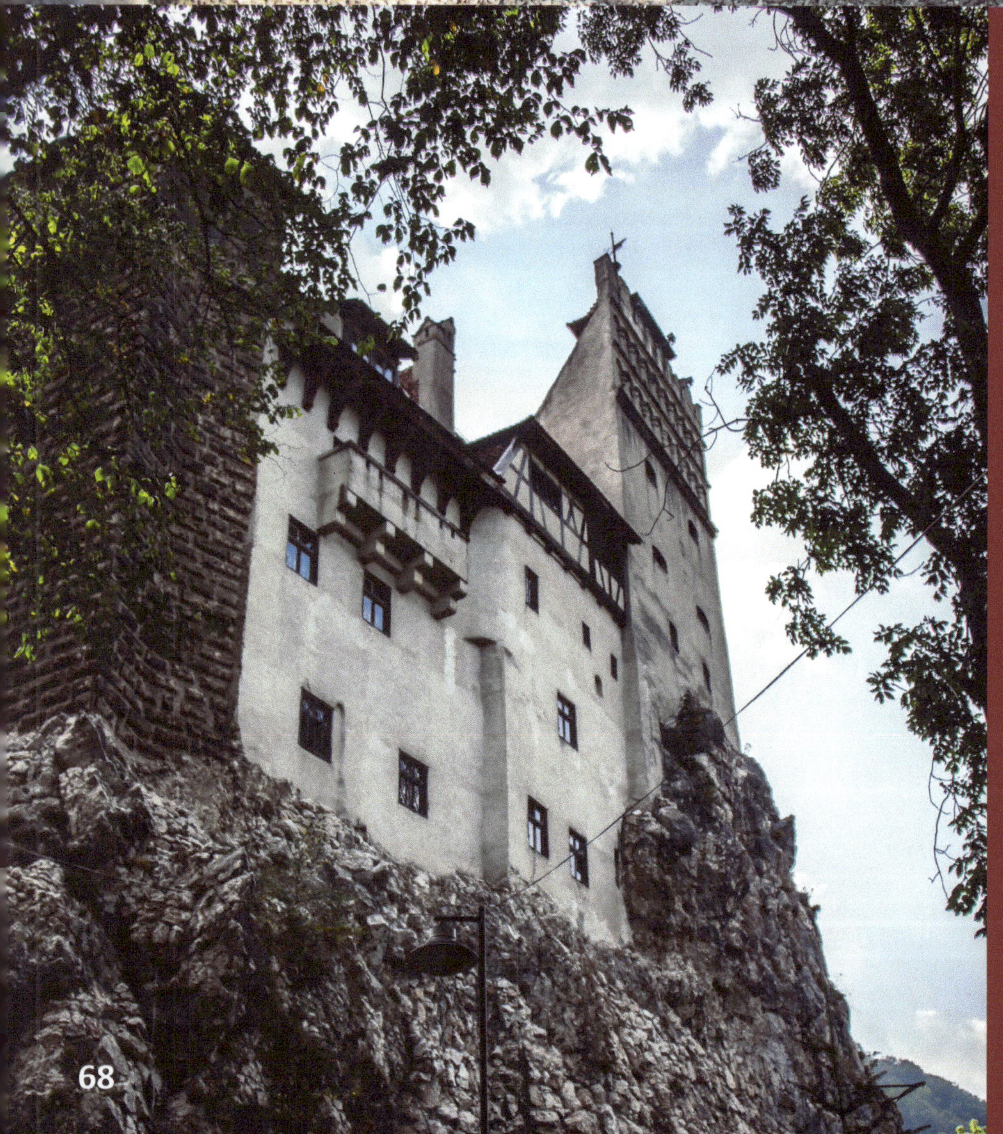

After that, you go to the town of Bran and visit the castle of Vlad the Impaler, Dracula's father. At that point, tourism really runs amok. The base of the castle is crowded with all kinds of booths and vendors. Everybody and his aunt want to sell you a cape and false fangs! Don't get me wrong—if I lived there, I would be in a little stall selling T-shirts and fangs myself, because you can make a good living from it.

They're profiting from *True Blood* and *The Twilight Saga* and all the other vampire films that have become so popular, but it is crass and disappointing.

Still, the castle itself is quite beautiful and imposing, perched as it is high on a rock and overlooking the town and countryside.

You have to climb a steep set of steps to get up to the entrance.

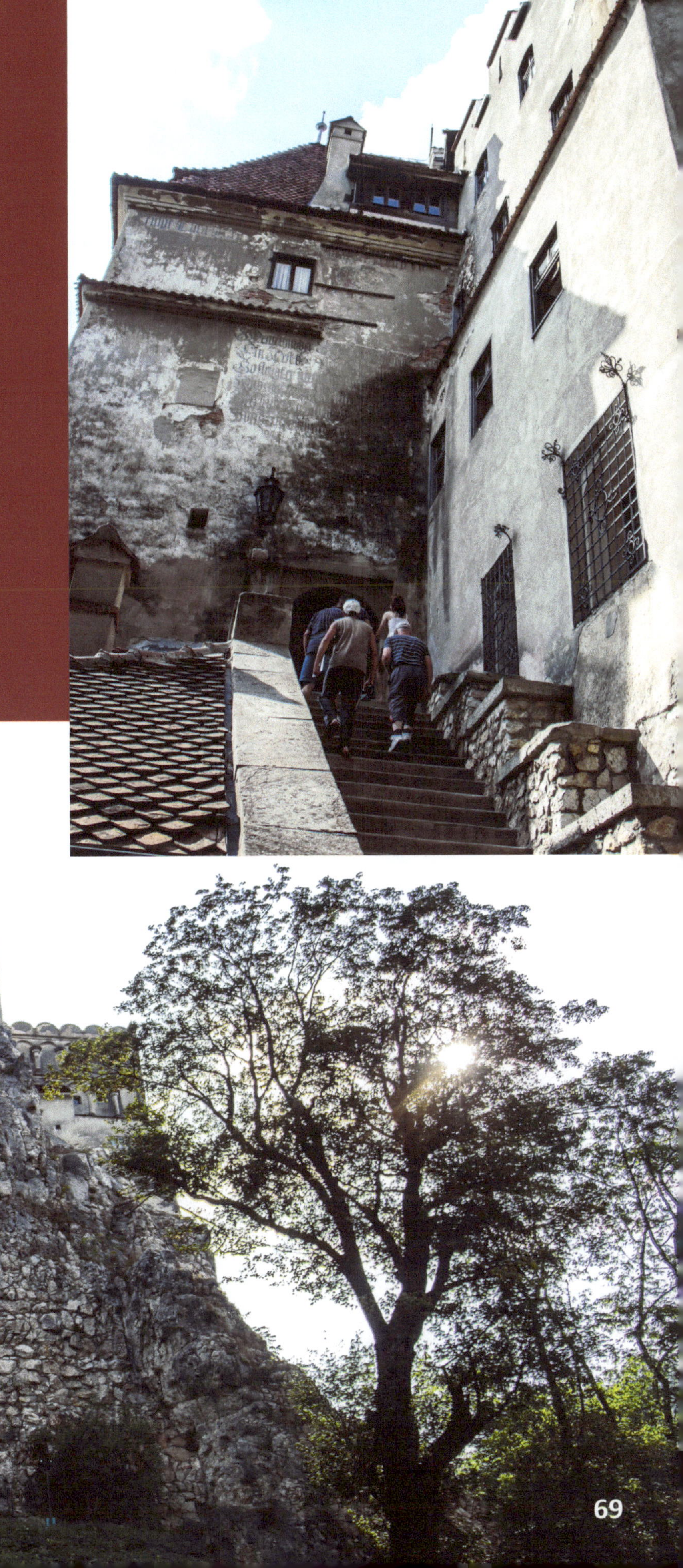

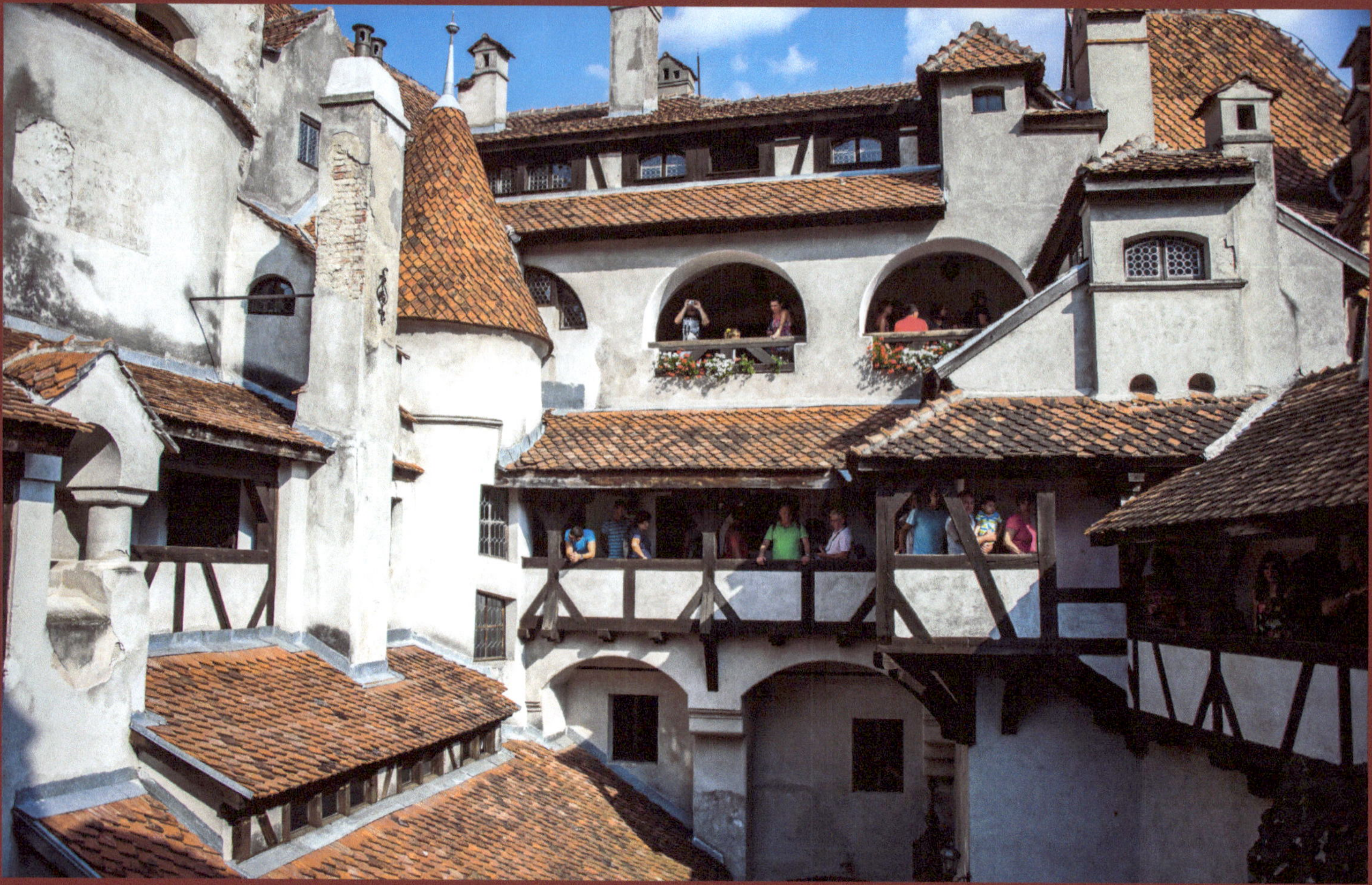

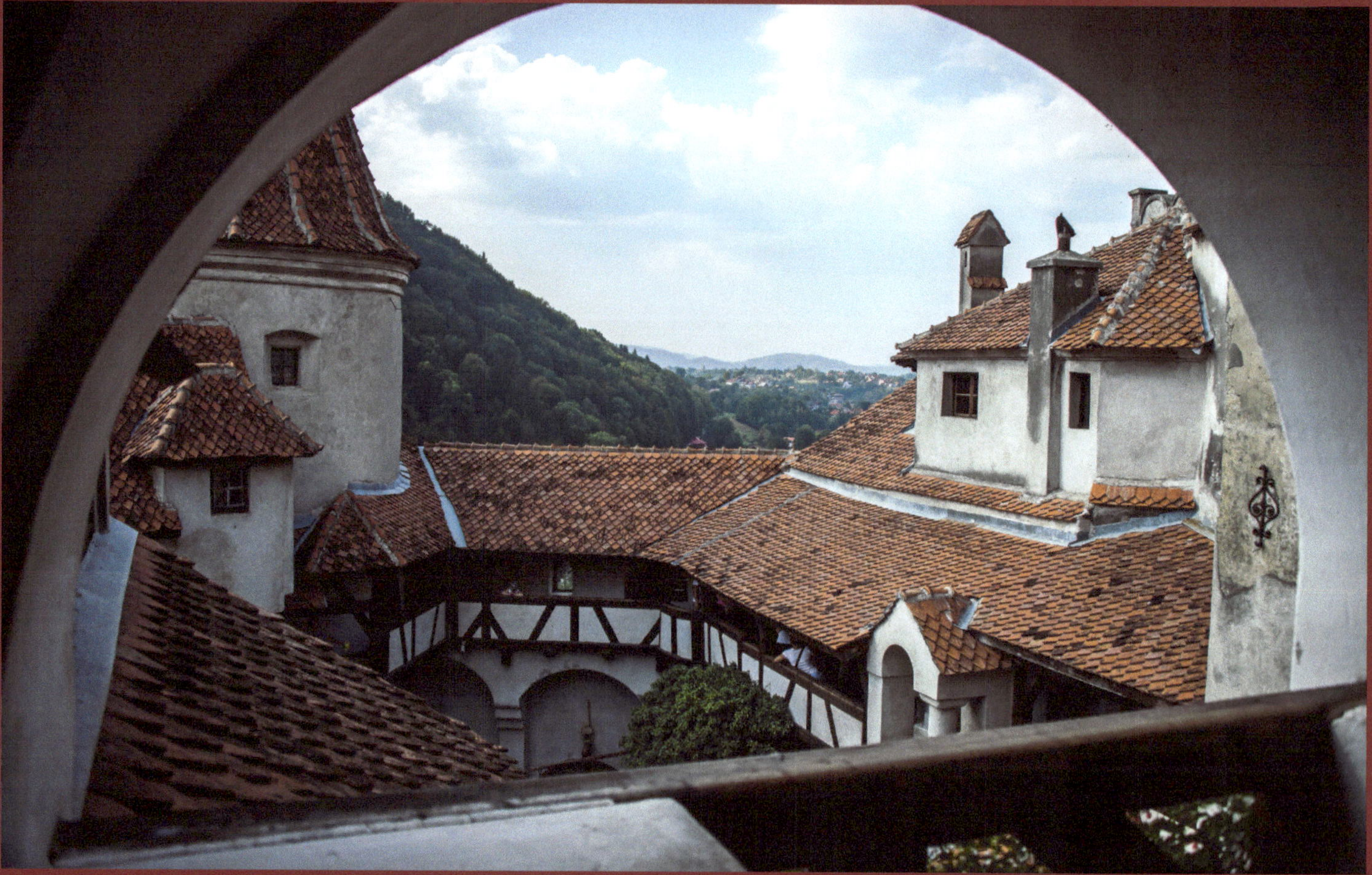

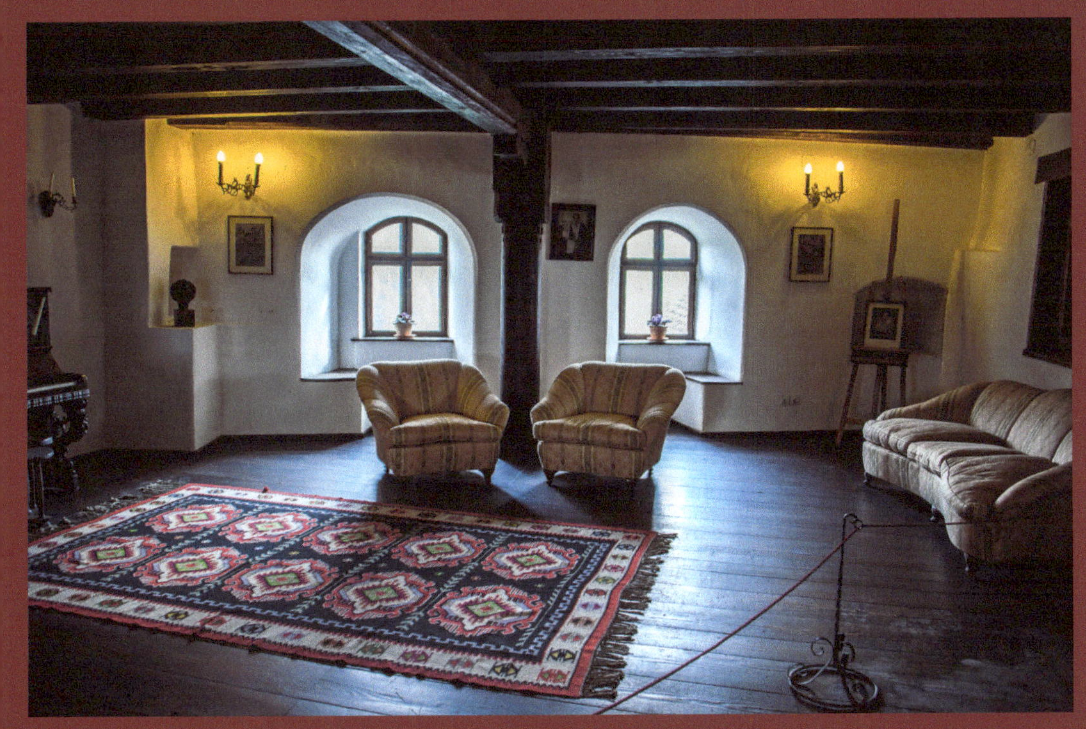

The courtyard of Vlad's castle is all enclosed. You can see how it is nestled into the mountains as you walk around. Inside, the rooms look quite cozy. I enjoyed the experience. But all the young visitors that went up to the castle really expected to see Dracula. They rushed from room to room, none of them caring about the history of the place. All they wanted was for Taylor Lautner or Stephen Moyer to stick his head around the corner, display his fangs and bite them. I was disappointed by that—they traveled all that way only to look for the wrong thing.

The Carpathian Mountains are beautiful, though. You shouldn't go to Romania without visiting them. They made up for all my disappointment with Romanian tourism.

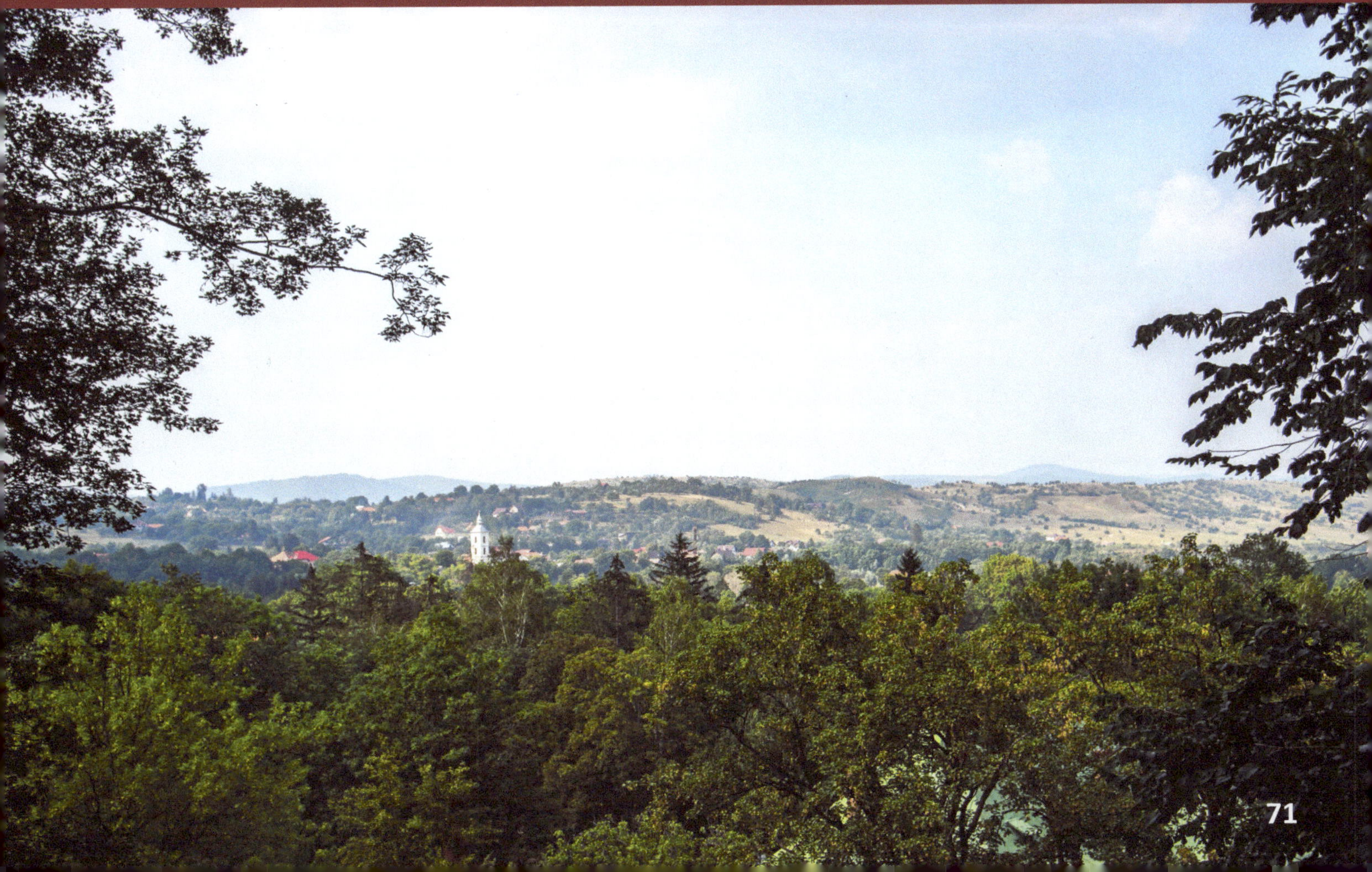

# 10

# ISTANBUL

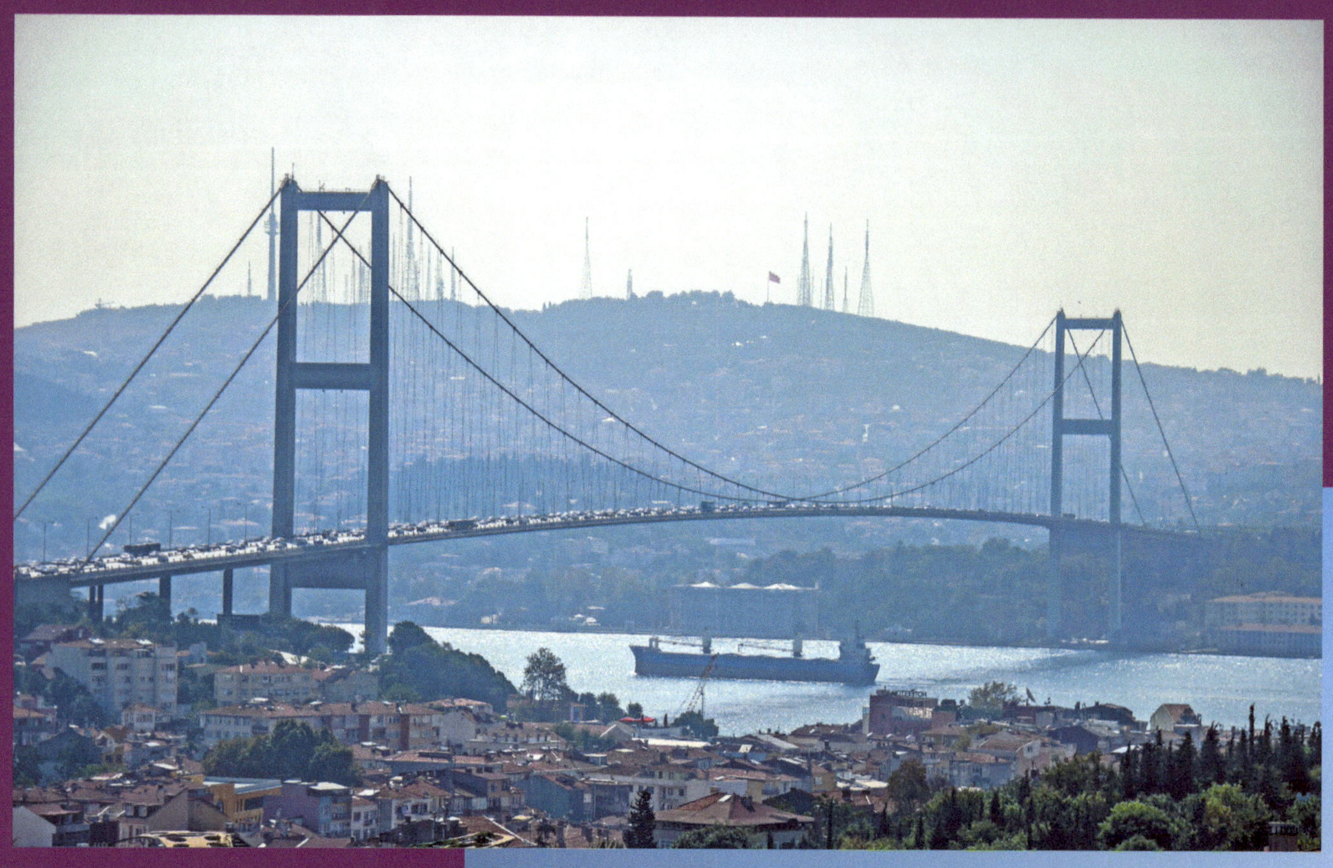

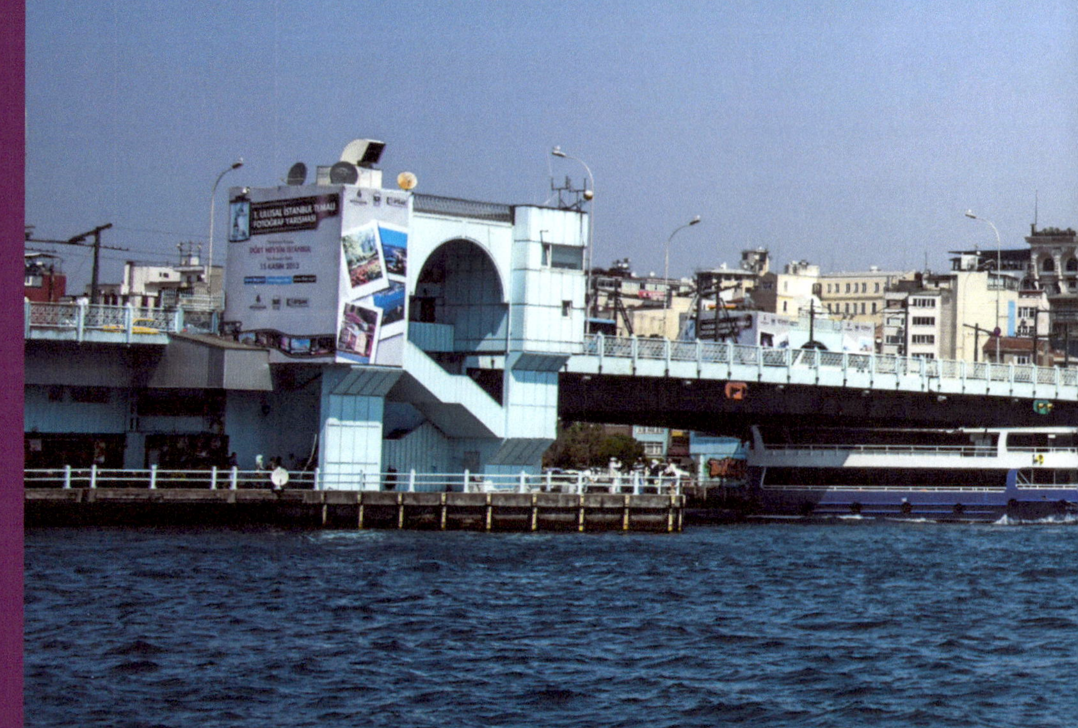

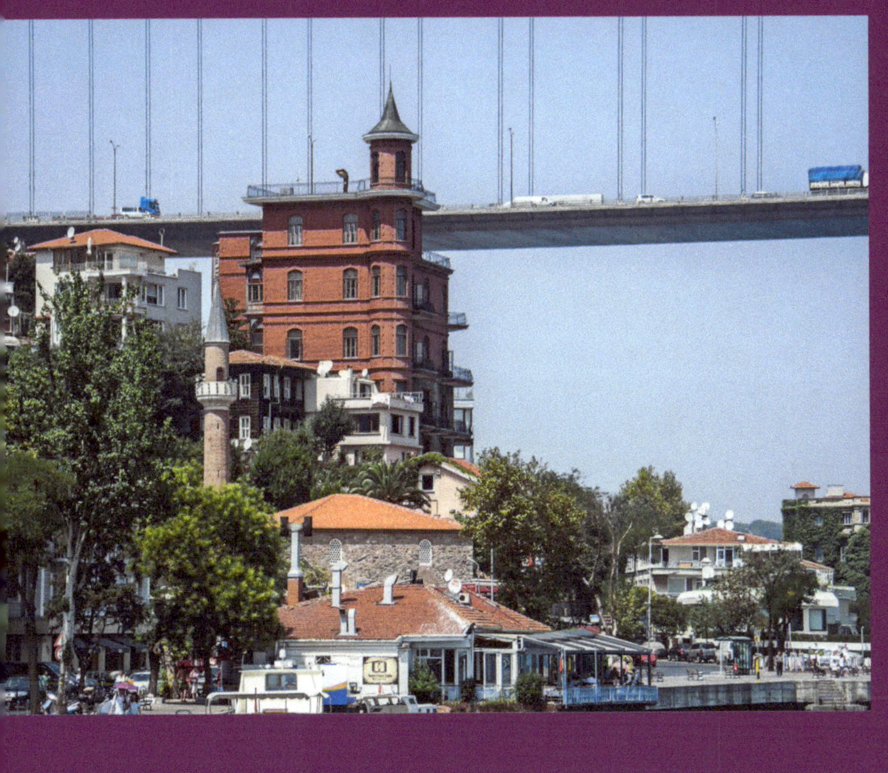

With Istanbul, I broke my rule of not going to any place I'd visited before. I had been there for two days in the early 1990s looking after the German rock band *The Scorpions*. I was so busy then I didn't see anything of the city. This time I wanted to do it on my own. Taking a flight from Bucharest to Istanbul, I didn't know that I would need a visa to enter Turkey. Fortunately, obtaining one was really simple. On arrival at Istanbul airport, you're directed to a counter where they sell you a visa (a stamp in your passport) for 15 Euros. Then you get back in the passport control line.

After Jerusalem, Istanbul is second on my list of favorite cities. There are 19 million people living in this nexus between Europe and Asia, and you get both Western and Eastern ambiance. The bridges span the Bosporus and Golden Horn, an ancient harbor on the northern side. You have to get out on the river to really appreciate the city. You get the best views from there. I took a cruise on the Bosporus, traveled across the Bosporus Bridge on a bus and got on a Hop On – Hop Off as soon as I could to see the city. It would have taken less time on foot. Everyone seems to be out at the same time, and there are traffic jams everywhere, but somehow it all works.

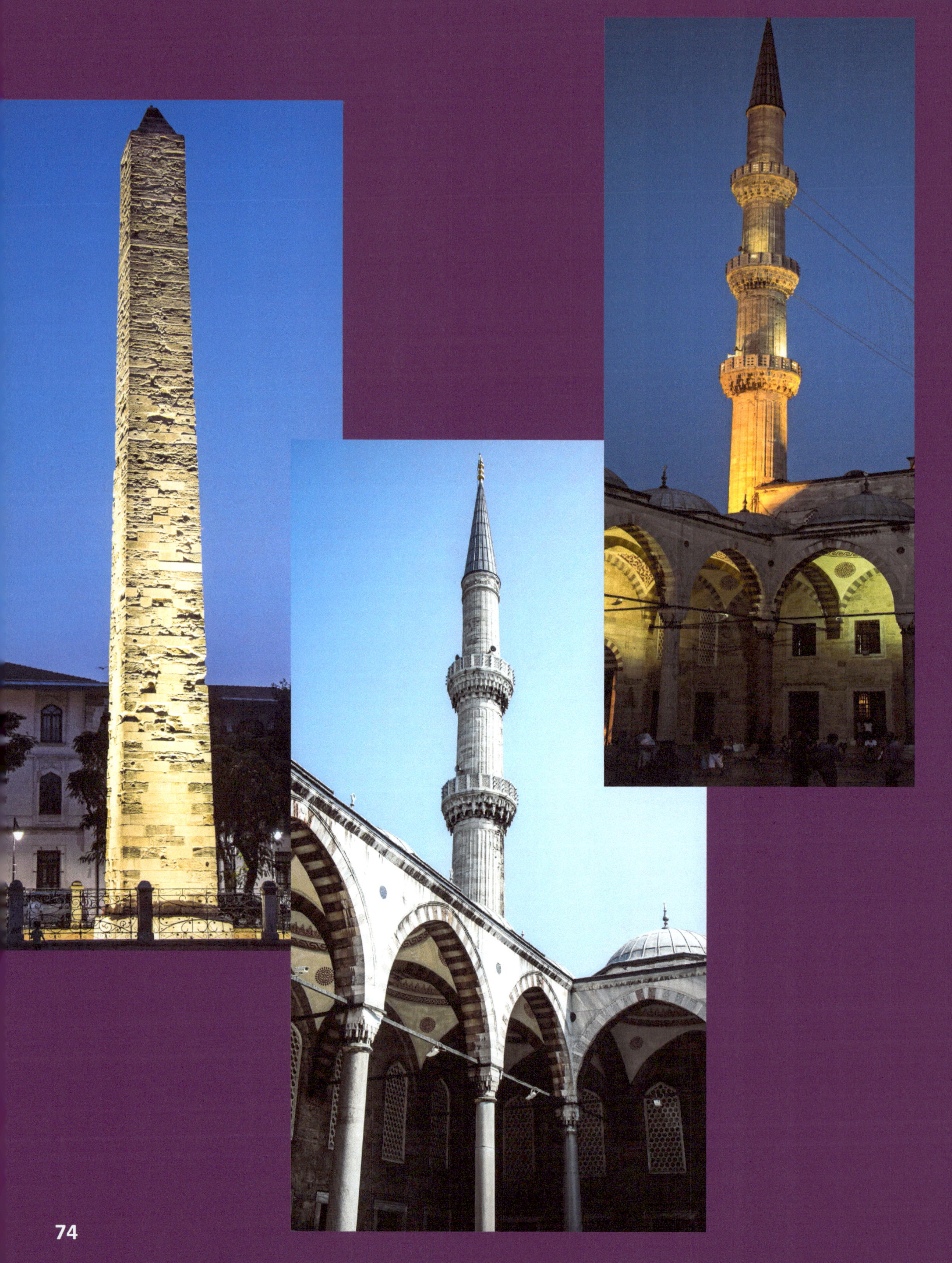

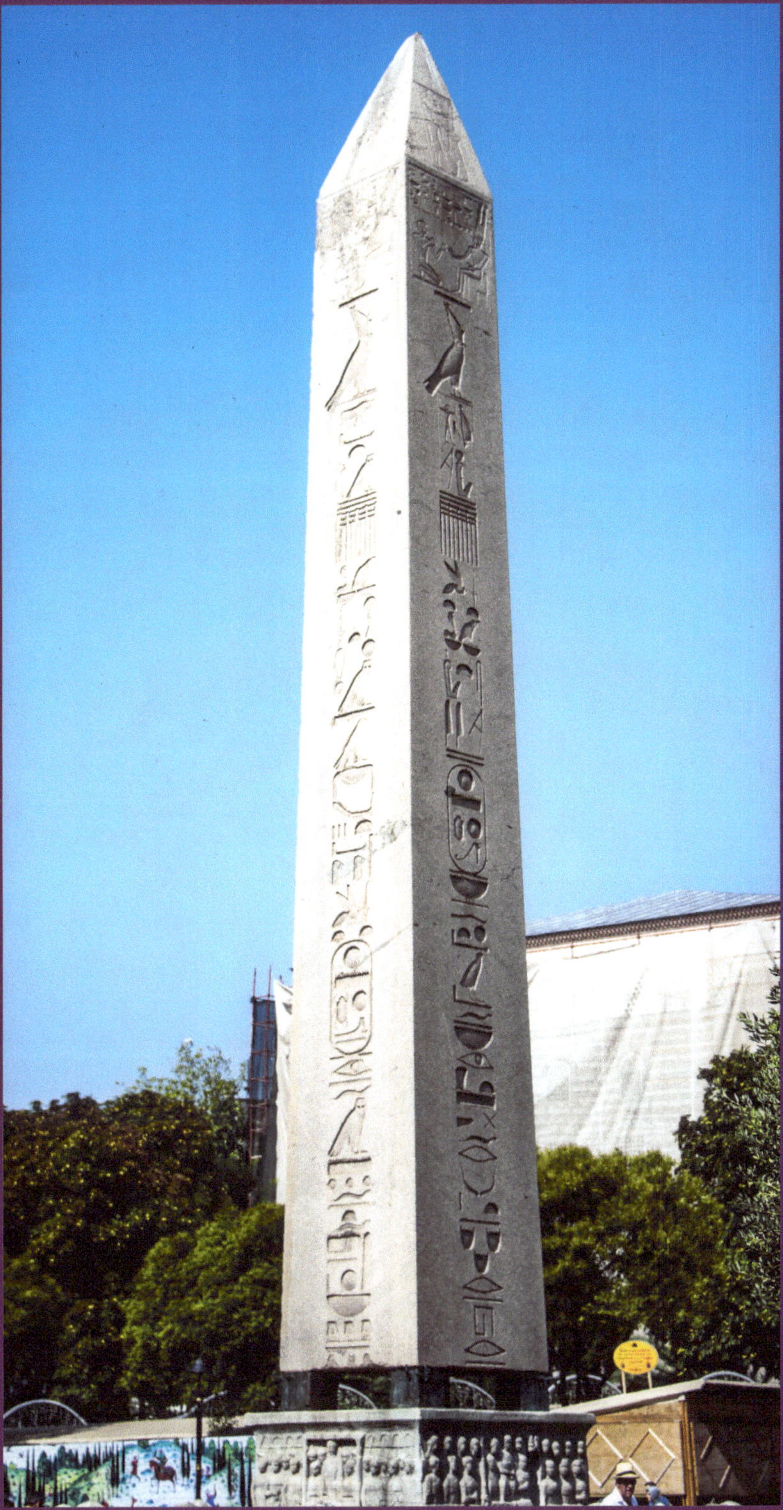

Wherever you look you see beautiful buildings—mosques, churches, obelisks and other architecture dating back to the ancient Roman, Byzantine and Ottoman Empires. Many are beautifully illuminated at night.

I was staying in the suburb of Sultanahmet, which is situated in the old part of the city, originally built up by the Roman Emperor, Constantine the Great. He gave the city its name—Constantinople—when he dedicated it in 330 A.D. When the Ottoman Turks conquered it in 1453, they renamed it Istanbul, which means "in the city" or "to the city."

The atmosphere was exotic and wonderful. I remember sitting outside at 5 o'clock in the morning listening to the clerics stand at the top of their mosque towers, singing and chanting though microphones, calling on everyone to go to morning prayers. Loudspeakers are attached to the outside of the mosques, and it's incredibly loud because everyone's doing it at the same time. I'm sure you get used to it if you live there, you don't even think about it; but for a tourist sitting on his balcony early in the morning, drinking his Turkish coffee, it's something special.

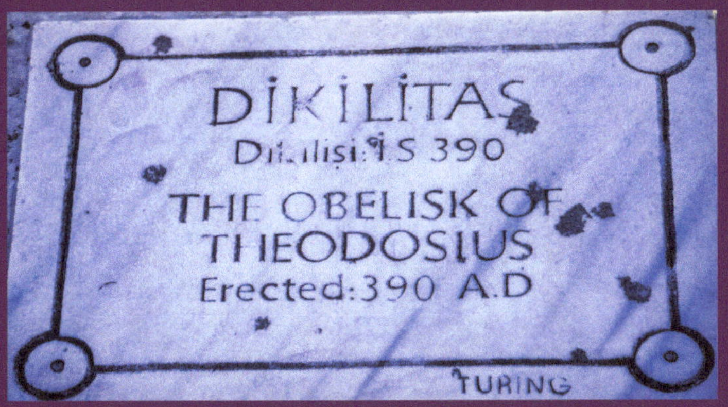

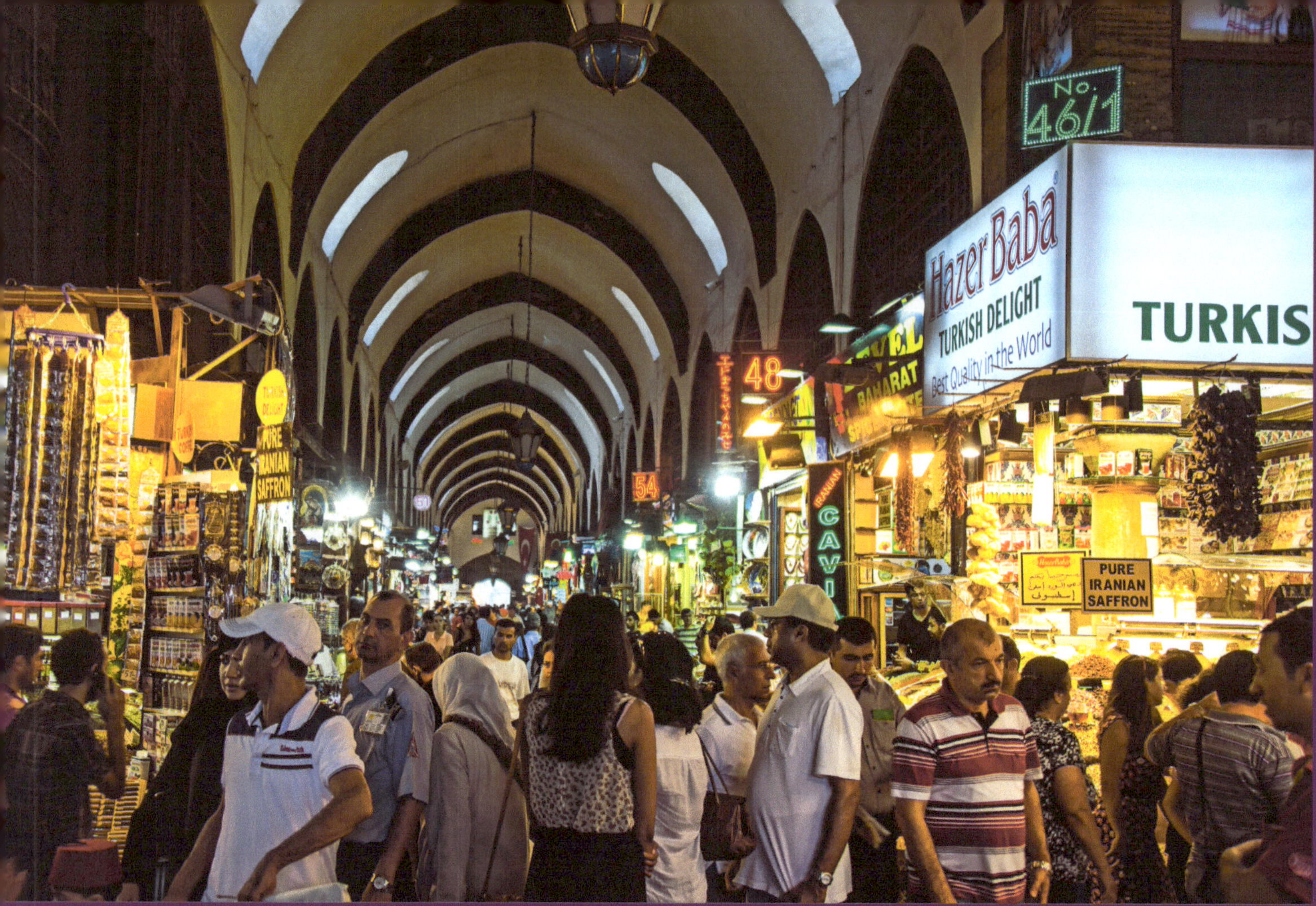

I remember getting off a Bosporus boat without a clue as to where I was going. I walked across the road into this covered market. As I mentioned before, I don't take a camera strobe with me, I use whatever lighting there is. Besides, you can't walk around these markets with a flash—it would get you ejected, or worse. Some of the vendors like to be photographed because they think it's good promotion; others tell you to get lost!

The pictures, counterclockwise: bottles and waterpipes, dried herbs, bars of soap. In the upper right corner: all kinds of candies.

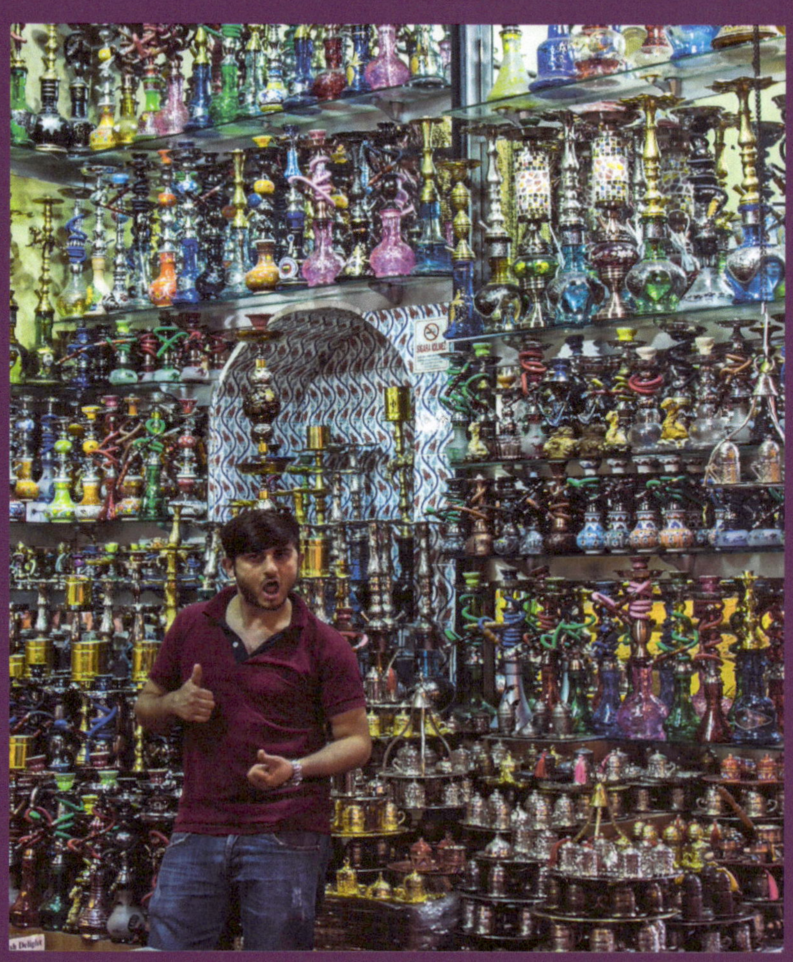

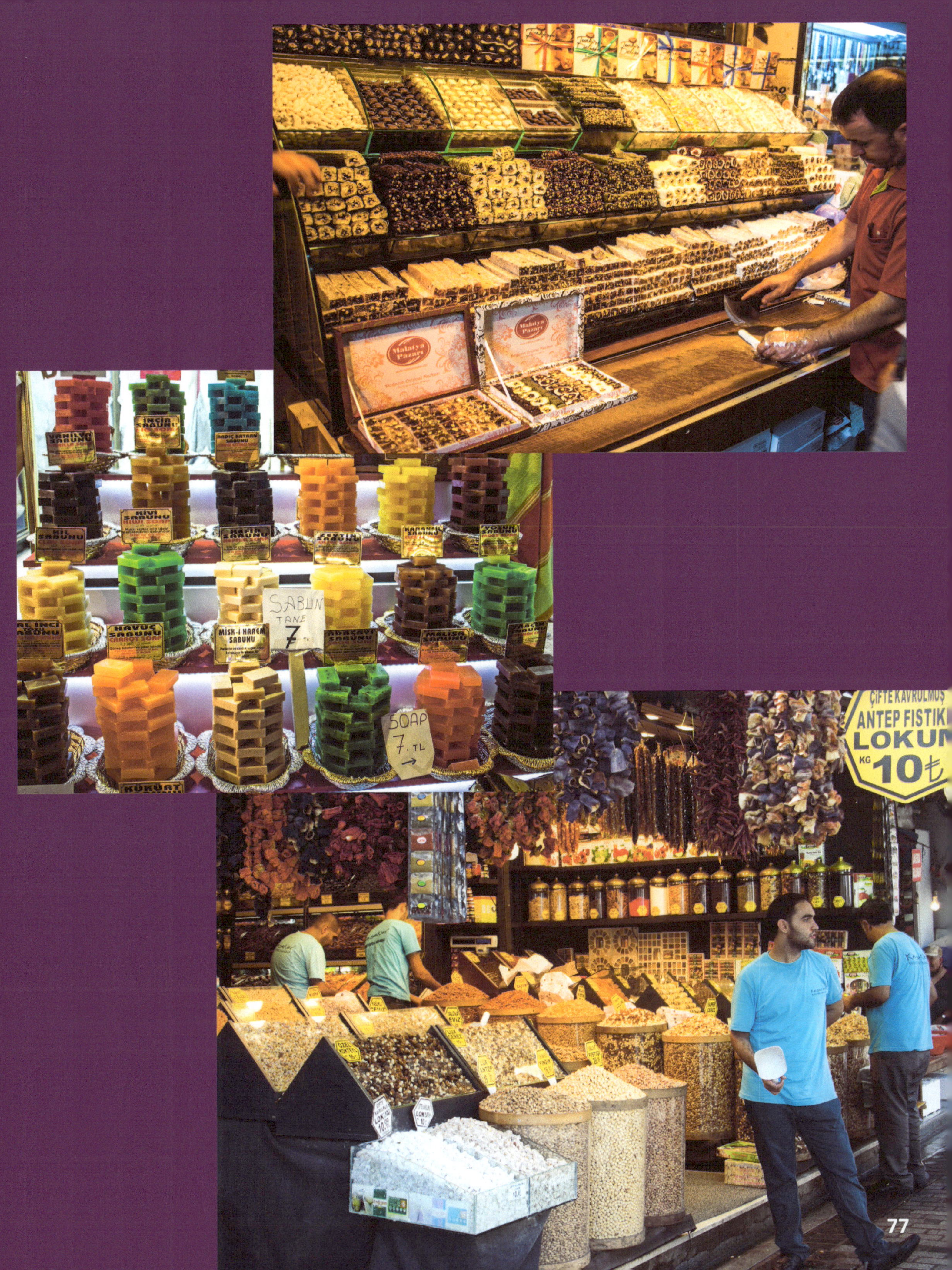
Malatya Pazarı
Malatya Pazarı
KİVİ SABUNU
KIWI SOAP
HAVUÇ SABUNU
CARROT SOAP
SABUN
TANE
7 TL
SOAP
7. TL
ÇİFTE KAVRULMUŞ
ANTEP FISTIK
KG 10₺

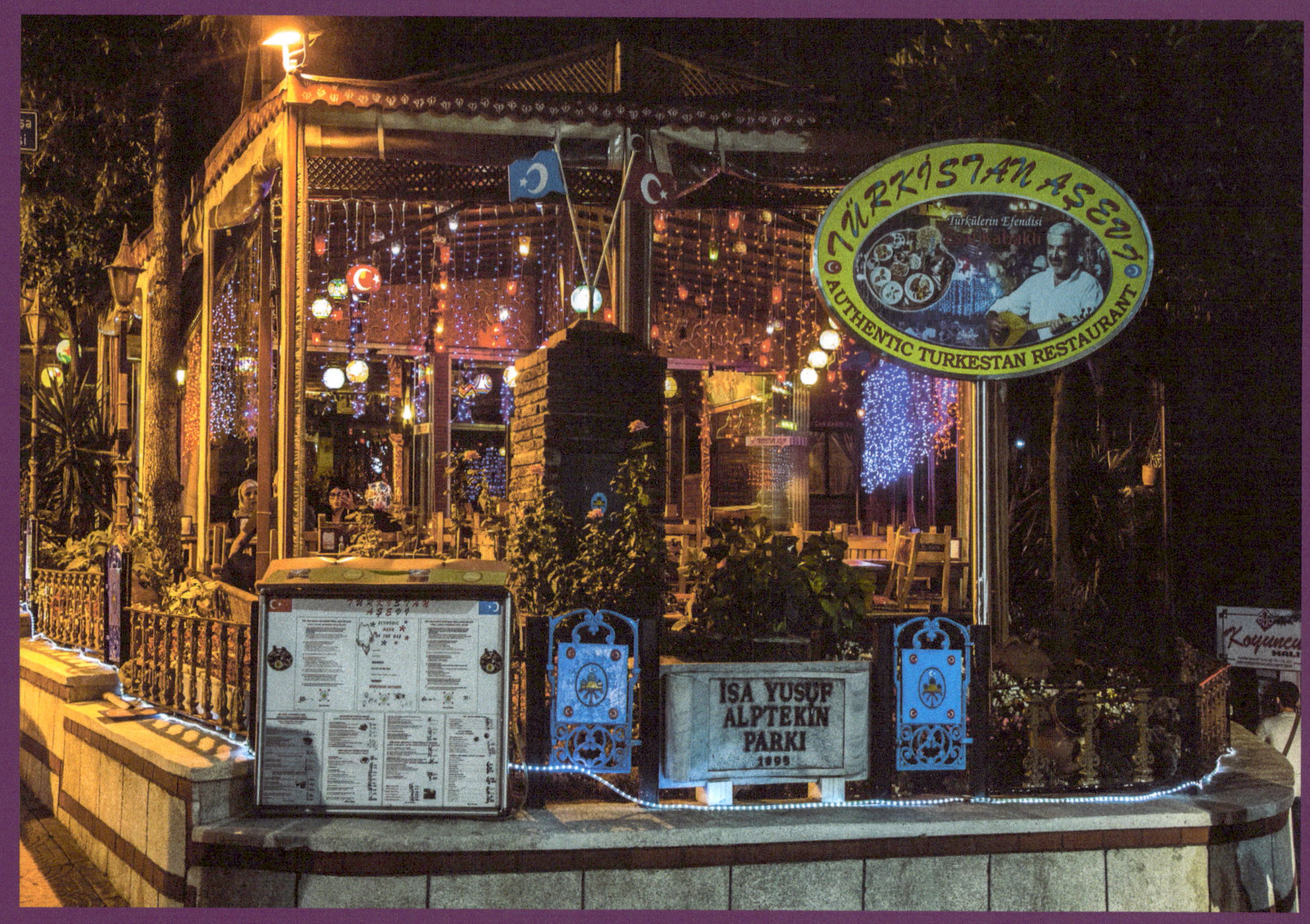


As I mentioned earlier, when I'm on the road, I snack a lot. In Istanbul, I had Turkish coffee wherever I went. After a couple of days, when I needed a break from the local cuisine, I'd end up in a pizzeria or Chinese restaurant.

Istanbul is an enterprising city, very different than 50 years ago. It's not the old, quaint and a bit dated Constantinople that everybody knew. It wants to be a cosmopolitan European city. Many of the younger generations of Turks have been to Germany and Northern Europe at some point in their lives as guest workers (the Germans call them *Gastarbeiter*) or tourists. They all speak English. The older generation sits around and makes for good, picturesque photographs, but the younger generation determines what's happening in the city.

Despite the recent resurgence of Islamic fundamentalism in Turkey, Istanbul is coming into the 21st century with a vengeance.

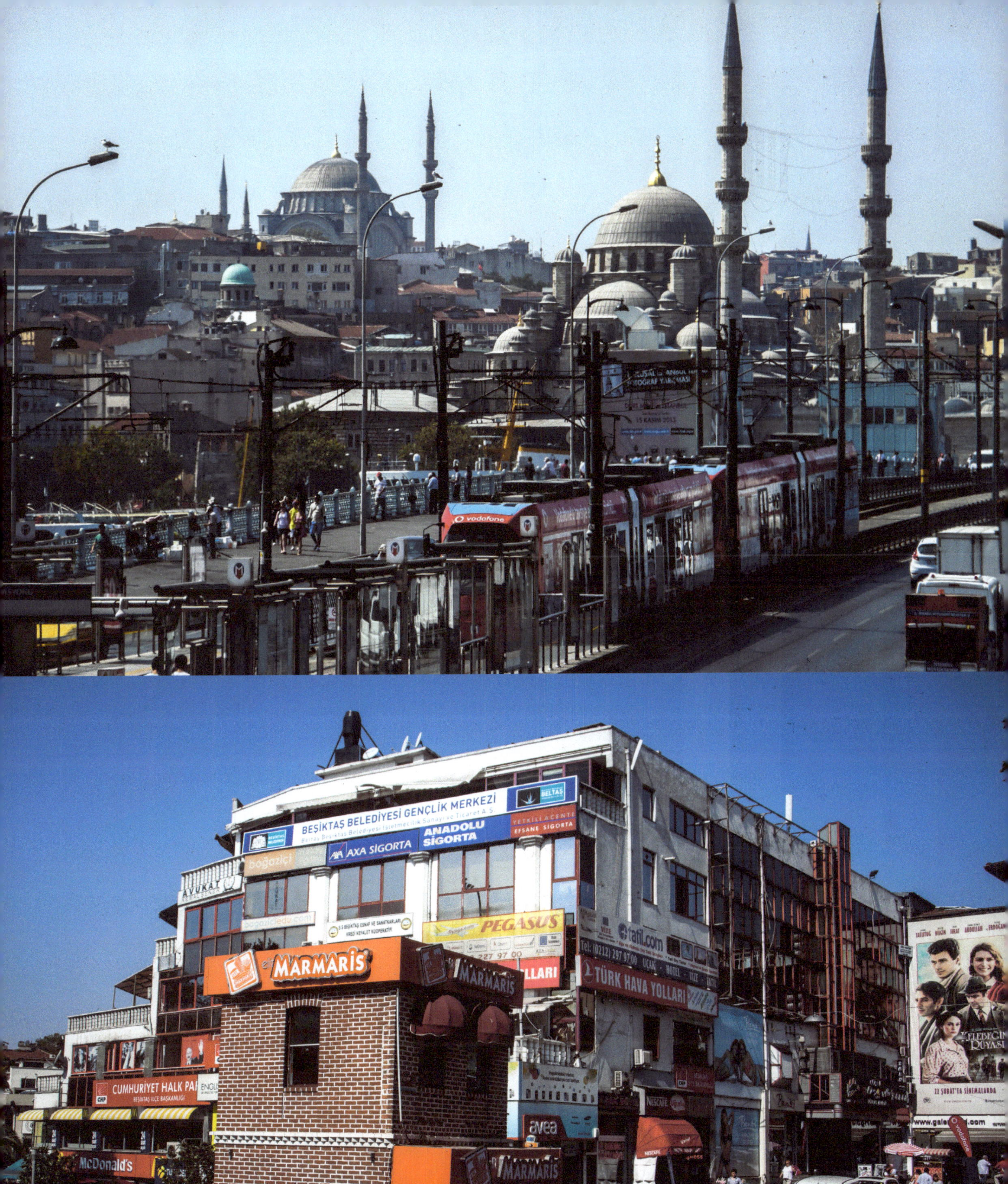
vodafone
BEŞİKTAŞ BELEDİYESİ GENÇLİK MERKEZİ
BELTAŞ
ANADOLU SİGORTA
AXA SIGORTA
EFSANE SIGORTA
AVUKAT
PEGASUS
MARMARIS
TÜRK HAVA YOLLARI
CUMHURİYET HALK PA
McDonald's
avea

# 11 SOFIA

I had always wanted to go to Bulgaria, so I took a short flight from Istanbul to Sofia. It so happened that I shared the plane with a team of Bulgarian wrestlers who were coming home from an international meet. They must have done well because they were in good spirits, but it felt very strange to be on a plane with these huge guys dressed in red uniforms wandering up and down the aisle.

I arrived on the morning of Holy Virgin Mary's Day. Nobody was working and the streets and pedestrian zones were empty. The middle of Sofia felt like a ghost town, and I missed the hustle and bustle of Istanbul, but I still managed to take some interesting and unusual photos. The little church on the opposite page looks like an empty ruin made of ancient stones and rubble, but note the air conditioner on the side.

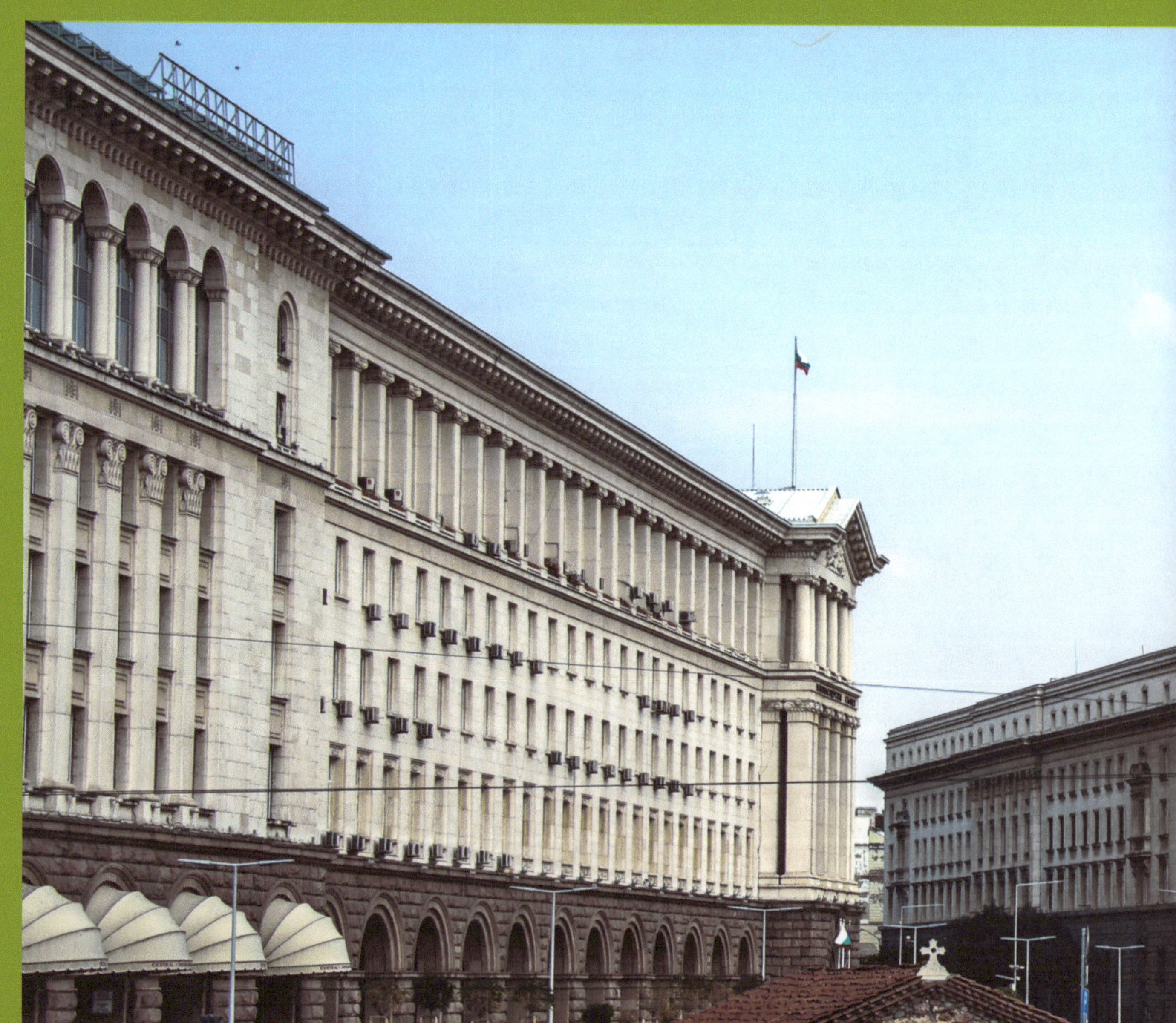

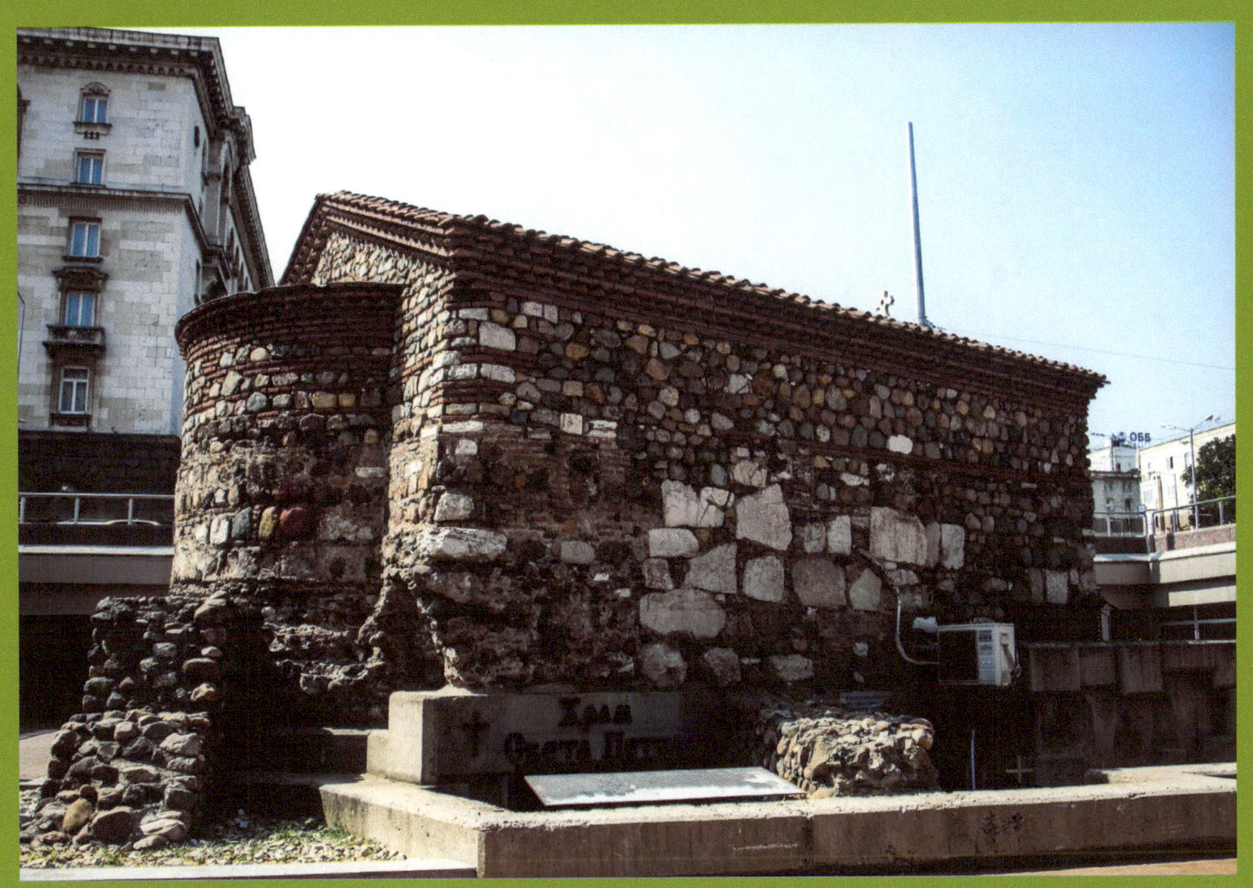
Храм

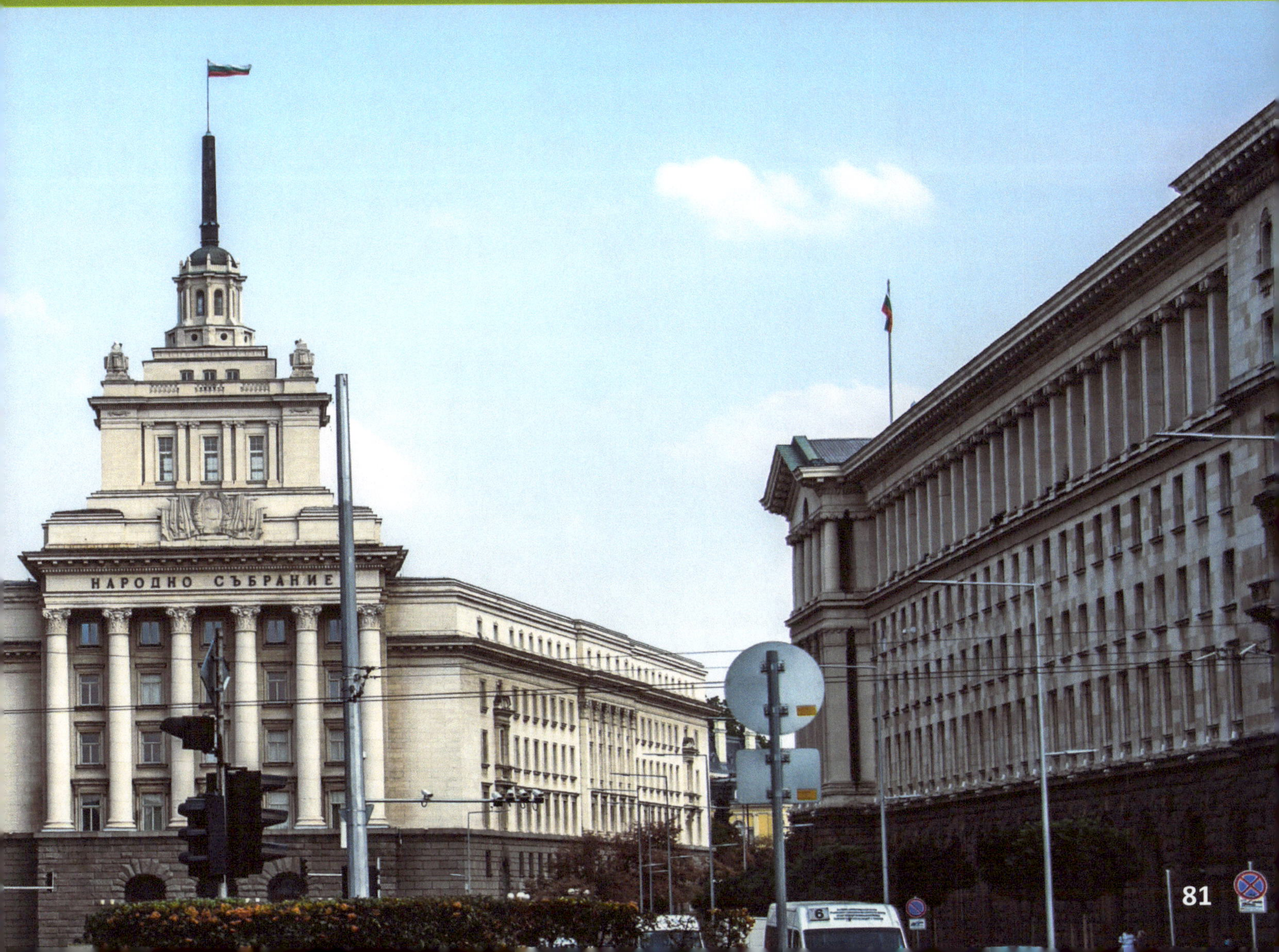

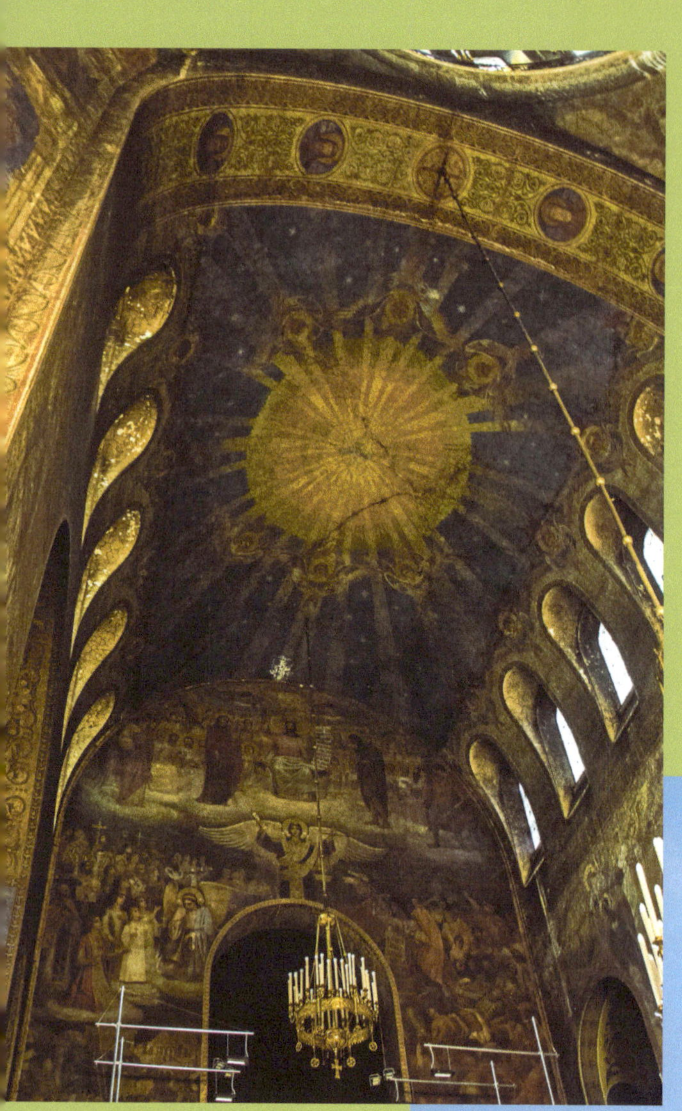

The only activity anywhere that day was in the churches, so I wandered inside some of them and started taking photos. No one seemed to mind. They had gorgeous interiors. Below is the famous Alexander Nevsky Cathedral. It's named after the 13th century prince of Novgorod and Kiev who defeated German and Swedish invaders—a famous movie about his victory against the Teutonic Knights of the Holy Roman Empire was made by Sergei Eisenstein with epic music by Prokofiev. Alexander Nevsky was sainted in 1547. Every town in Eastern European with a Russian Orthodox population has a church named after him, and they all look alike, but this one was huge.

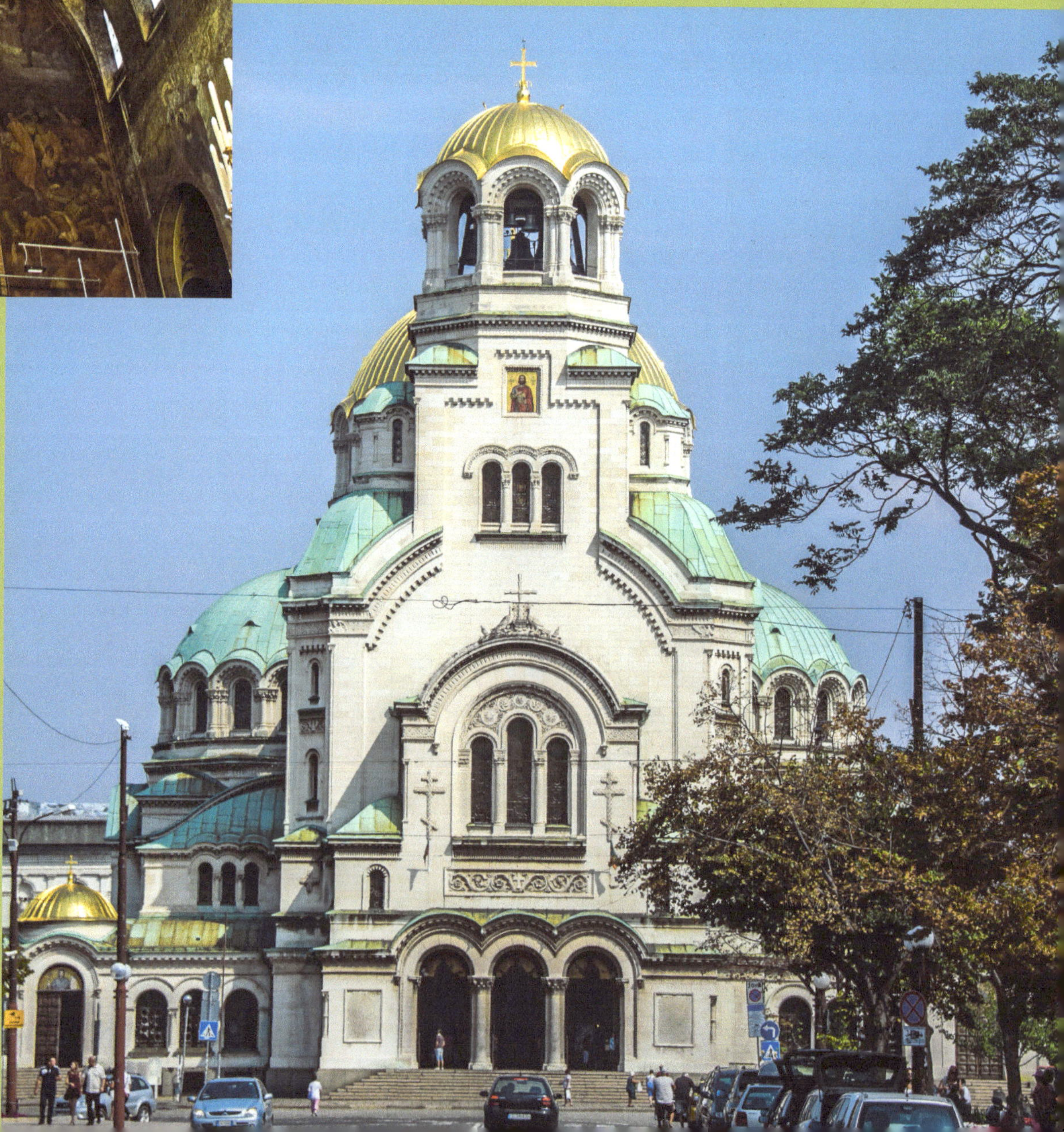

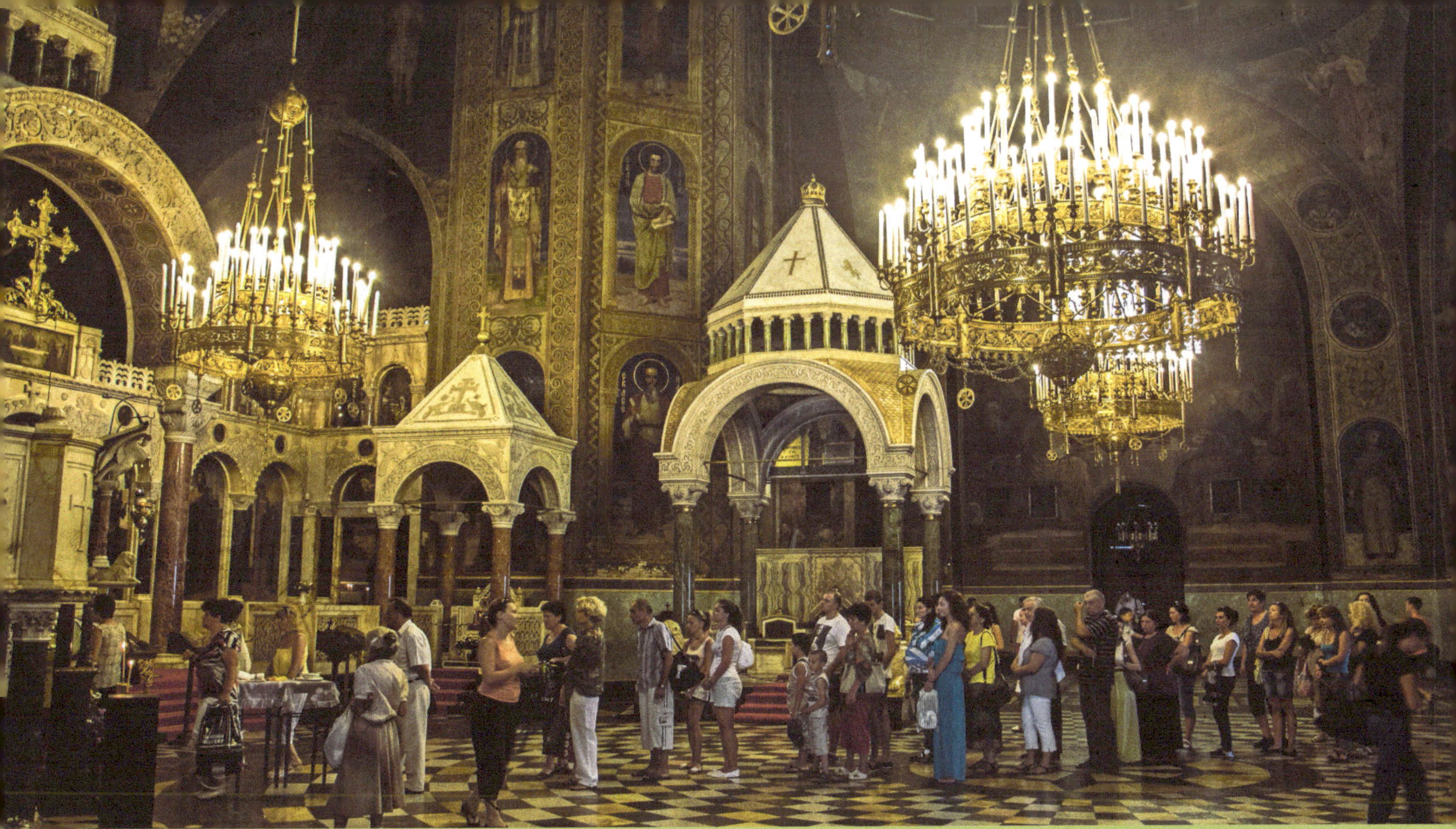

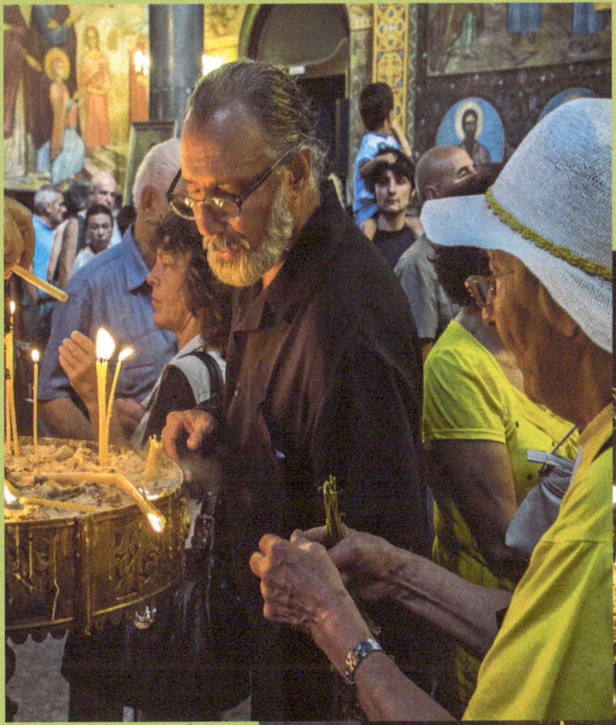

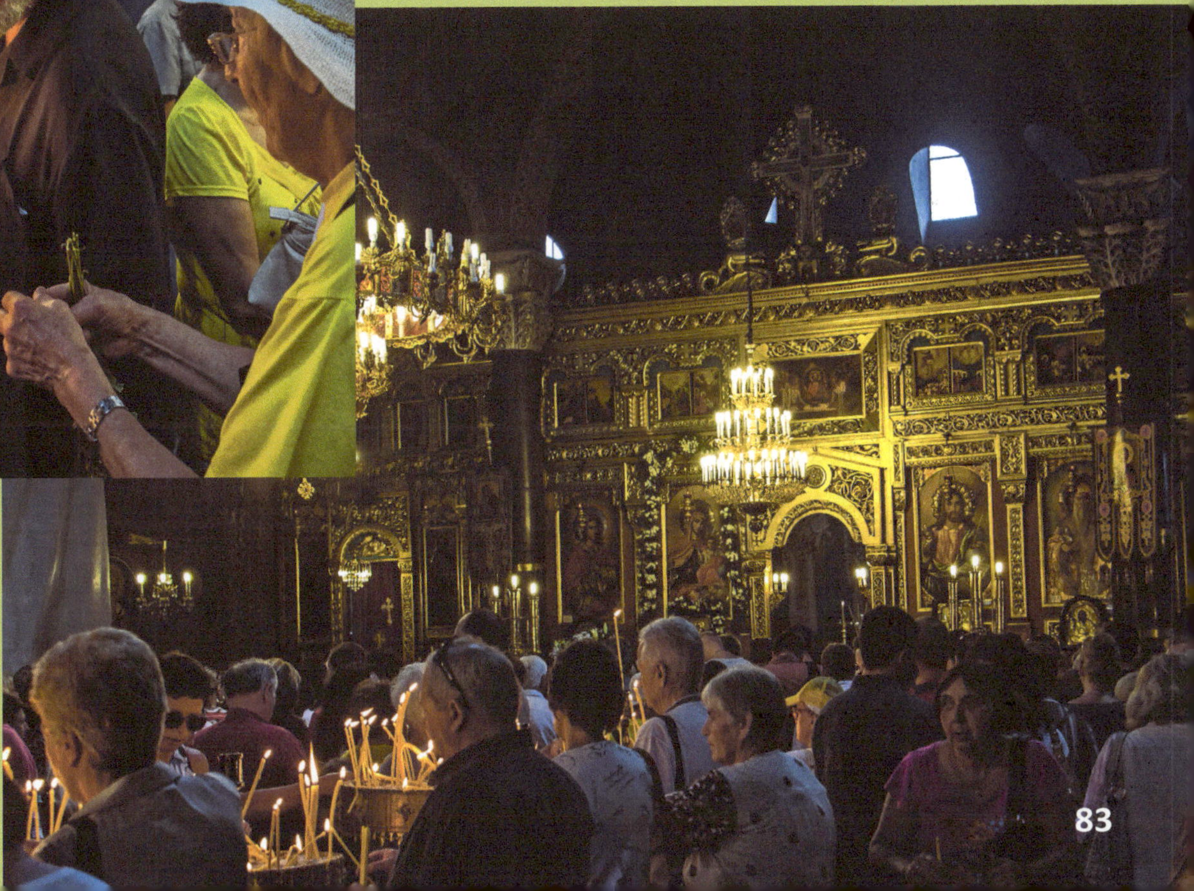

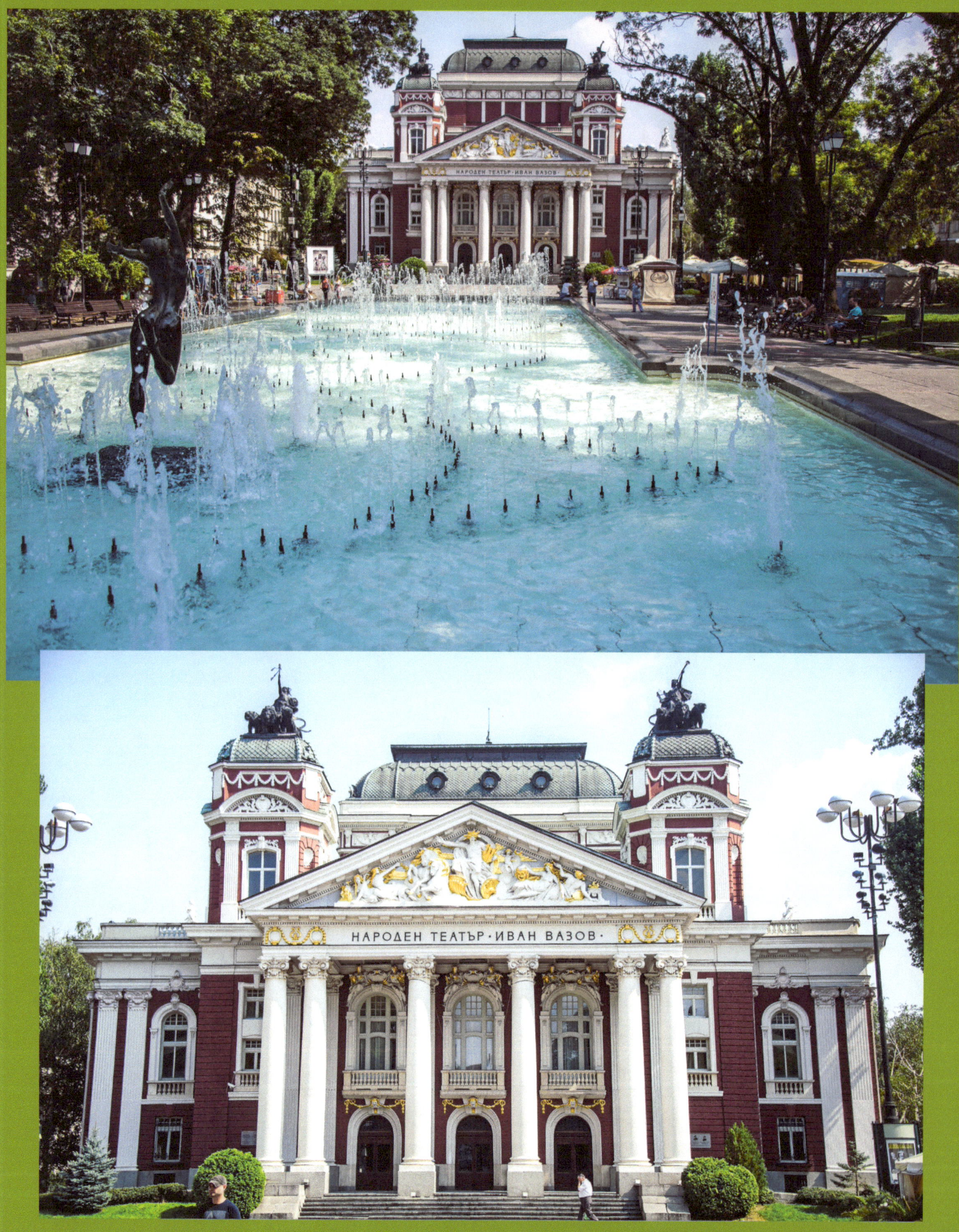
НАРОДЕН ТЕАТЪР · ИВАН ВАЗОВ ·

I liked this fountain in front of a theatre with a beautiful facade. Later I hired a taxi and asked the driver to take me to another church. He drove up into the hills to the one on the right.

Sofia, like Bucharest, is trying to get out from under the shadow of Communism and the USSR, but it's very difficult. After the Cold War ended, you couldn't just destroy every Stalinist building and put up new ones. I probably didn't give Sofia enough of a chance, although it turned out to be a big turning point in my trip.

I figured I'd go to Moscow before heading to Estonia and bought an online airline ticket and reserved a hotel there, prepaying for five days. The evening before I left, I got an e-mail from my travel agent in Britain asking if I had gotten my visa. I hadn't and couldn't buy one at the airport as I did in Istanbul. The hotel wouldn't refund my money and I was out over $600, so I cancelled the flight and decided to conserve my funds and continue my journey by bus.

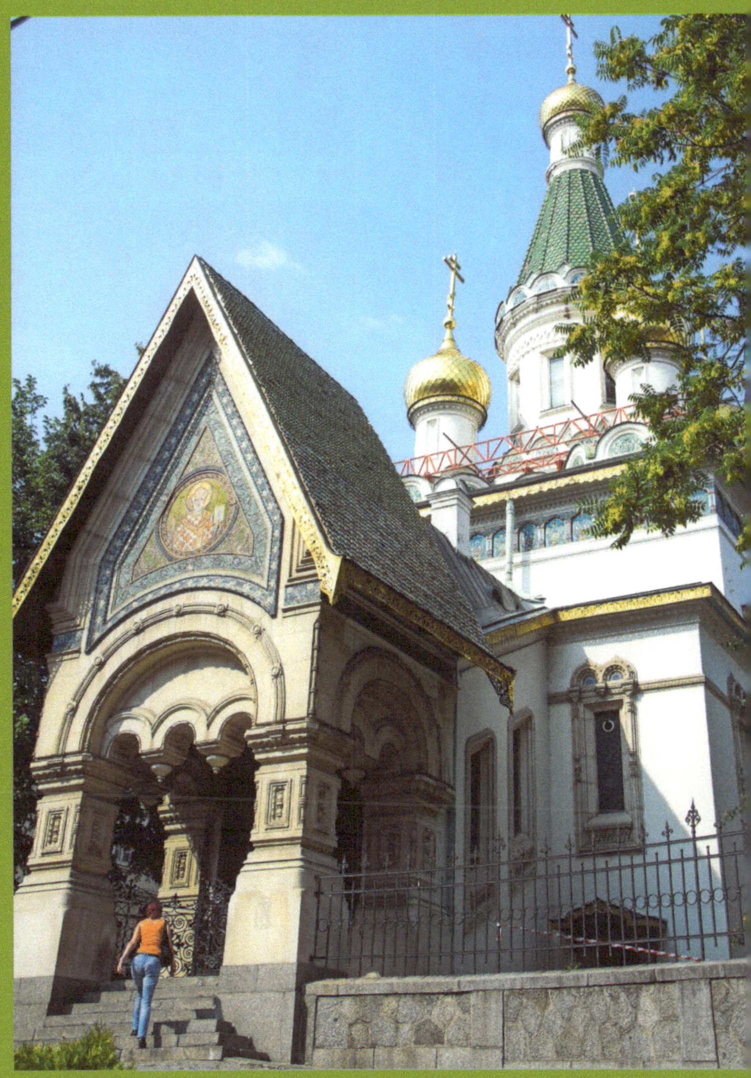

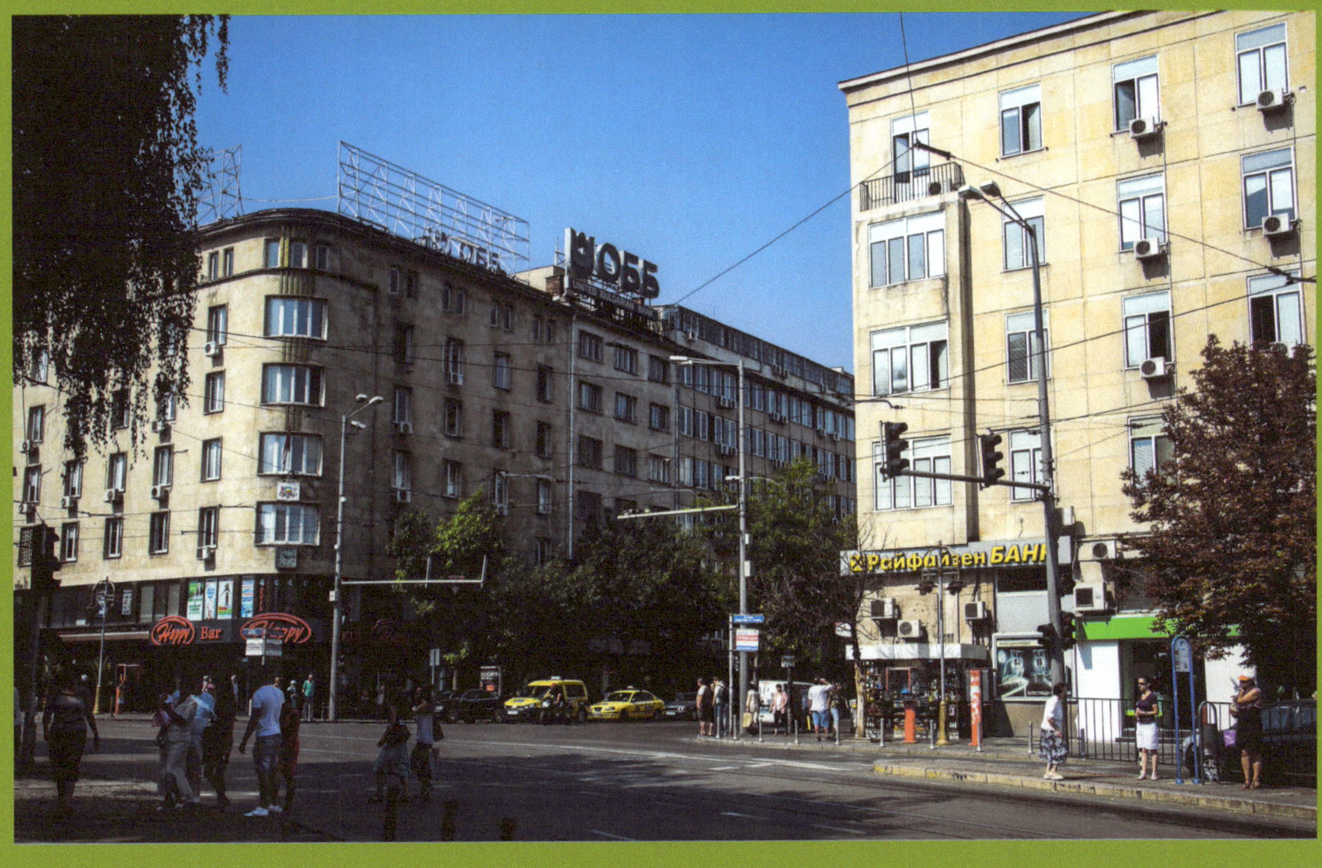

# Churches and Cathedrals

I found the interiors of Catholic and Orthodox churches in Eastern Europe an amazing feast for the eyes—Brasov and Krakau on the opposite page are just two examples. In contrast below is the great gothic Cologne Cathdral I'd come to love through the many years I lived in Germany. It may look more austere, but in its own way it's just as majestic and impressive.

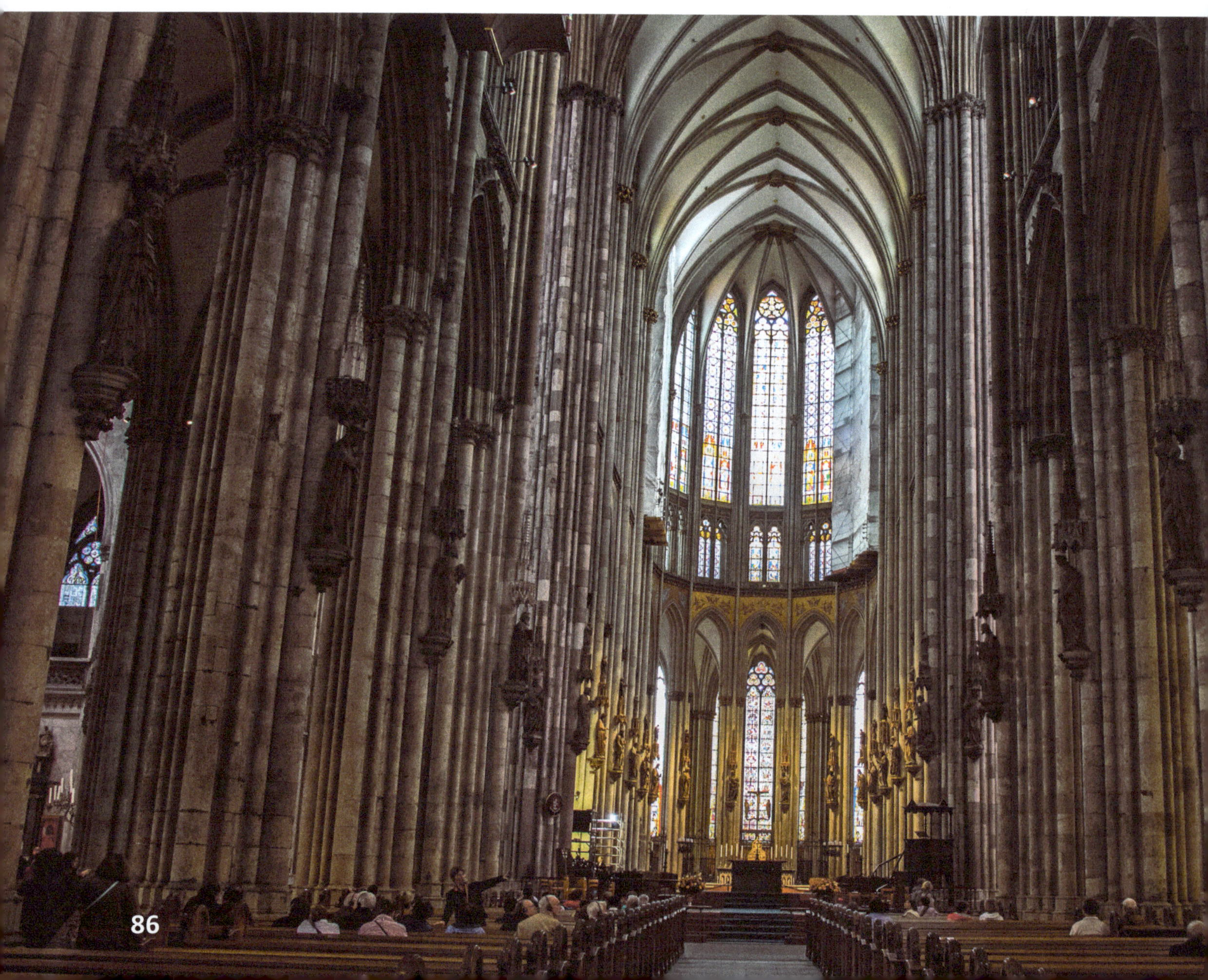

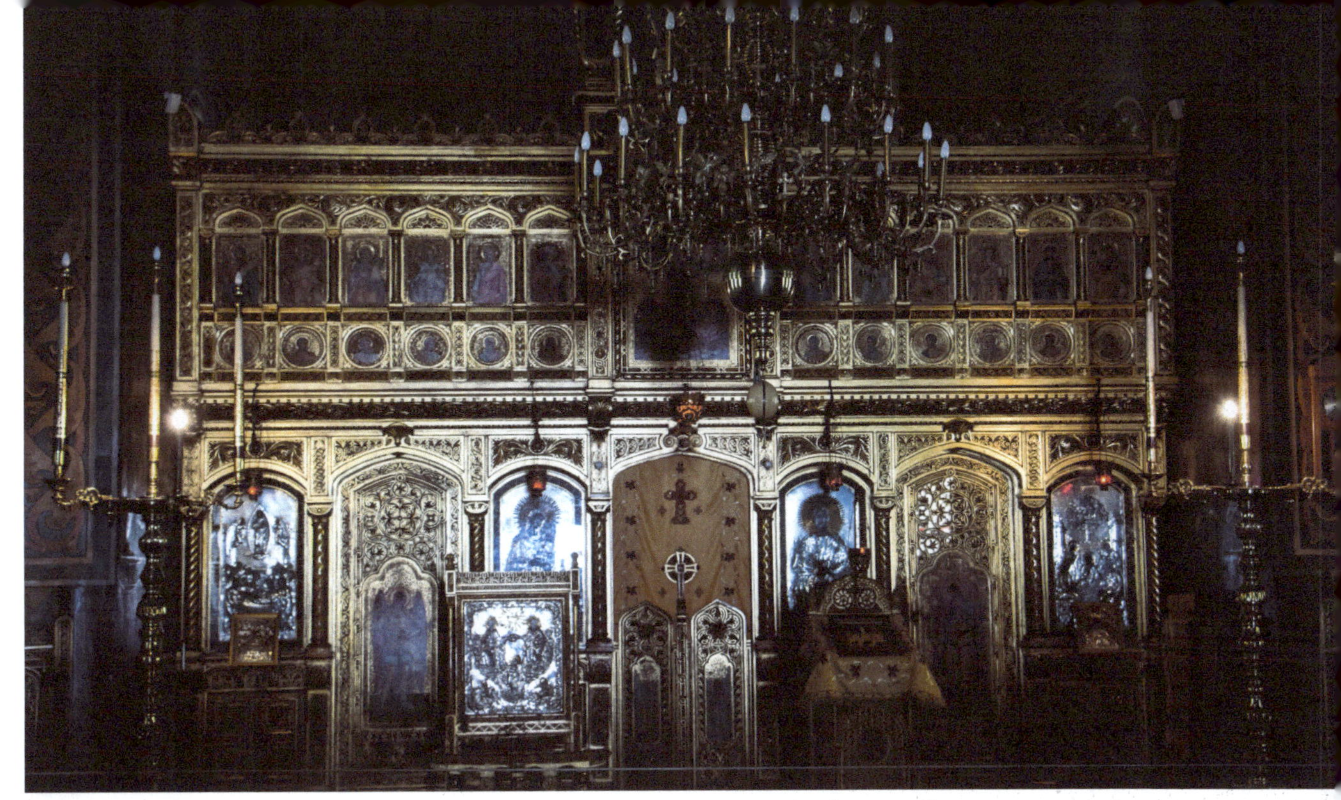

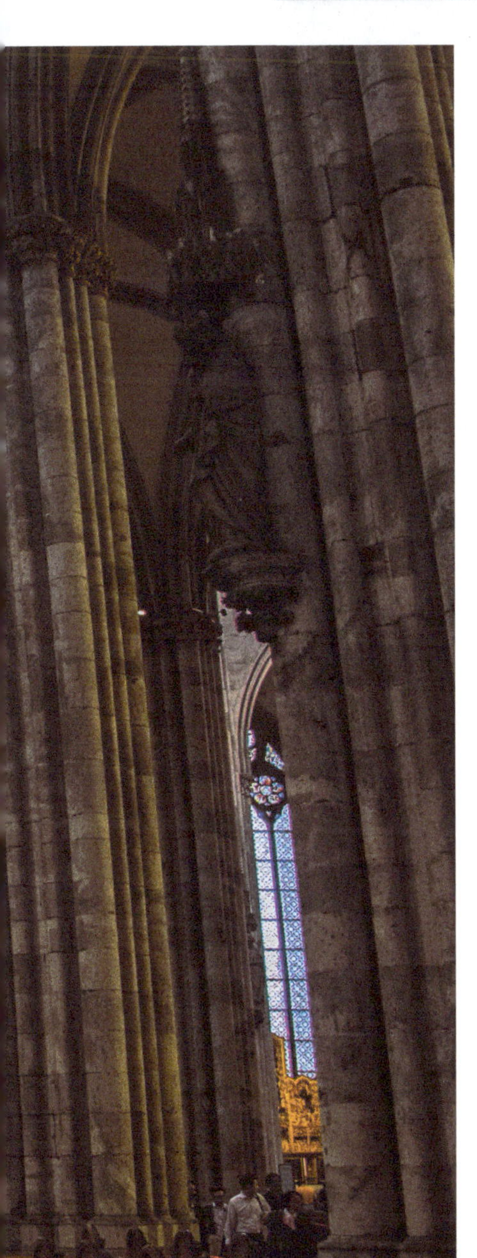

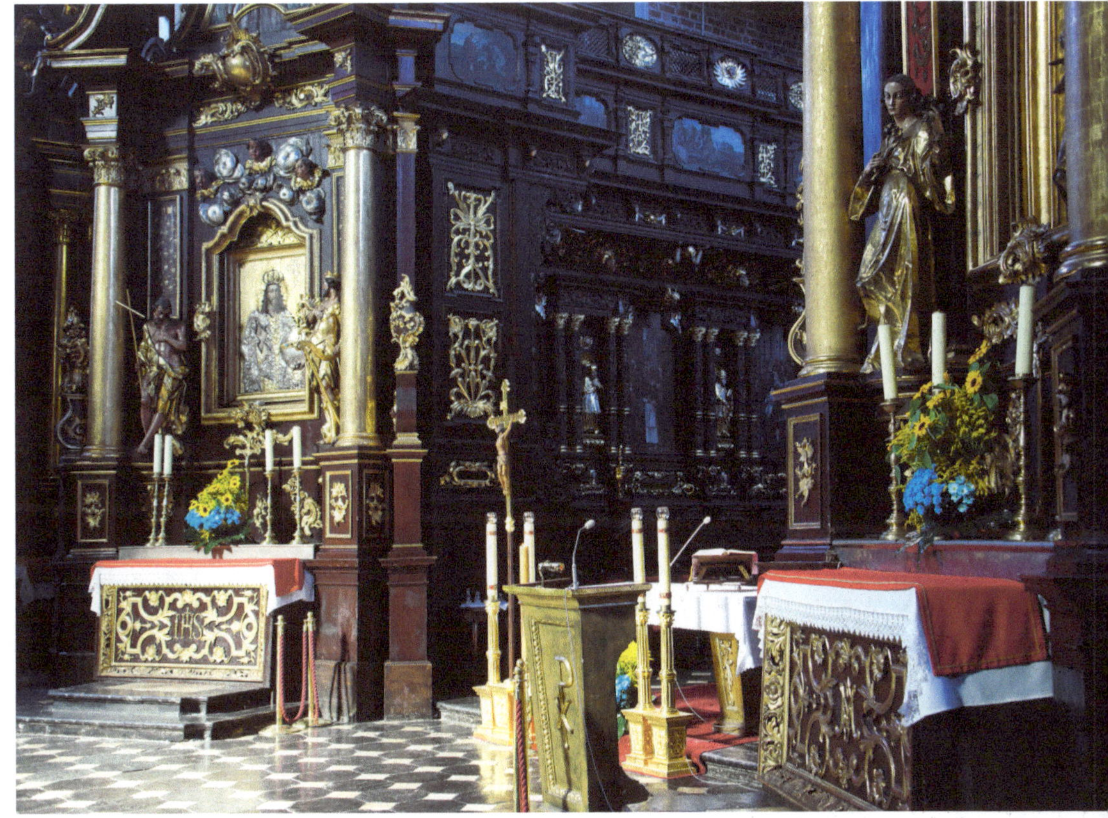

The bus to Poland went through Serbia, Hungary and Slovakia. Going into Serbia, I experienced one of those throwbacks to Iron Curtain times. Not being part of the European Union, the country is still very much living in the 1950s. The authorities hold you up at the borders for hours going through customs. When you're in a tourist bus, as we were, you at least get into a separate lane from the cars; otherwise we'd still be sitting in the line today.

It took us about half an hour to get to the border, at which point the guards took our passports and disappeared with them into an office. It was a scary moment. We got them back after exiting the bus and walking the 20 yards to the next checkpoint. The officials make a point of keeping you waiting to intimidate you, and it works. Without your passport, you feel naked and frightened; and very annoyed afterwards!

It happened twice—first going from Bulgaria into Serbia, and then again when we crossed the border into Hungary. I would have liked to stop there for a day or two, but I had promised my wife, whose family comes from Budapest, that I would not visit it on my own. She gave me strict instructions not to go there without her!

By the time we reached Poland, we had been in the bus for 22 hours. There was an IT student from Warsaw University on the bus—Piotr (Peter)—who told me to get off at Krakow because it would be an interesting experience. Also, the trip from there to Warsaw would take seven more hours because the bus switched from express to local, stopping at every telephone pole to drop off and pick up passengers. I took his advice and I'm glad I did, because Krakow became number 3 on my list of favorite cities..

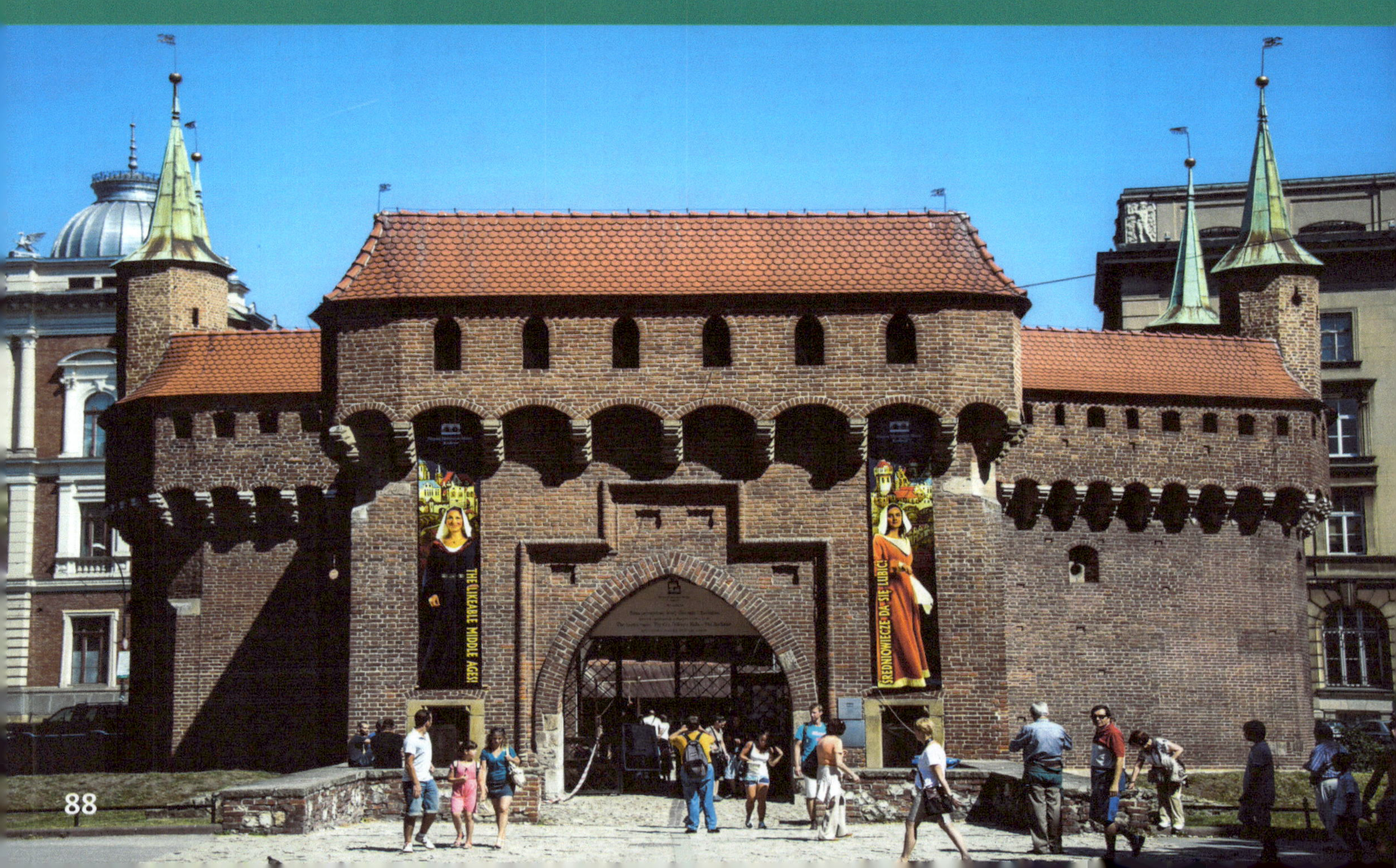

# 12

# KRAKOW

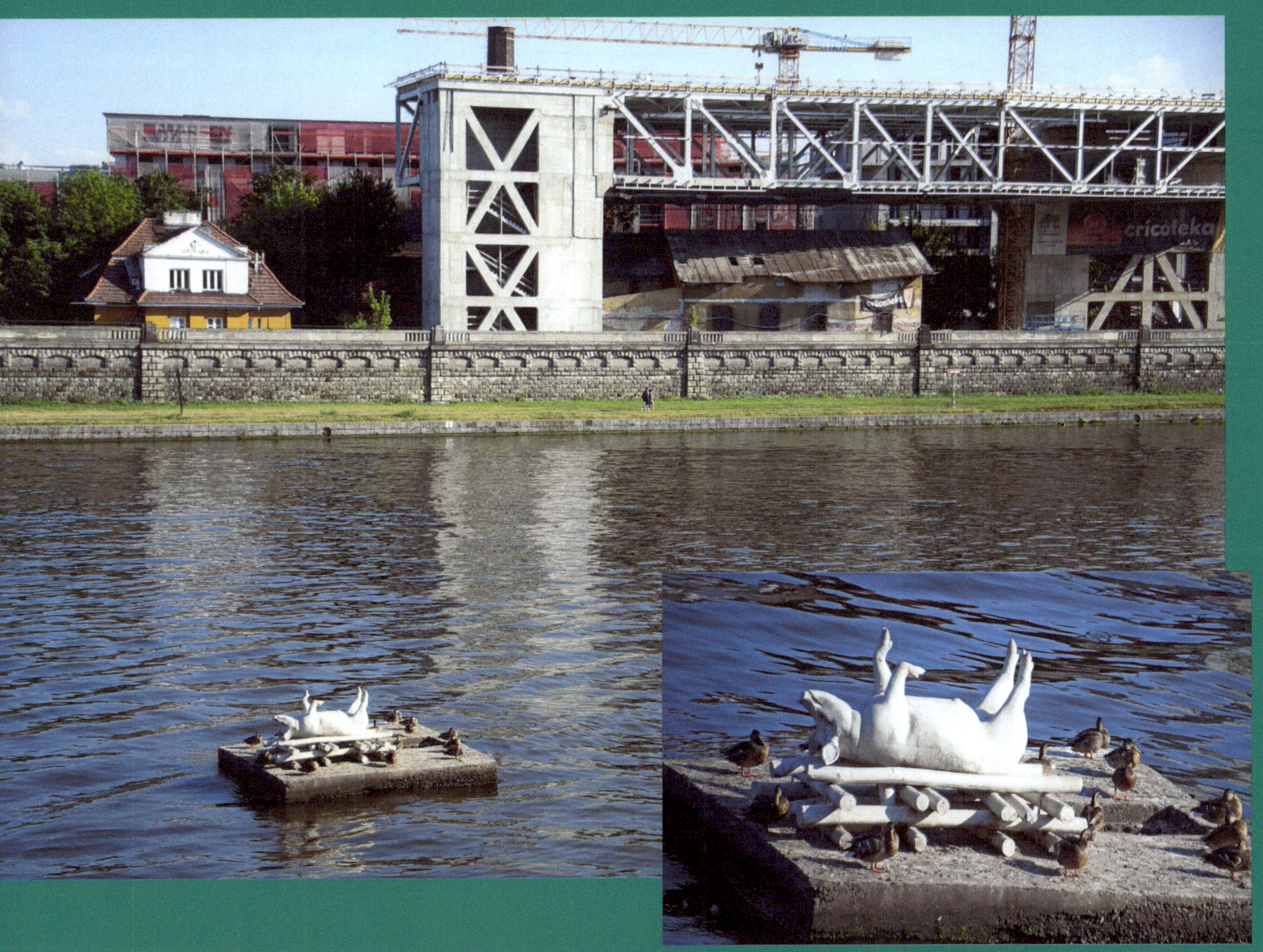


Located in the southern part of Poland, Krakow dates back to the 7th century. It was the Polish capital from 1038 to 1569 and has always been one of the country's leading academic, cultural and economic centers. Krakow is a combination of old and new, contemporary installations and ancient legends, and downright wonderful Polish weirdness. No one seems to know, for example, what the floating pig sculpture on the wooden pyre in the middle of the Vistula River means, but it doesn't seem out of place and is, of course, a favorite tourist attraction.

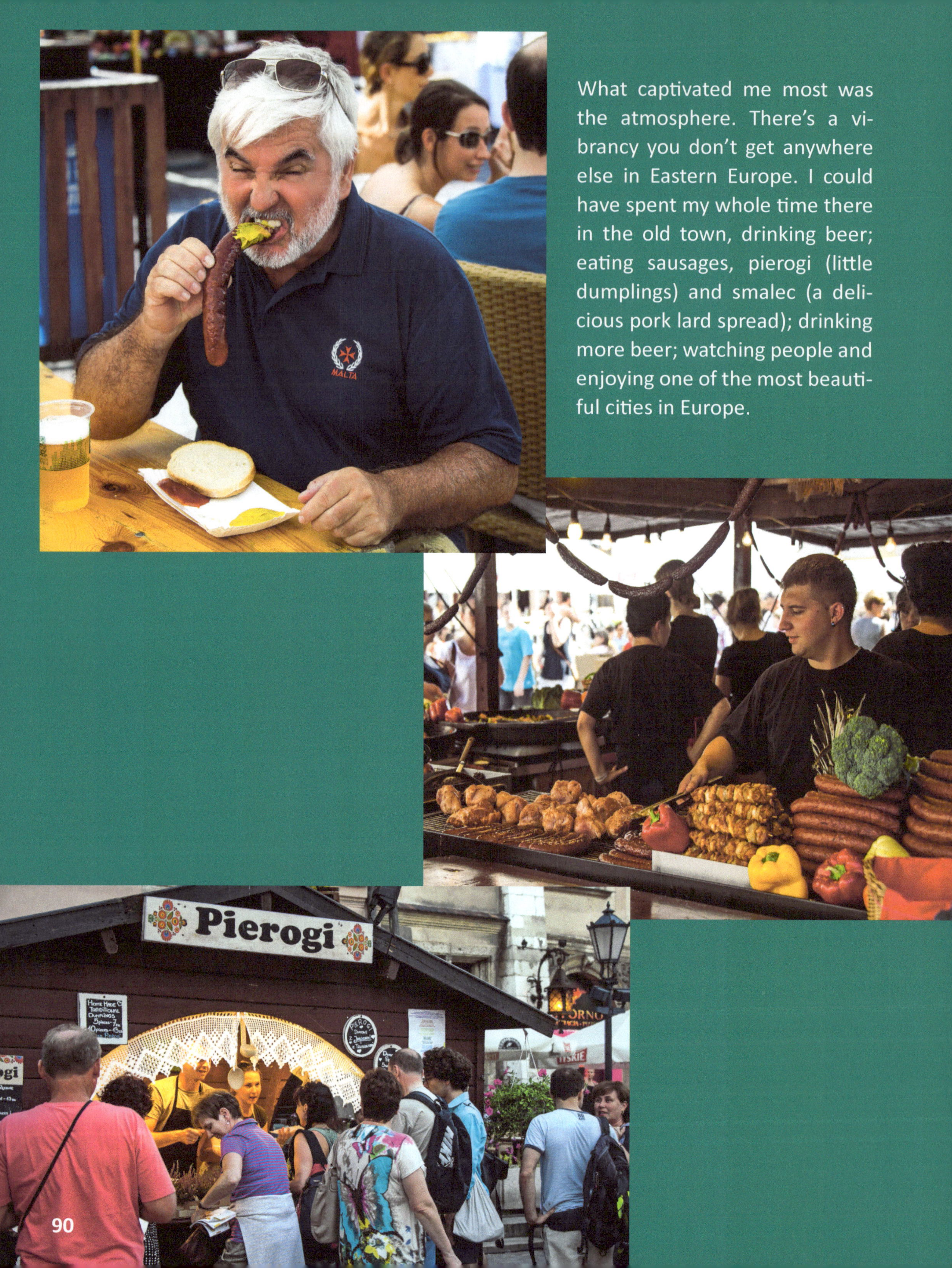


What captivated me most was the atmosphere. There's a vibrancy you don't get anywhere else in Eastern Europe. I could have spent my whole time there in the old town, drinking beer; eating sausages, pierogi (little dumplings) and smalec (a delicious pork lard spread); drinking more beer; watching people and enjoying one of the most beautiful cities in Europe.

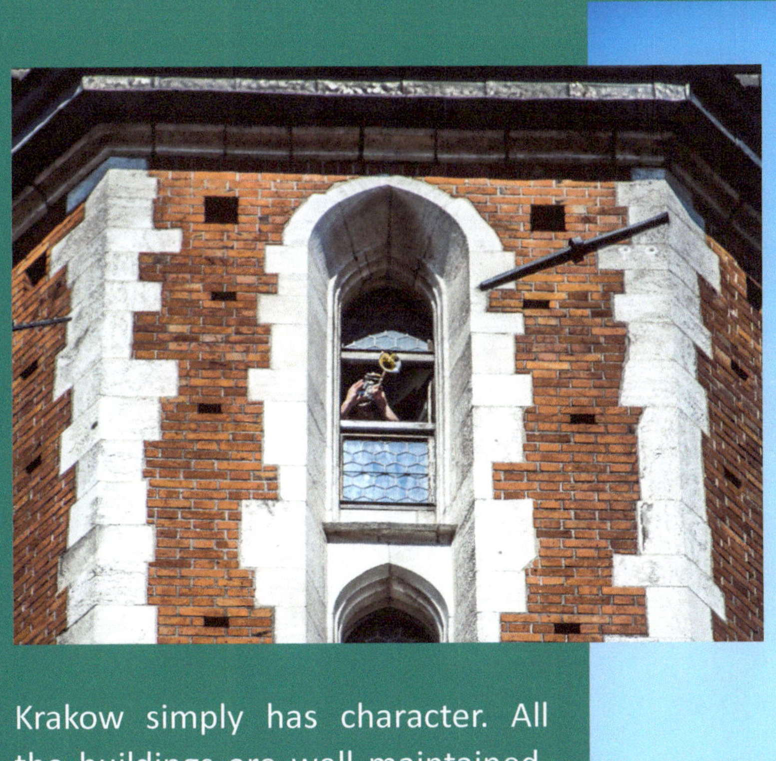

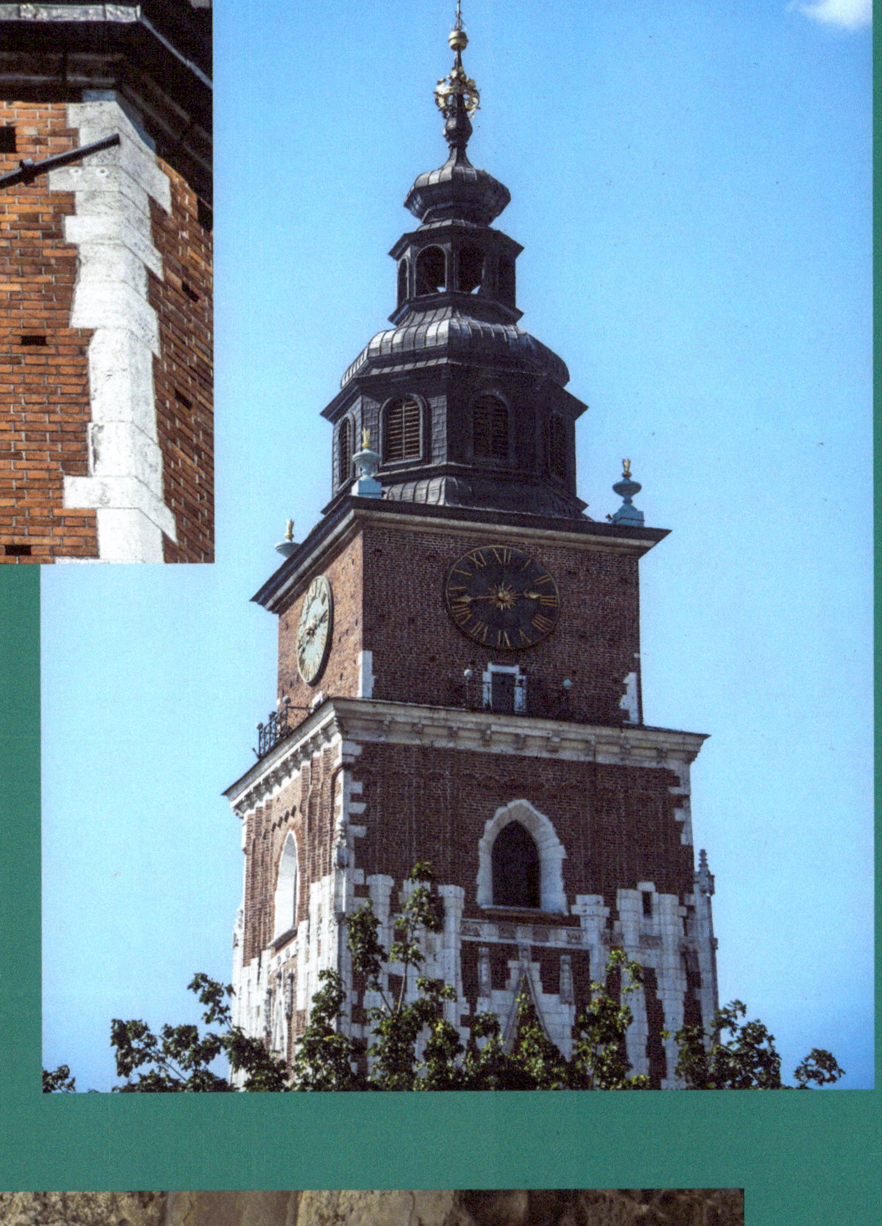

Krakow simply has character. All the buildings are well maintained, the people are colorful and friendly. On the main square, every hour a trumpeter comes out in the bell tower and plays. I think they are student musicians who take turns and earn a bit of pocket money doing it. You never see them, just this long, thin trumpet sticking out.

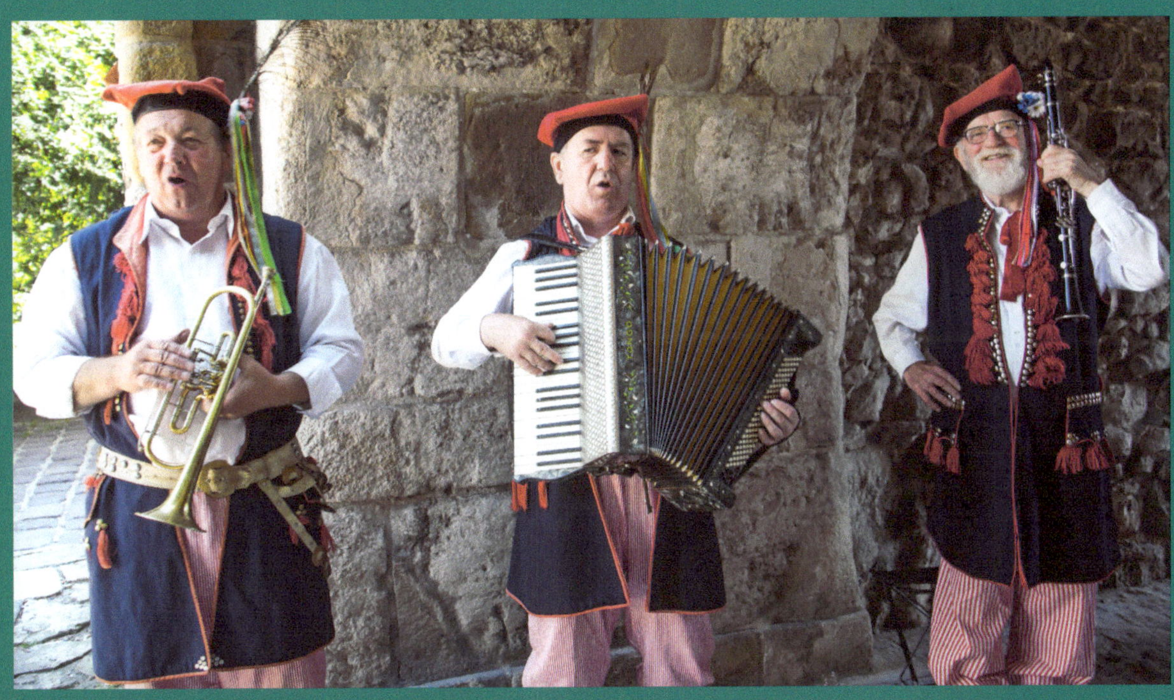

In the evenings, the central part of town takes on a special, magical atmosphere. The hustle and bustle of the daytime continues unabated with people milling about and having a good time.

The illumination of the city buildings at night is also impressive. I liked these stepping stones in a fountain that were lit up, making it look like gold was pouring down.

On the lower right is an indoor shopping mall.

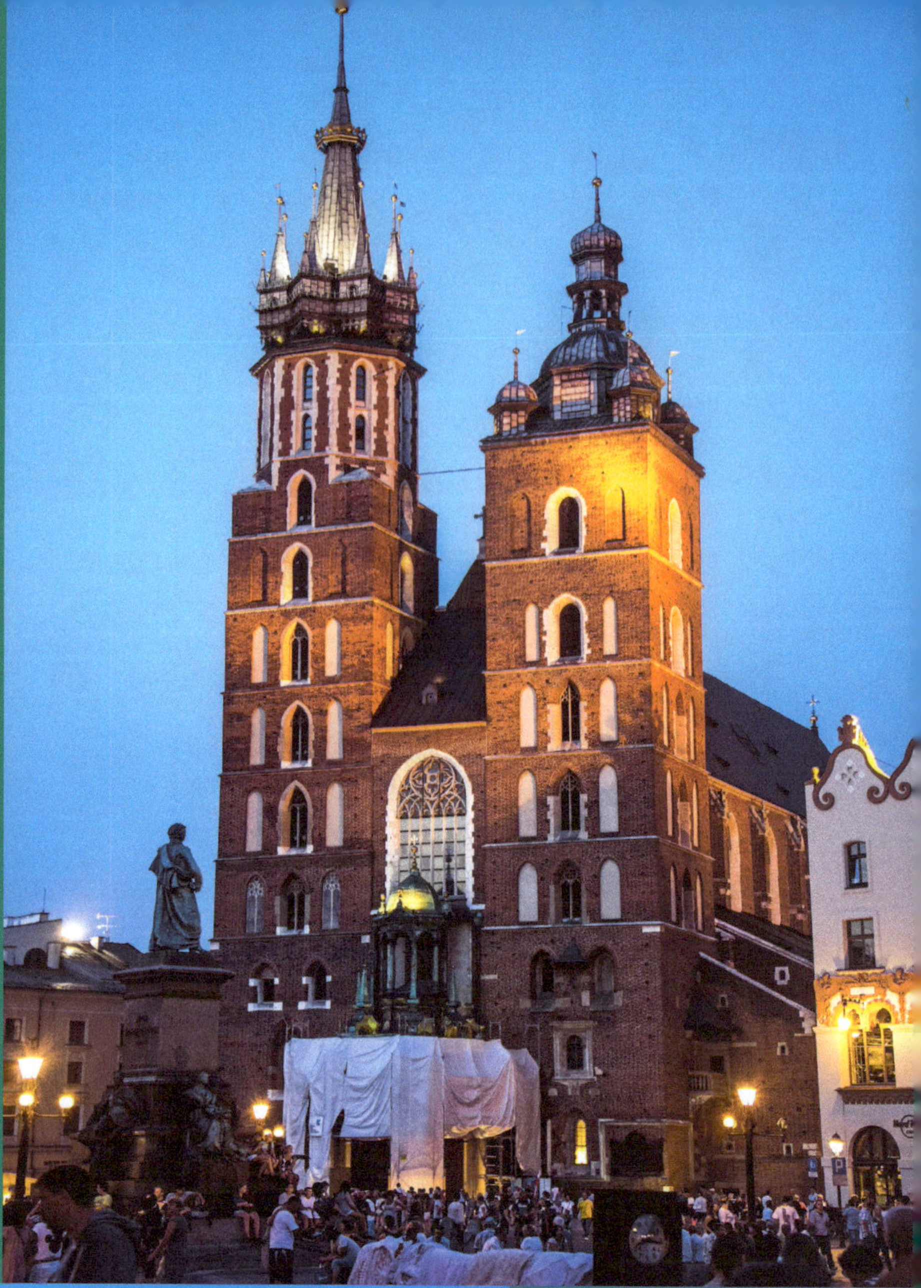

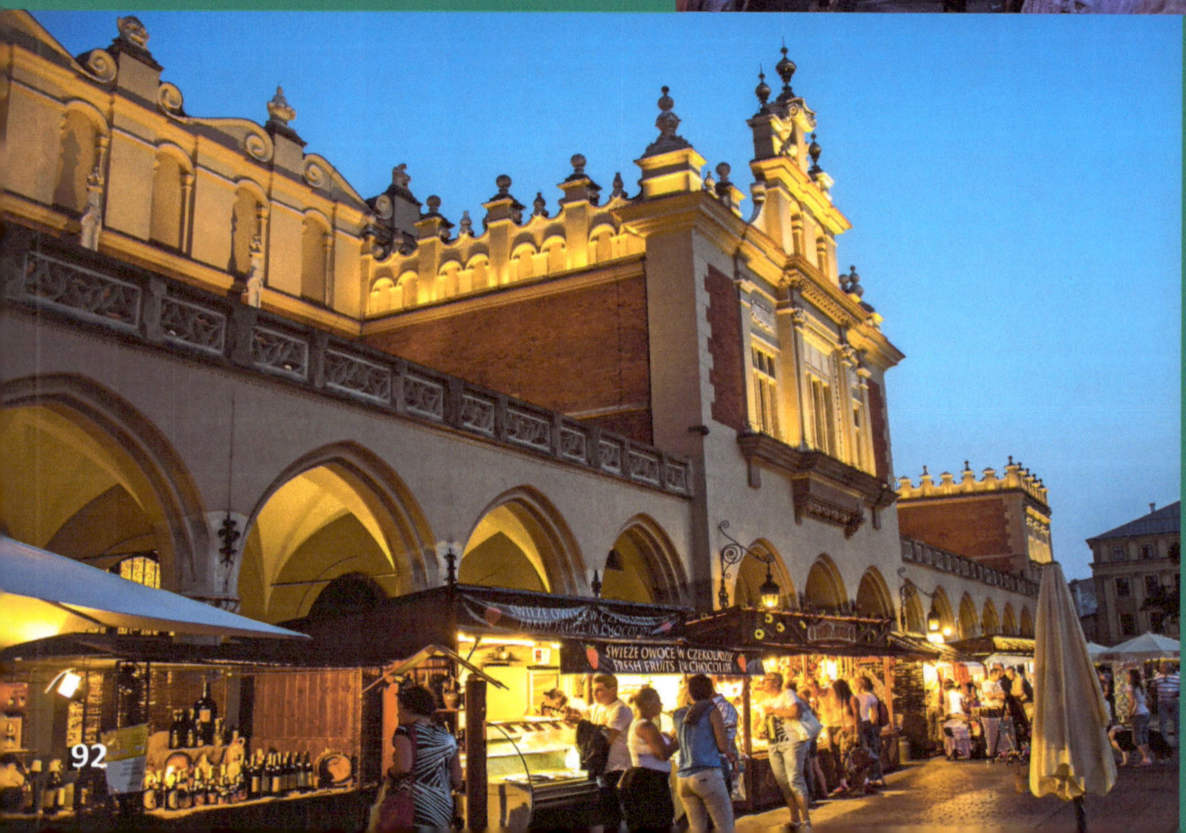

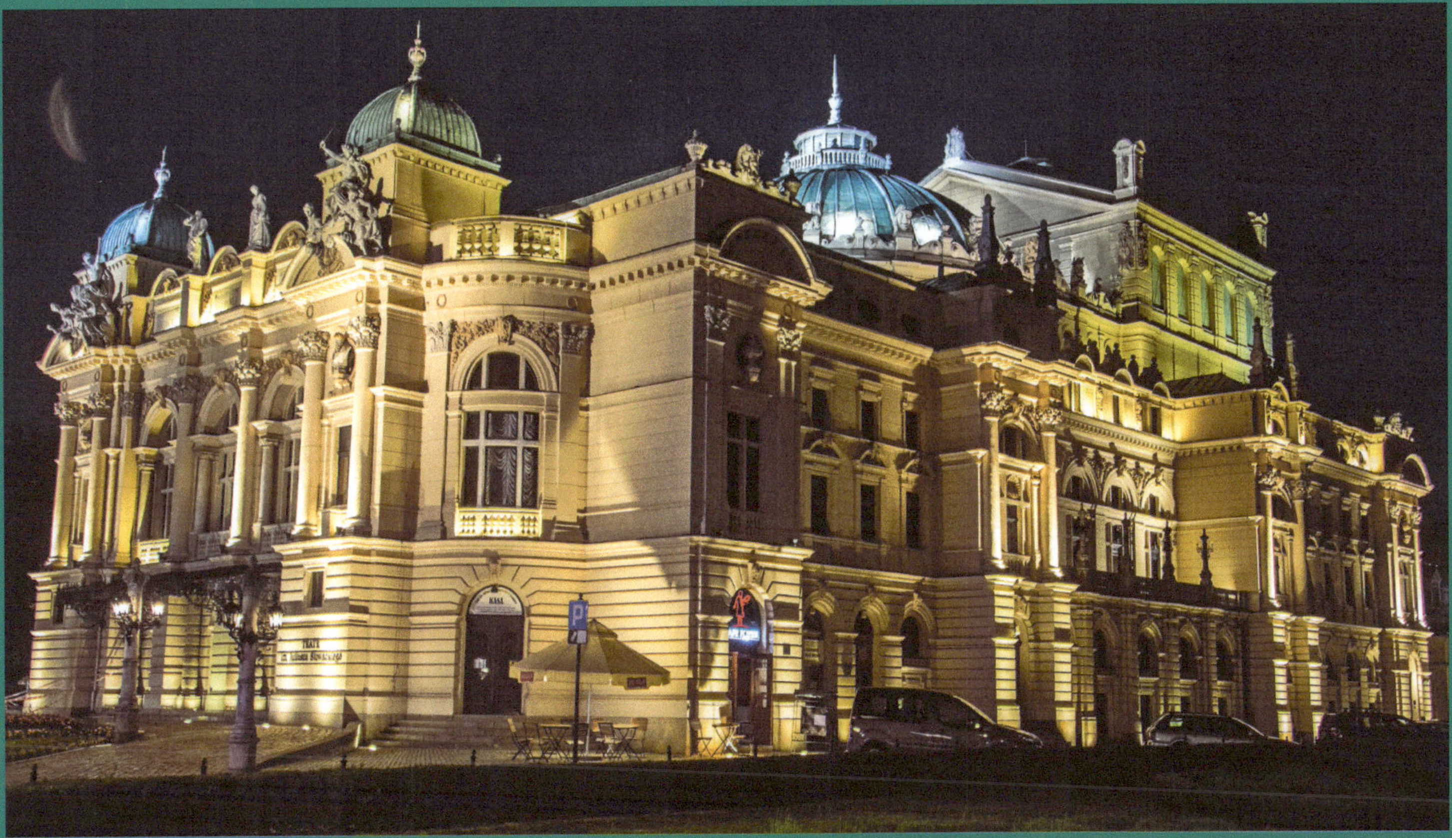

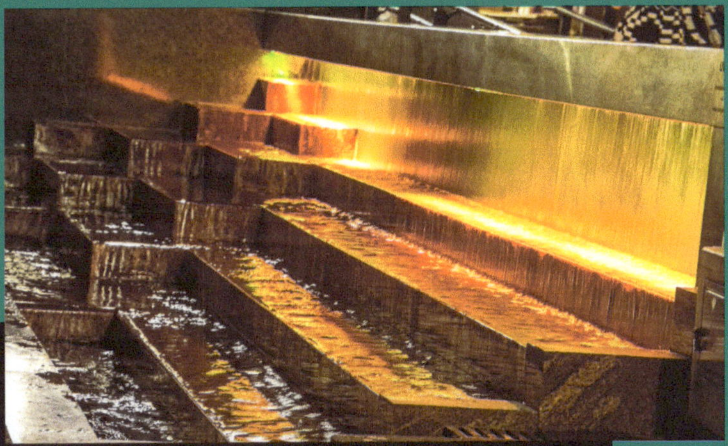

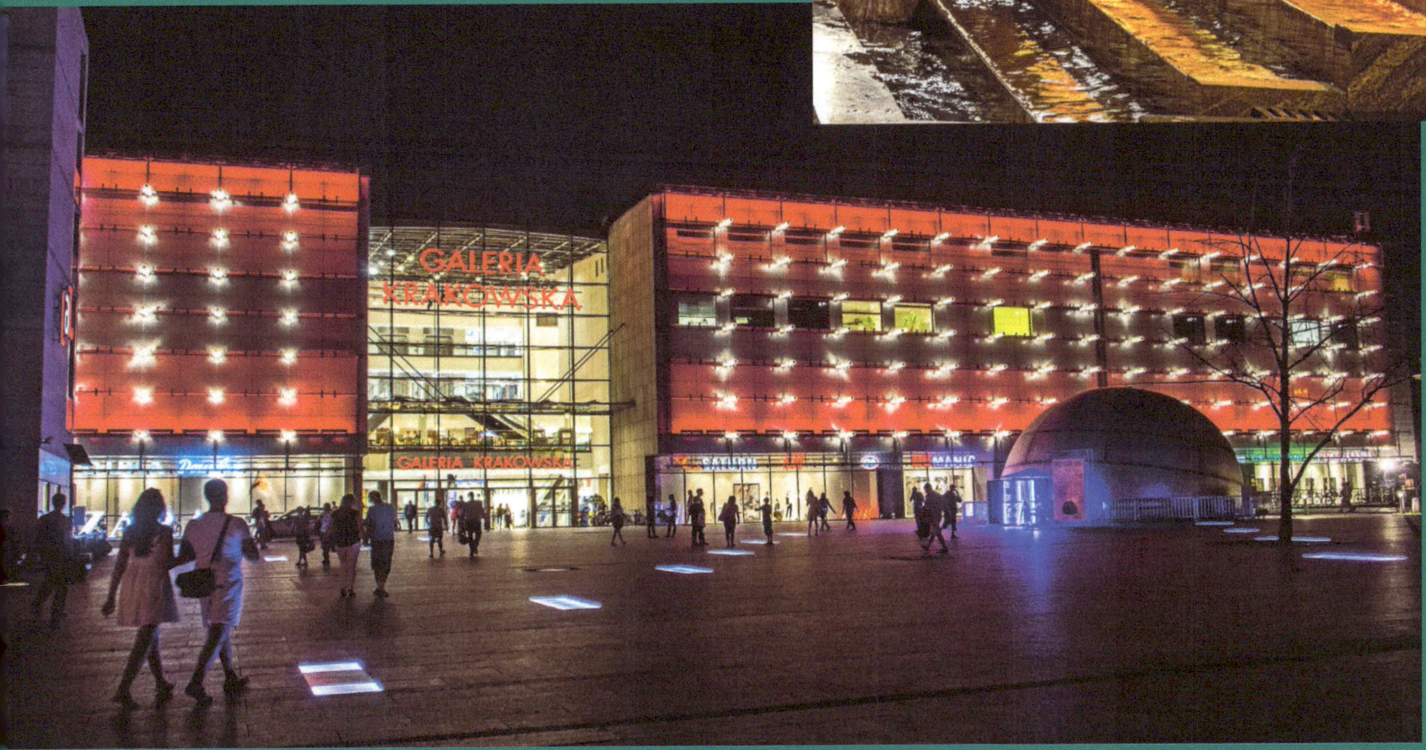

# 13

# KRAKOW
## The Jewish Ghetto

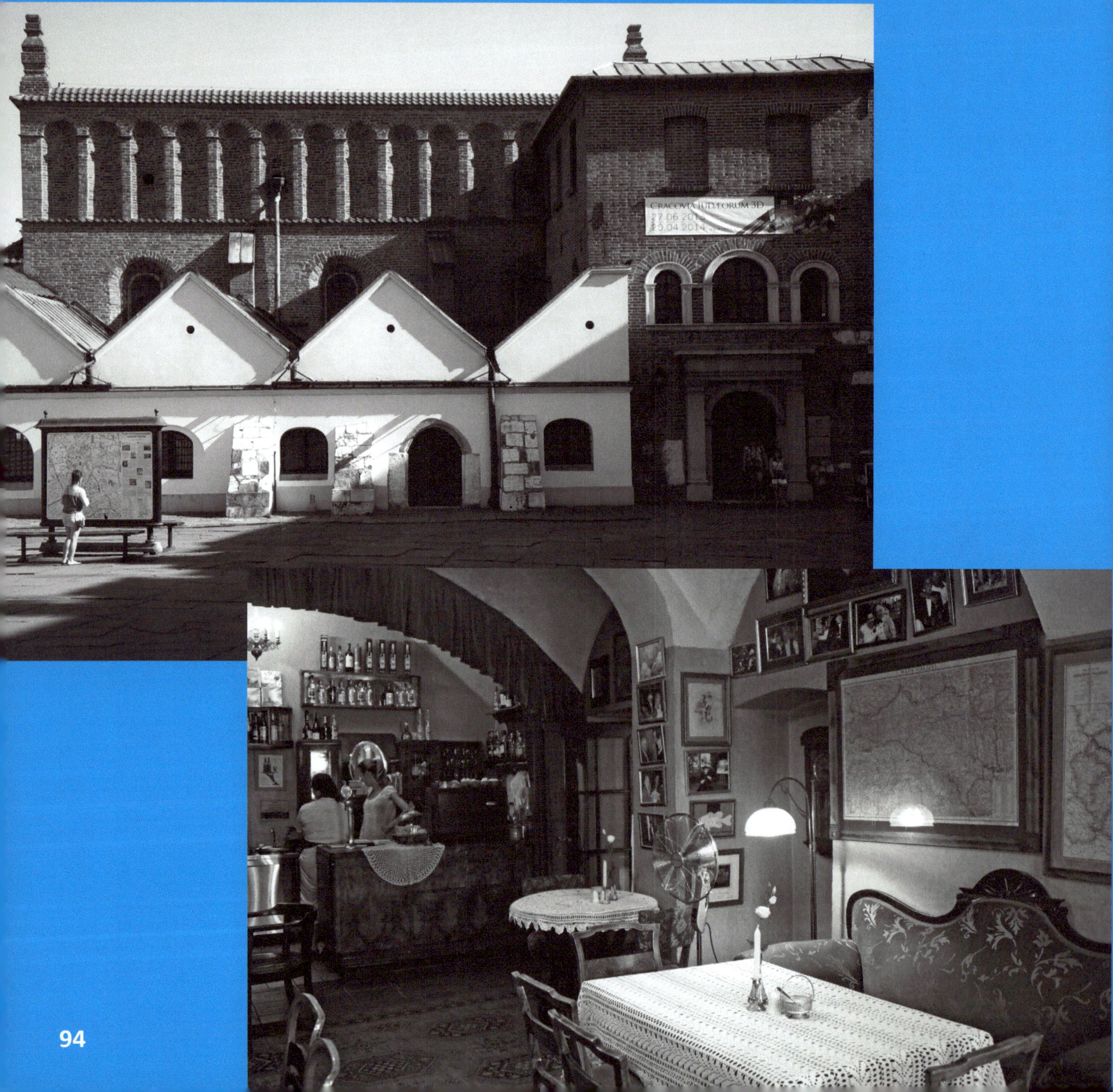

A friend of mine, Margot Zarzycka, an accomplished violinist, has a pal in Krakow. His name is Wojtek Markiewicz, and she said he'd show me around the town, including some of the places that Steven Spielberg used for the filming of Schindler's List. Wojtek and I walked around the areas that included the old Jewish ghetto, cemetery and the factory buildings you can see in the movie.

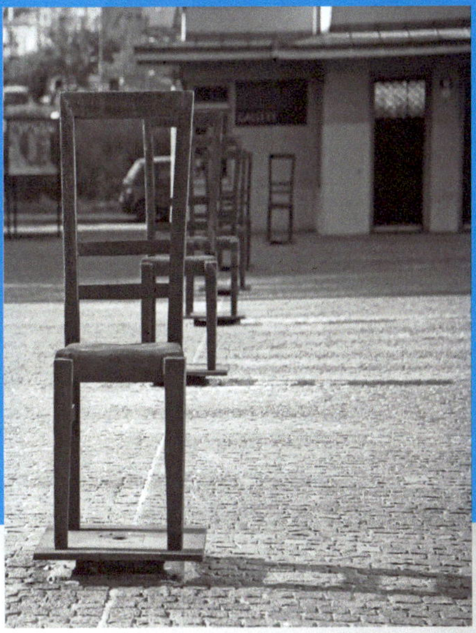

The entrance to the old Jewish ghetto has a bookshop, restaurants, and an old factory that was built before World War II. They've opened up a lot of little museums as well. When you go inside the little café, you can feel the presence of the Jews who sat there not knowing if they'd be alive the next day.

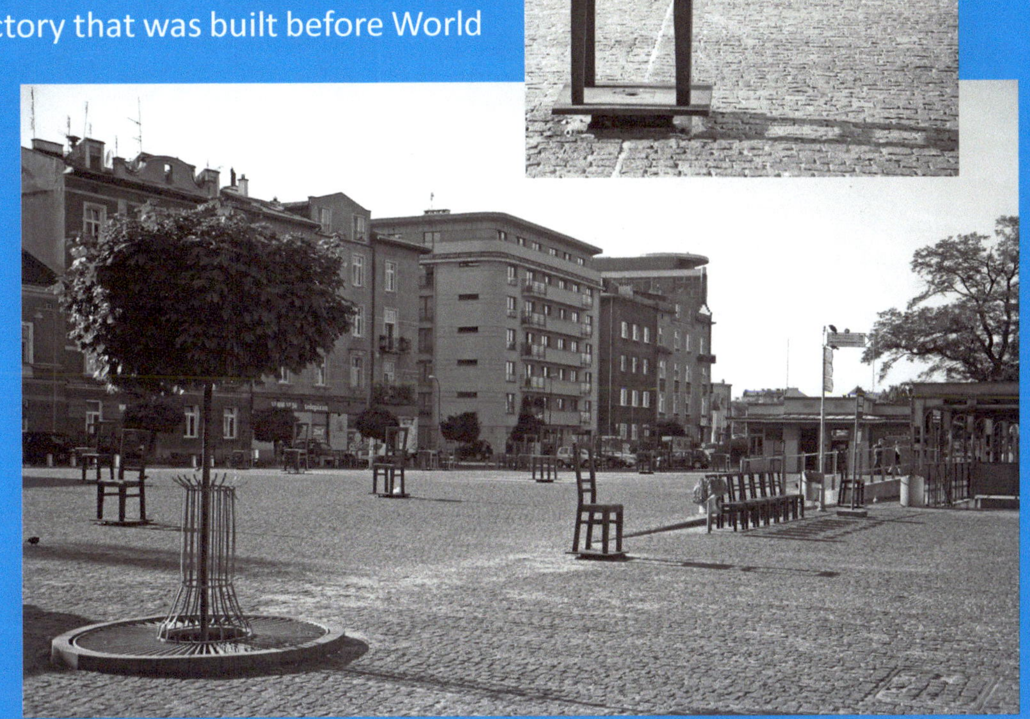

In the *Platz Scudi*, where a great many Jews were massacred during World War II, each chair represents 1,000 victims.

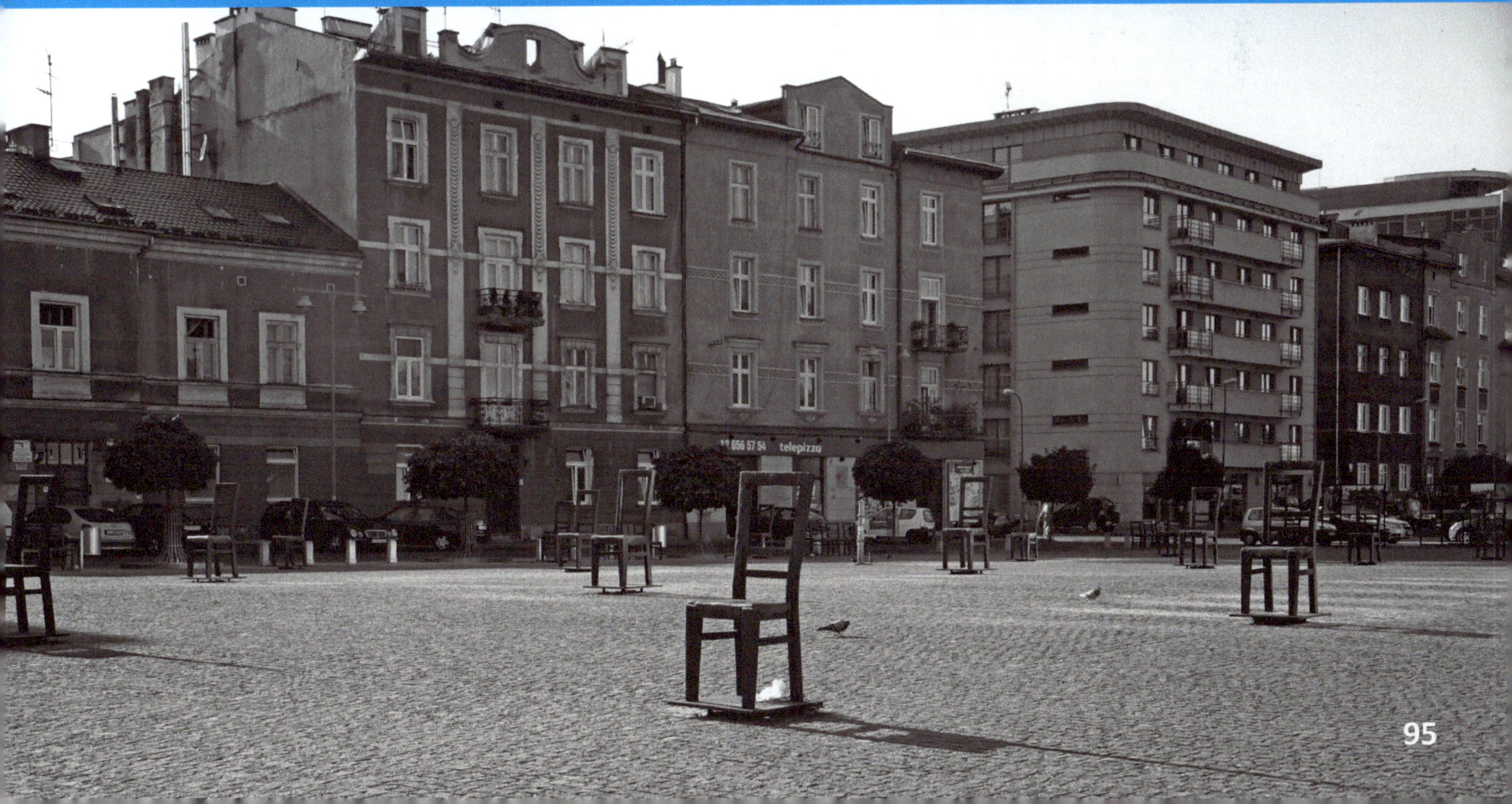

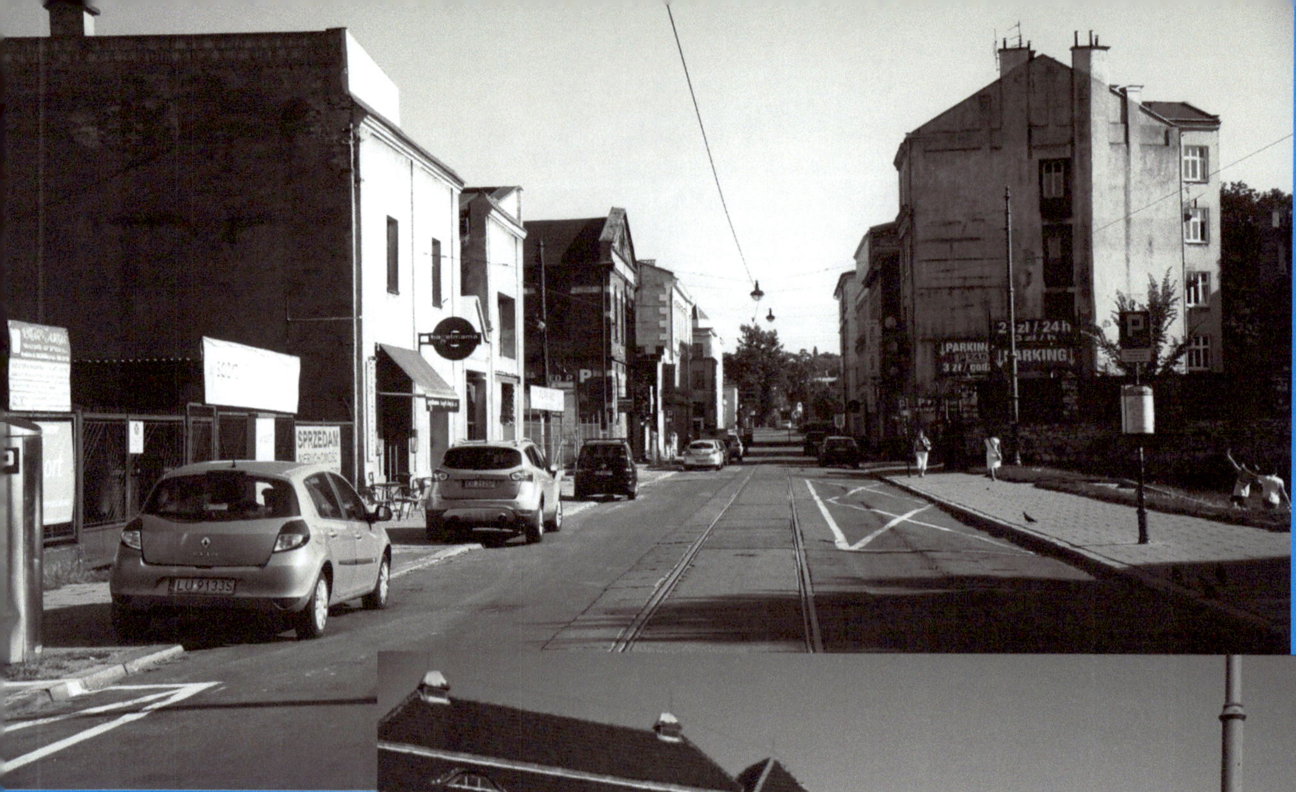

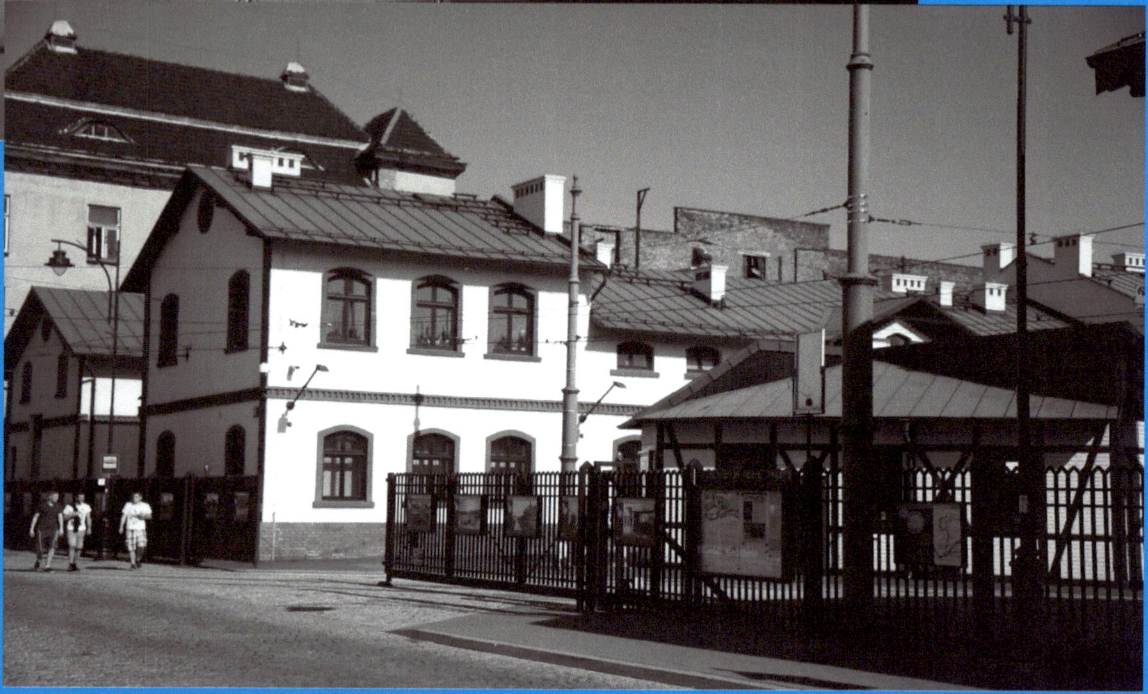

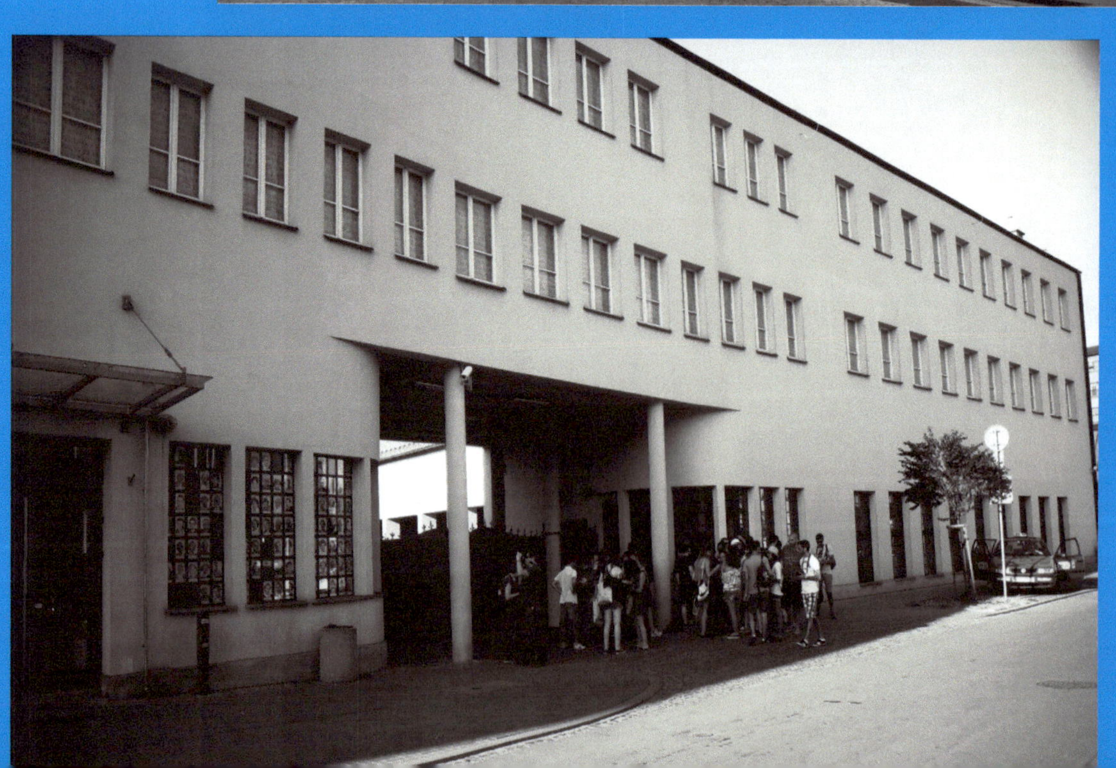

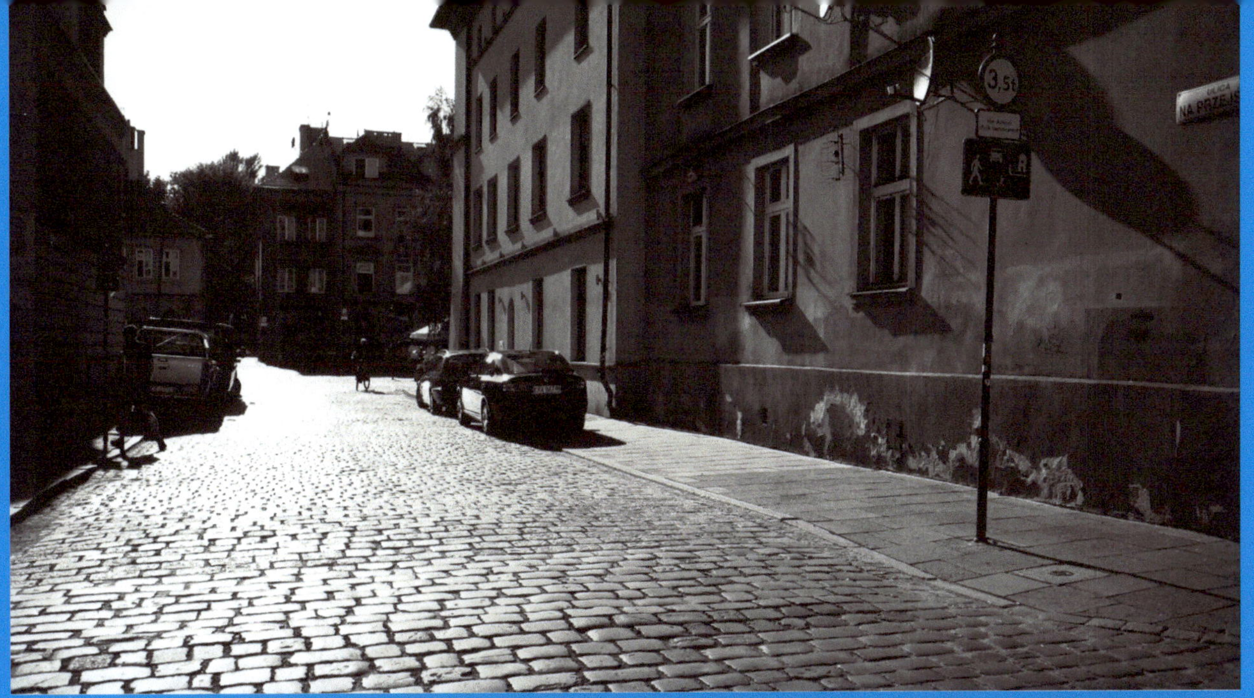


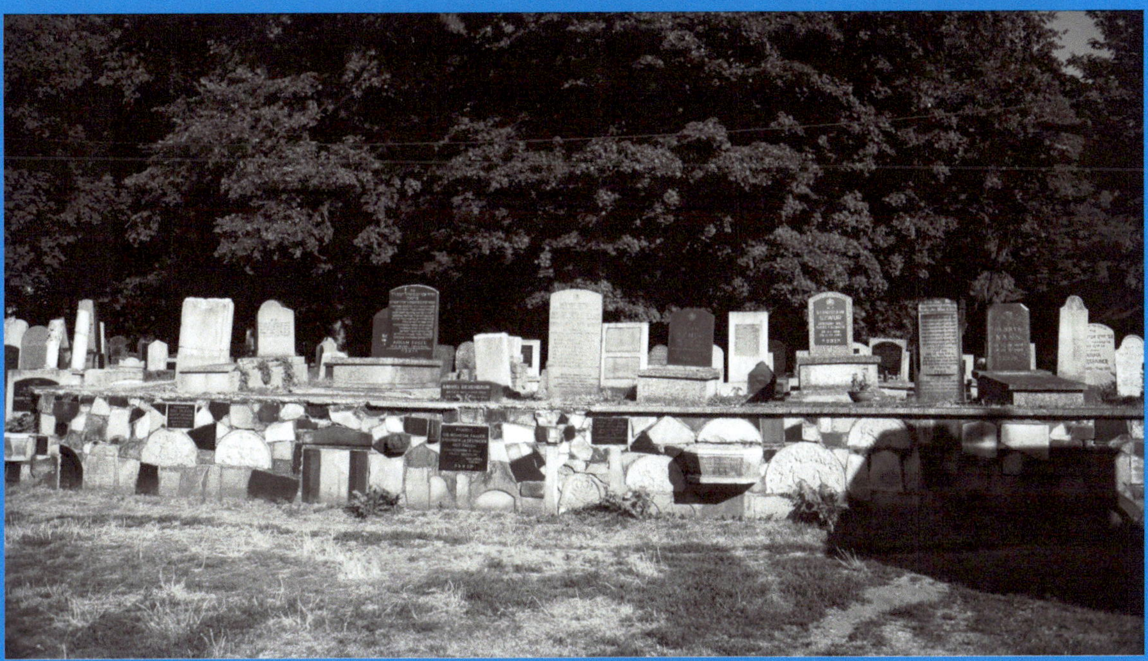

We walked for miles. Bottom left is the factory entrance that you actually see in Schindler's List, where one of the Jewish workers stands and says to Oskar Schindler, "Please take care of my mother and father for me."

The Jewish cemetery contains thousands of gravestones and big monoliths with the names of people killed during the Nazi occupation.

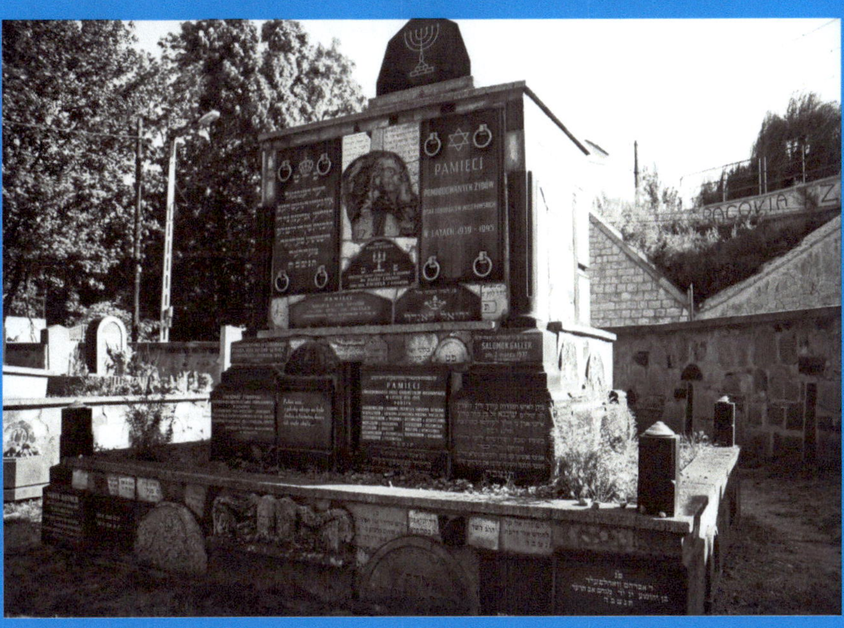

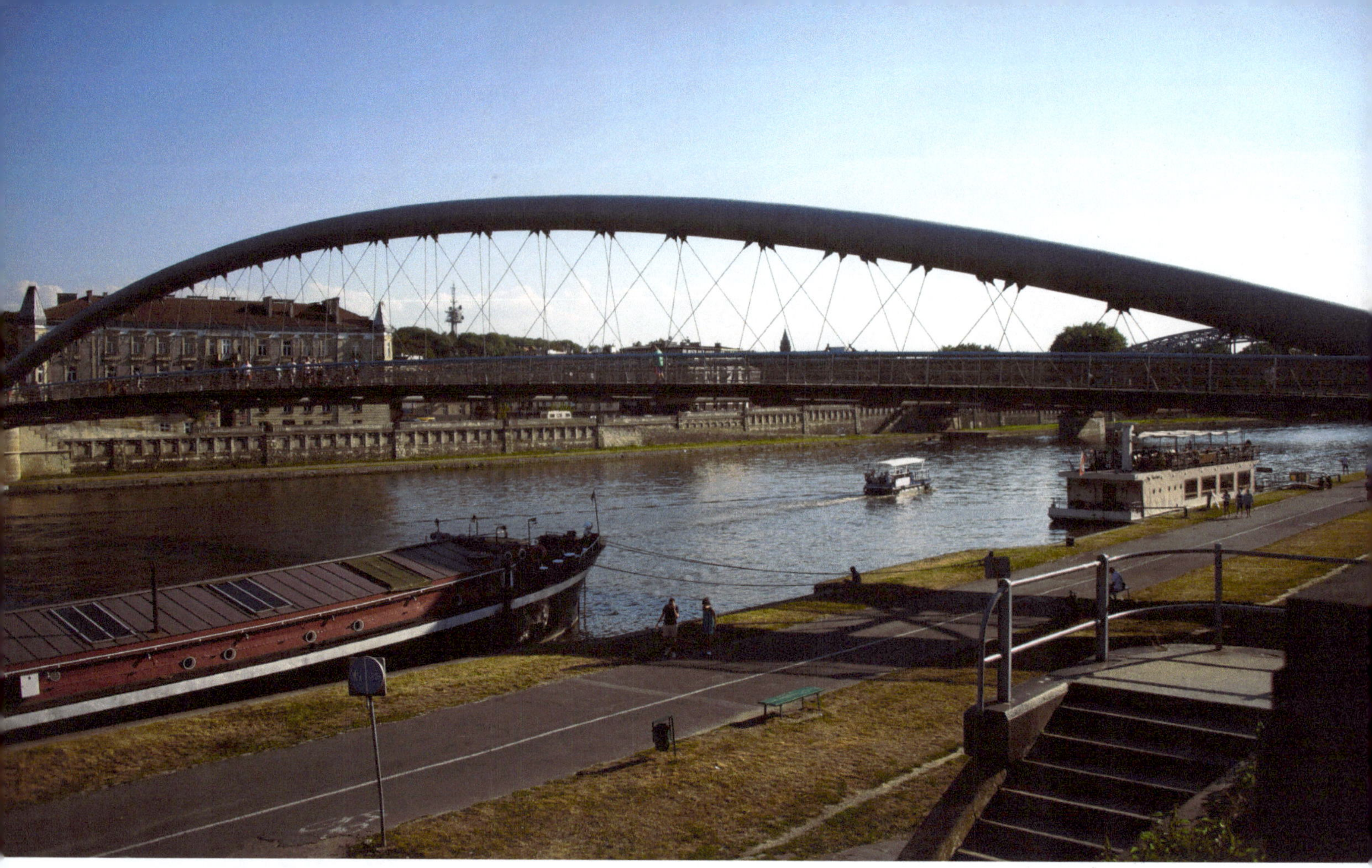

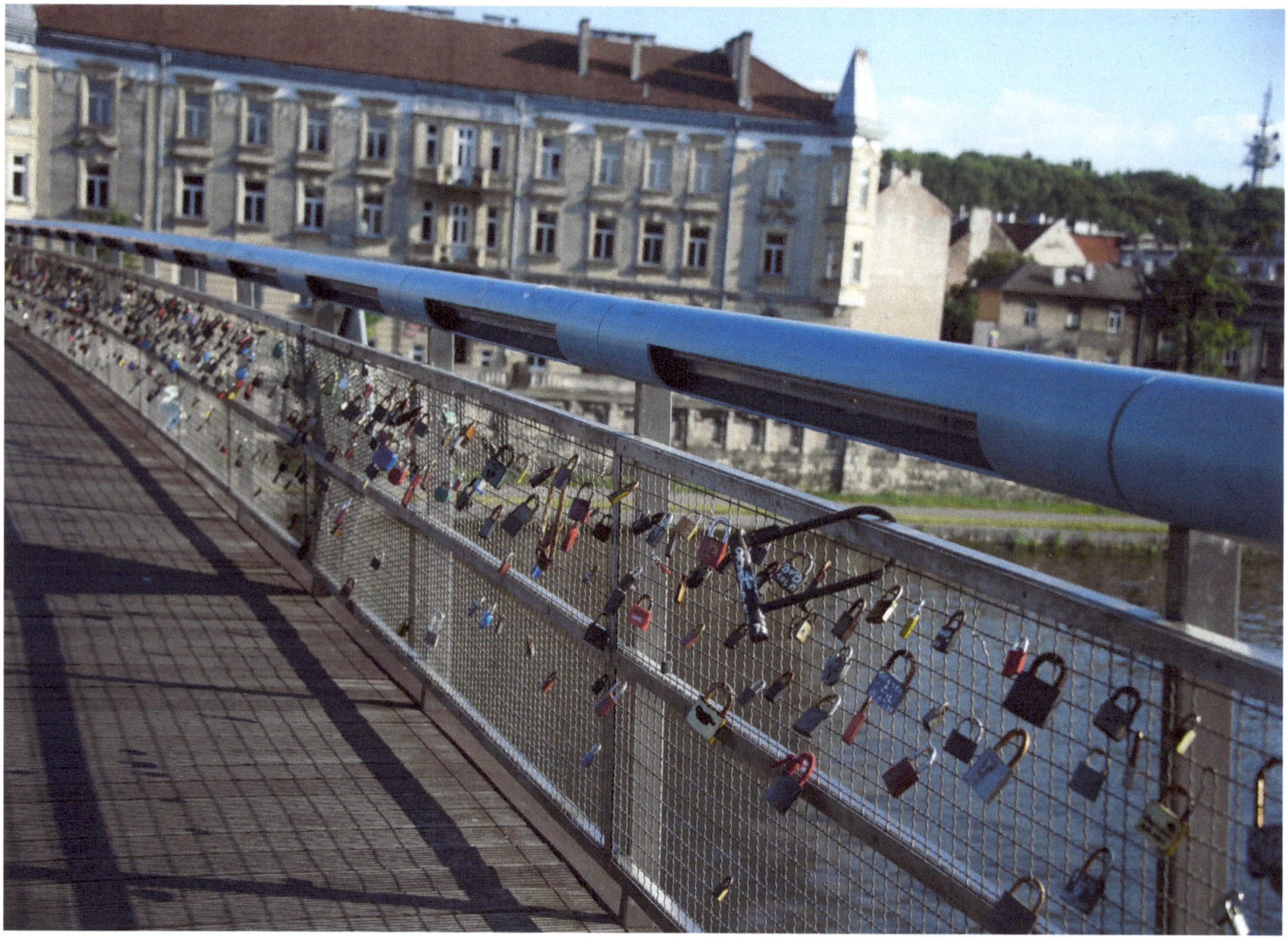

# Love Locks

I was crossing a bridge in Krakow when I came upon a phenomenon I had encountered on my previous travels: love locks or love padlocks.

Since early 2000, they have popped up in European cities and other parts of the world. Sweethearts usually inscribe their names on them, lock them to a bridge, fence or gate, or other public fixture, and then throw away the key to symbolize their "unbreakable love."

Some local authorities regard them as a nuisance, littering problem or even vandalism, but when they try to remove them, the outcries and protests usually make them think twice. That 's what happened in Paris and In Brooklyn, New York, when municipalities tried to get rid of the locks because their weight became a problem.

I took the picture below later when I was walking around Hamburg, Germany.

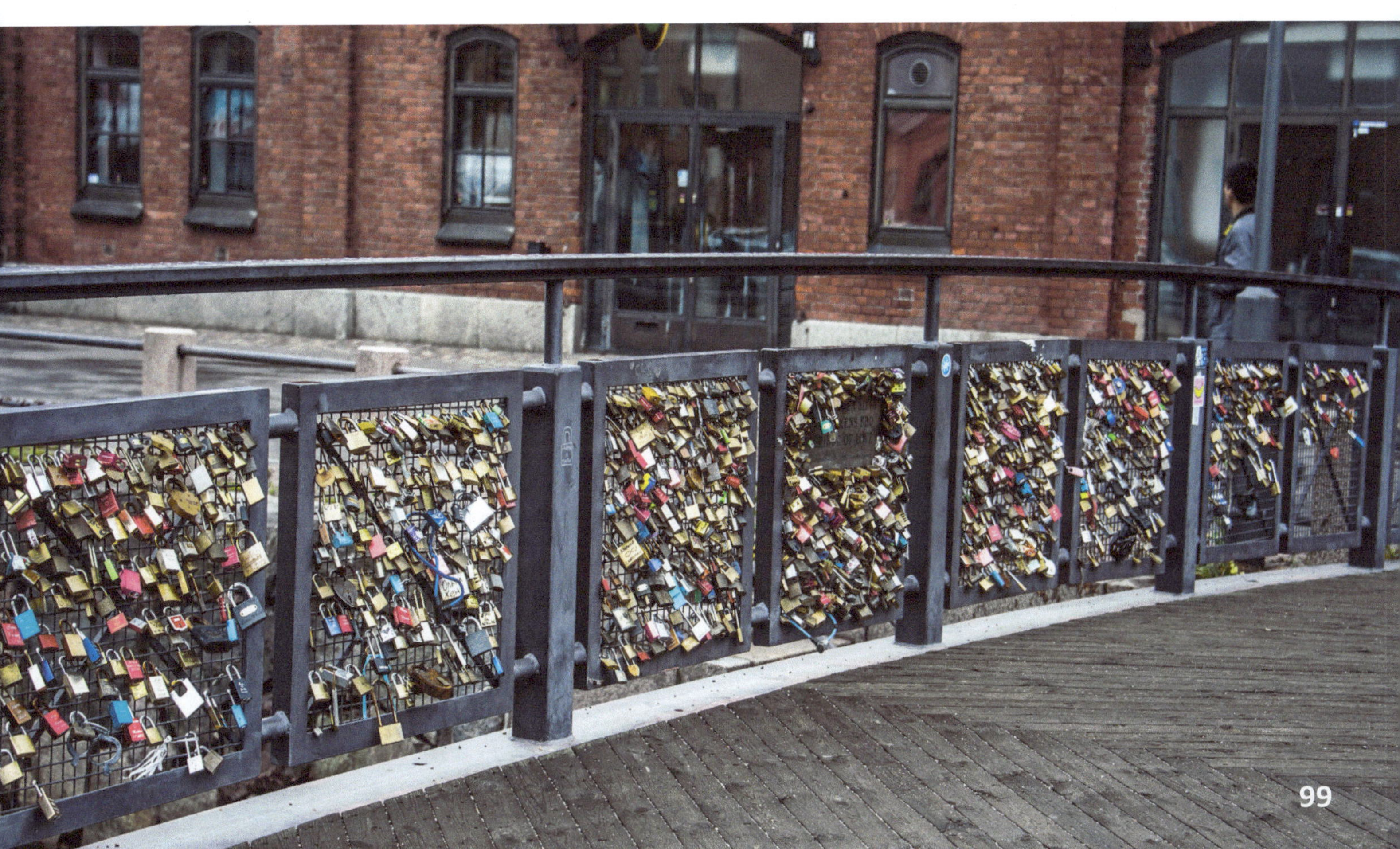

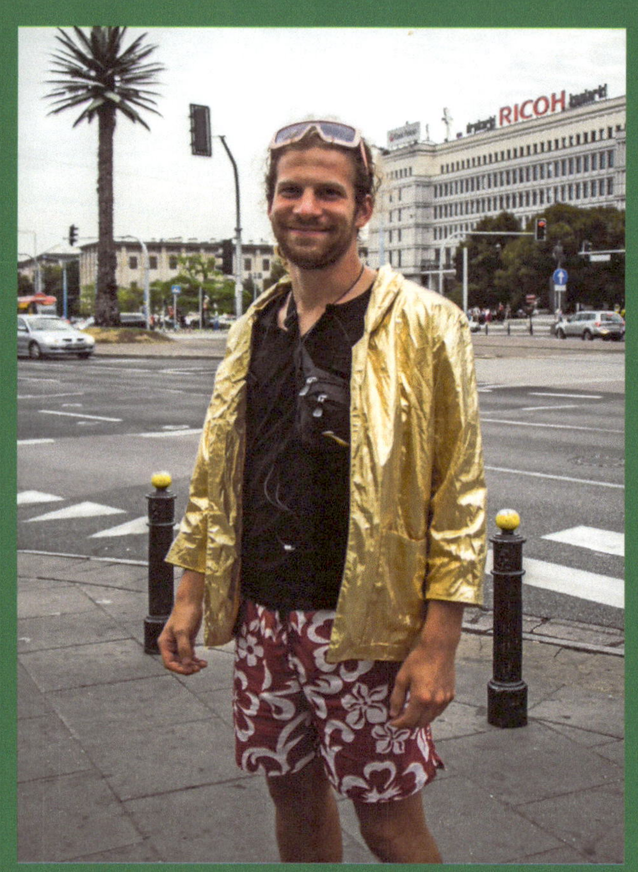


I took the three-hour train ride to Warsaw. After Krakow, the Polish capital was disappointing. I had dinner with Piotr, the IT university student who had traveled with me from Sofia. We went to a fabulous Beer Garden and when darkness fell, he showed me round the city. He is also the man in the center of the photo below, in the middle of the Barbican, the fortifications of Warsw's Old Town. That's how I got these beautiful illuminations—with no tripod or special lenses. Thank goodness I have a steady hand!

The Europeans take a lot of trouble lighting up the buildings of their cities at night. I loved the warm colors on the old city wall and the moat, foundations and walls of Warsaw castles.

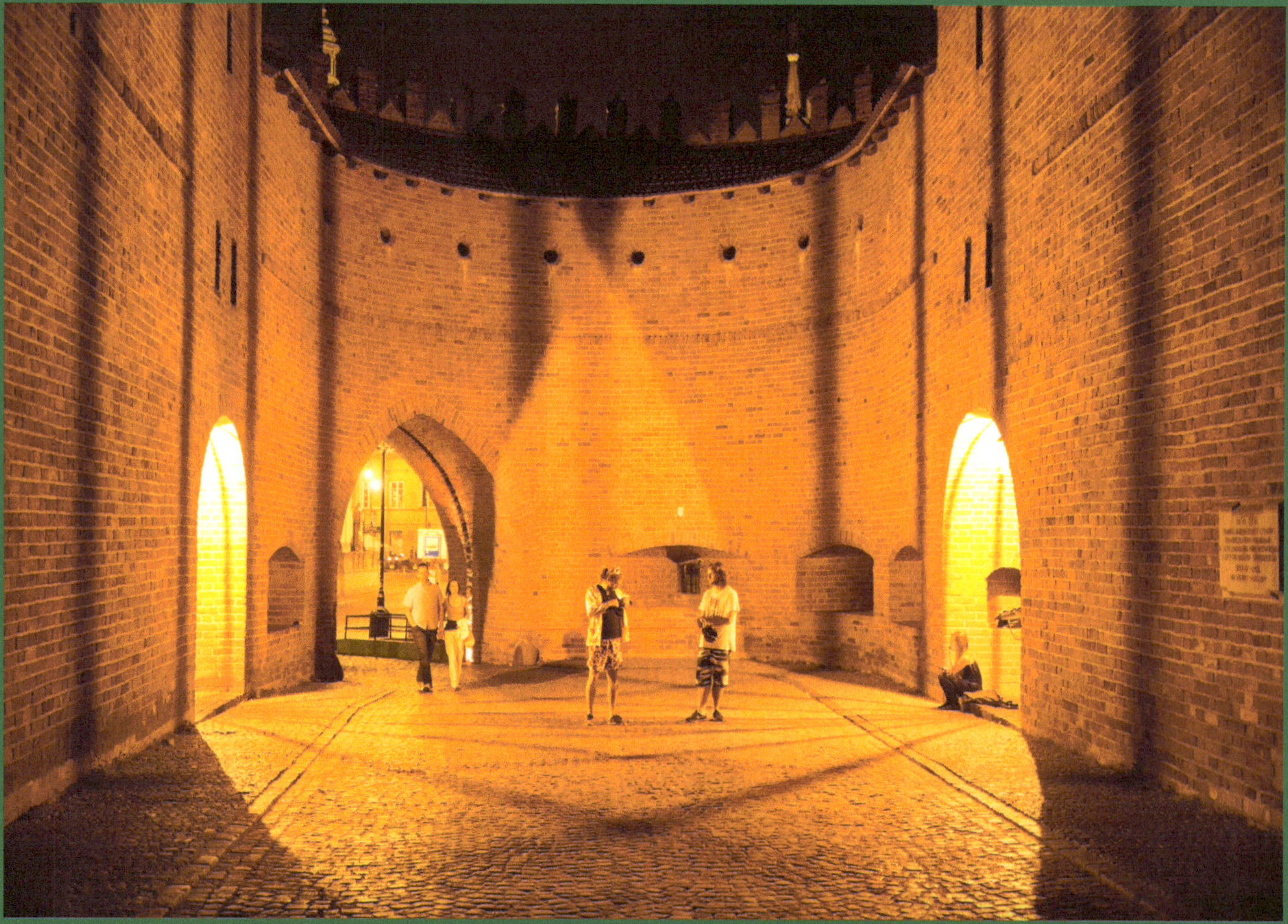

# 14
# WARSAW

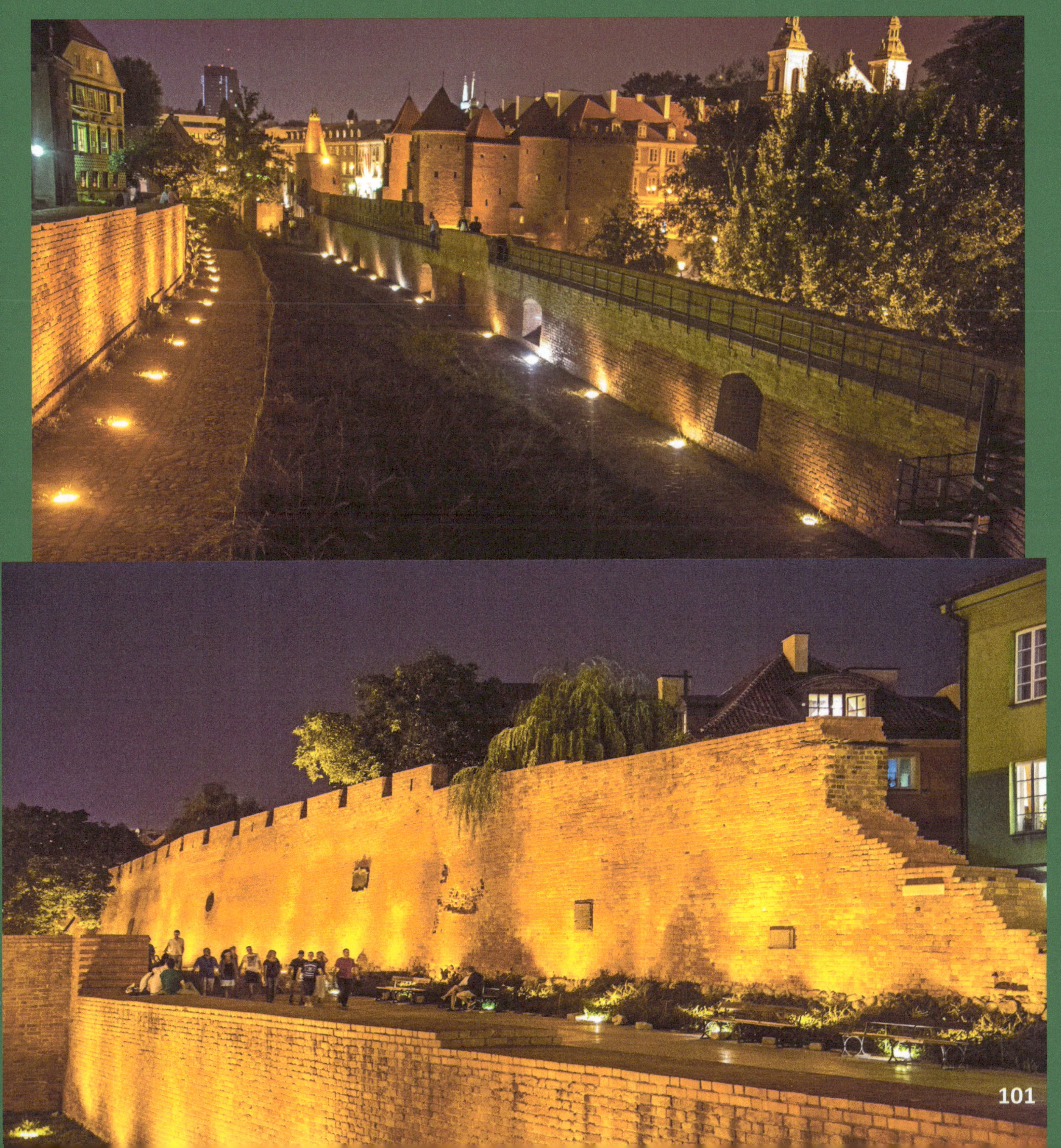

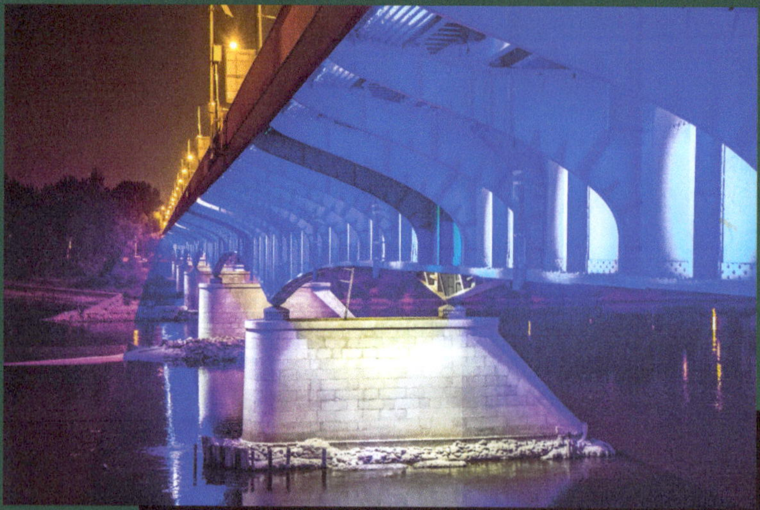

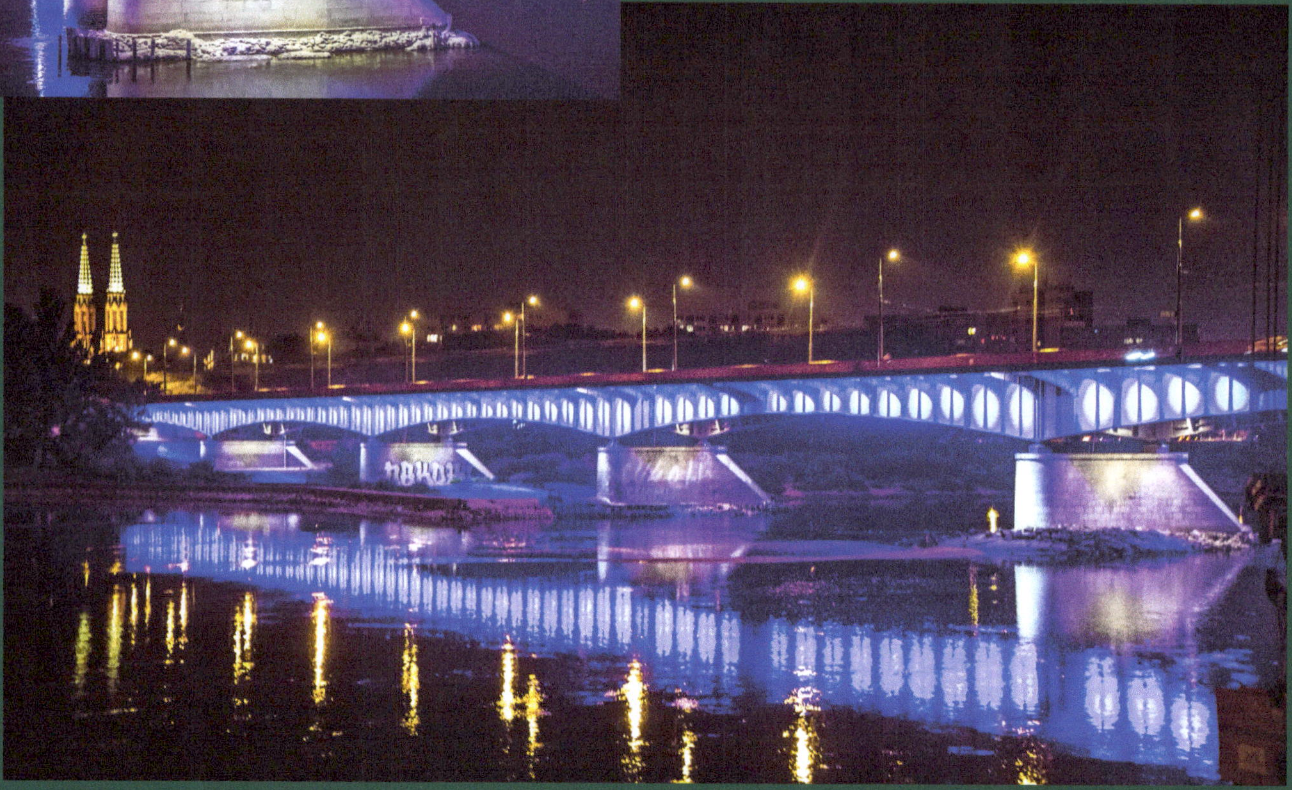

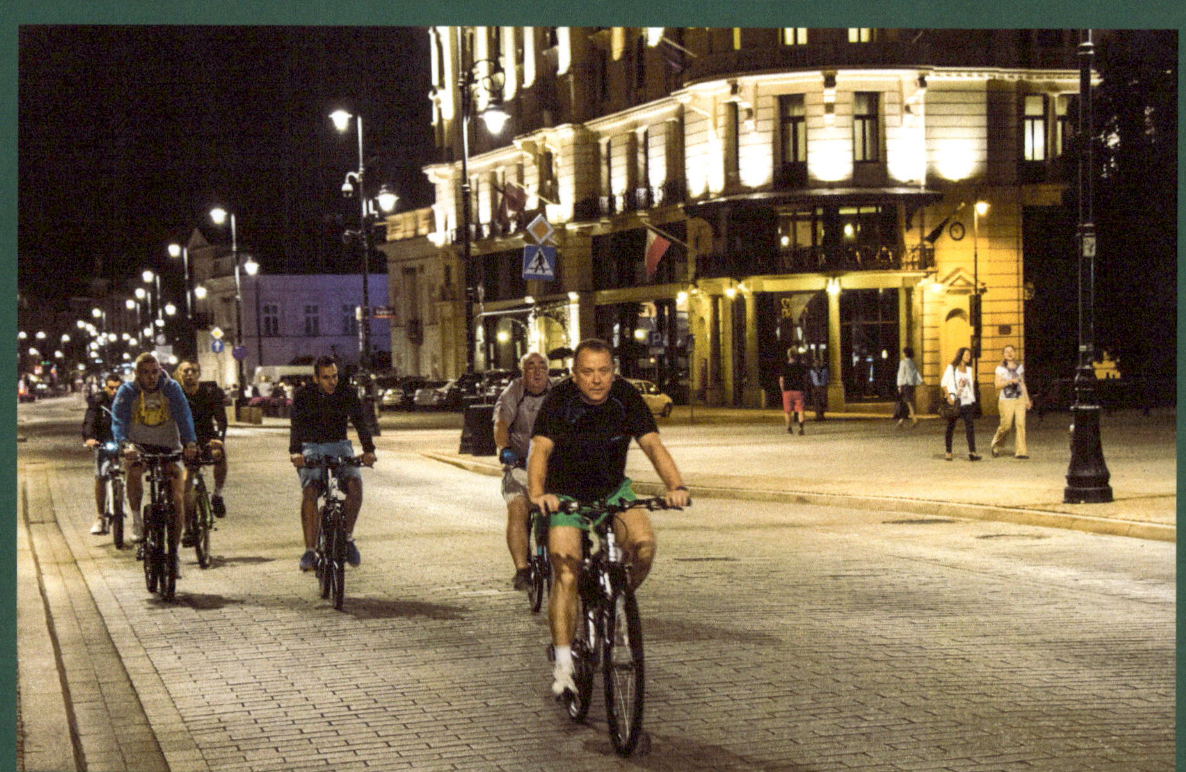

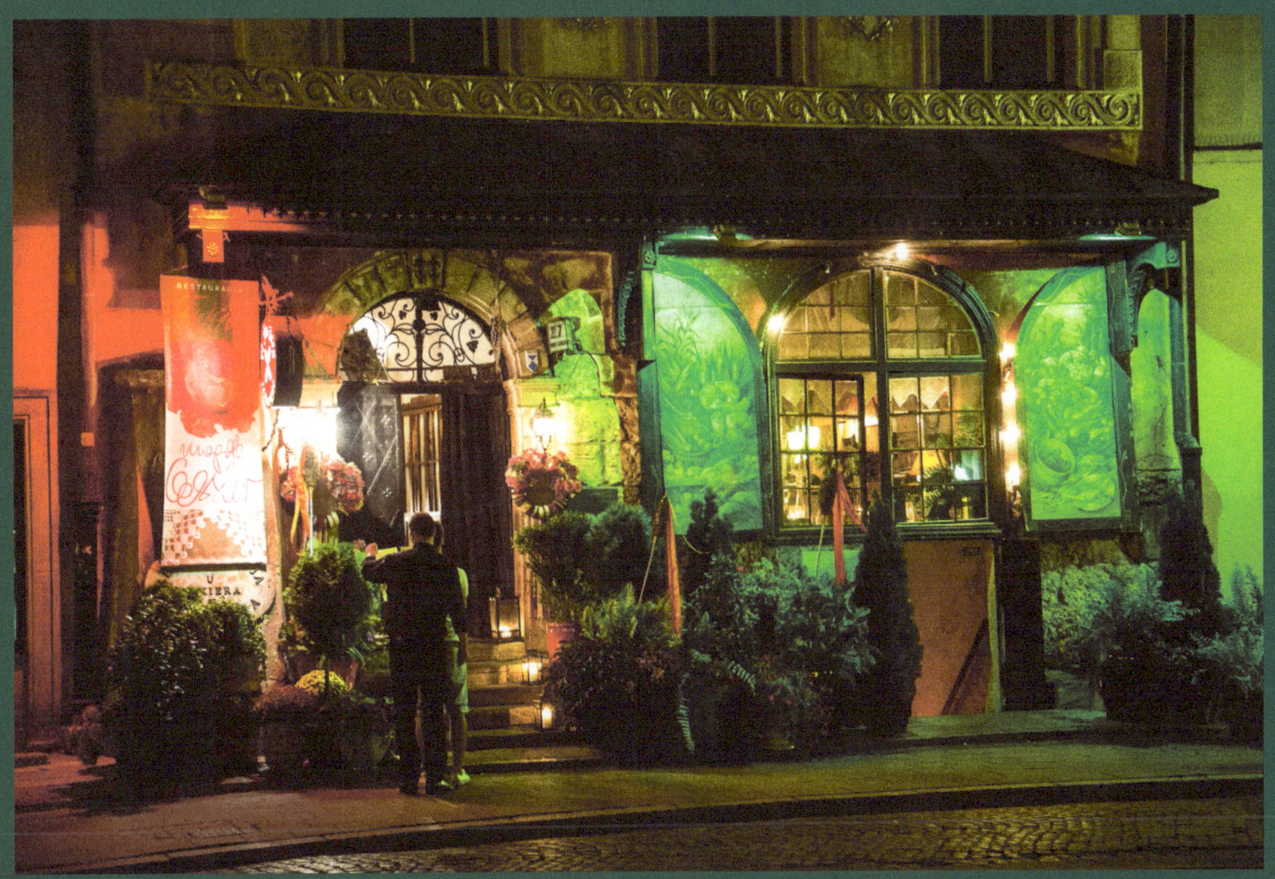

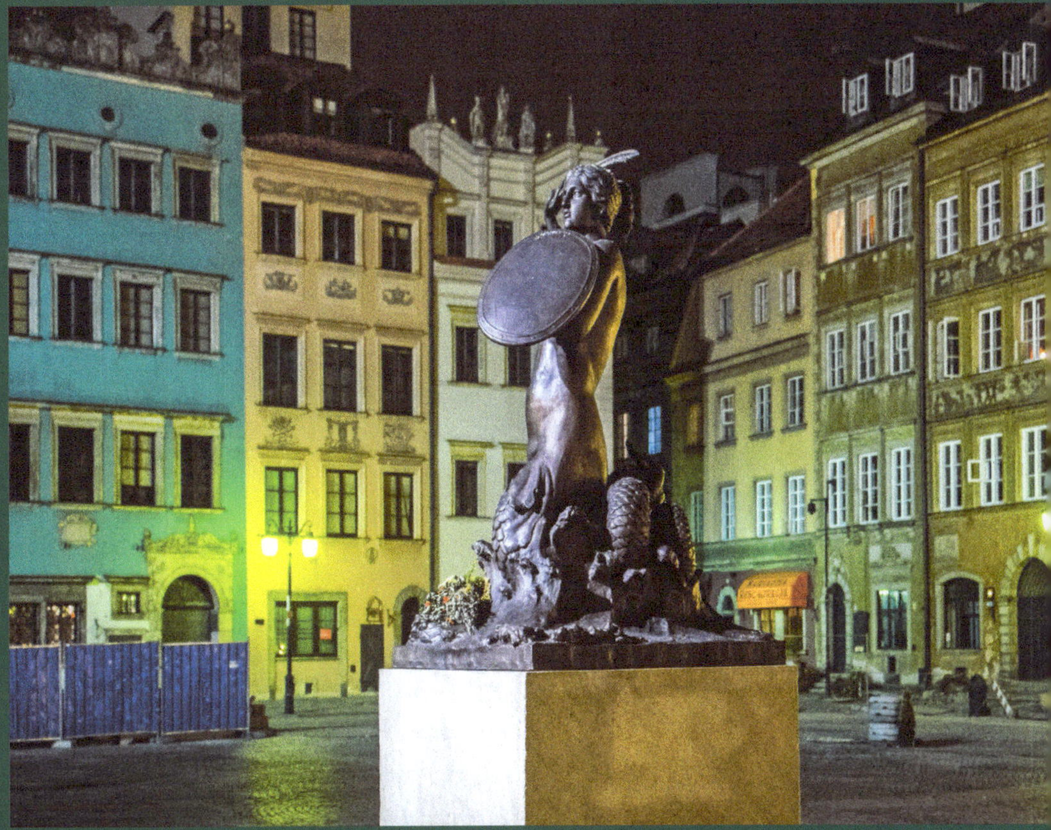

As you can see, they pay special attention to illuminating their bridges. I also liked the way this little restaurant looked in the old part of Warsaw that wasn't destroyed during World War II.

I was walking down the street when a group of cyclists came towards me. I liked the idea of them cruising in the middle of Warsaw on a balmy August night.

There are three statues of the mermaid, which is the symbol of Warsaw. Legend has it that in the 14th century Prince Kazimierz got lost hunting in the marshlands that are now Warsaw, and a mermaid guided him to safety. This one is in the Old Town Square (another is on a bridge by the river, and the original stands in the historical museum).

I took a guided bus tour around Warsaw, which of course included a visit to the Warsaw Ghetto. This monument is located in front of the Museum. Normally you can't get a picture like this because there's usually a big crowd of people in front of it, but I caught it on a quiet day.

Below is the entrance to POLIN, the Museum of History of the Polish Jews, which had opened just four months earlier. Polin in Hebrew means either "Poland" or "rest here."

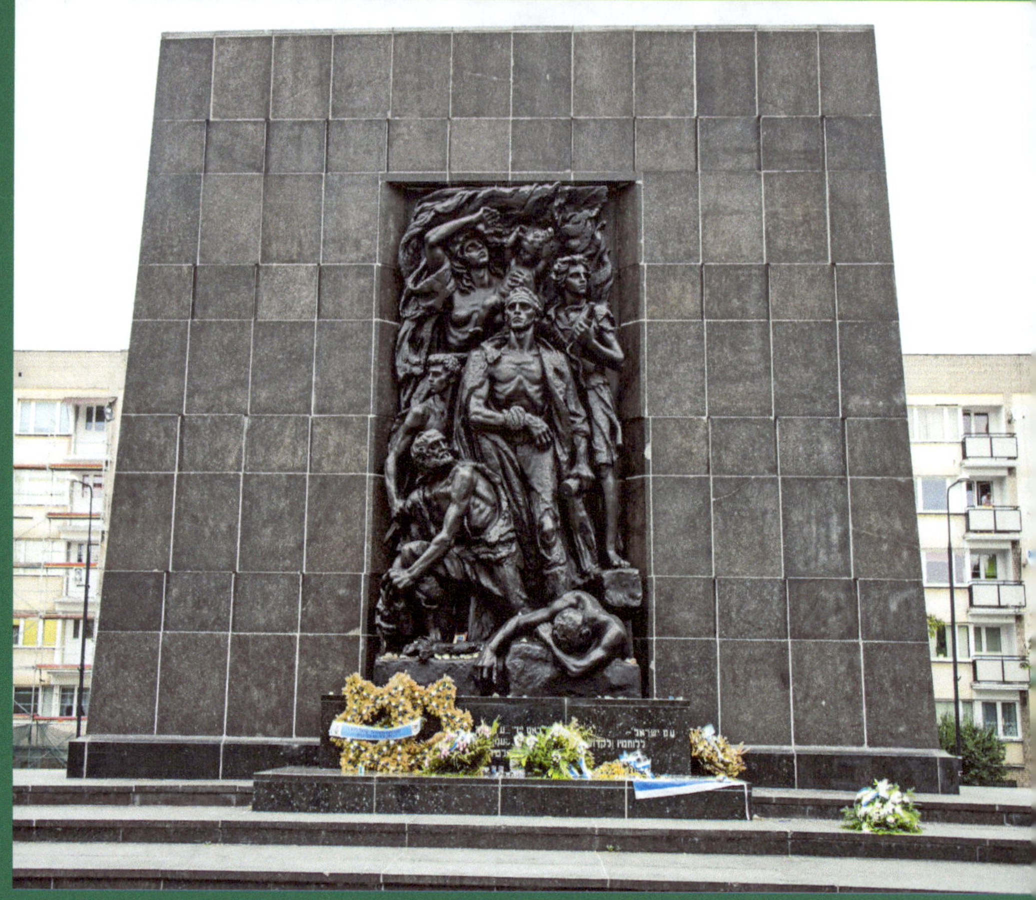

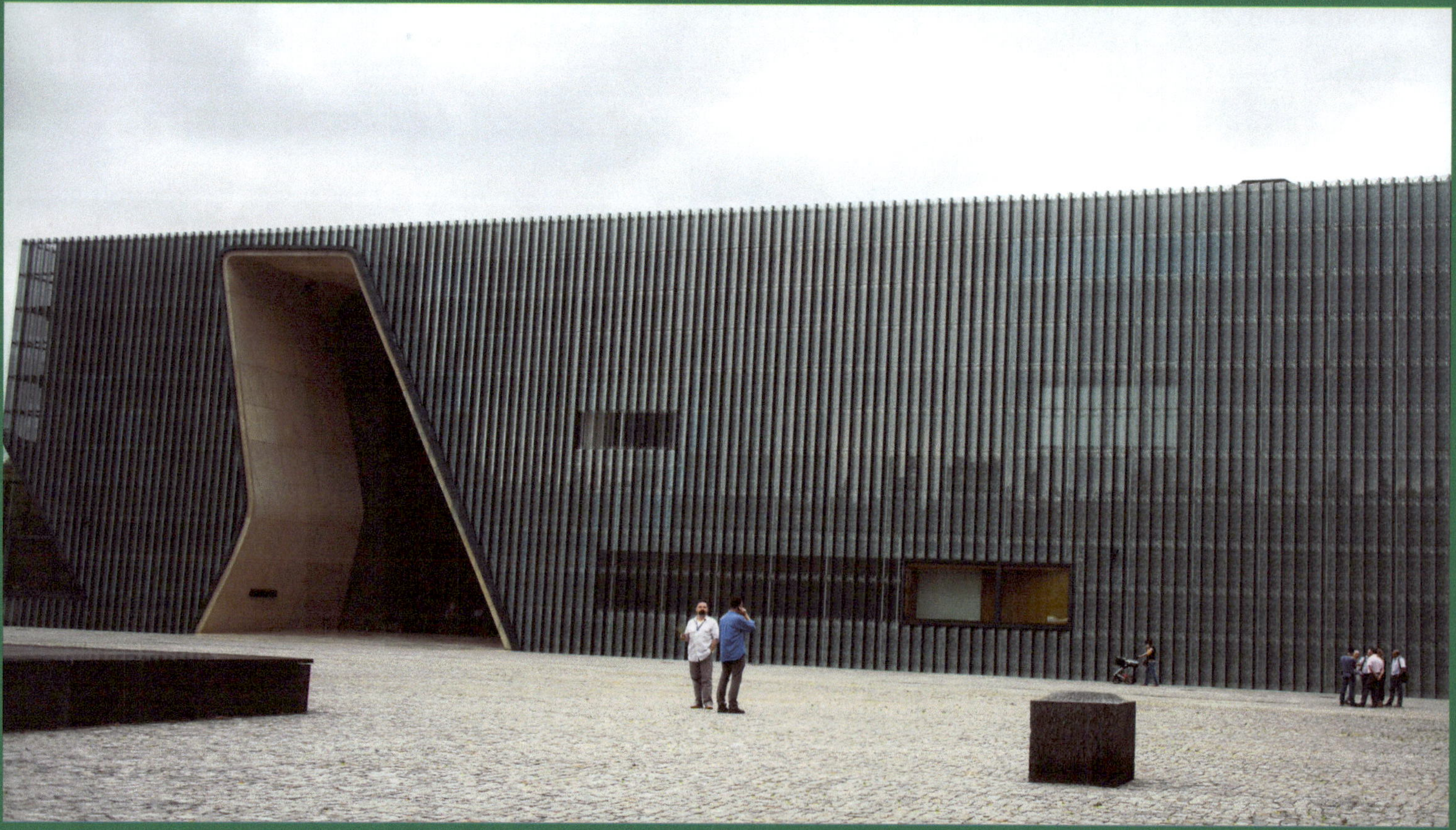

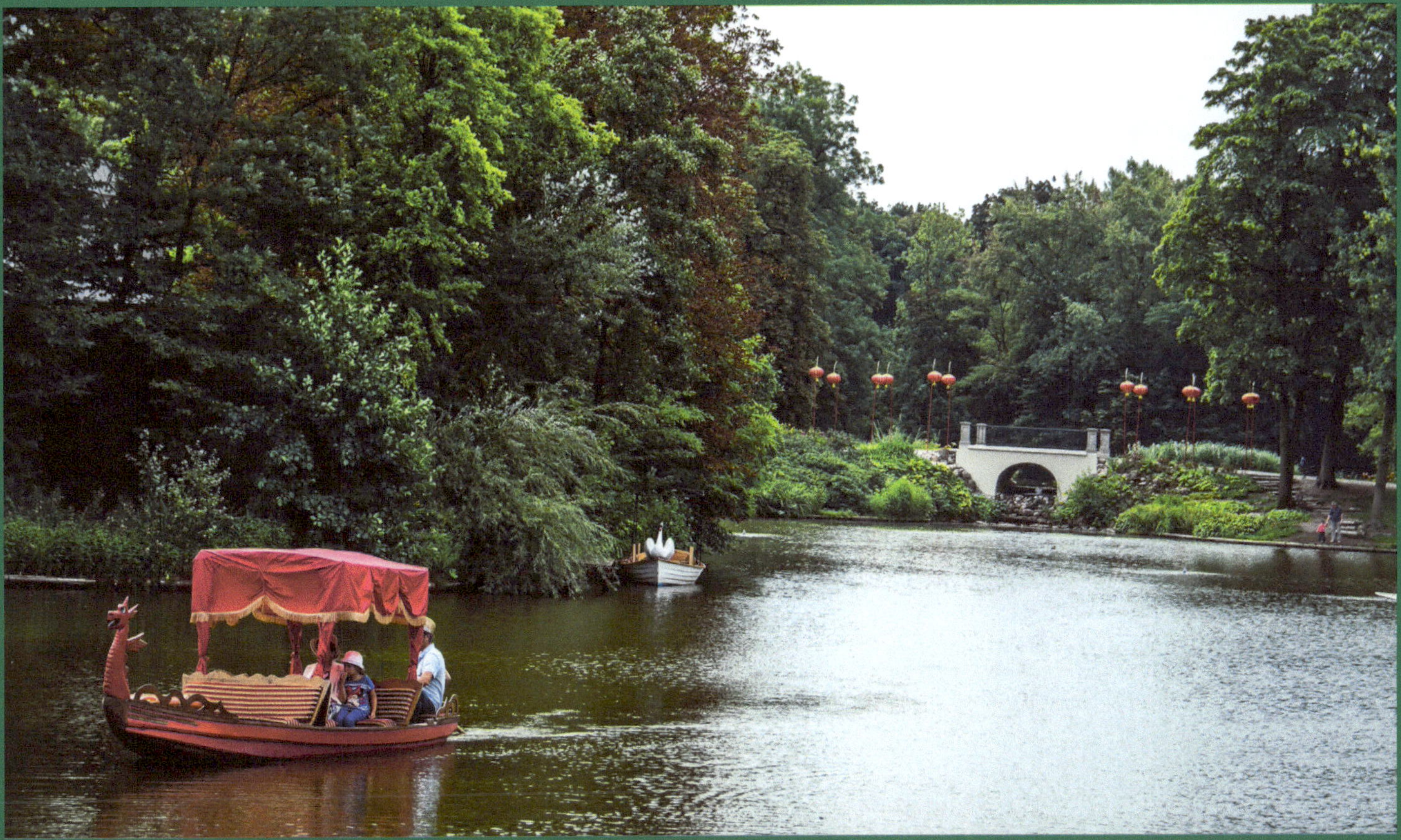

This is the Chopin Garden, a beautiful place with a gorgeous walk. It's very well-known and popular. But by this time I was anxious to get to the Baltic States, however, so I don't think I gave this beautiful city my full attention. Maybe I'll return one day.

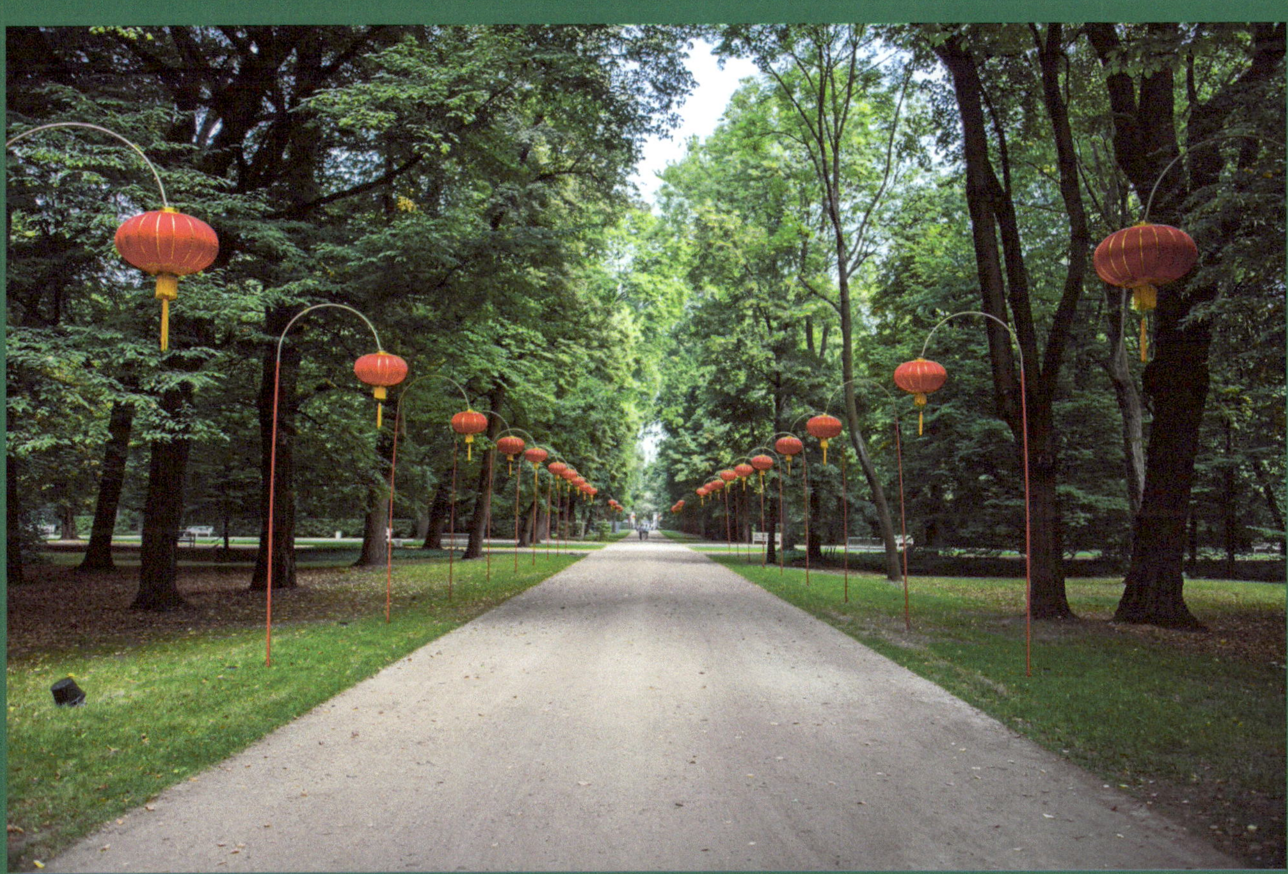

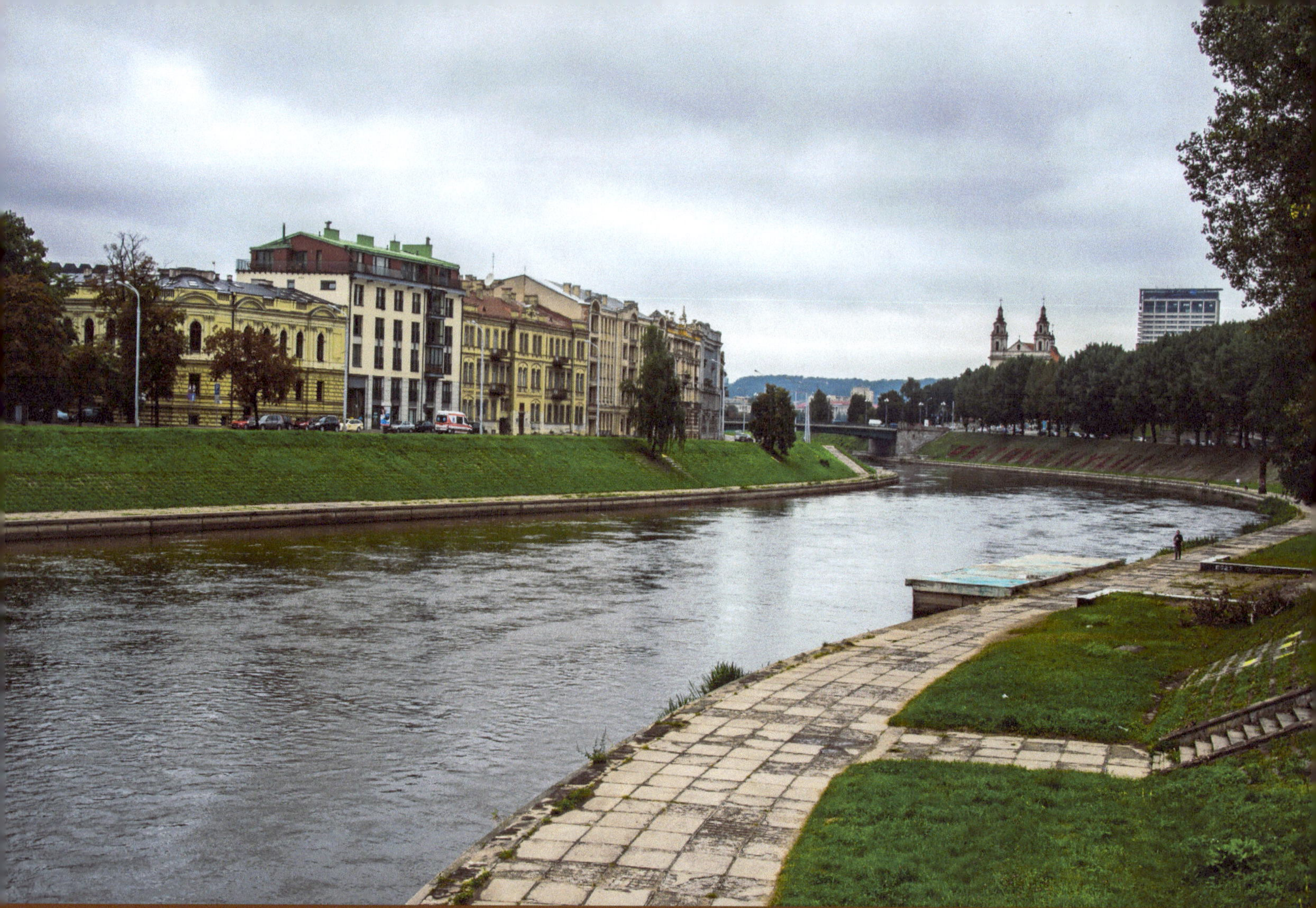

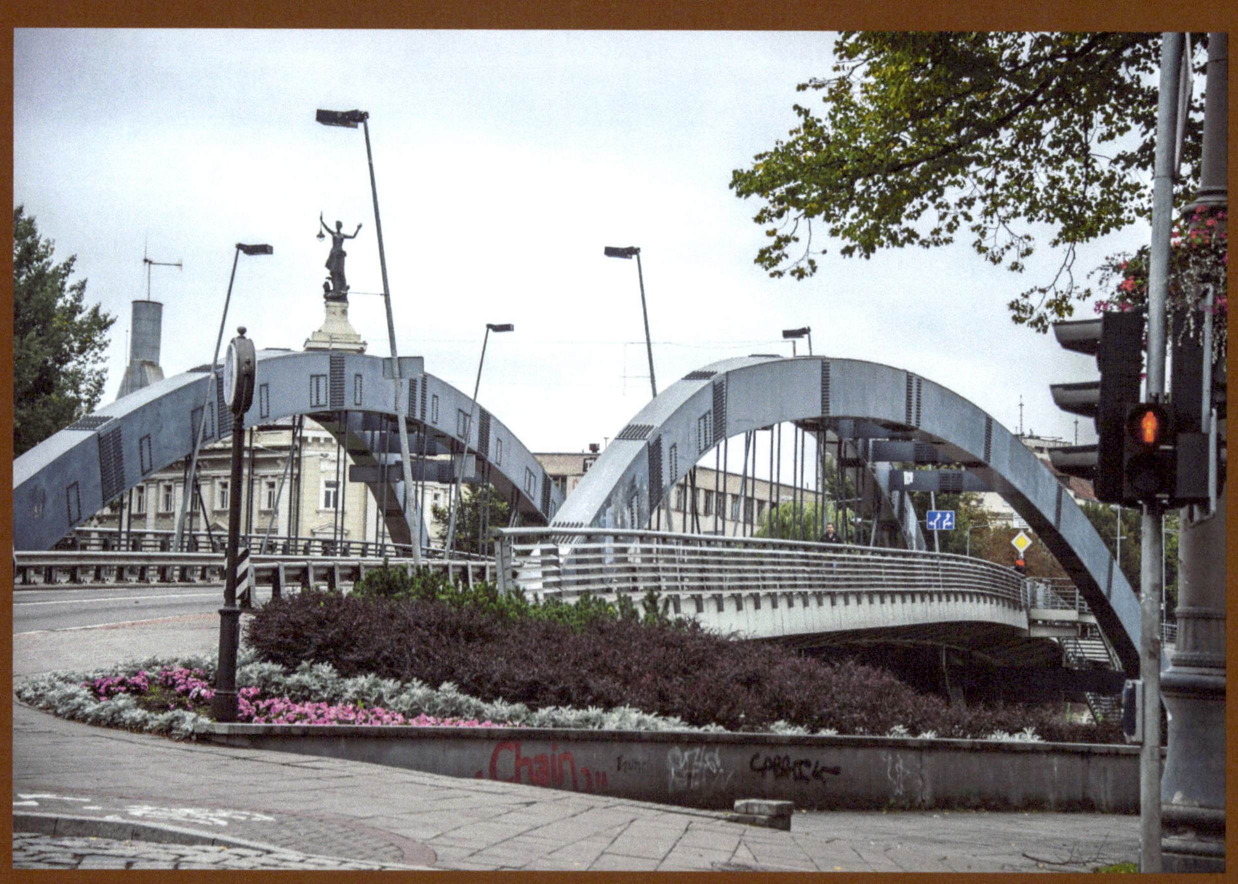
Chain

# 15

# VILNIUS

I took the night bus from Warsaw to Lithuania. Lux Express is the biggest operator of international express bus routes in the Baltic region, and a good, practical way to travel. You can book at different levels of comfort. The more expensive option will give you a recliner with video screen, the basic ticket will squeeze you in like sardines. The overnight coach from Warsaw got me to Vilnius, the capital of Lithuania, at six in the morning. My room at the hotel wasn't ready, so I left my luggage there and, tired as I was, walked around the city and along the Neris River, trying to get impressions and breakfast. The weather was changing. For the first time in all the weeks I had been on the road, it rained.

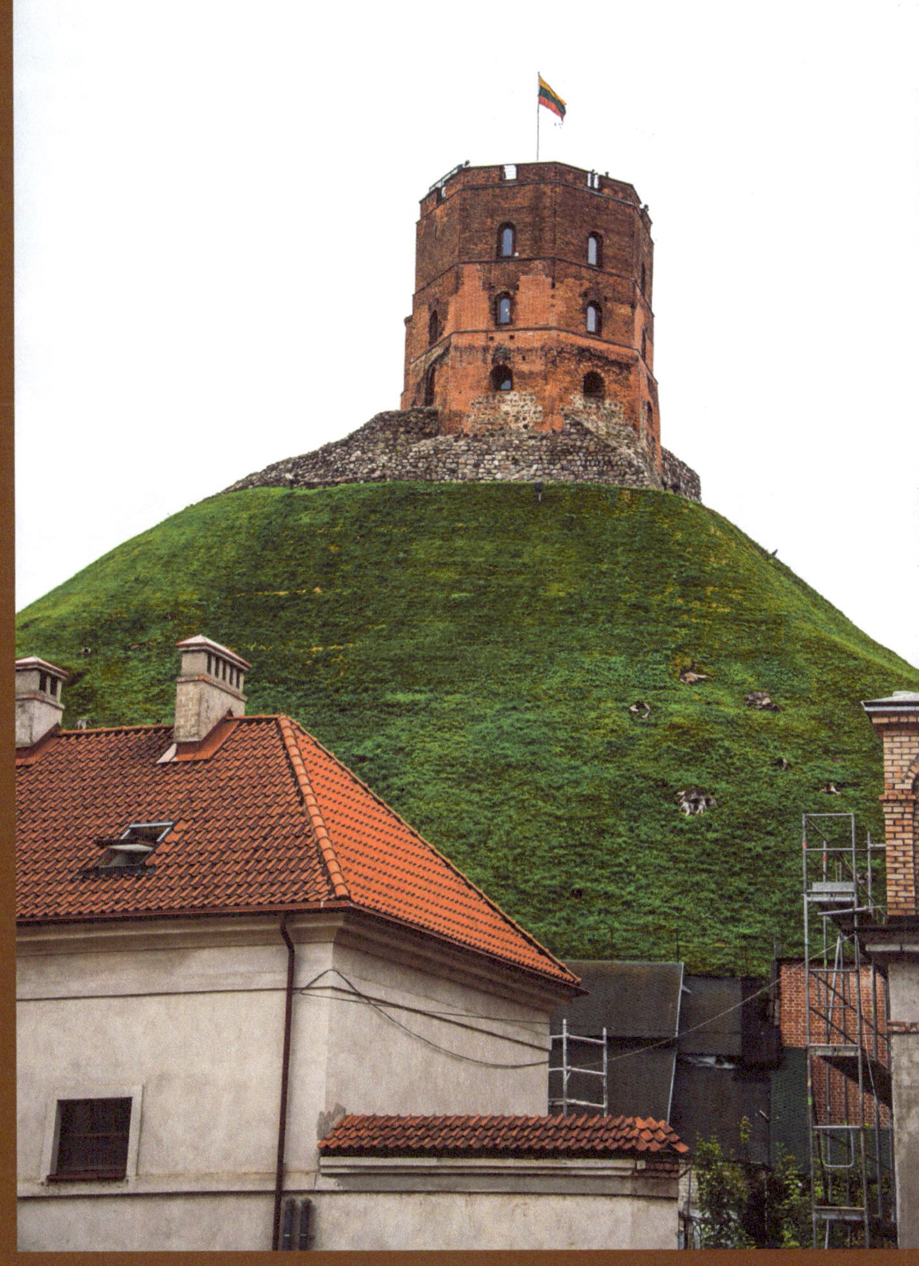

There's a lot of troubled history in all the Baltic States. They've been tossed around among Russia, Poland and Germany like the proverbial bad penny. But unlike many other Eastern European cities, Vilnius has a feeling of being more contemporary, more Western looking, even with its many historical buildings. The tower on top of the hill is all that's left of Gedimina's Castle, named after the Grand Duke who founded Vilnius in 1323. It's the symbol of the city, and the flag displaying the coat-of-arms of Lithuania flies from above its parapet.

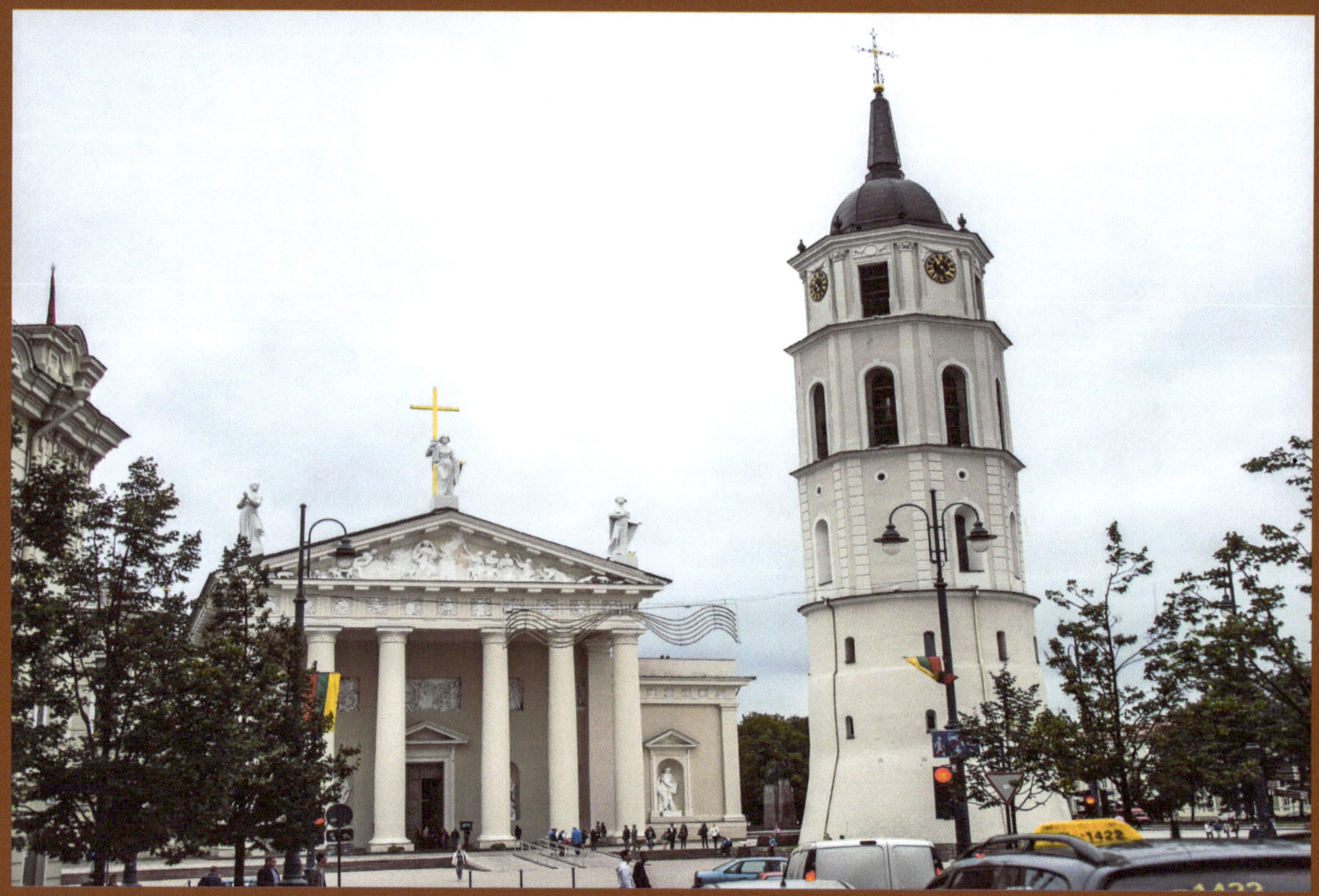

Vilnius has its own leaning tower on Cathedral Square in Old Town. It's unusual to have a separate bell tower in northern Europe—that's more common in Italy—and this one is a mix of architectural styles from the 13th century at the base to the 19th century at the top.

Walking round the city, I noticed a lot of modern sculpture. The voluptuous statue of *Barbora Radvilaitė* by Vladas Vildžiūnas is a depiction of a 16th-century Queen of Poland, who was also Grand Duchess of Lithuania. The piece next to it by Gintaras Mikolaitis is called "Bird's Nest."

The "Three Muses" by Lithuania's most celebrated sculptor, Stanislovas Kuzma, sits atop the main entrance to the National Drama Theatre. Although there are nine muses altogether, these three are thought to represent the three pertaining to the theater—Calliope (music and dance), Thalia (comedy), and Melpomene (tragedy). To me they looked scary.

I bought my wife a lovely amber necklace. Amber is the main gem stone that is made in Lithuania—it's actually petrified tree resin distinctive for its rich, golden-brown color.

I also took the Hop On – Hop Off, but after two-and-a-half days, I'd had enough. I didn't find Vilnius inspiring. I'm sure there are wonderful things to discover, but I just didn't feel in the mood at that point. The weather depressed me so much I didn't go out to experience any of the nightlife. Instead, I spent my time in my hotel room and edited pictures all evening, and was glad to leave the place behind after two days.

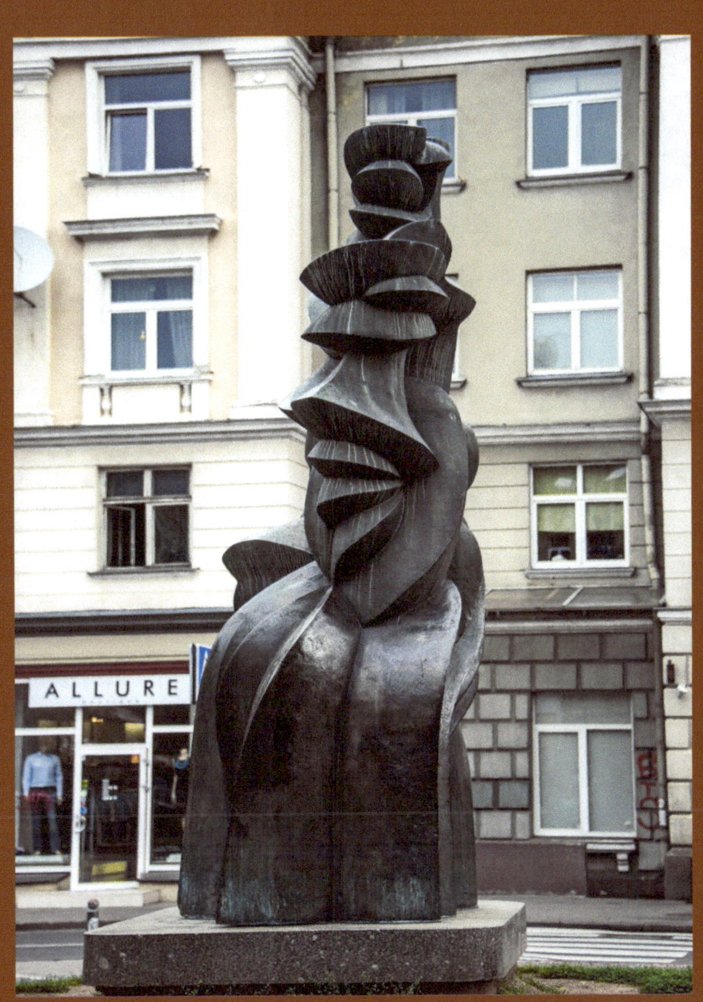
ALLURE

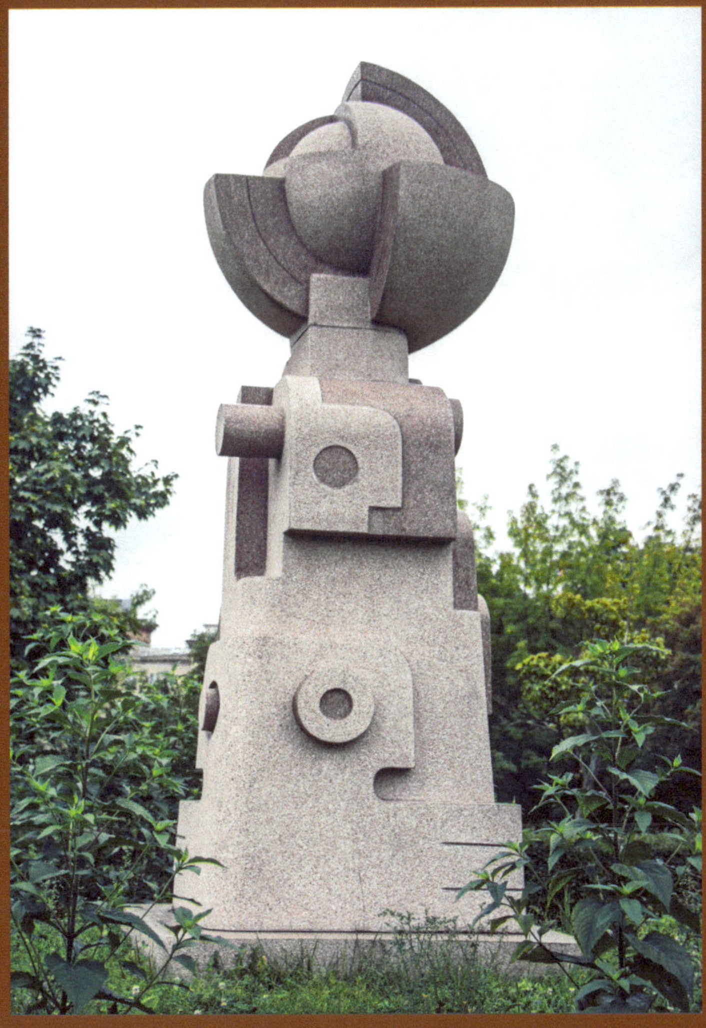

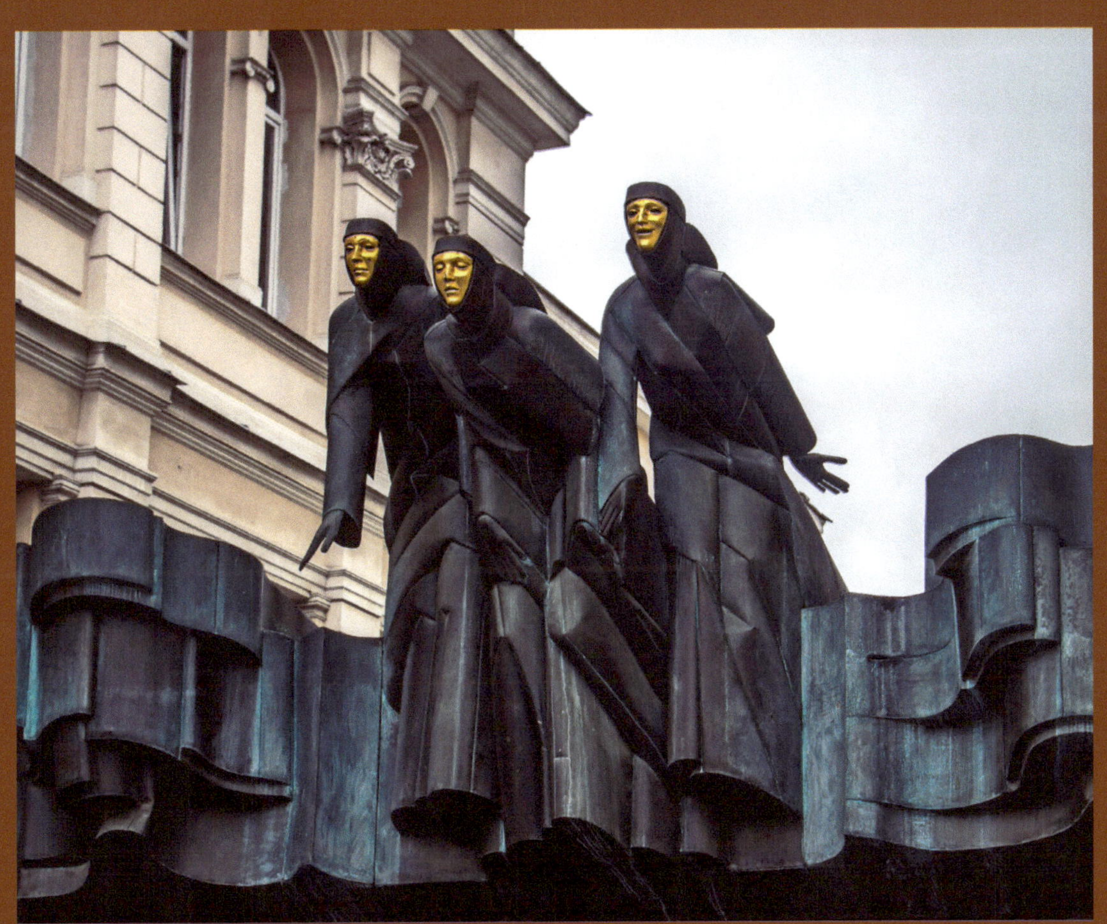

# 16
# RIGA

Riga, the capital of Latvia was Number 4 on my list of favorite cities. I liked it because it's attractive, clean and modern, yet maintains its old European atmosphere—spectacular bridges, a wonderful Old Town, beautiful illuminations, which I liked very much. It was also by far the most expensive city I visited.

Since it was founded in 1201, Riga has always been a mercantile city, starting out as a Viking trade center. The River Duagava, which runs through it, was part of the Viking navigation route to ancient Byzantium. From the 13th to the 17th century, Riga belonged to the Hanseatic League, a confederation of Northern European merchant guilds and their market cities.

Like many places in that part of the world, Riga has been owned by just about everybody, but has managed to maintain its own personality, adding color and flair to its architecture. Riga is a lot like Krakow.

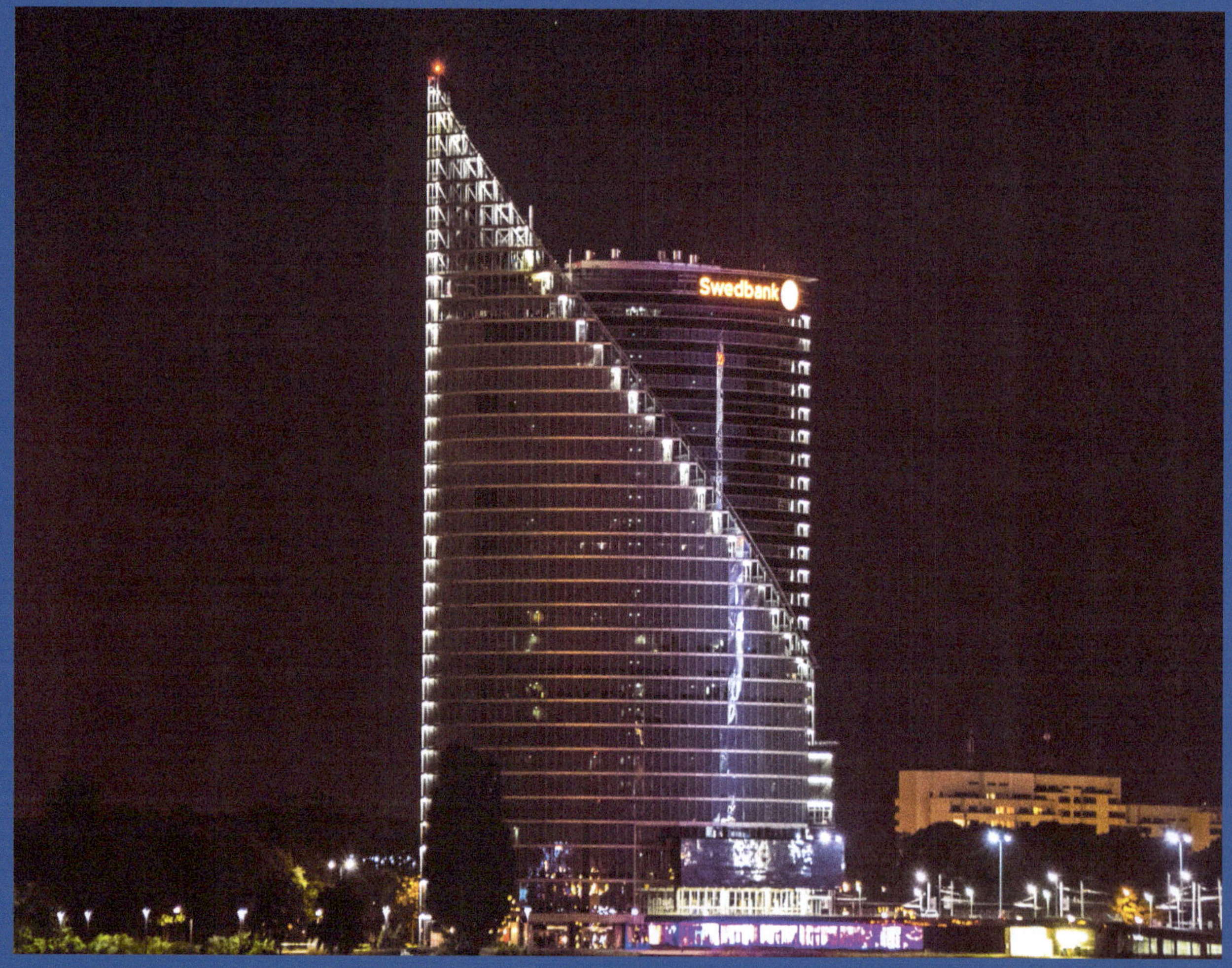

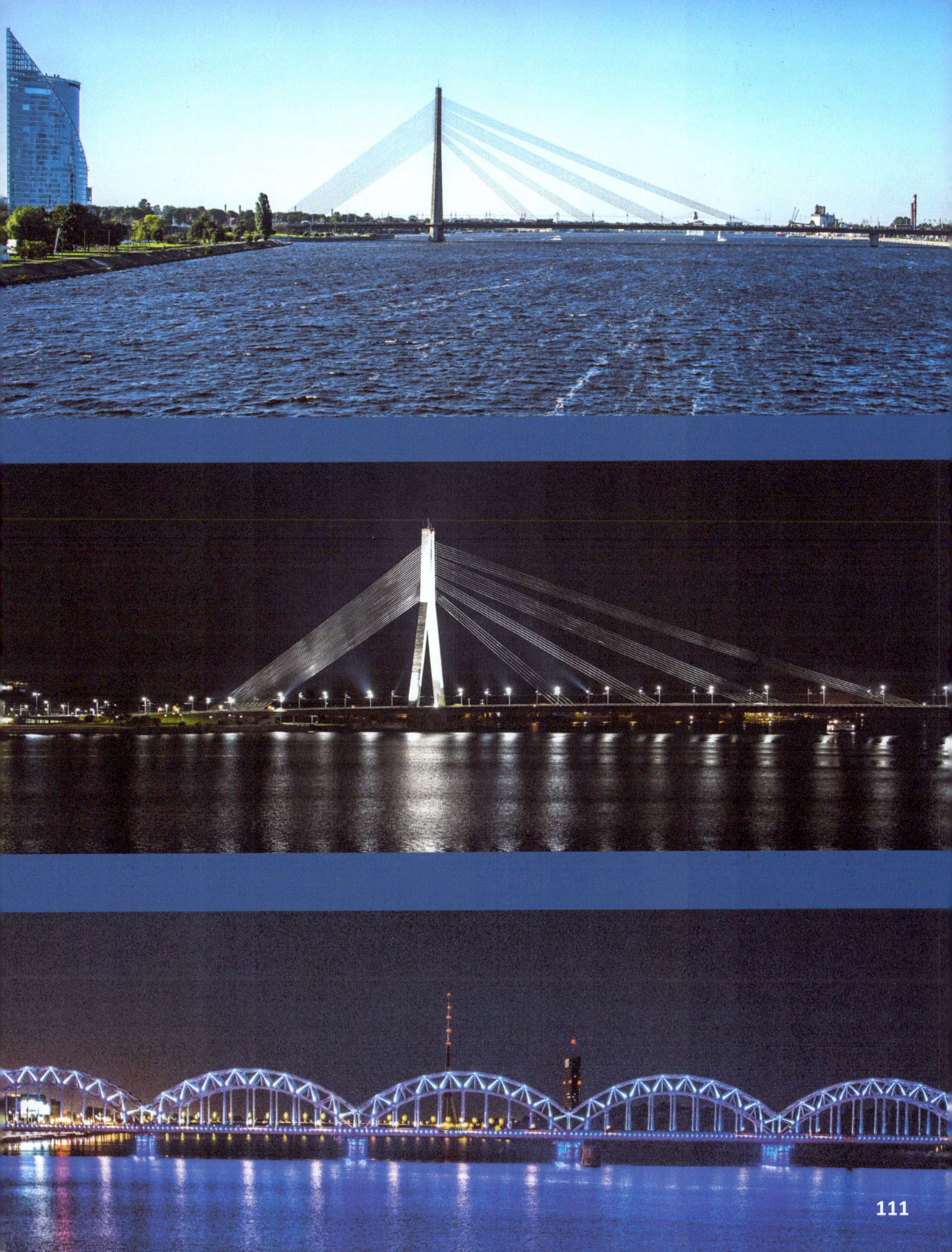

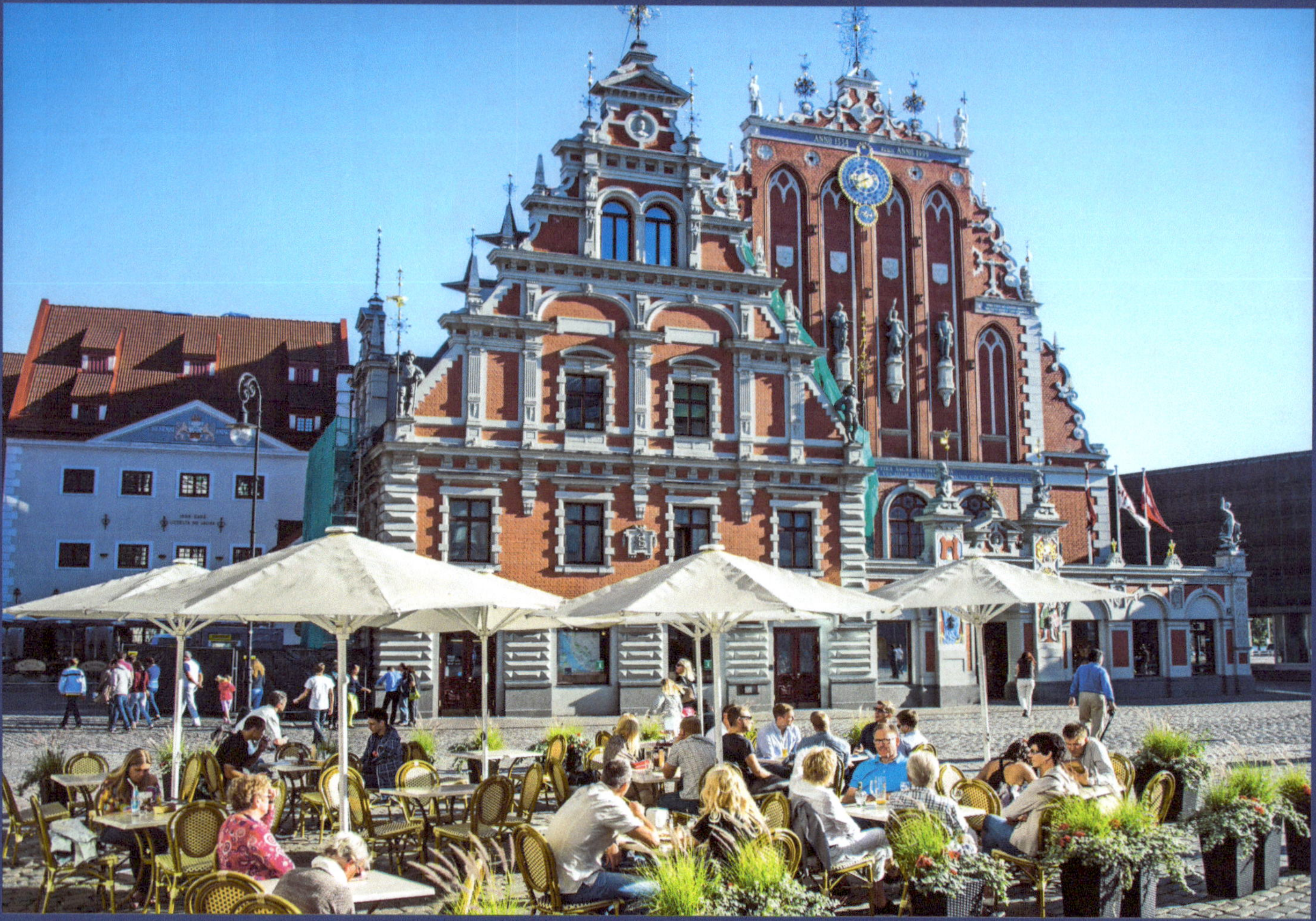

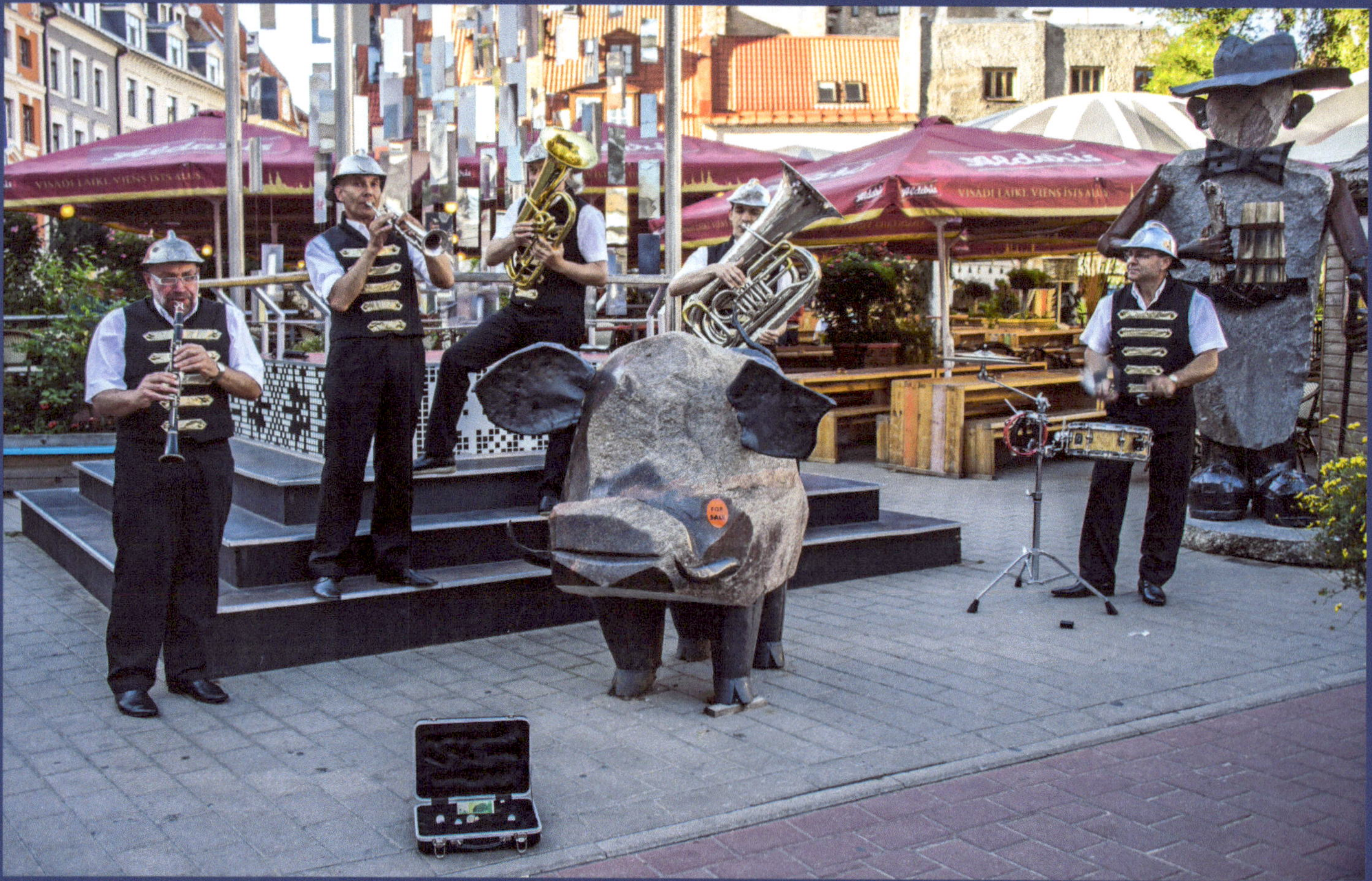

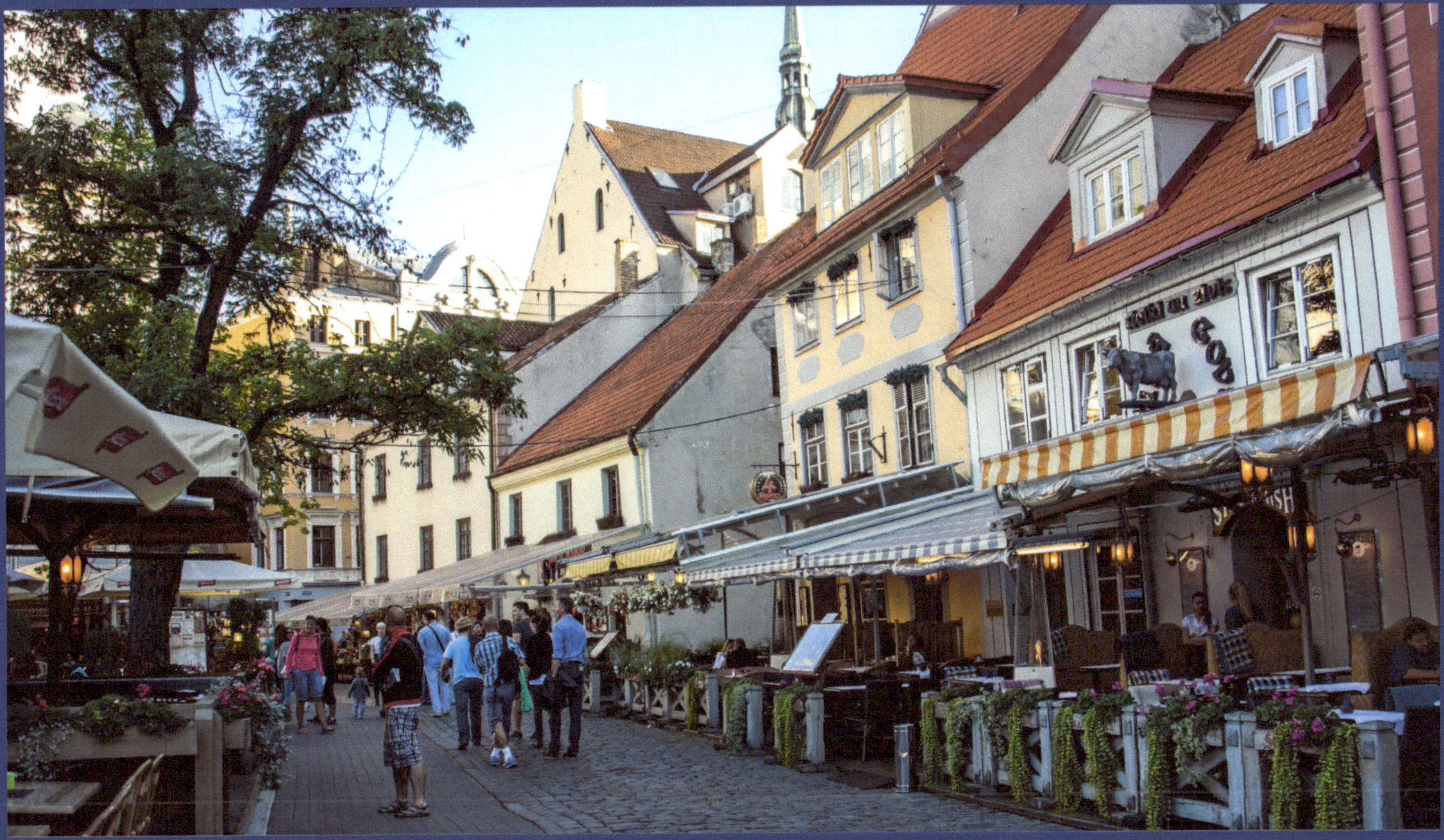

The sun came out for me again, and if it hadn't been for my feet starting to hurt from all the walking I'd done, it would have been a perfect visit. I spent a lot of time in the Old Town, sitting in a little café for hours to get the feeling back into my feet, enjoying the people and the scenery.

On the opposite page is one of the city's most famous buildings, the House of the Blackheads, who were a 14th century guild for unmarried German merchants in Riga. It was bombed by the Nazis during World War II and completely demolished by the Russians in 1948. This is actually a reconstruction done in the mid-to late 90s.

In the Old Town, there were exhibits of stone animals with little orange stickers telling you they were for sale. I shot this one with a band playing nearby. Everywhere you looked there were great jazz bands.

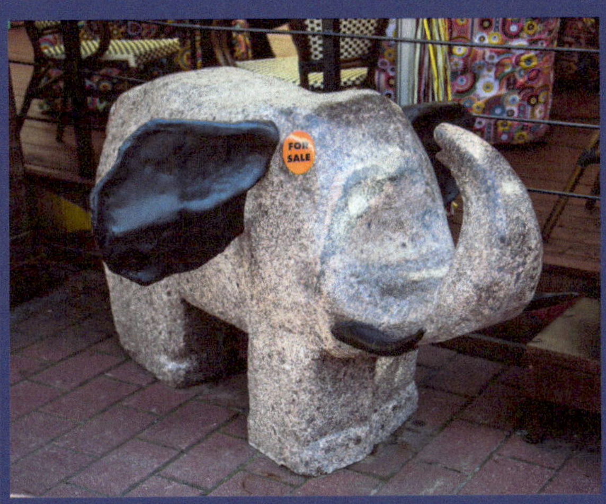


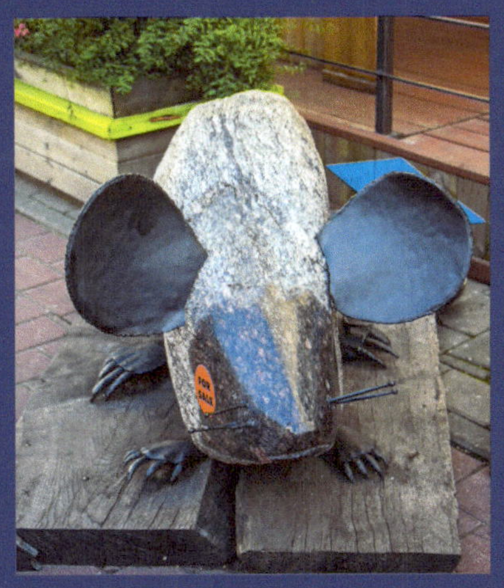

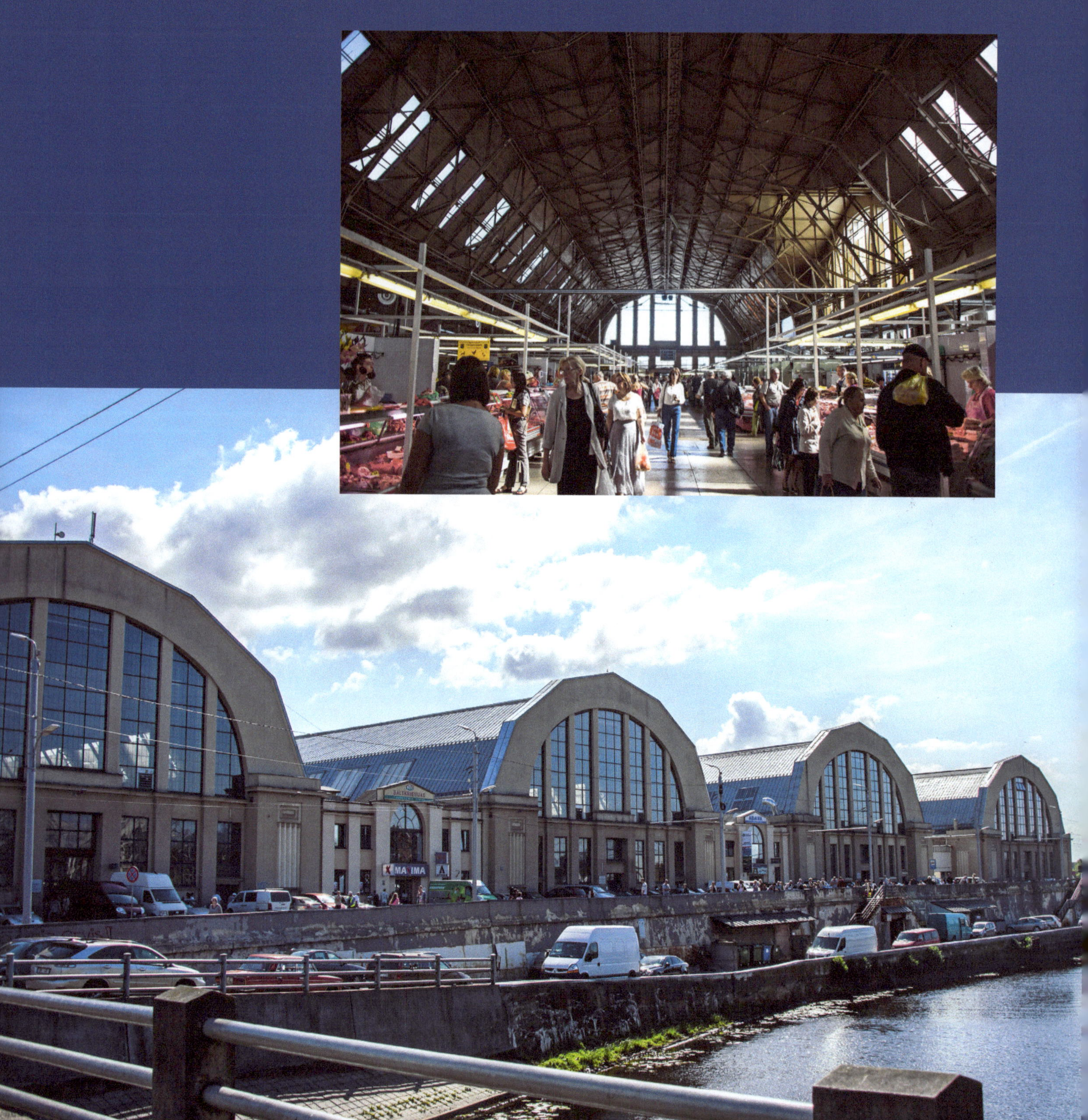

The Riga Central Market is Europe's largest shopping arena. Each of the covered structures is as big as a football field and there are more than 3,000 trade stands and booths. The buildings were constructed in the 1920s, reusing old German Zeppelin hangars. I walked around the Market five times in three days—I couldn't get enough of it! Such a beautiful part of the city; so much energy and color.

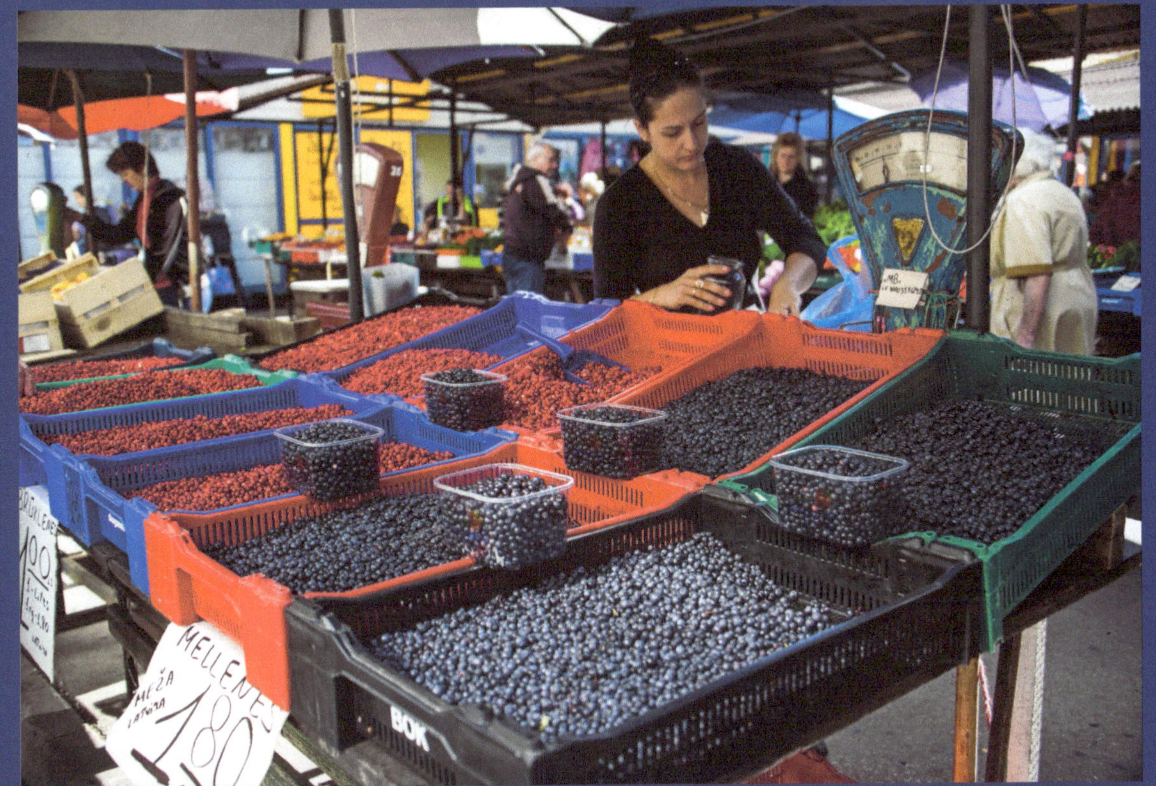


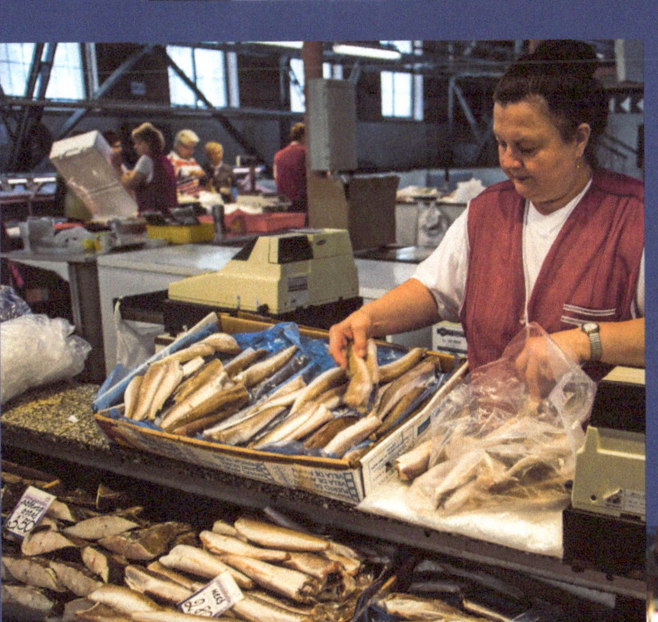

Inside the market halls, they nearly threw me out for taking pictures. Some of the female vendors didn't like being photographed, and a few of them told me to get lost (but in much stronger terms!). So I secretly shot a lot of photos from the hip.

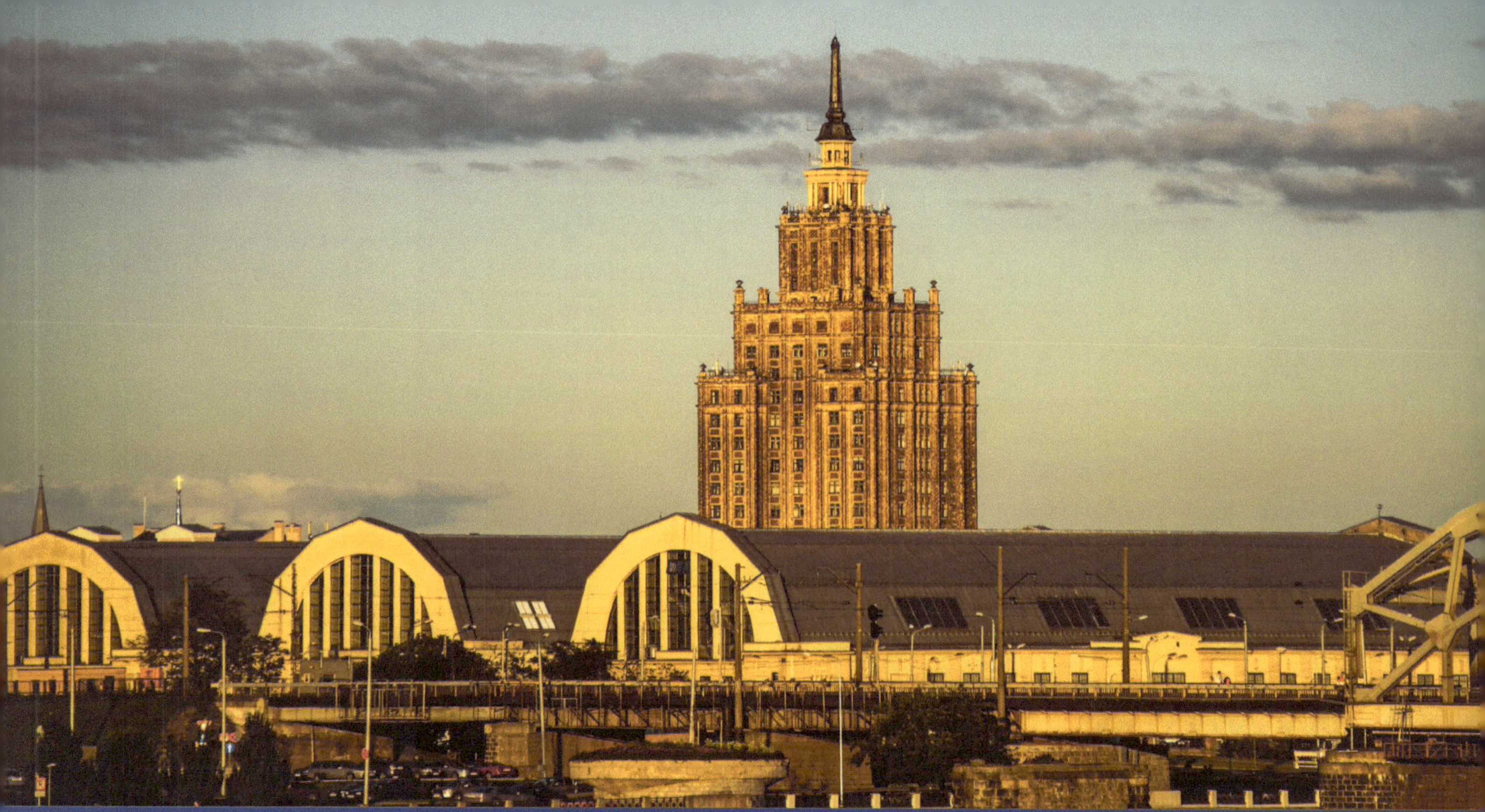

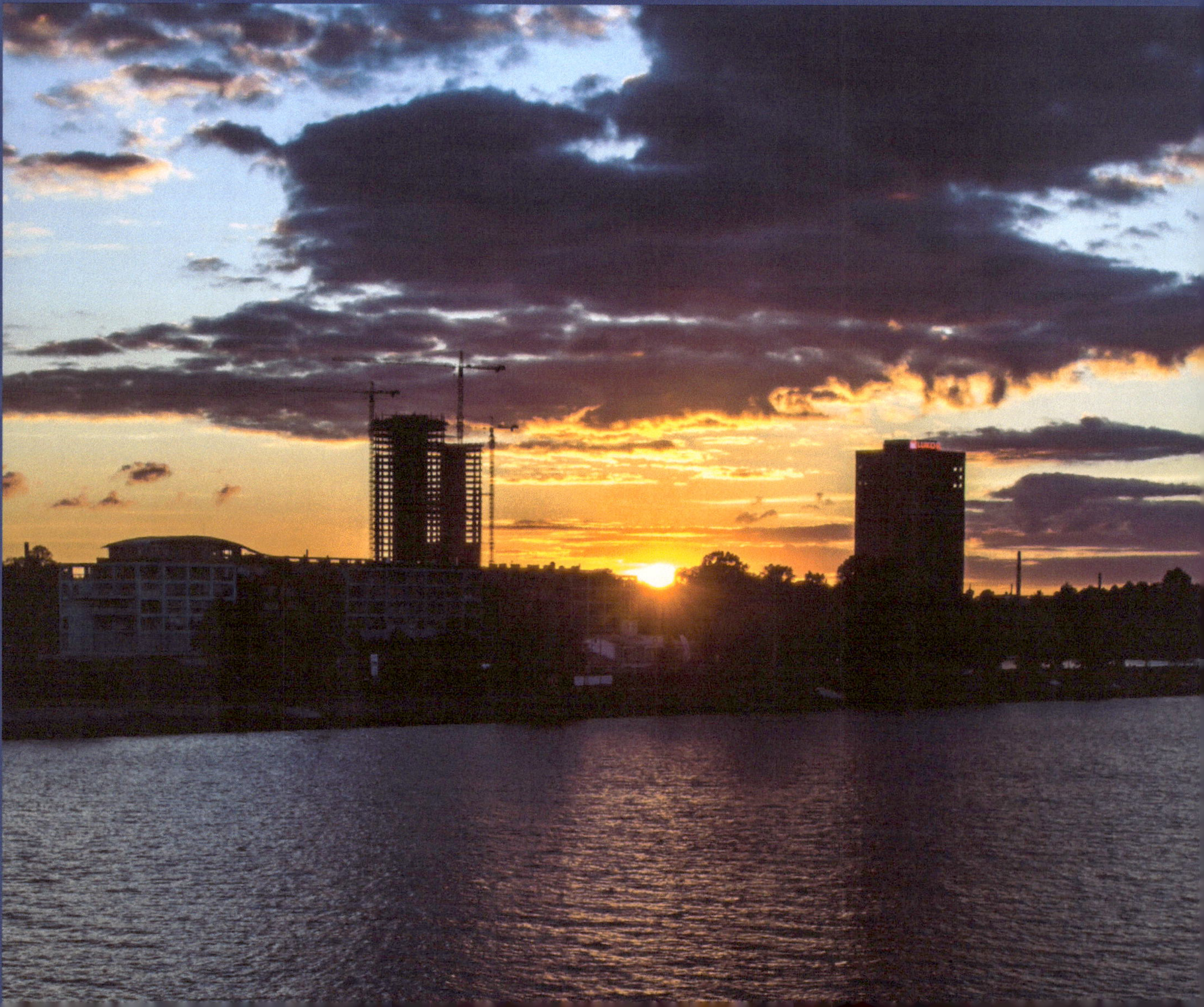

Whatever you do, do not say "Thank you" in Russian to the locals—they'll tell you to go you-know-where in no uncertain terms. When I asked, someone explained to me that you have to say, "Paldies." That's "Thank you" in Latvian.

I spent four days wandering around and enjoying Riga. The Hop on–Hop off helped me a lot, and it included a trip on the river, which I loved. I would say to anybody planning a trip to Europe, "Go to Latvia and Estonia." Those two countries really impressed me.

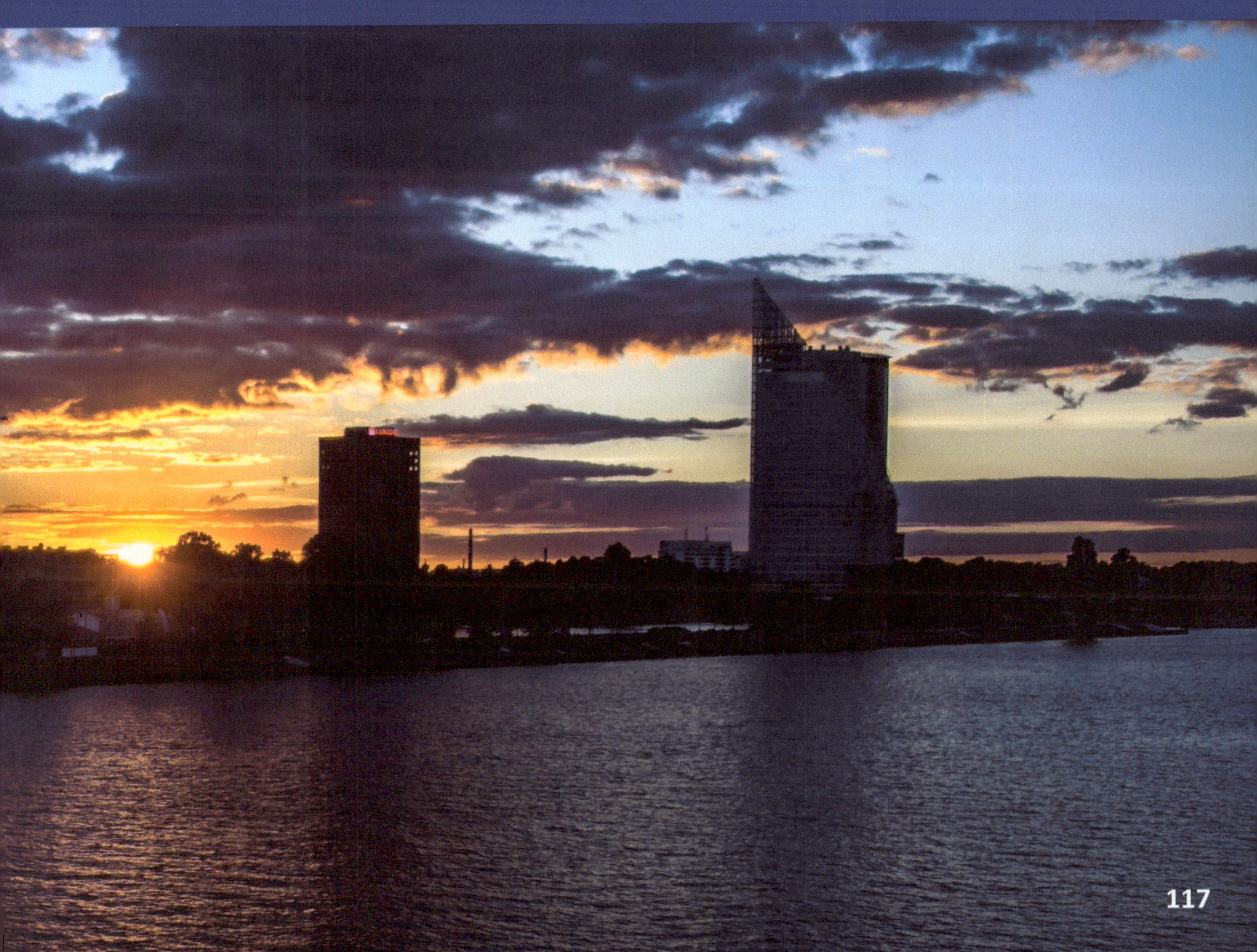

# 17
# TALLINN

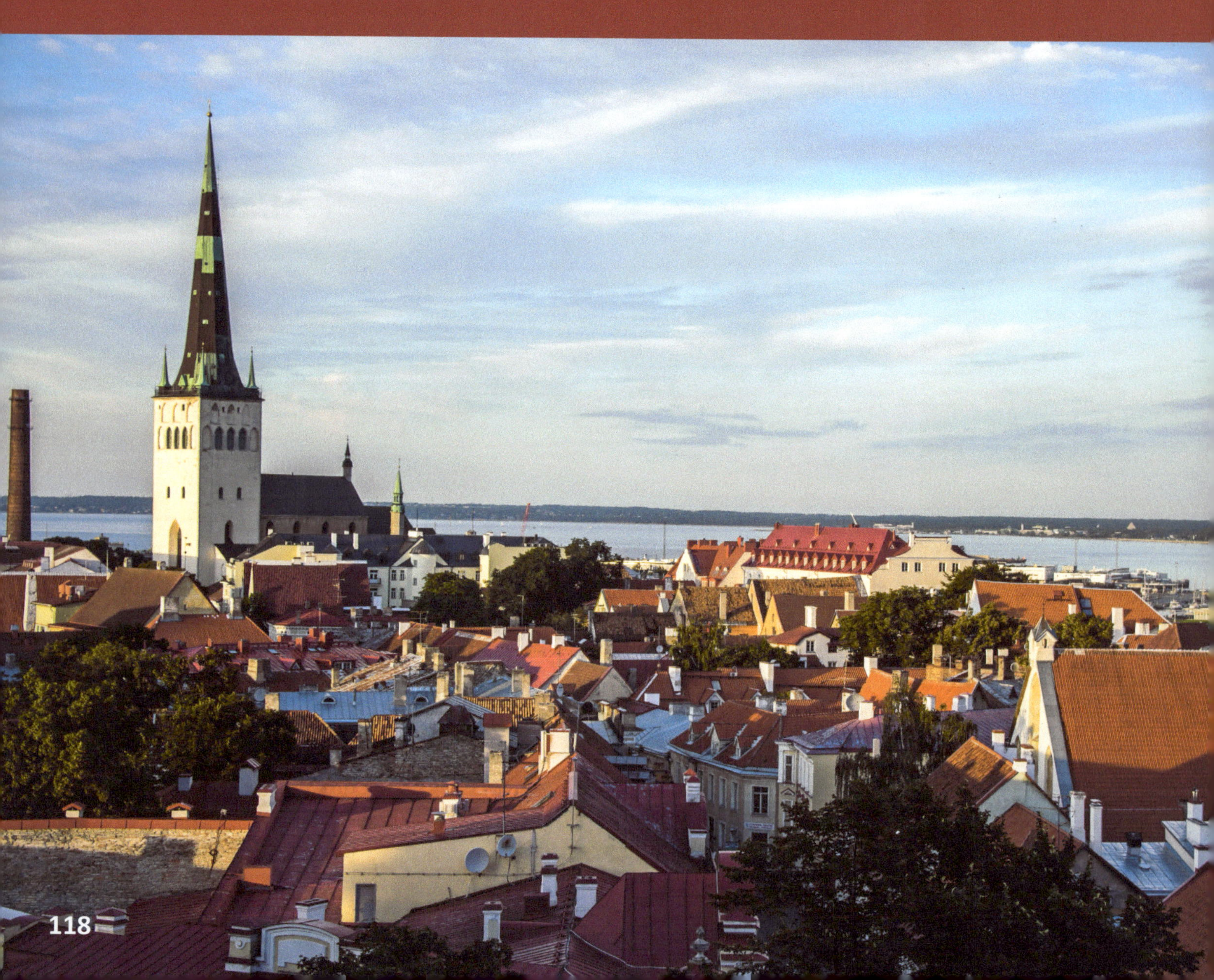

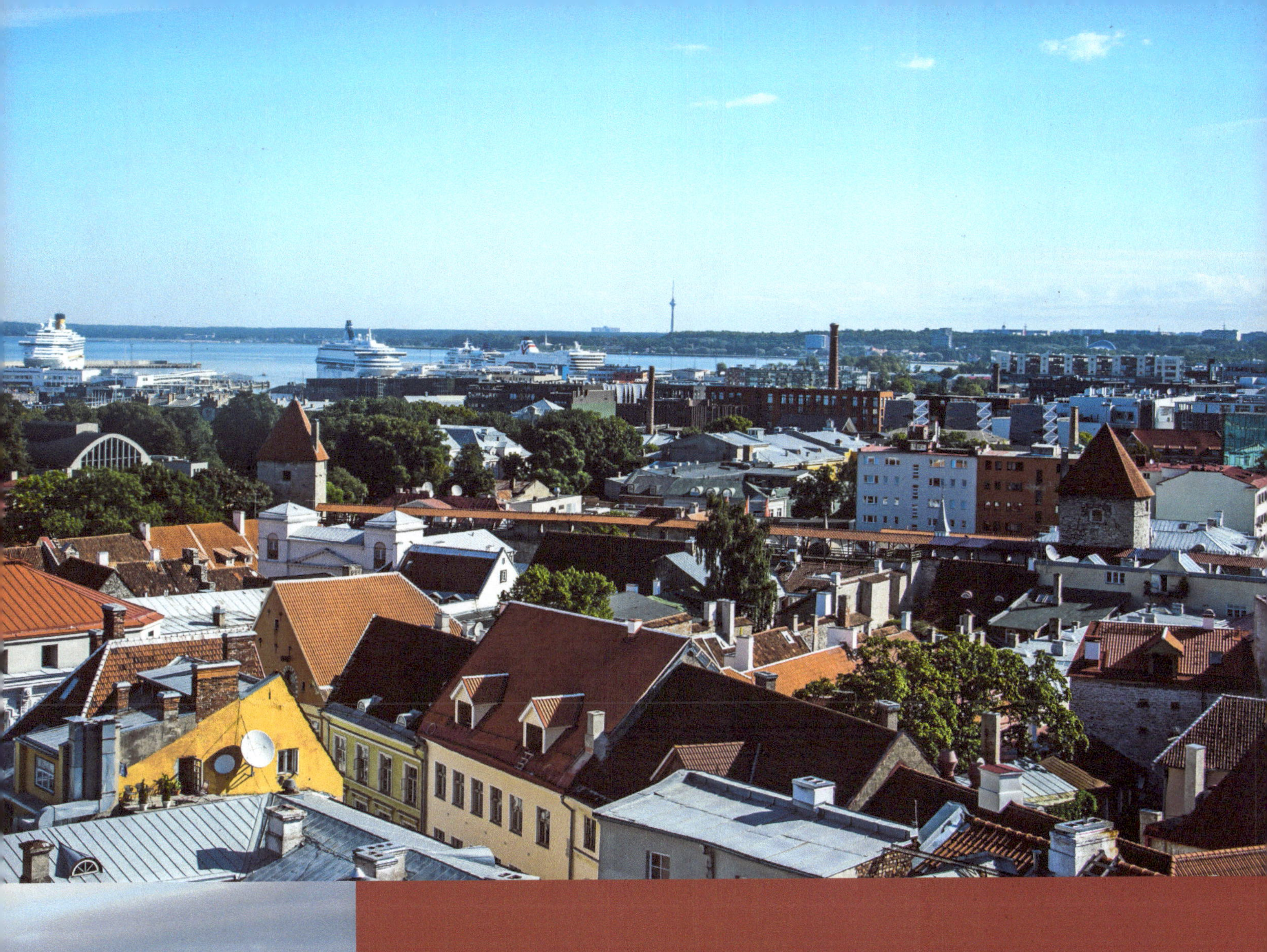

I took an afternoon bus from Riga to Estonia's capital, Tallinn. Of the three Baltic capitals, it has the most beautiful Old Town, a well-preserved example of a medieval northern European trading city dating back to the 13th century. The old defensive walls surrounding the heart of the city are still standing—over a mile of them—including 20 towers and four gateways.

Because Tallinn is the stop for cruise ships in the Baltic Sea, it has become something of a tourist trap. Wherever you go you see vendors catering to tourist fantasies. But there also are a lot of good little restaurants and colorful houses, doorways and courtyards. Without question, Tallinn really is a beautiful town, and people love it for good reason.

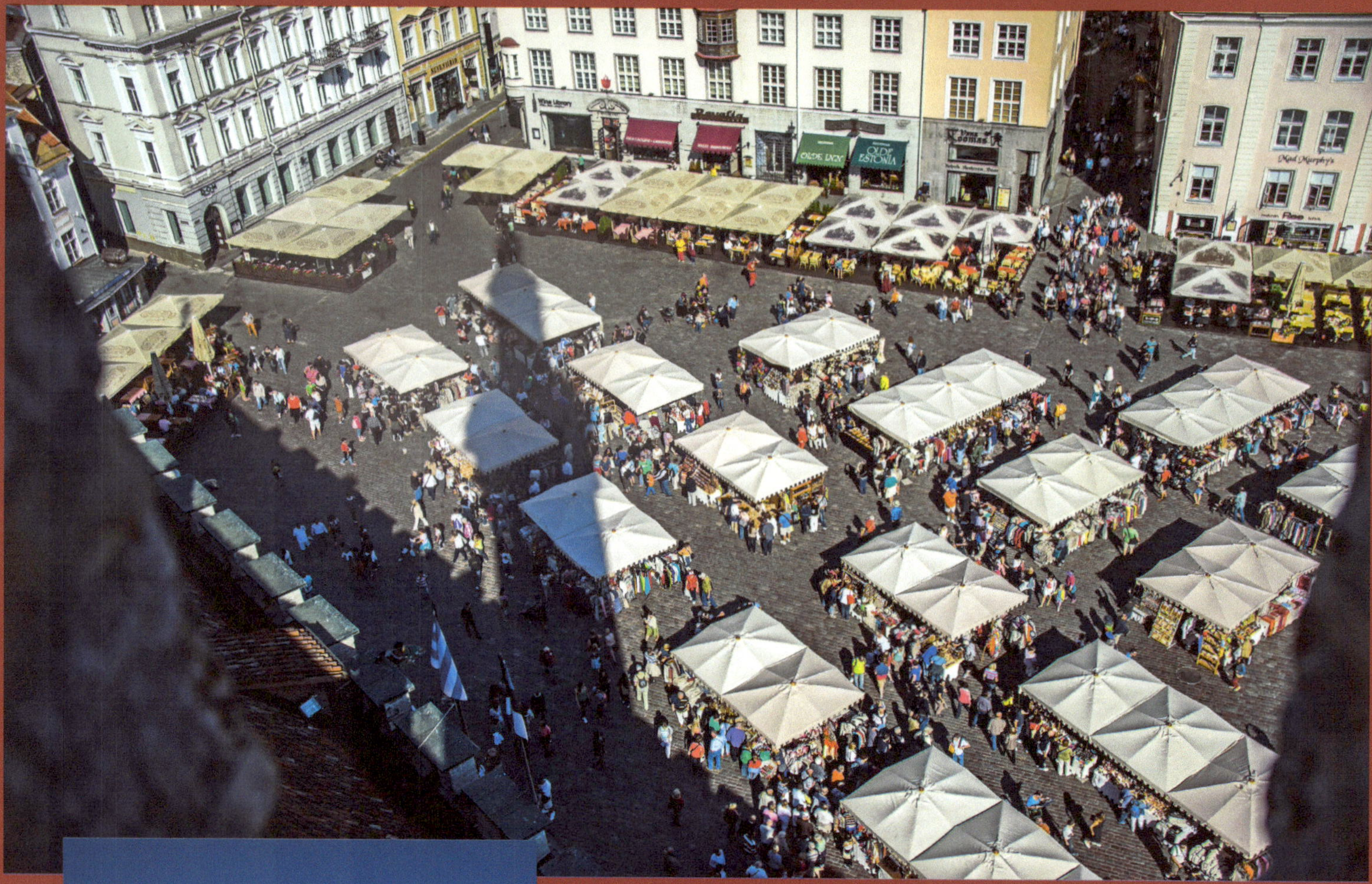

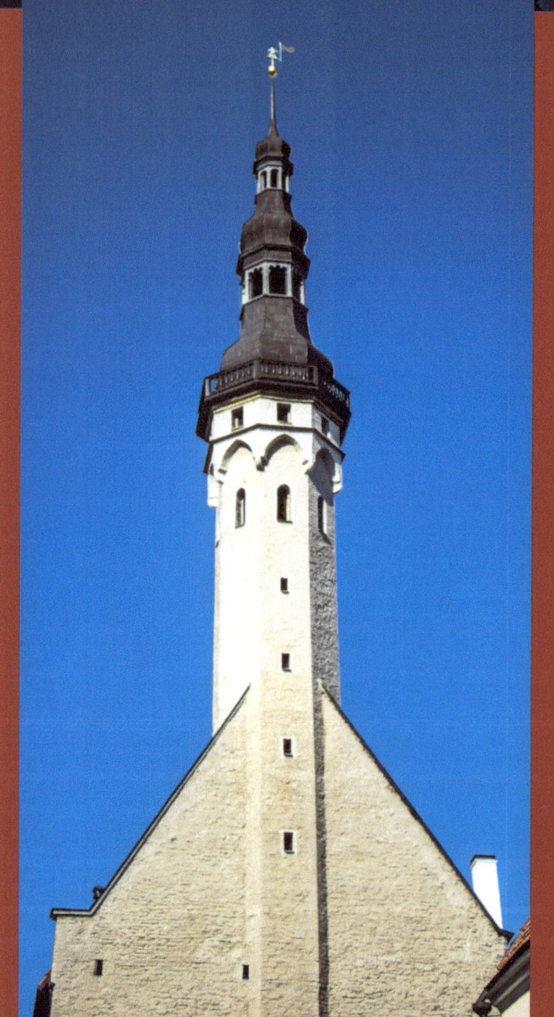

One of the hardest climbs I've ever made was the 366 stone steps inside the church bell tower on Tallinn's marketplace to get the aerial shots of the city on the previous two pages and the stalls in the picture bove, but it was worth it. Note the shadow of the tower on the white tent tops of the booths.

The bronze statue of a bull on a wooden bench—also known as the cow sculpture—sits in front of the only classic American steakhouse restaurant in the Baltic States and Scandinavia. Created in 2011 by Tauno Kangro, an Estonian sculpture, its official name is "Black Angus."

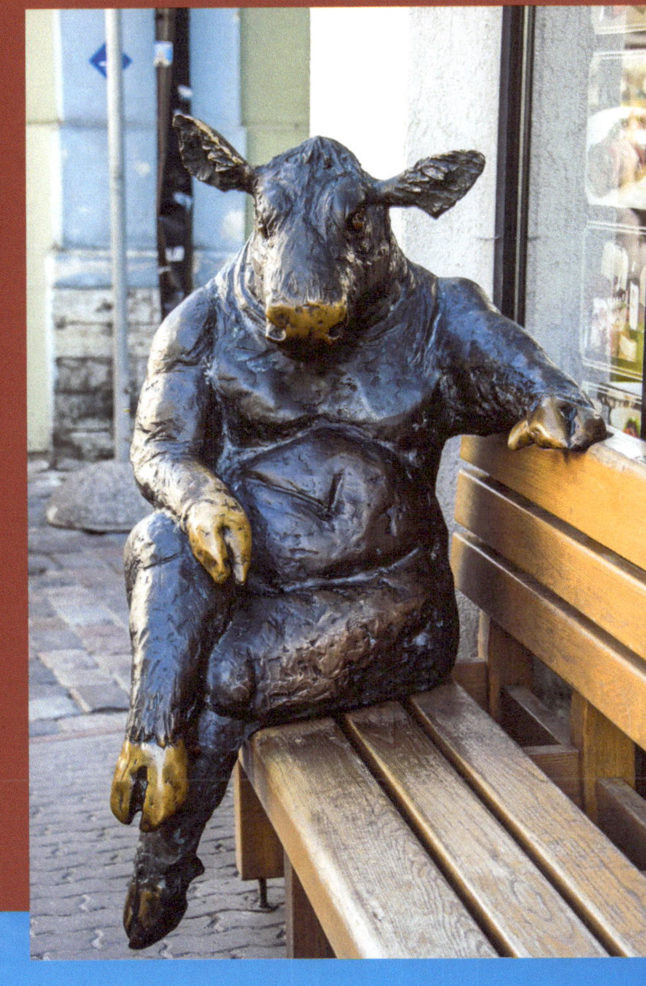

Because it's located just inside the Viru Gate, the entrance to the old city, it's a favorite of the tourists that pour from the cruise ships into town. They like to have their picture taken sitting beside it.

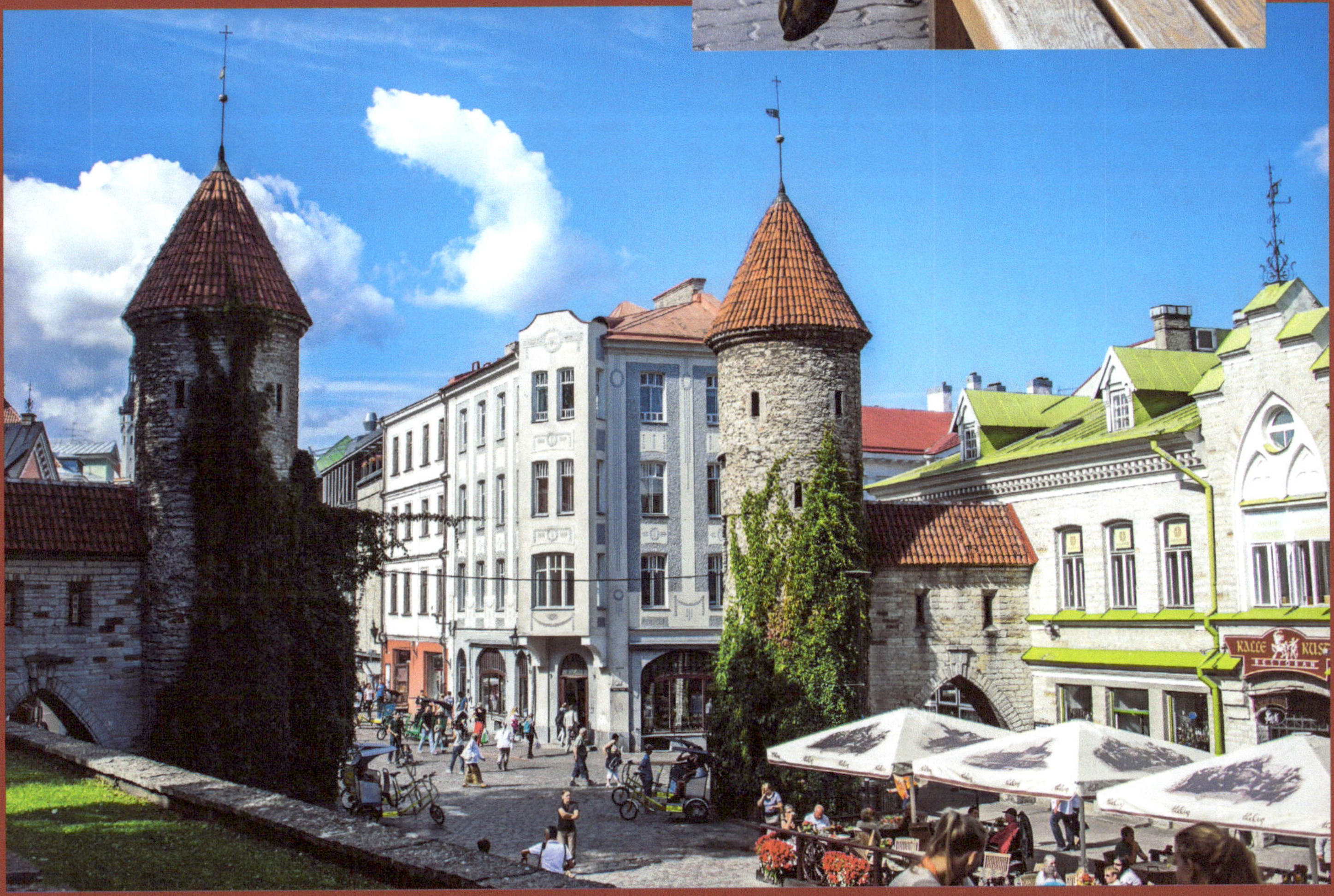

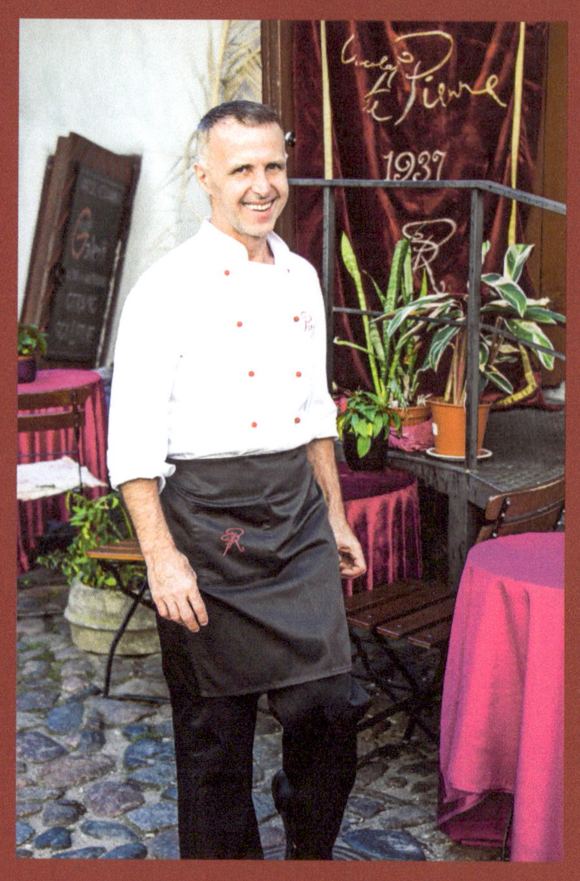


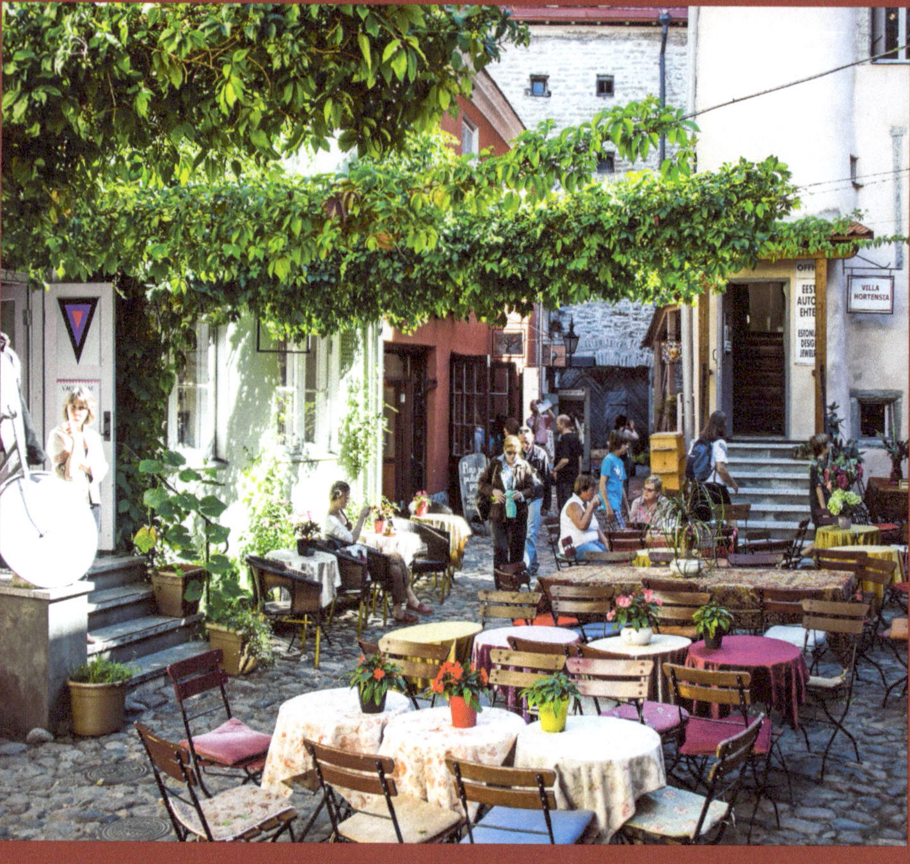


One of my favorite places was *Pierre's Chocolaterie*—that's Pierre himself up left. It's a very well-known café in Tallinn, where you can sit and enjoy delicious hot chocolate, coffee and pastries.

I enjoyed my stay in Tallinn. Like Riga, it has been owned by everybody at one time or another—Germans, Swedes, Danes, Russians. Yet it has become one of the most modern cities in Europe, combining the old and new with charm and elegance.

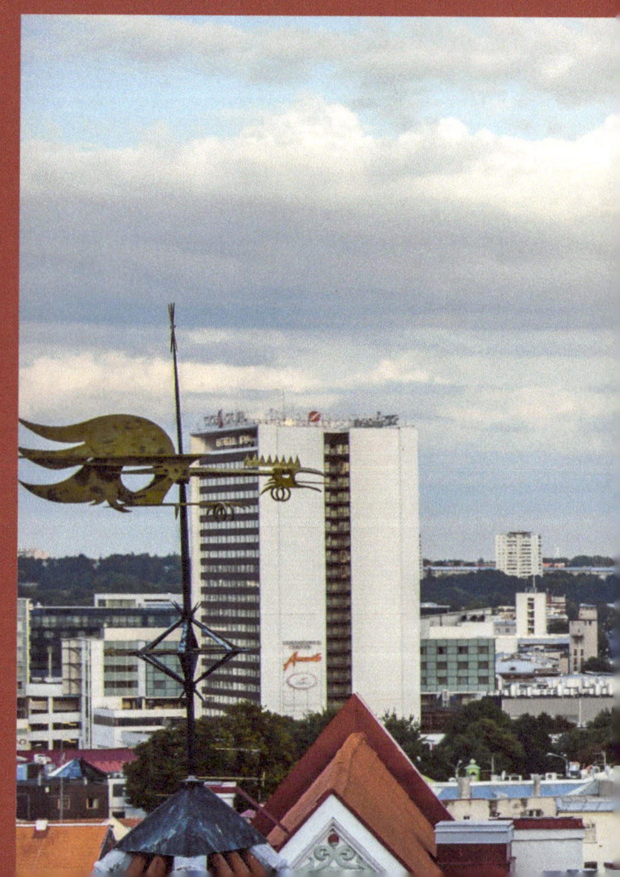

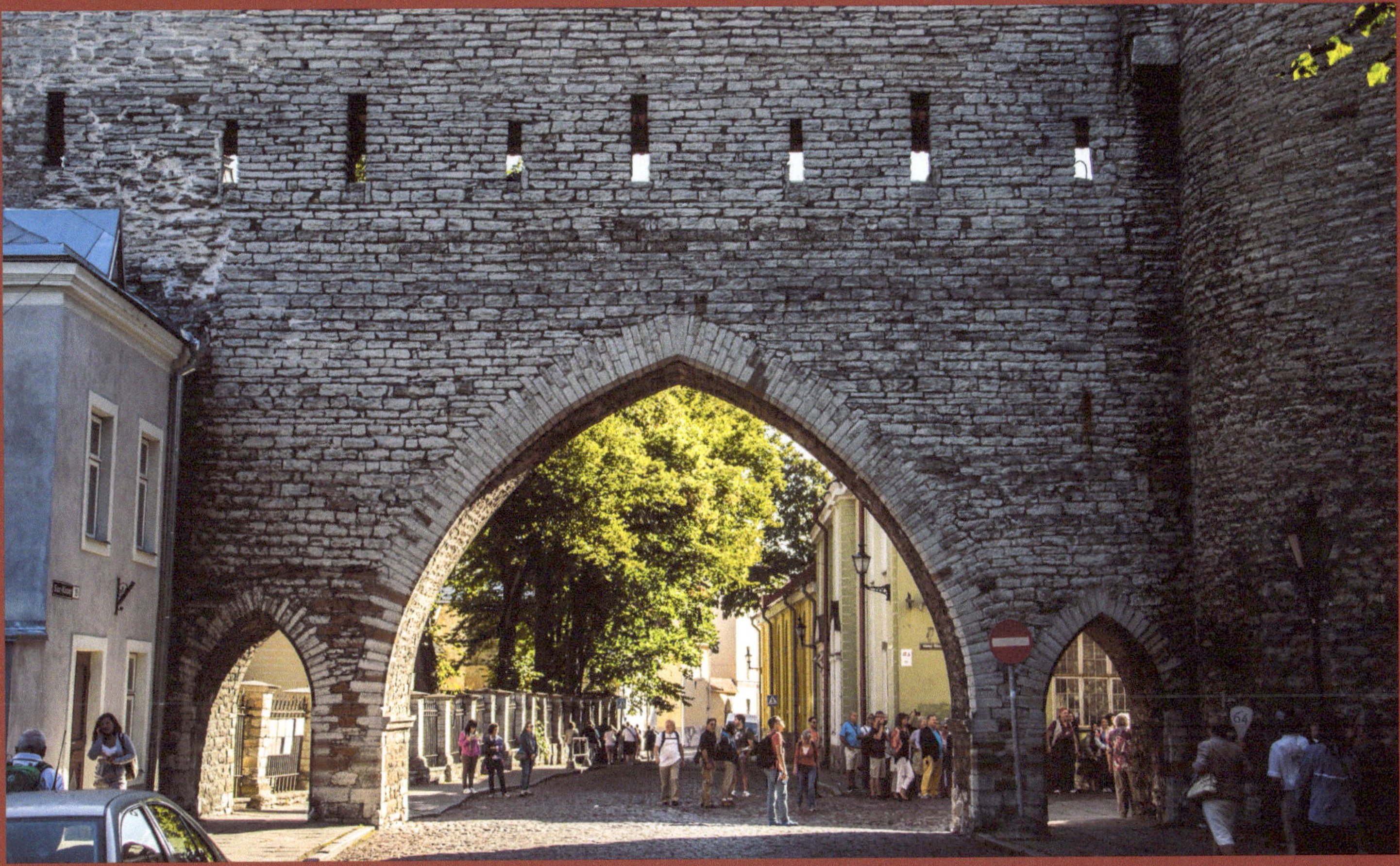

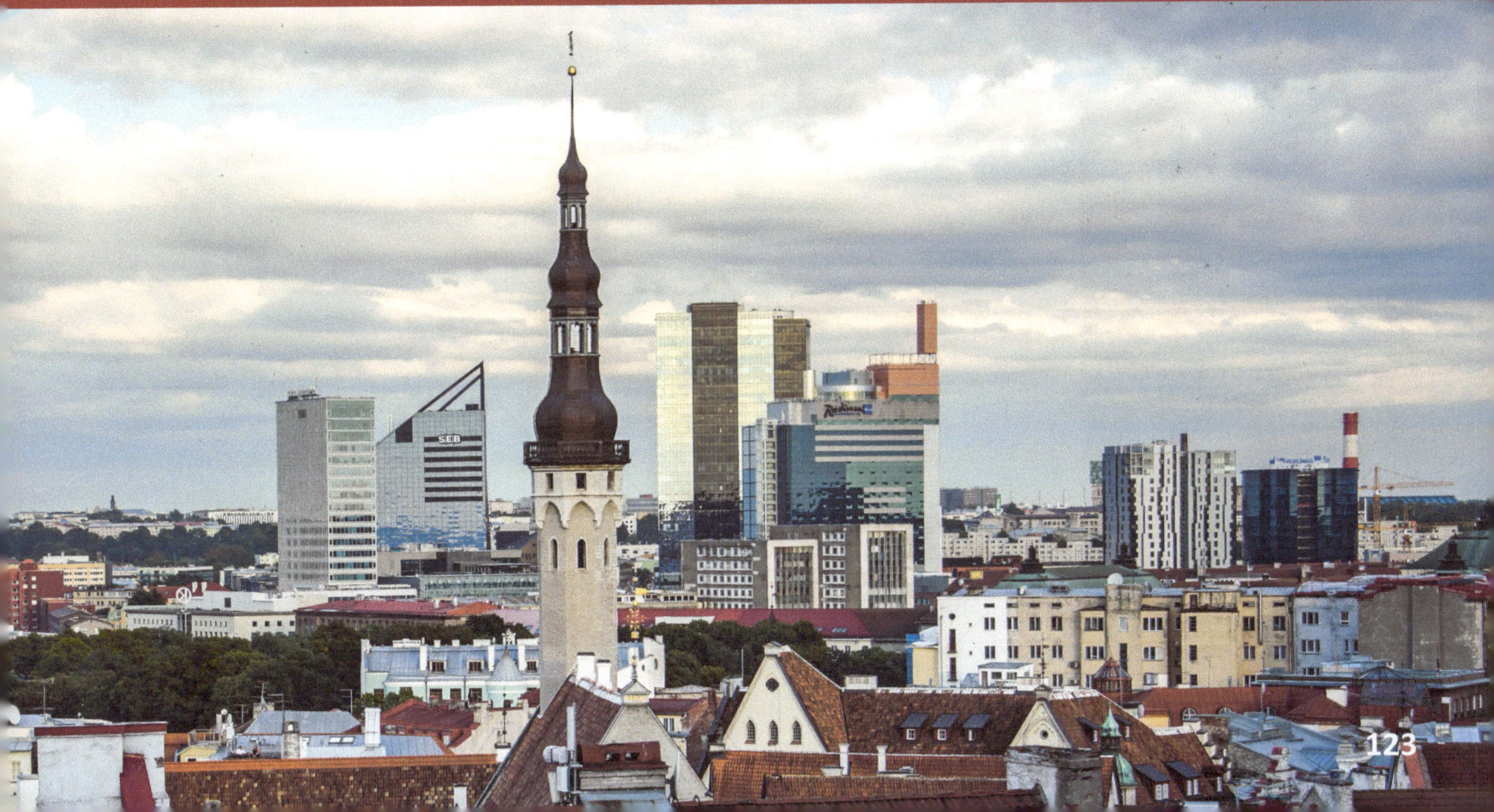

# Old and New

Because of its history, wars and recovery over the centuries, all cities in Europe combine the old and new in more or less elegant fashion. It often feels like you're in a collage of overlapping centuries. Sometimes the results are delightful, at other times the contrasts are rather bizzare.

The three examples, clockwise, starting on this page, are from Bucharest, Tallinn and Hamburg.

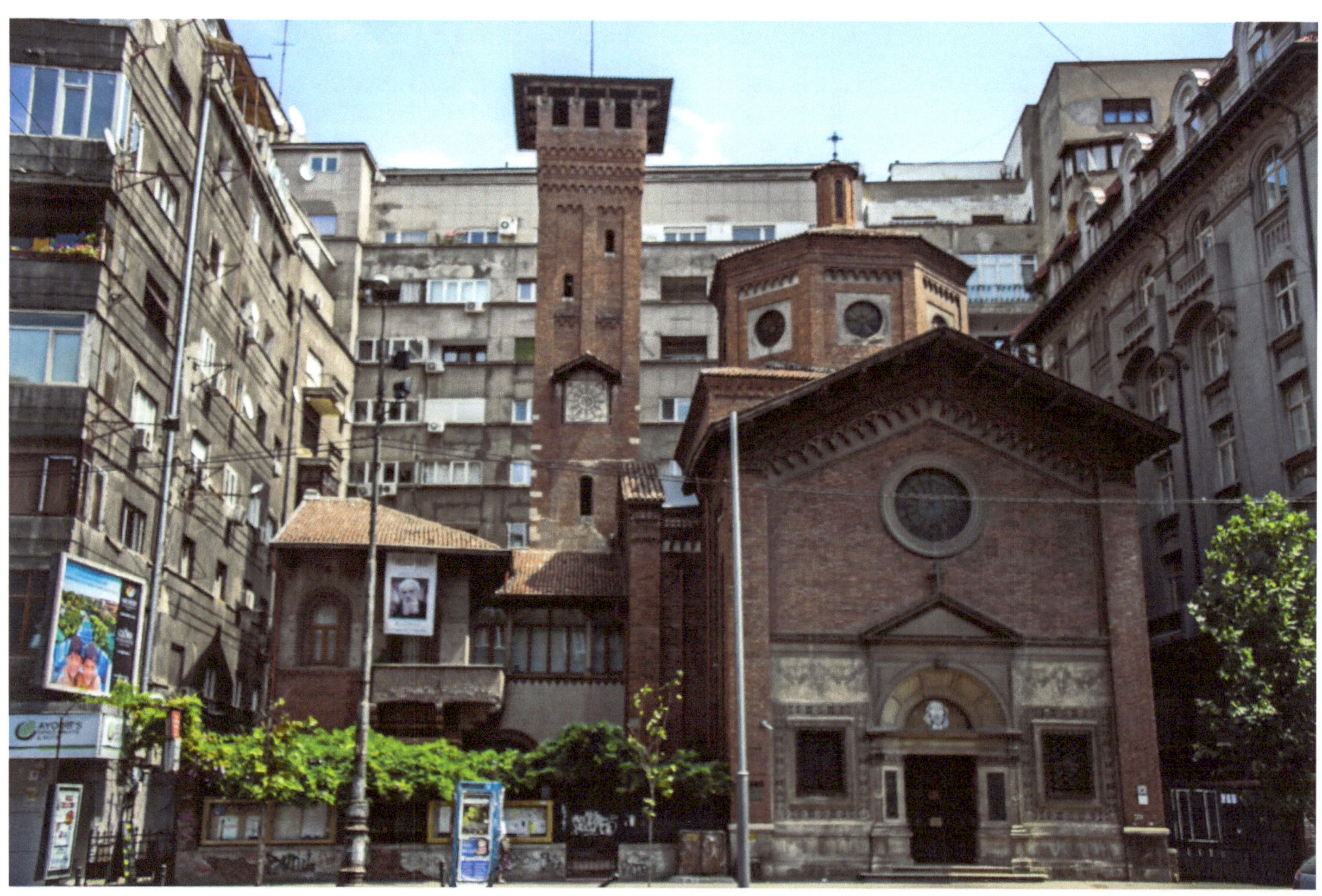

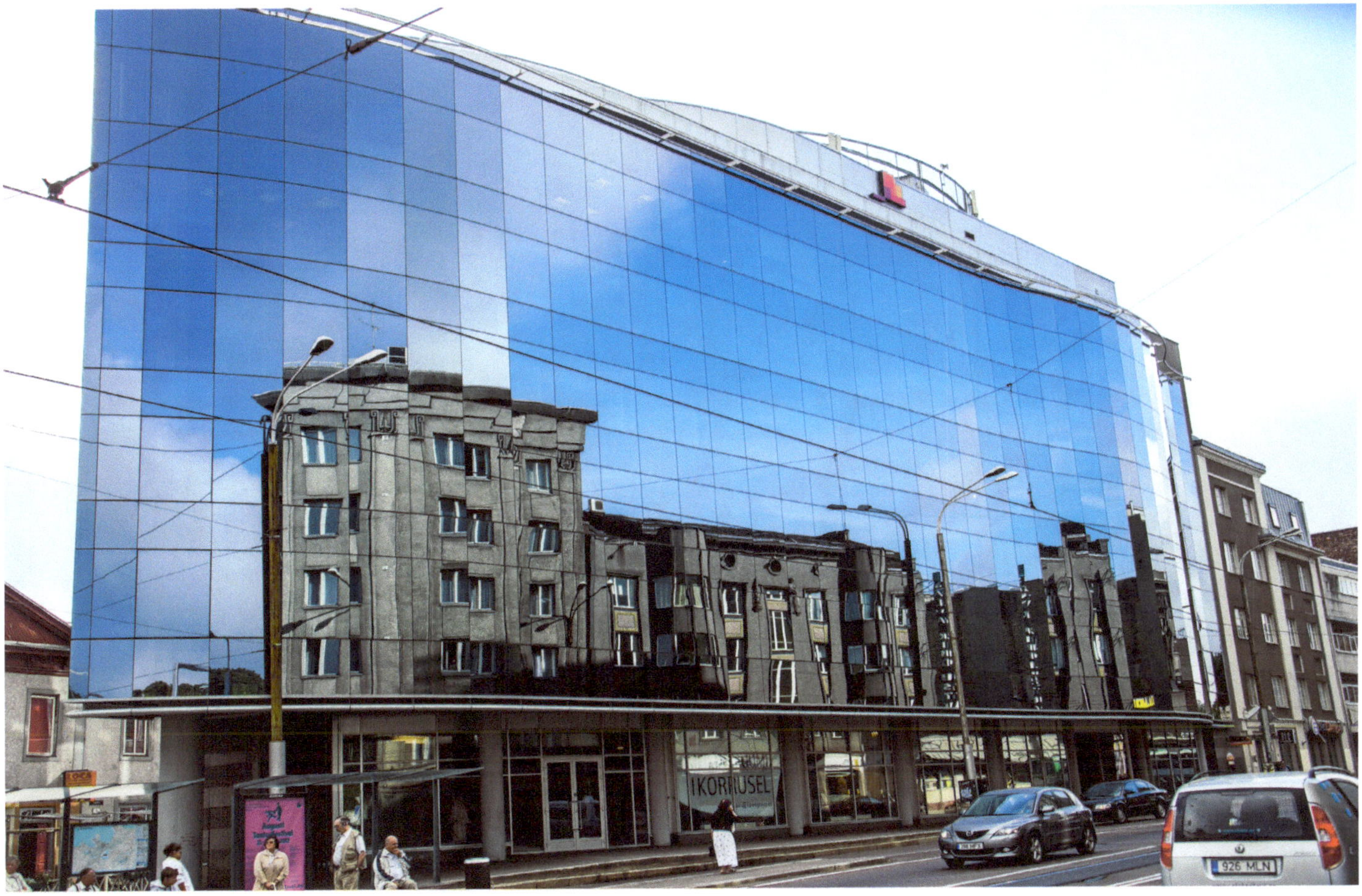

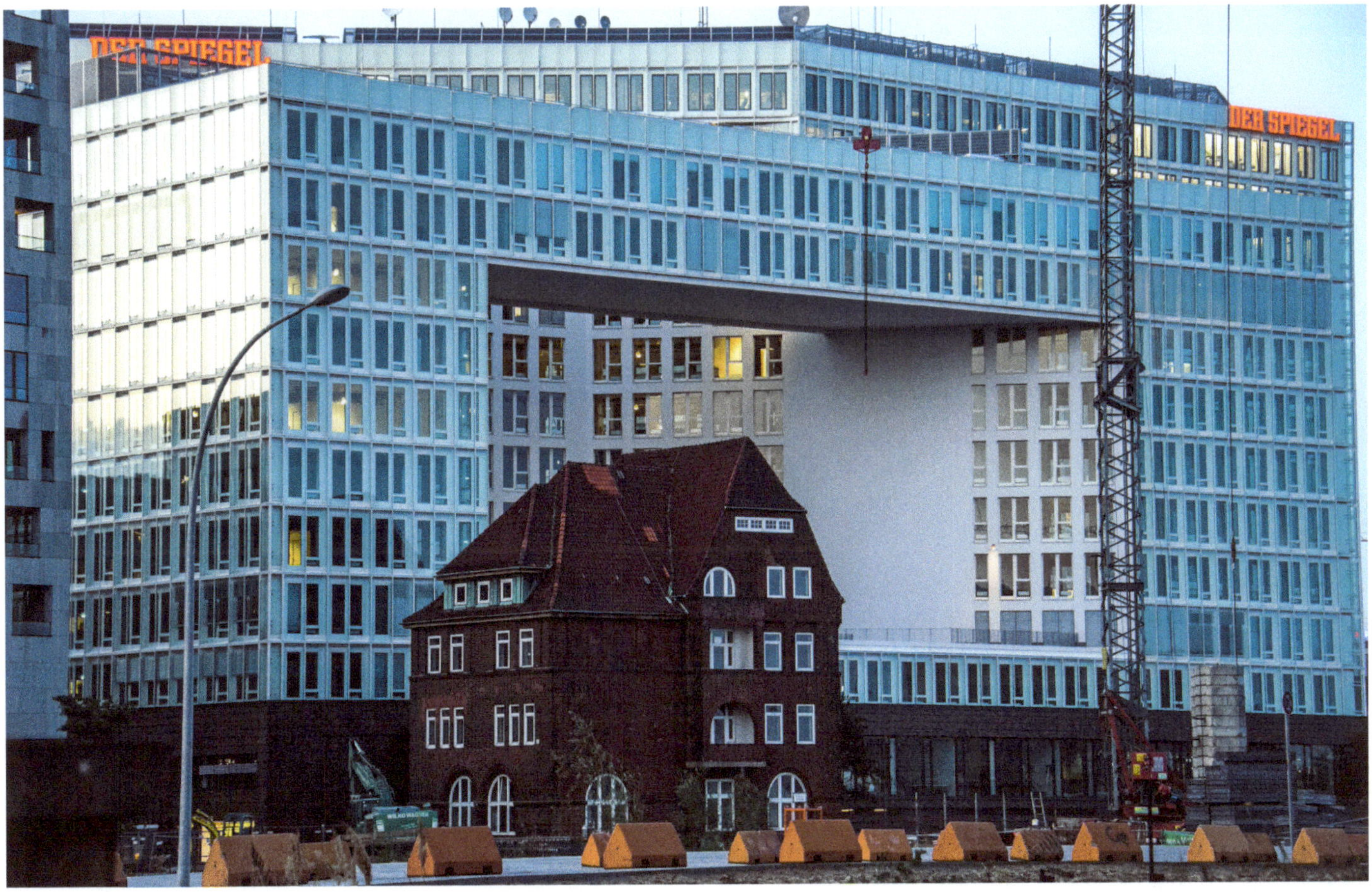
DER SPIEGEL
DER SPIEGEL

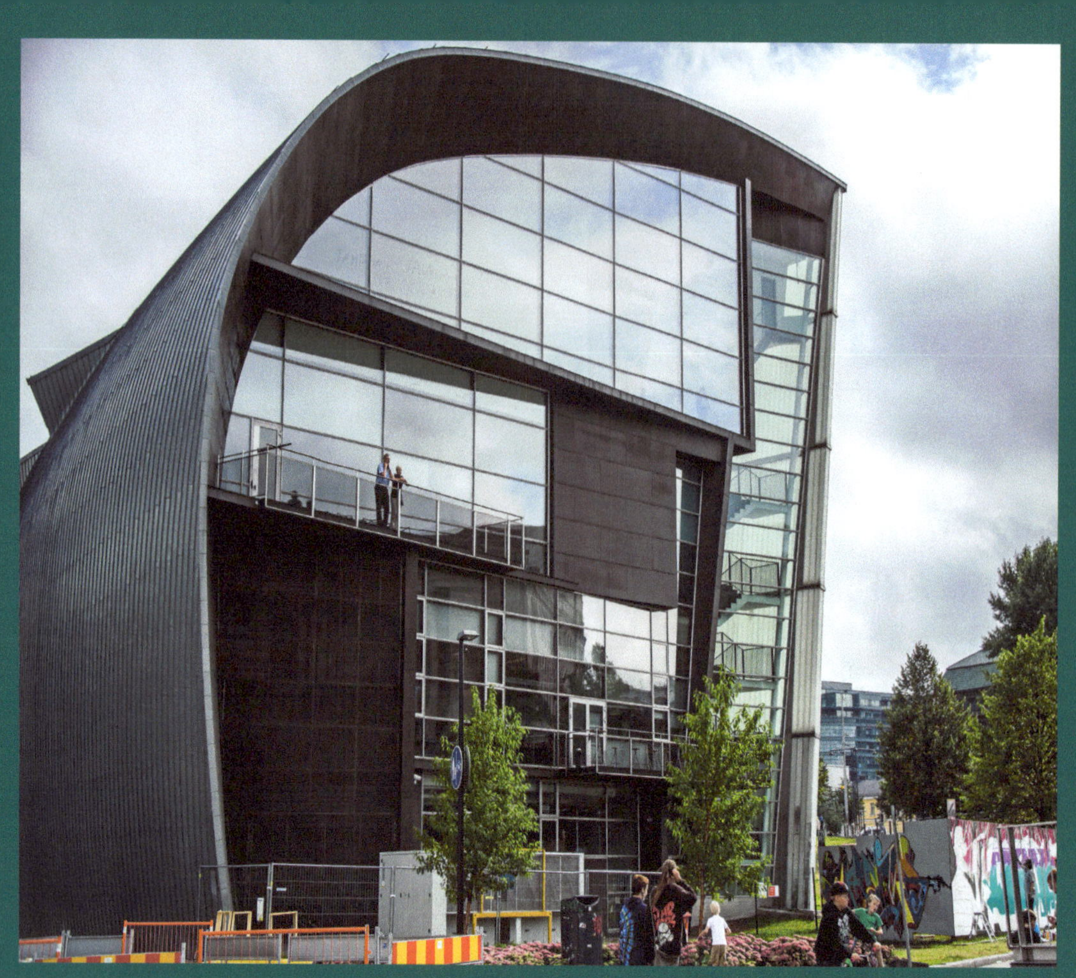

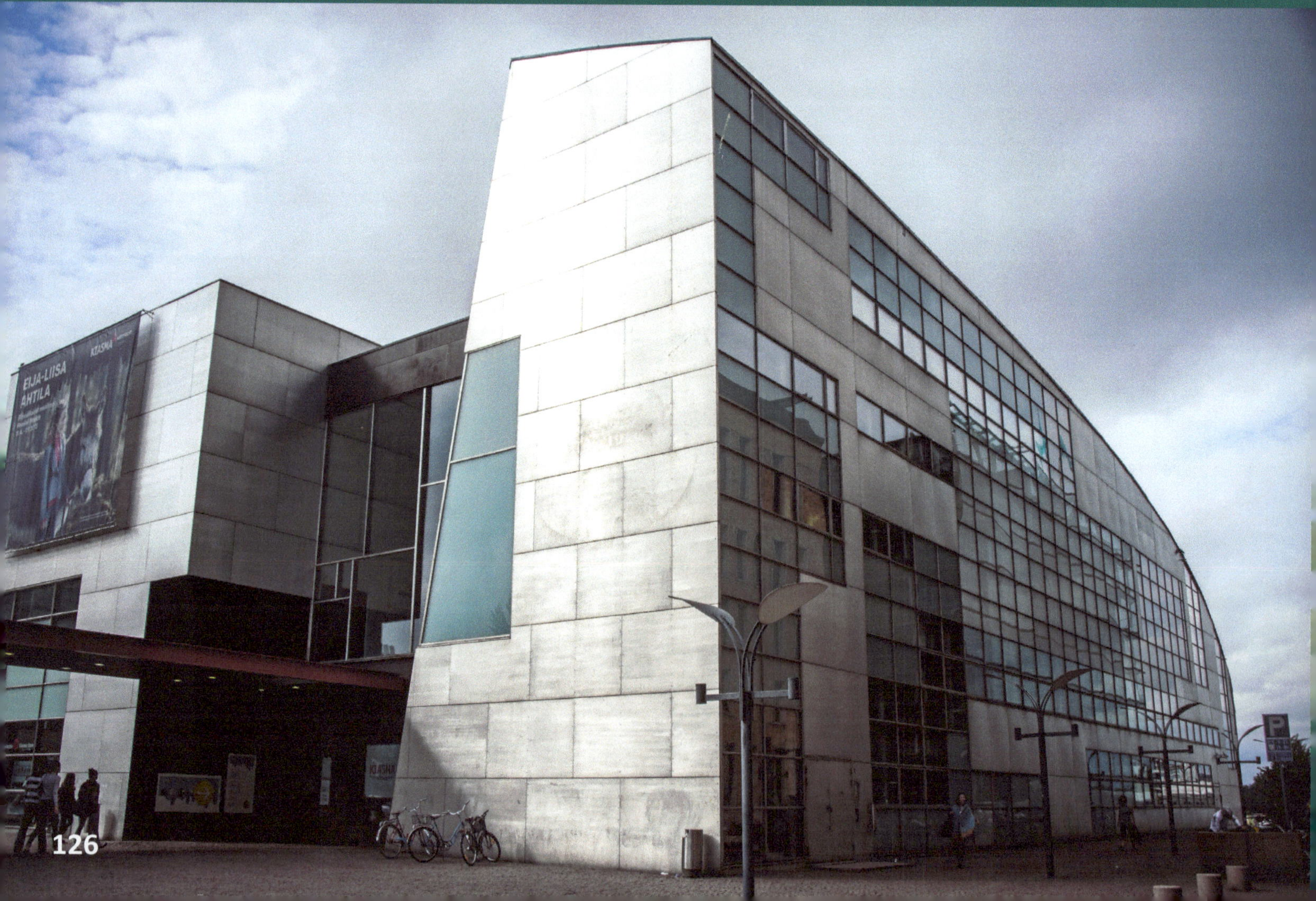

# 18

# HELSINKI

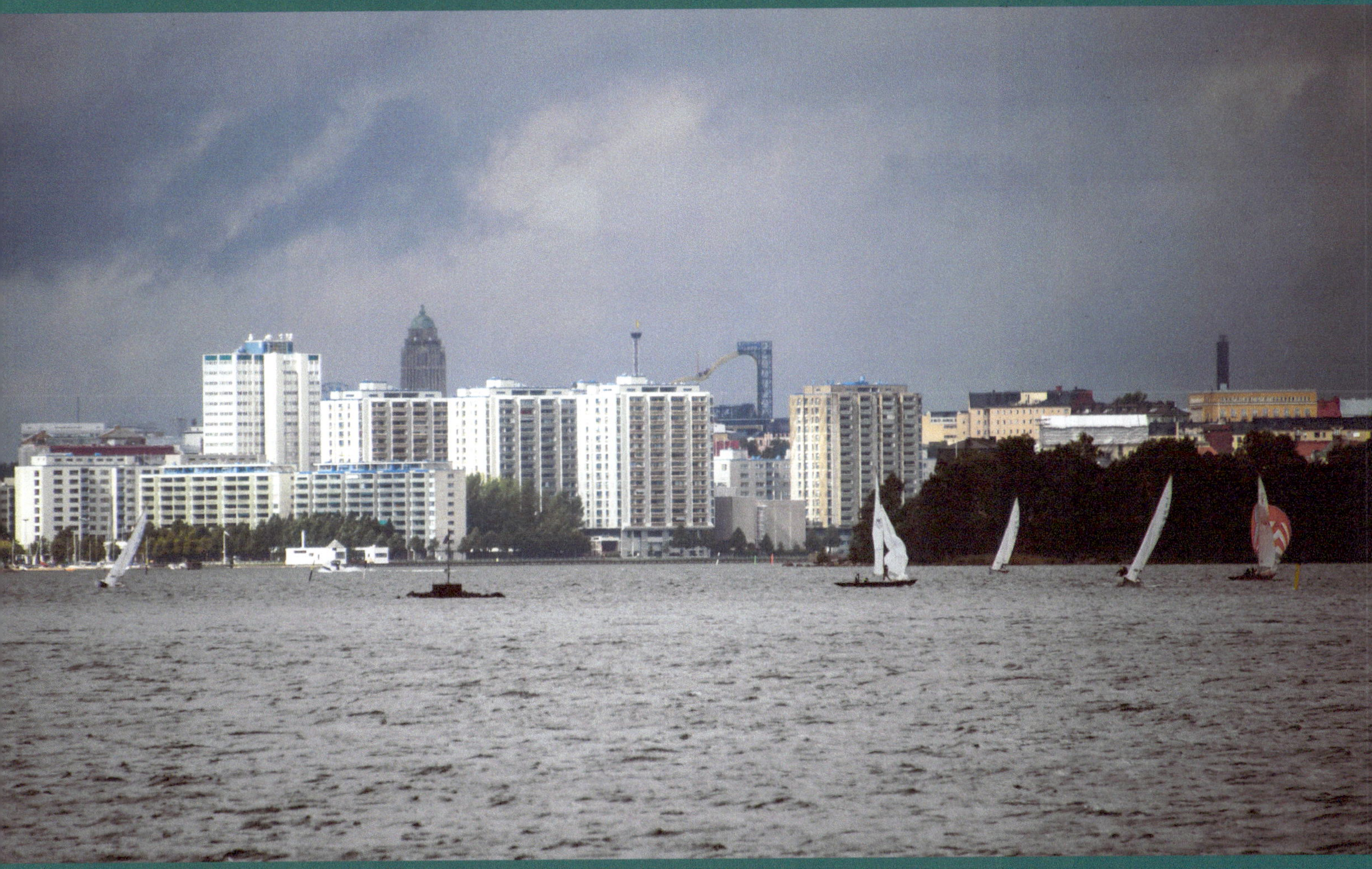

I took the ferry from Tallinn to Helsinki, a short, two-hour trip across the Gulf of Finland. The Finnish capital is a beautiful city—very clean, cosmopolitan and prosperous.

Everything is modern and inviting. You become so intent on seeing as much as you can, you almost forget to take photographs. Being a port city, it allowed me to sit in the harbor and take tours, although the weather started getting rainy again.

The Kiamsa Myseum for Contemporary Art on the opposite page was built after an architectural competition was held in 1993. It had 516 entries, and the winning design was by the only American participant, Steven Holl. The name is Finnish for "chiasma" and refers to an anatomical crossing or point of overlap.

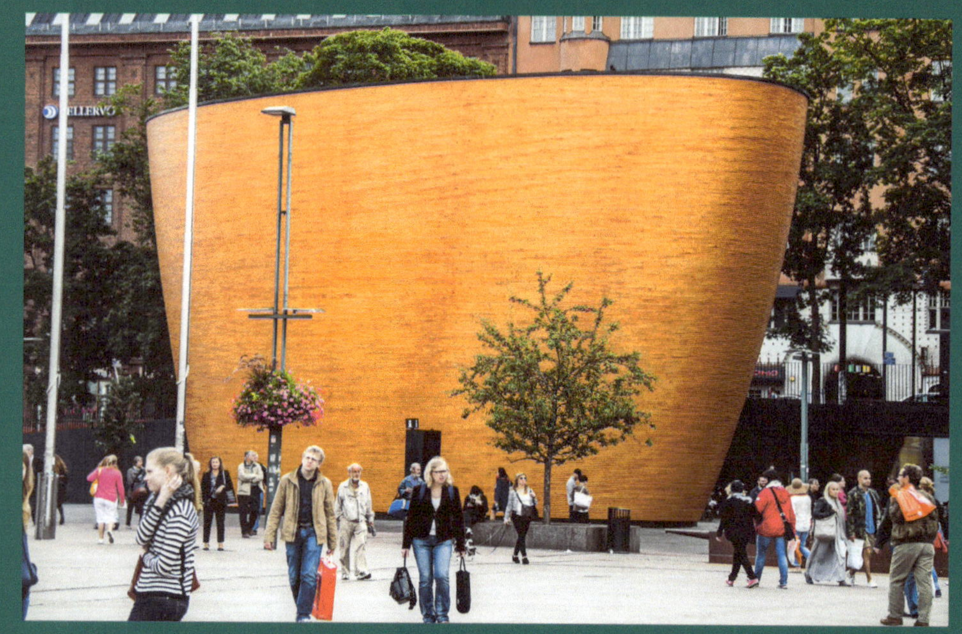

The Kamppi Chapel, also known as the Chapel of Silence, is located near the entrance to a large, underground shopping center in one of the busiest areas of Helsinki. Constructed in 2012, it offers respite and calm to anyone who wishes to make use of it, regardless of religion or philosophy. The Metro is part of the underground city.

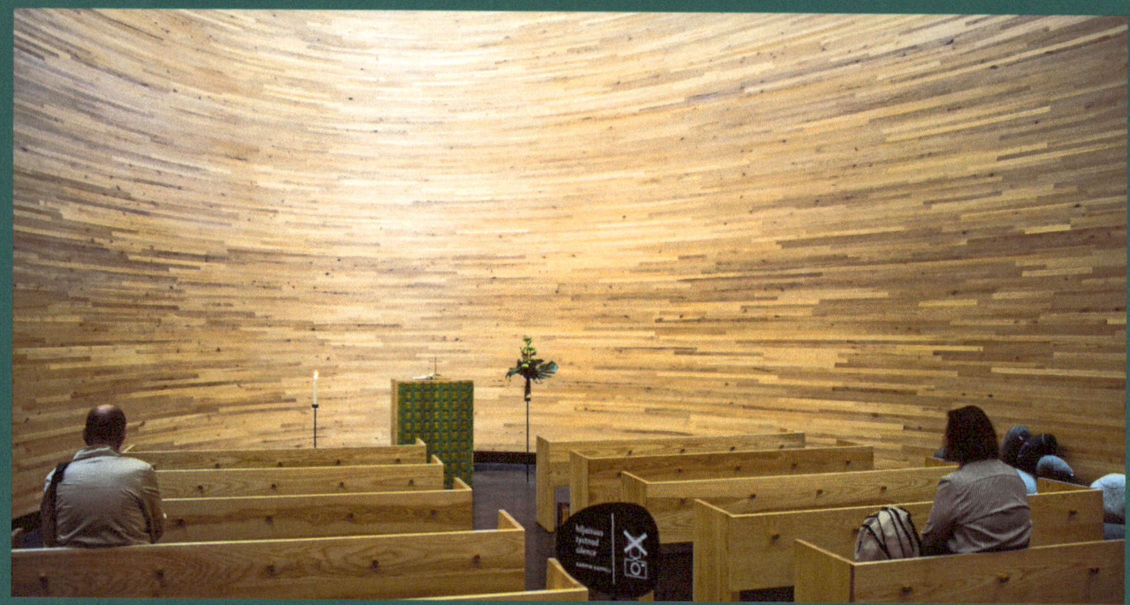

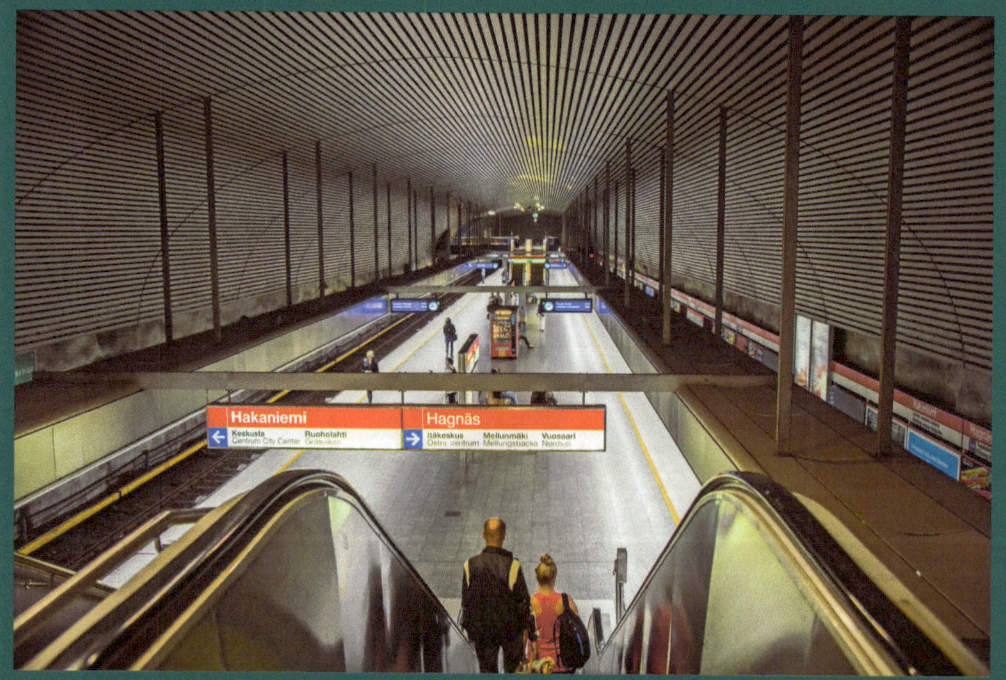

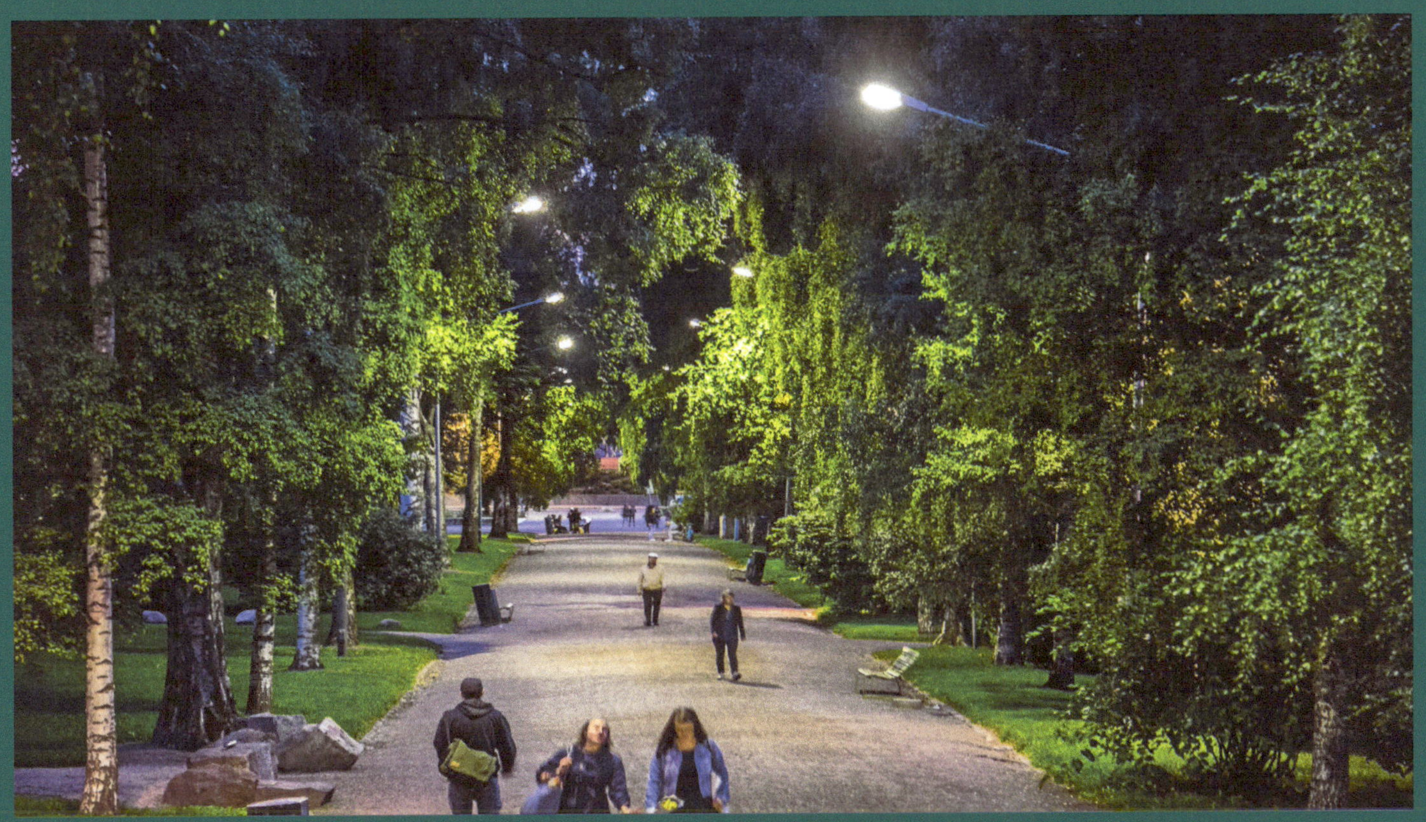

Helsinki has other areas of tranquilty throuhgout the city, like the beautiful Botanical Gardens, open late into the night. The women below are having a picnic in a park near the main square, waiting for the rain to stop.

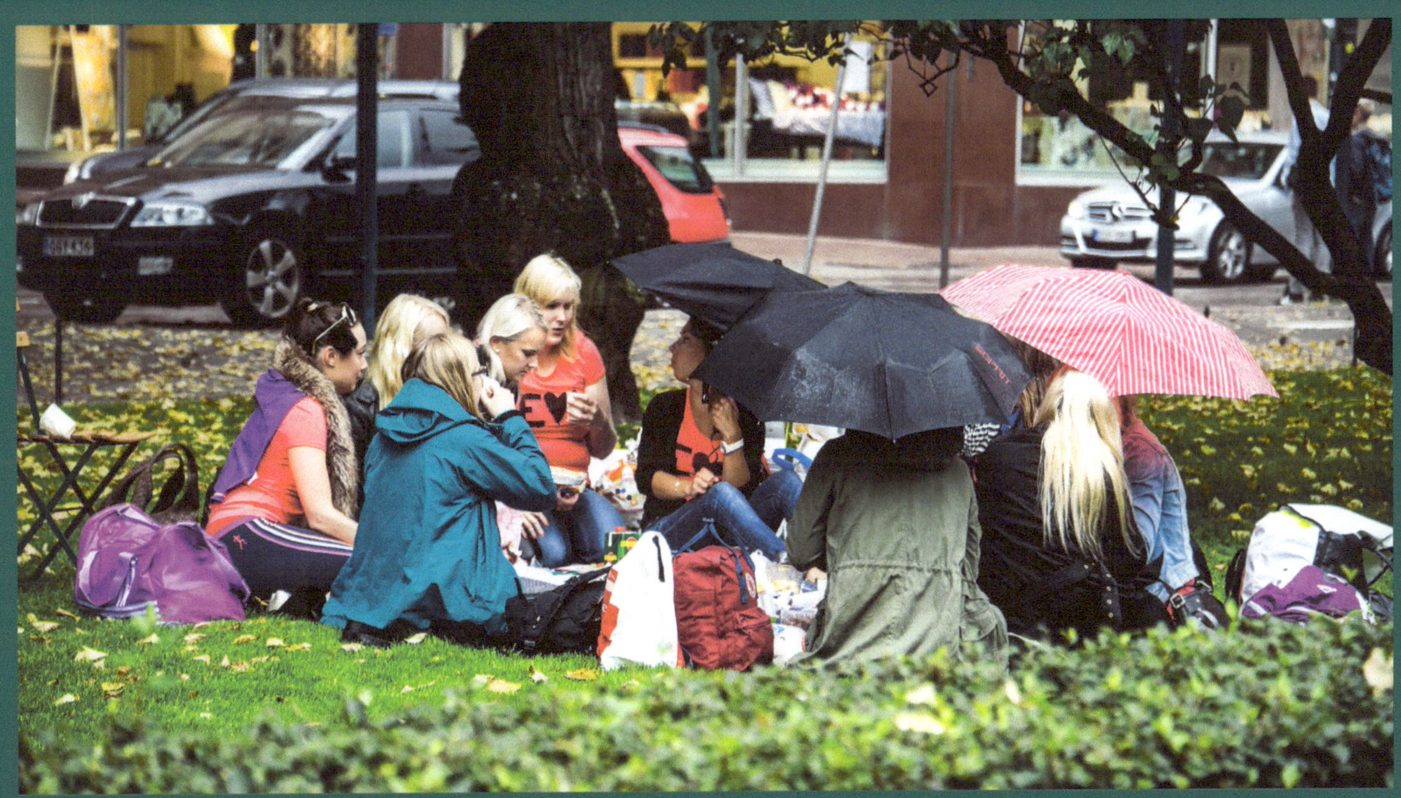

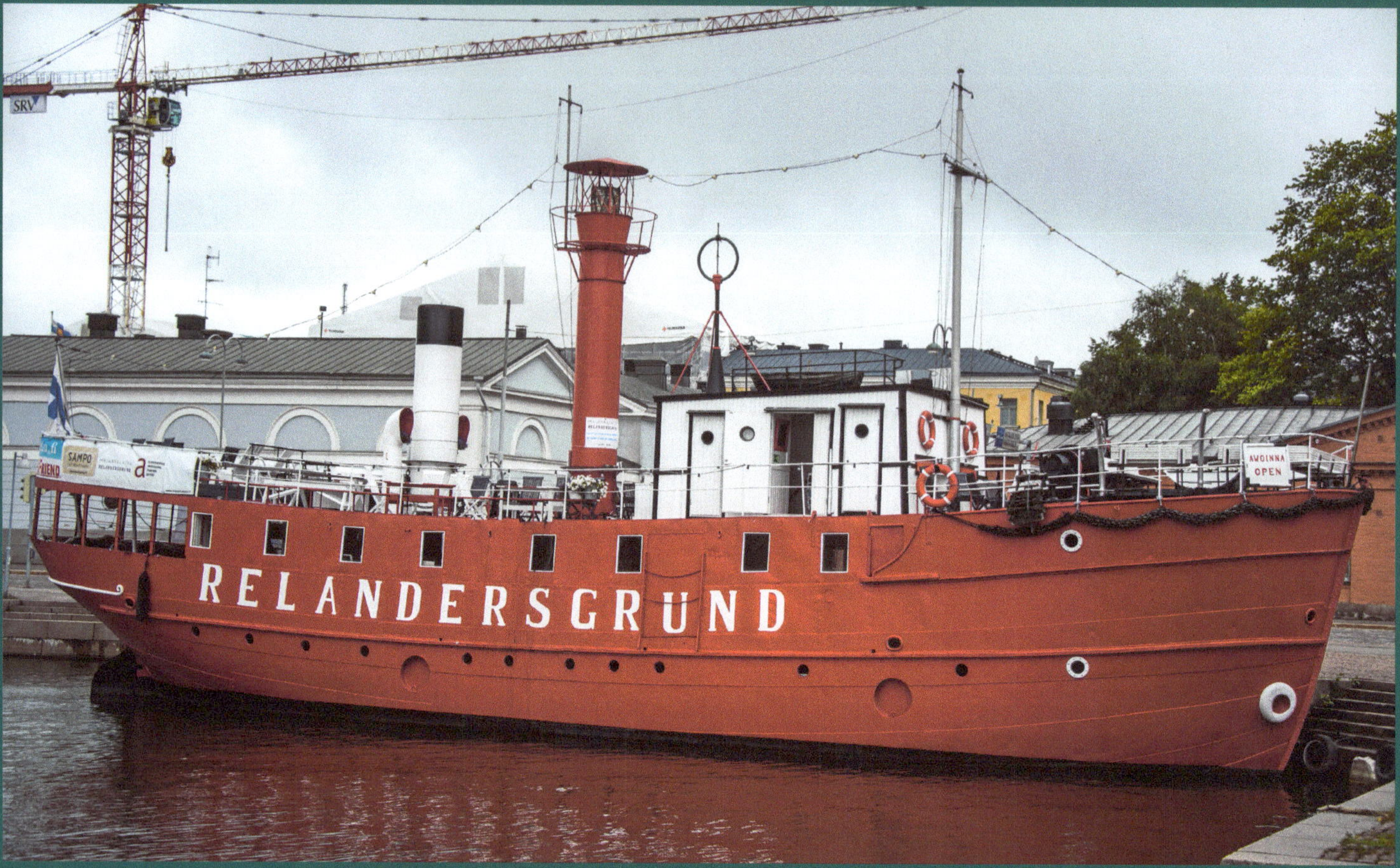
RELANDERSGRUND
AVOINNA
OPEN

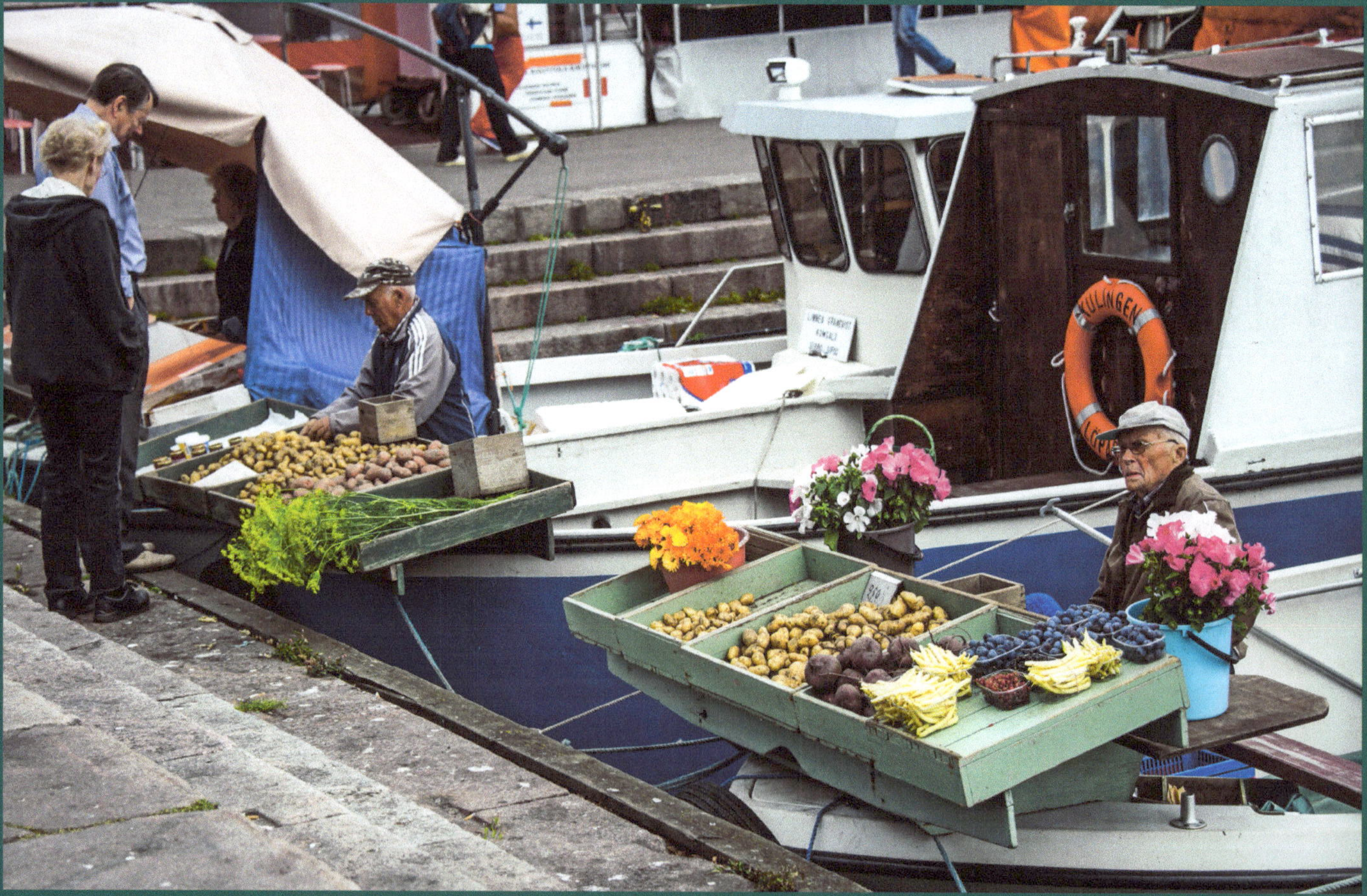

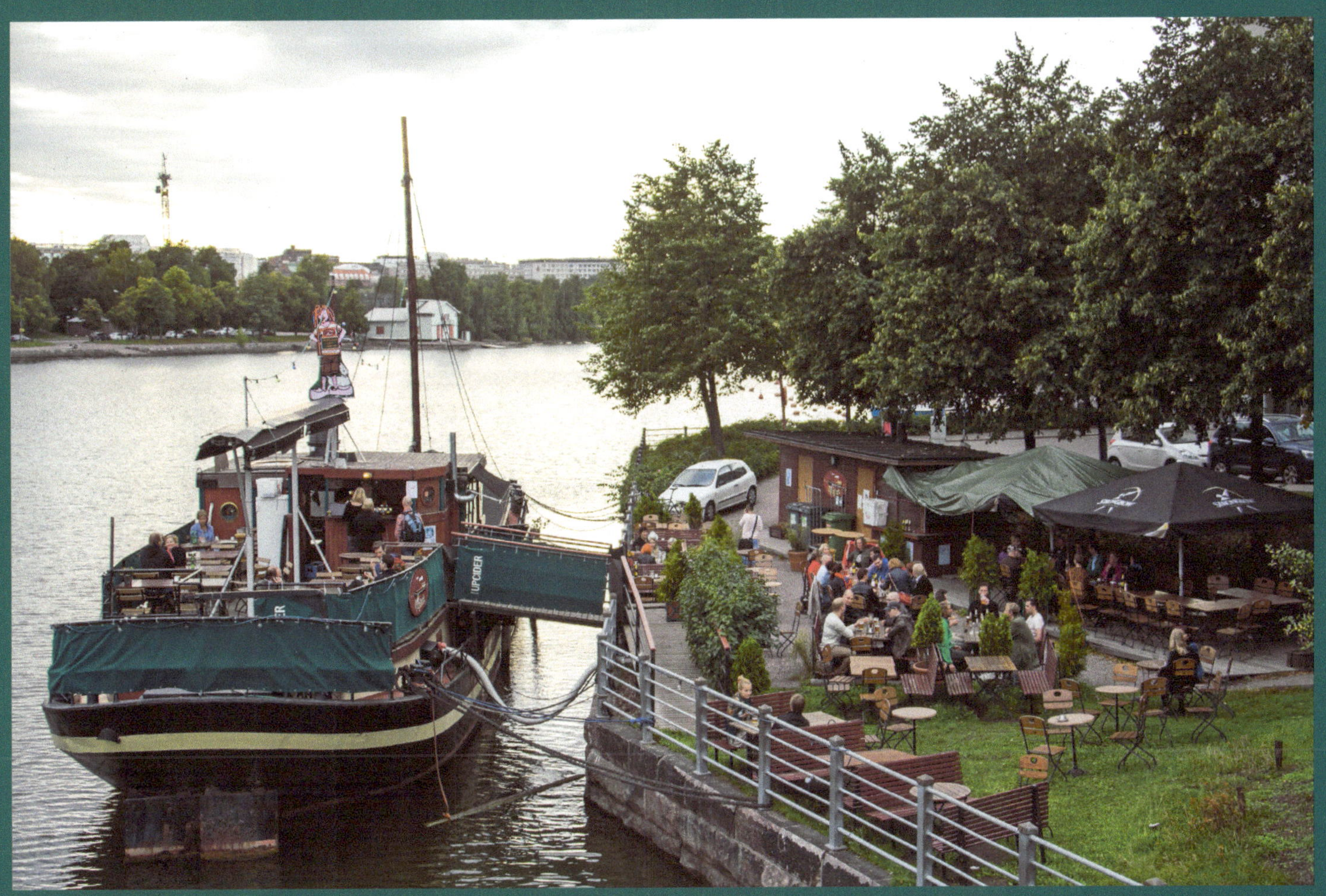

At the harbor, how could I not take a photograph of a boat freshly painted in such a wild color!?

On my way back to my hotel, I walked along the riverbank and found that restaurant-café on the river. In Helsinki harbor there is a big market all the time. You can buy crunchy little sardines and eat them with bread and beer.

I loved Helsinki, but I knew the trip was coming to an end and I had a decision to make. I had been on the road close to six weeks and could have gone to the other Scandinavian countries, but it was getting late, and I wanted some time to check out my old stomping grounds—Berlin, Hamburg, Cologne. So I decided to go home.

I inquired about a return flight to the States using my Lufthansa miles and was told there were seats on September 11 or 27. As I had a big photo job on the 27th, I had to go with the earlier flight, despite its association with the worst terrorist attack on the United States. My return flight was from Frankfurt.

I knew that I wanted to go to Berlin, Hamburg and Cologne before returning to the United States. They were my home, and I was curious as to how they had changed, so I got on a plane and flew to Berlin.

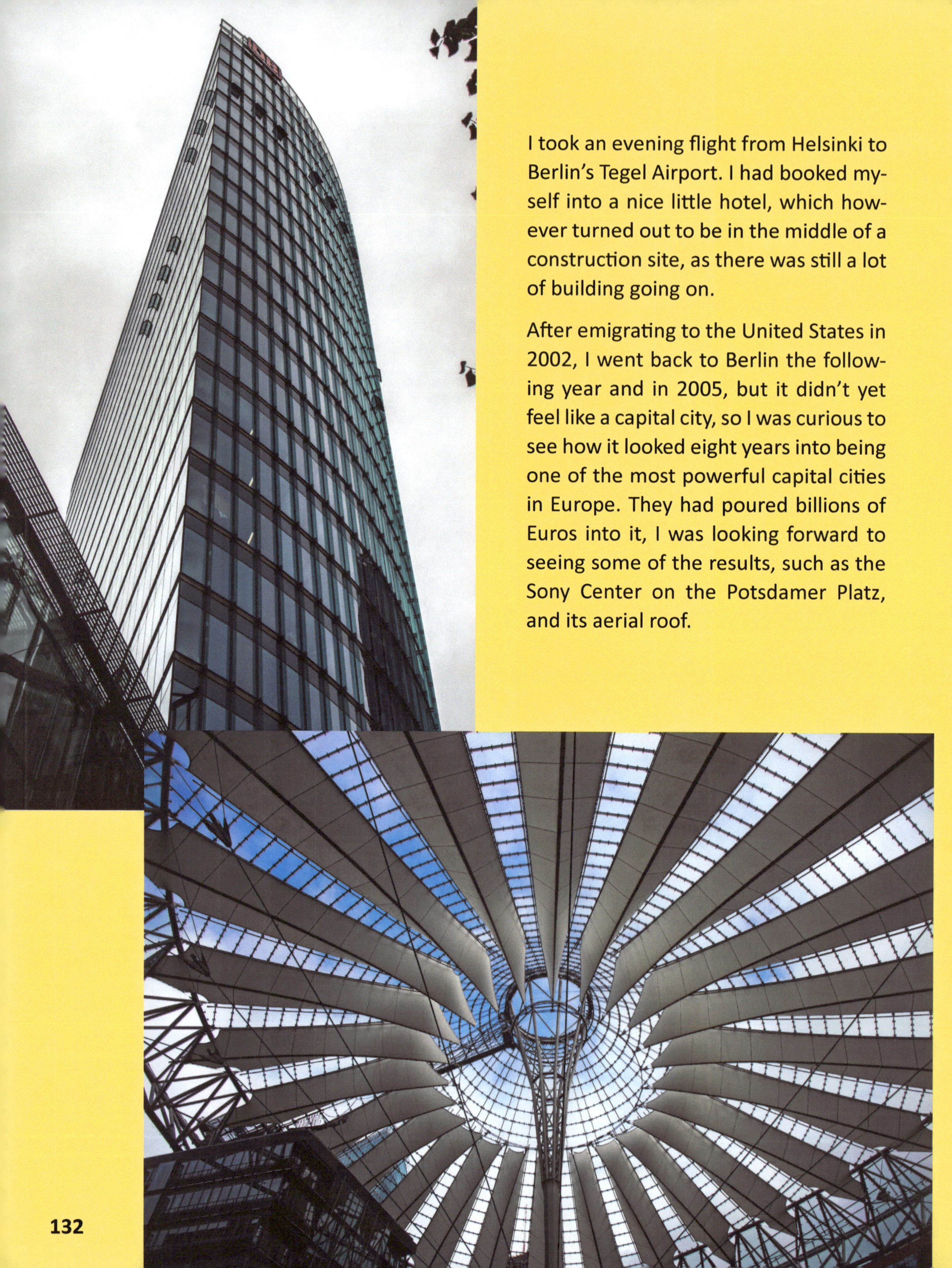

I took an evening flight from Helsinki to Berlin's Tegel Airport. I had booked myself into a nice little hotel, which however turned out to be in the middle of a construction site, as there was still a lot of building going on.

After emigrating to the United States in 2002, I went back to Berlin the following year and in 2005, but it didn't yet feel like a capital city, so I was curious to see how it looked eight years into being one of the most powerful capital cities in Europe. They had poured billions of Euros into it, I was looking forward to seeing some of the results, such as the Sony Center on the Potsdamer Platz, and its aerial roof.

# 19

# BERLIN

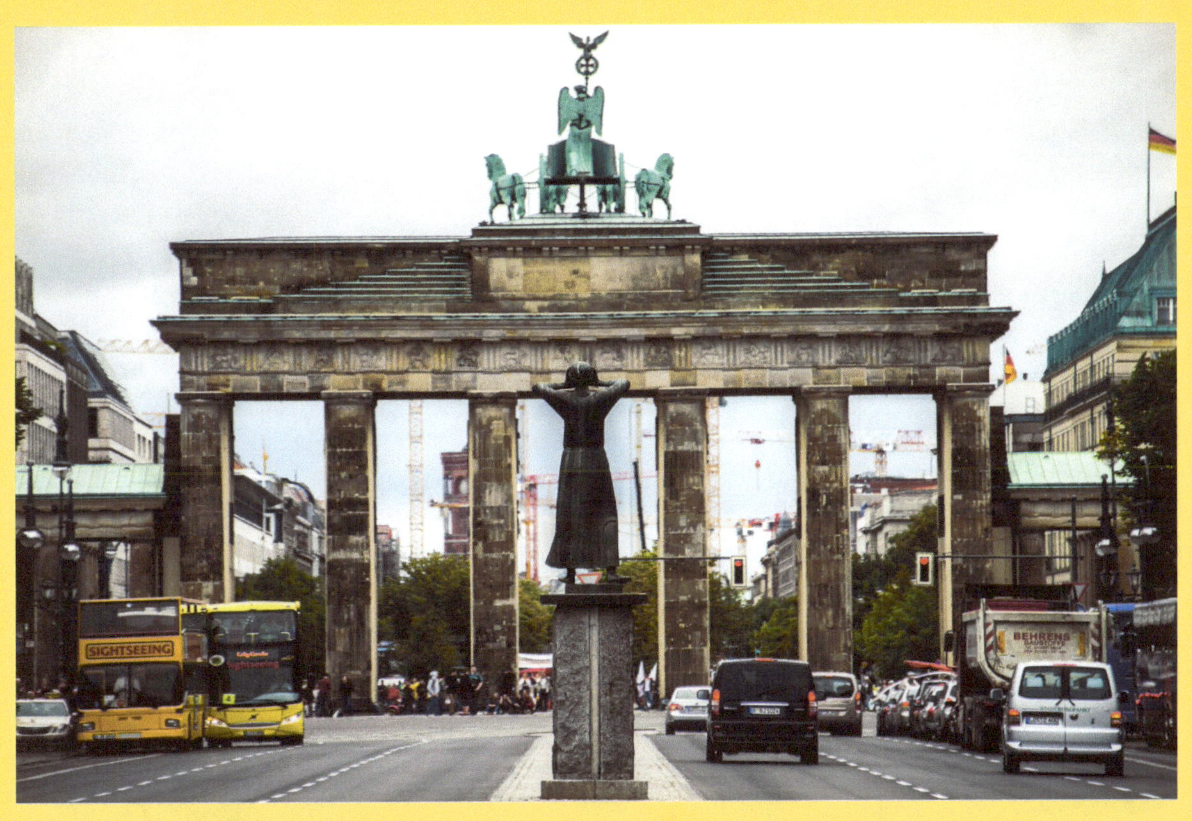


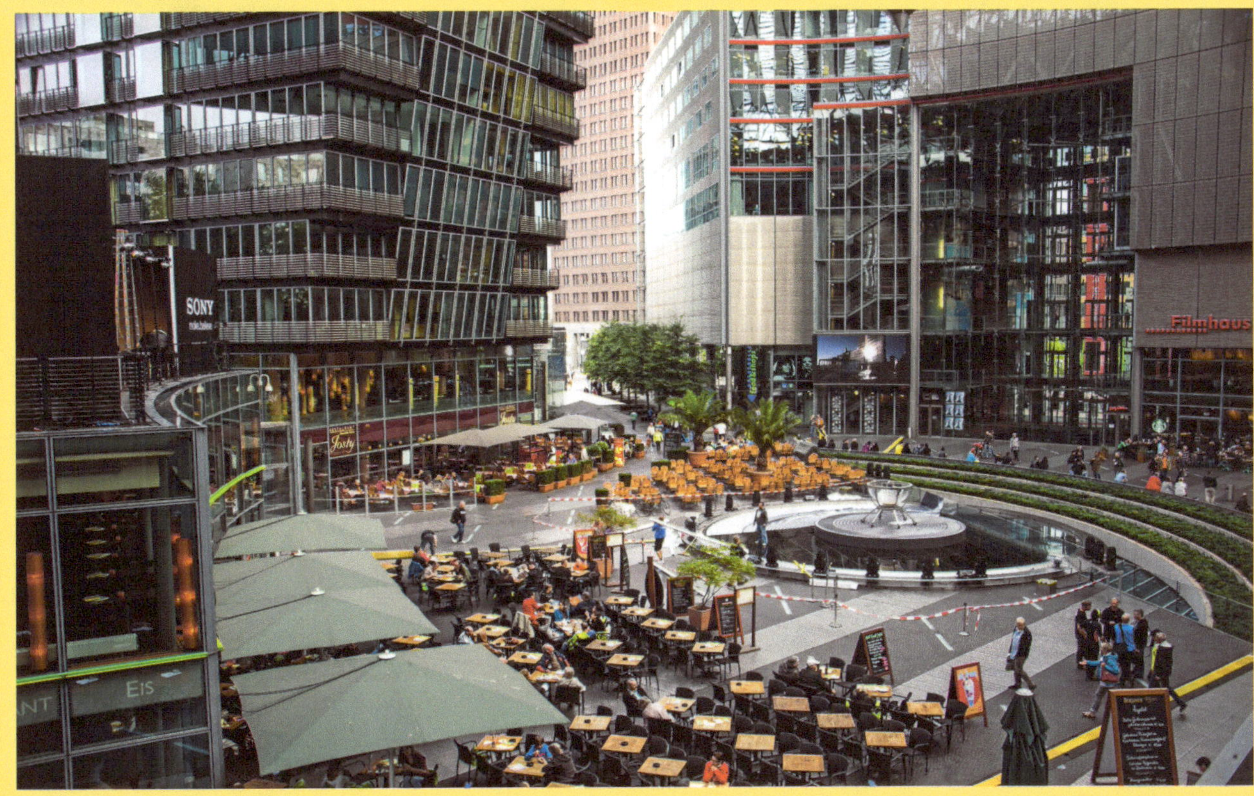

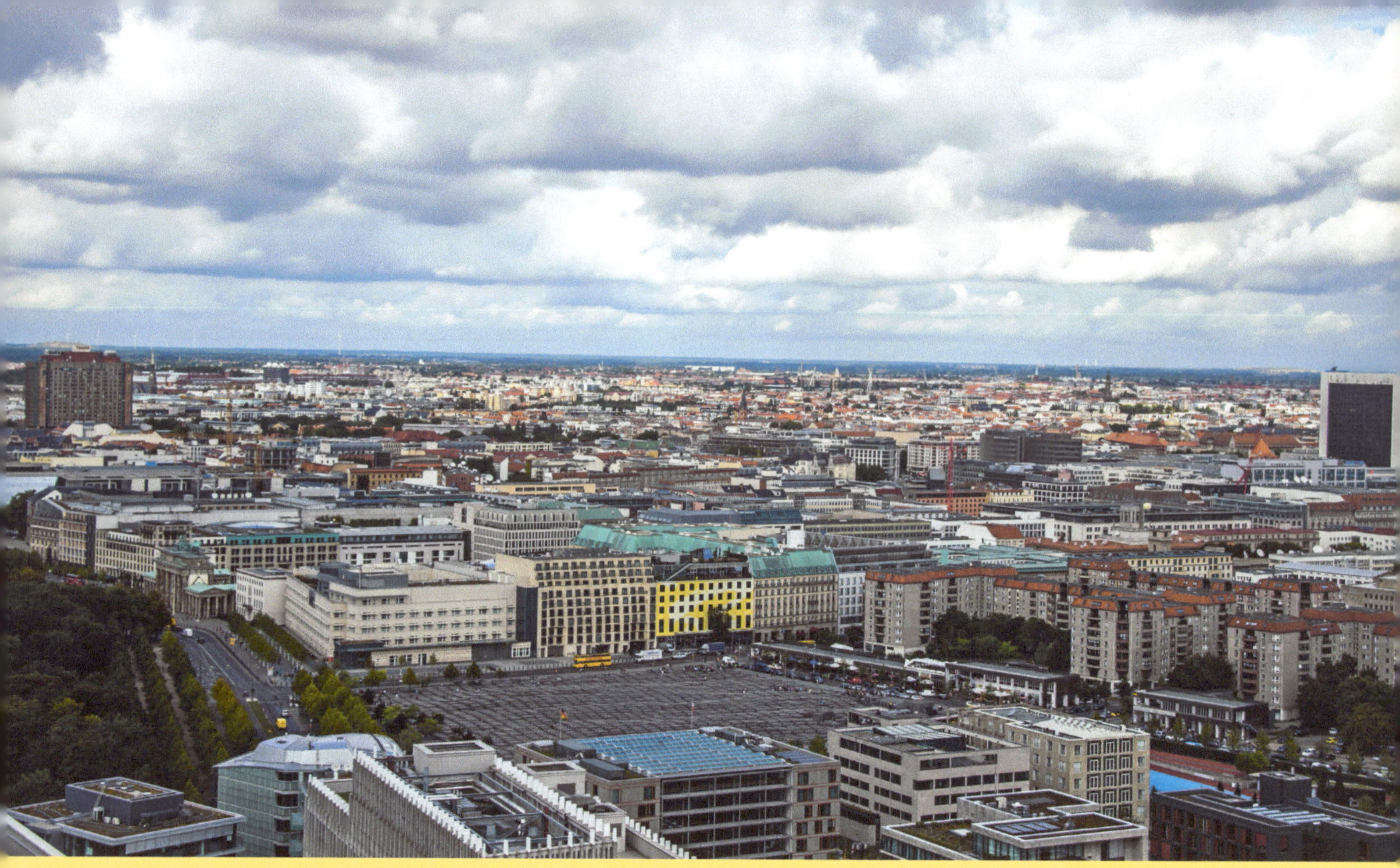

At the *Potsdamer Platz* is the 25-story-tall Kollhoff Building whose elevator—the fastest in Europe—takes just 20 seconds to get to the top. There, visitors can go to an open-air platform for amazing panoramic views of Berlin.

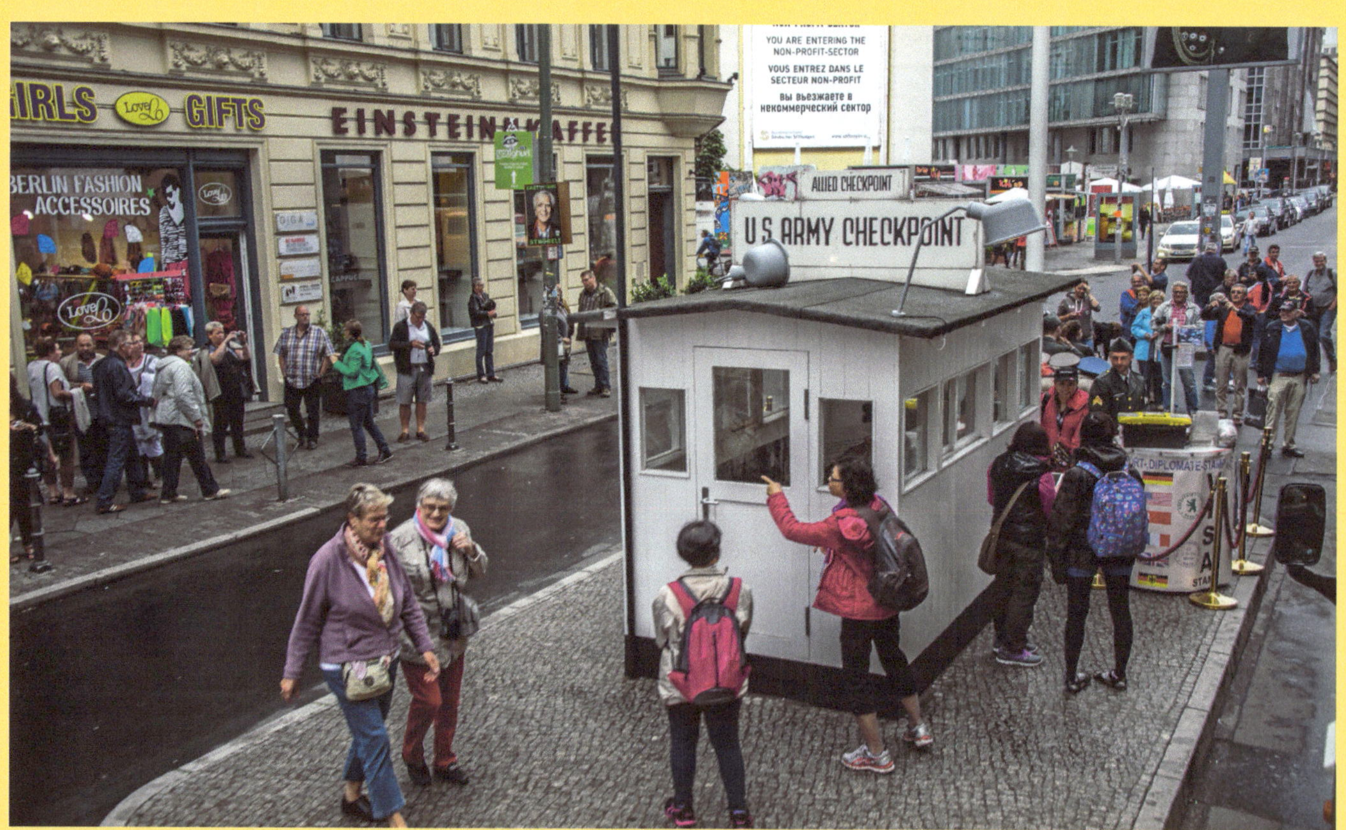

I met with some old colleagues from the music business and did a lot of walking by myself, and I'm glad I did. It was wonderful coming home and feeling that nothing had changed in my attitude toward Germany and Berlin, which was becoming a fantastic capital city.

*Unter den Linden*, the most famous boulevard in Berlin, was a construction site. I went through the Brandenburg Gate (previous page), but I couldn't see the famous *Gedächtnisskirche* (World War II memorial church), because it was surrounded by scaffolding from exterior renovations.

Checkpoint Charlie is a reminder of the Cold War and the division of Berlin into East and West, as is this sculpture with its broken links. Created by husband-and-wife sculptors Martin Matschinsky and Brigitte Matschinsky-Denninghof, and installed in 1987, it's called "Berlin." Even though the Wall came down in 1989, it has been kept there as a reminder of that era in German history.

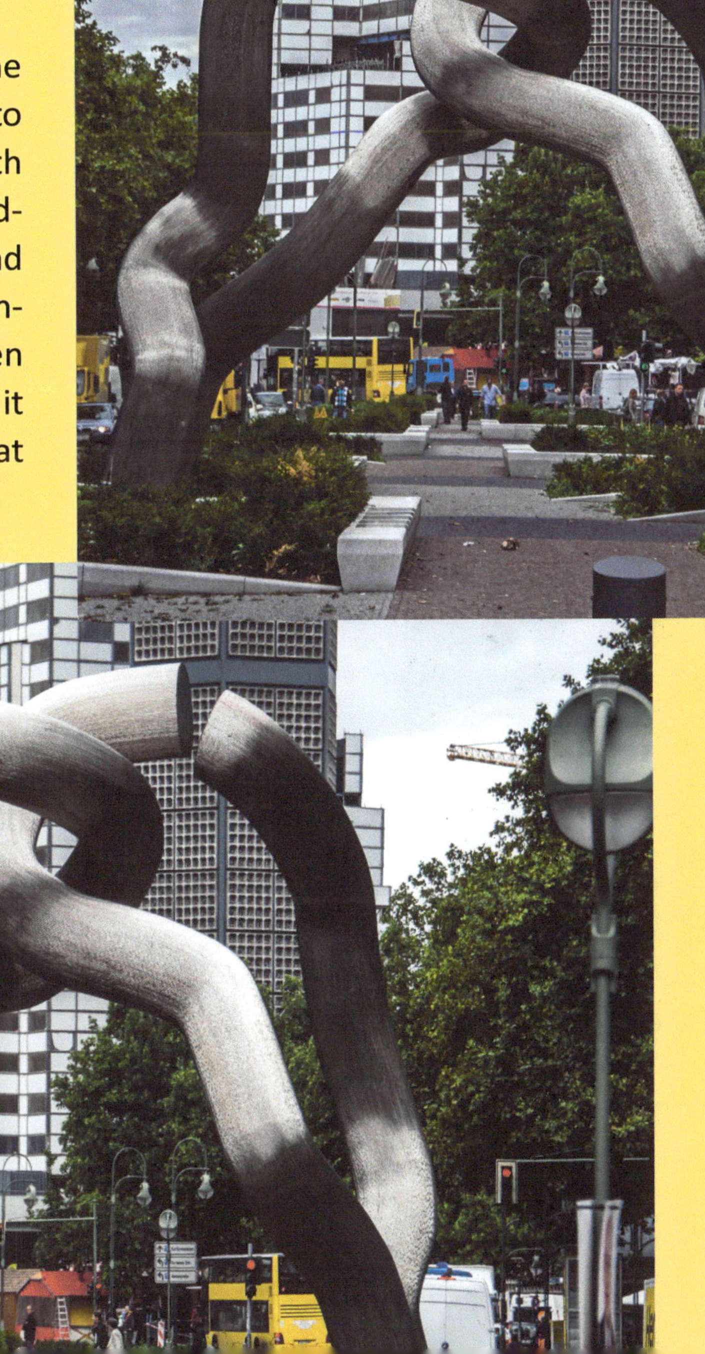

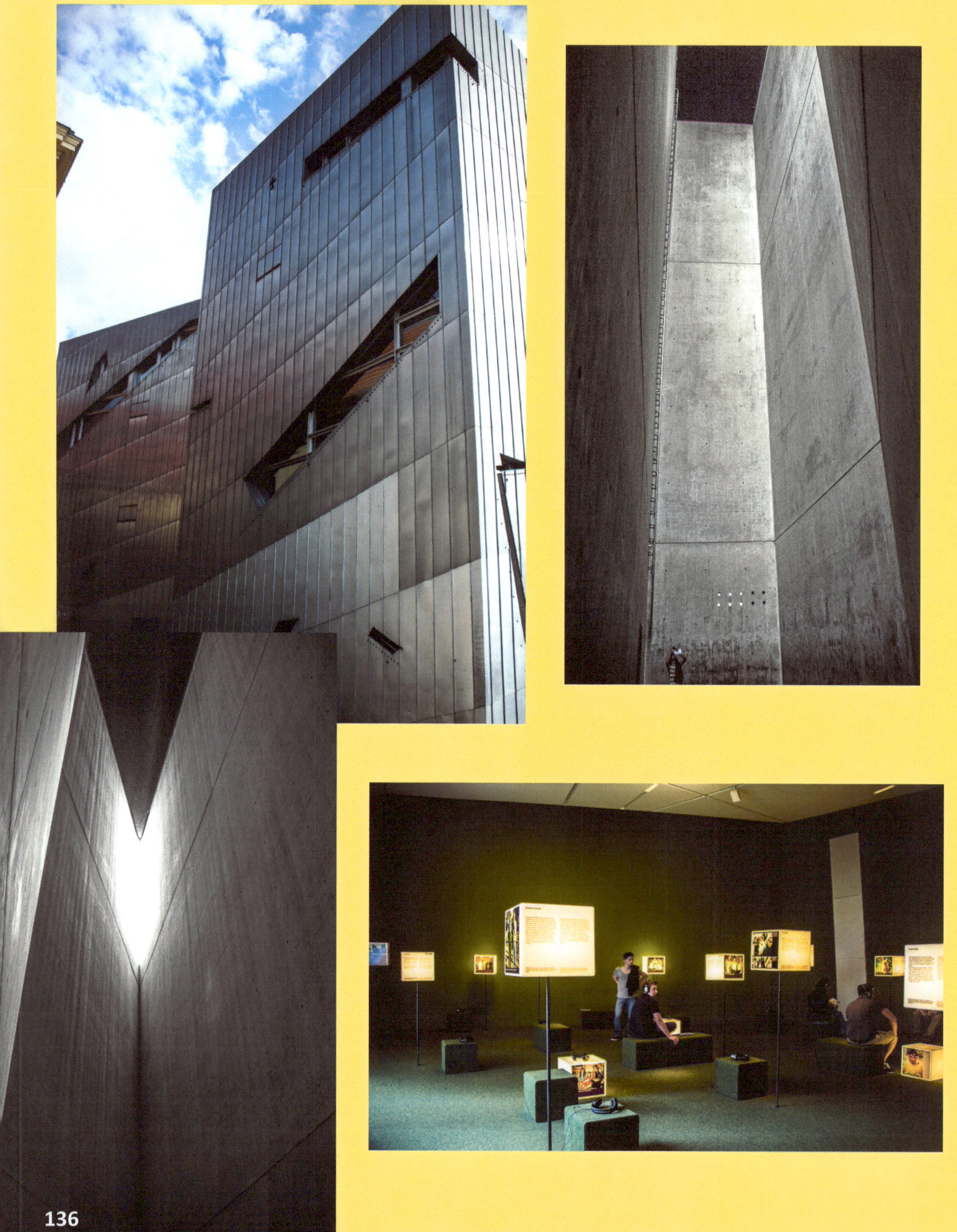

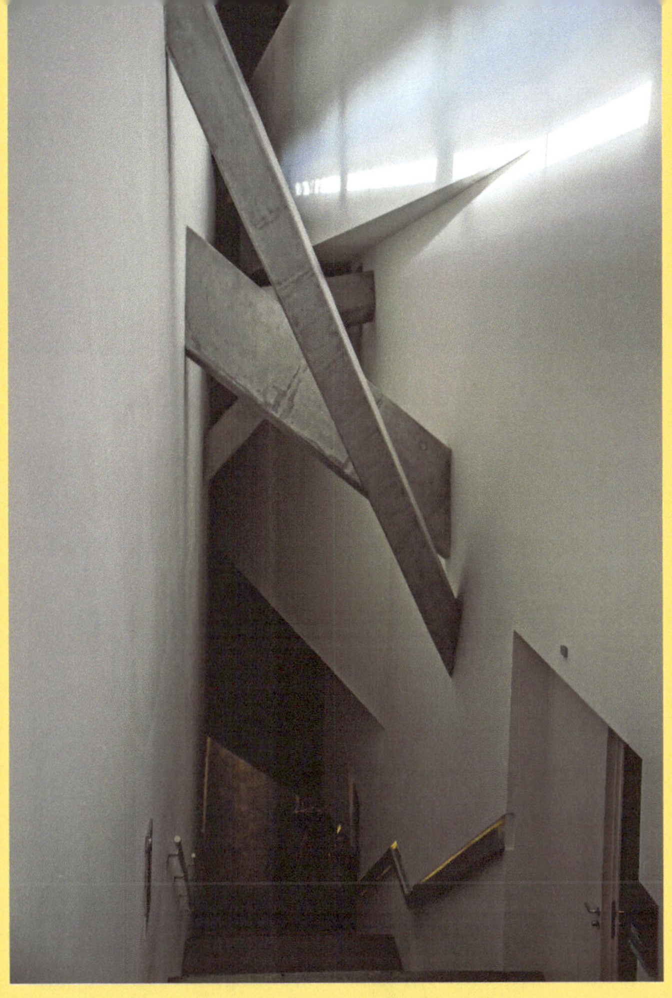

I hadn't been to the new Jewish Museum on Berlin's *Lindenstrasse*, which opened in 2001 and is one of the largest Jewish museums in Europe. It was definitely one of the highlights—the architecture, the emotions it evokes when you're inside it. As I walked around a corner inside the museum, I saw the man below sitting there on his own in this dark green environment, and I thought it looked beautiful. He was looking at the video screen display, which is constantly changing.

I stayed in Berlin for three days and bought a German rail pass at the newly built Berlin central train station, which is a work of art in itself. I got there early and spent two hours wandering around before I got my train to Hamburg.

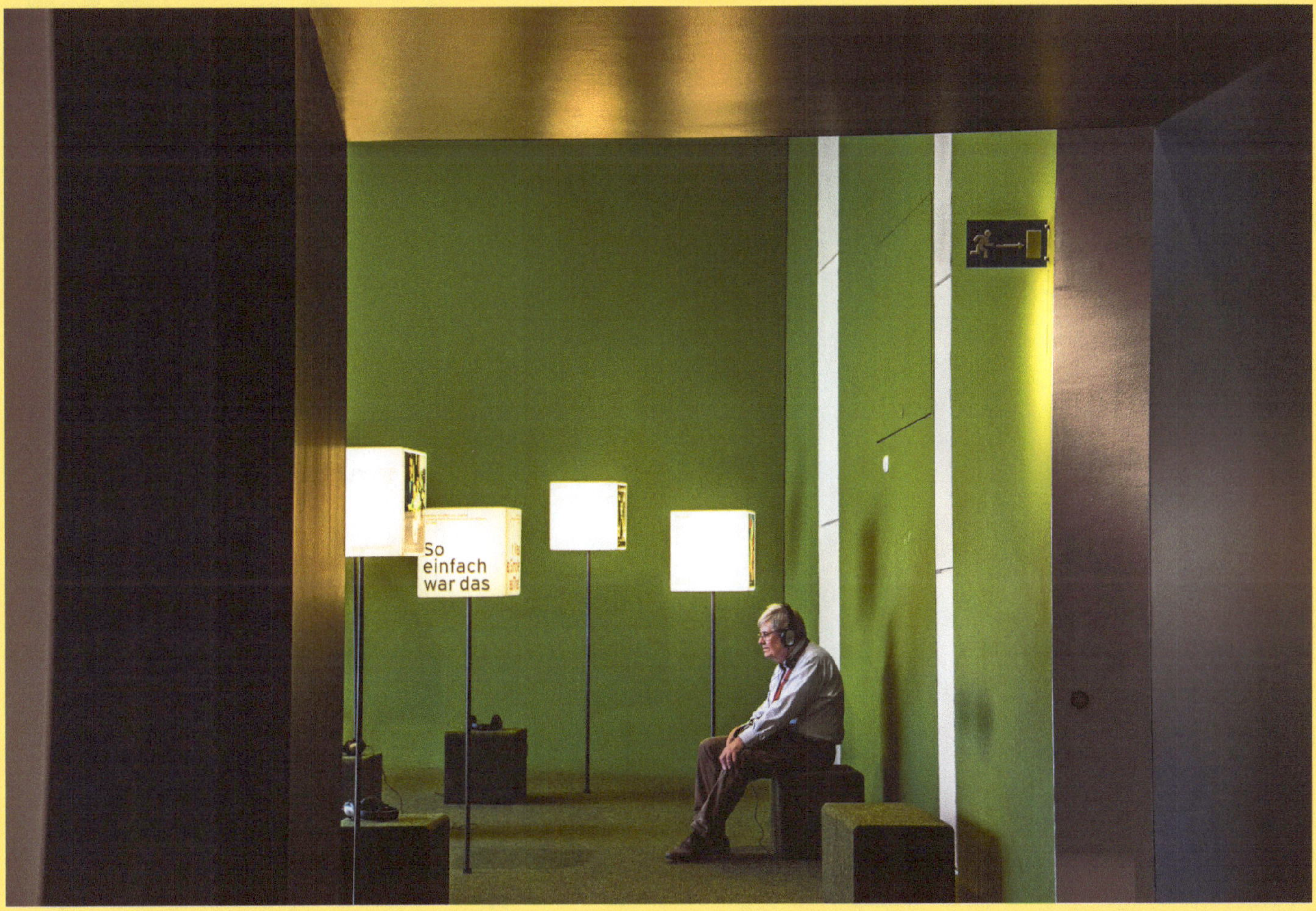

# KITSCH

For all its modernity and 21st-century edginess, Europe has plenty of oldtime displays of sentimentality and *Gemütlichkeit* (coziness).

The Germans gave us the word *kitsch* for tacky art and knickknacks, and they have plenty of it, as the two versions of the Berliner Bear, the totem animal of the city, here demonstrate, and the row of metallic sun worshippers and ice cream cone in Cologne below.

But there are lots of examples in other parts of Europe. The blonde, braided Brunhilde is from Estonia. The tippler in green Lederhosen stands in Bucharest. The donkey is from Santorini.

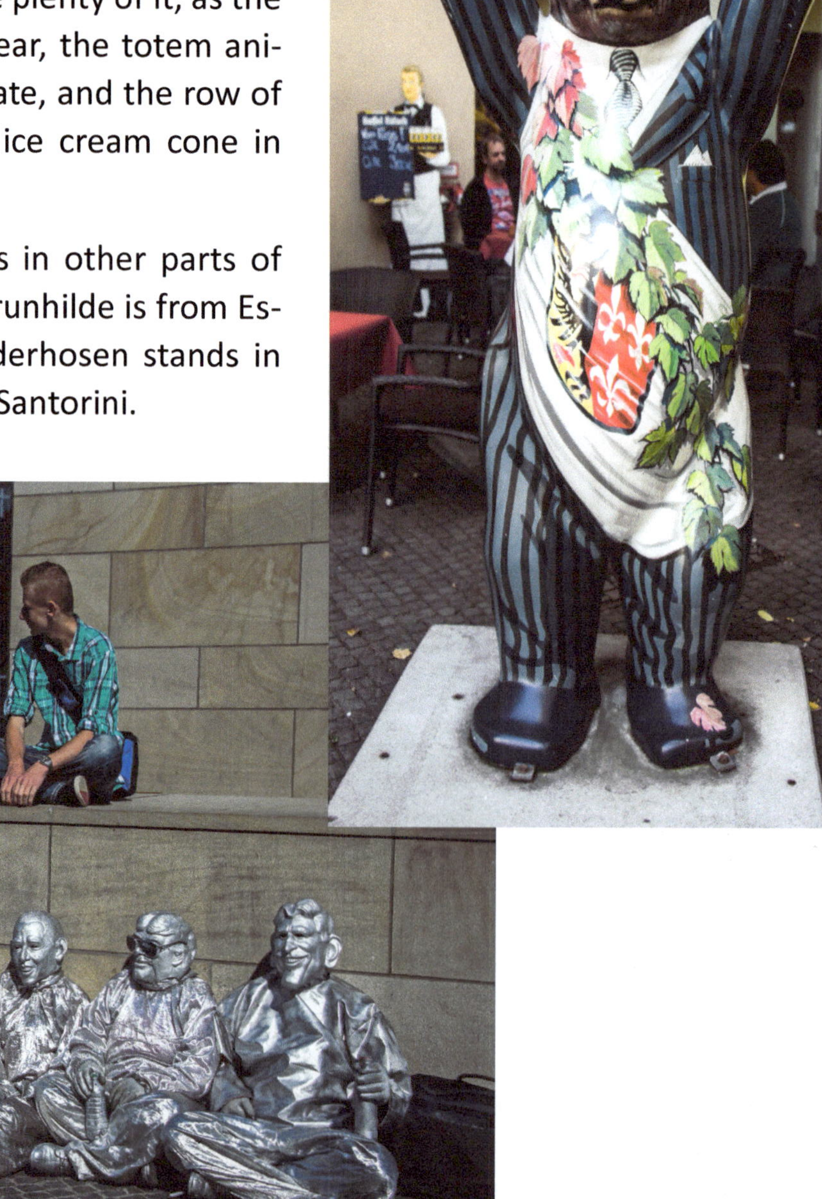

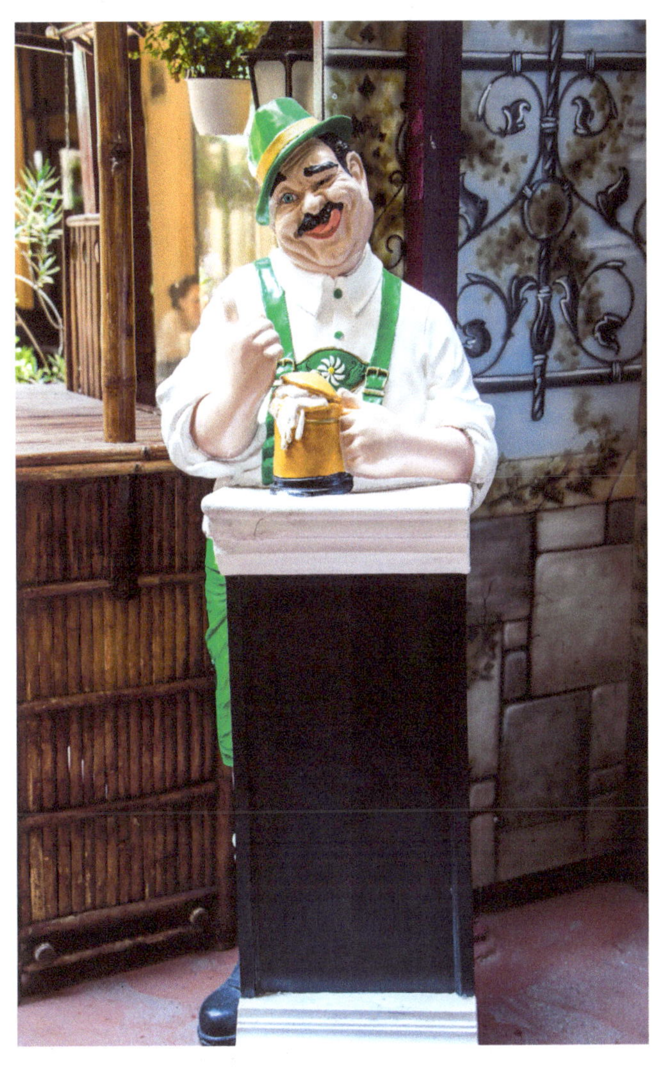

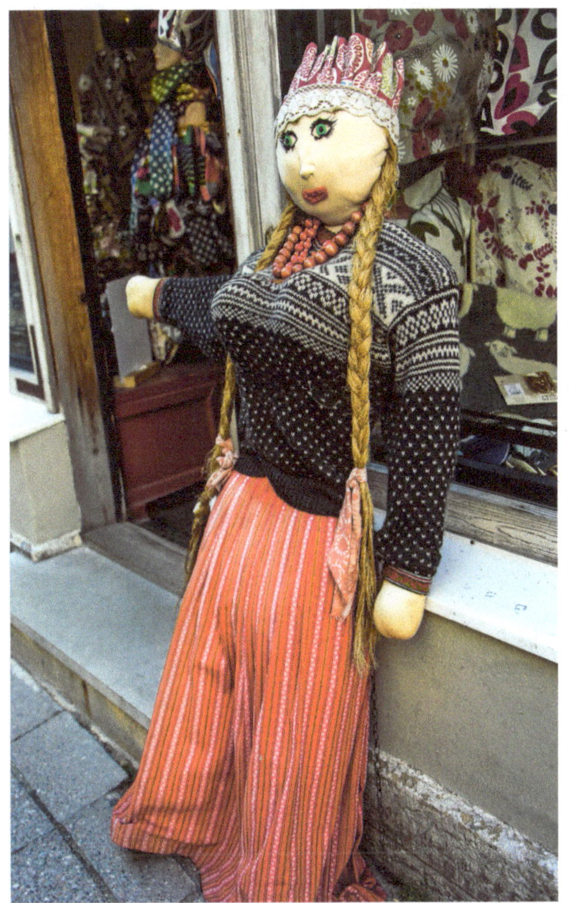

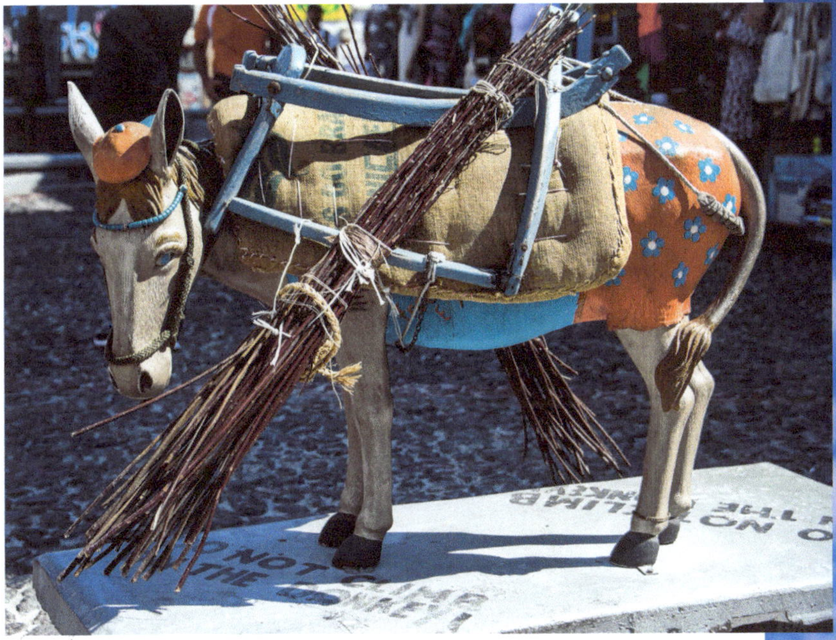

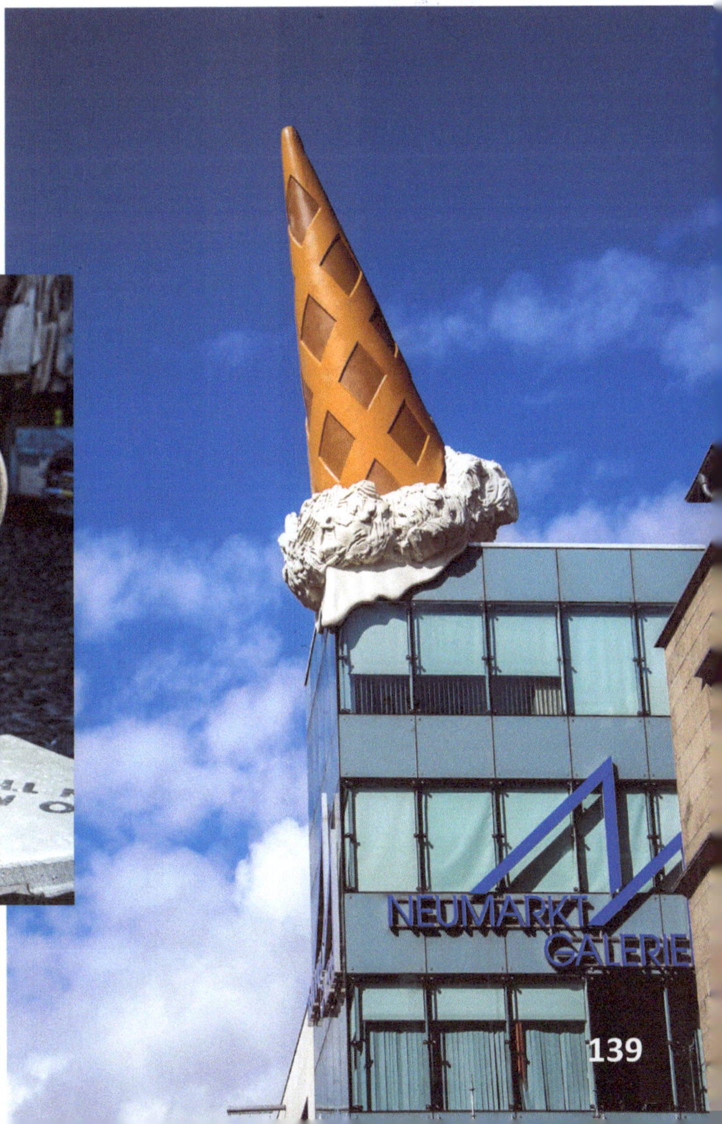

# 20

# HAMBURG

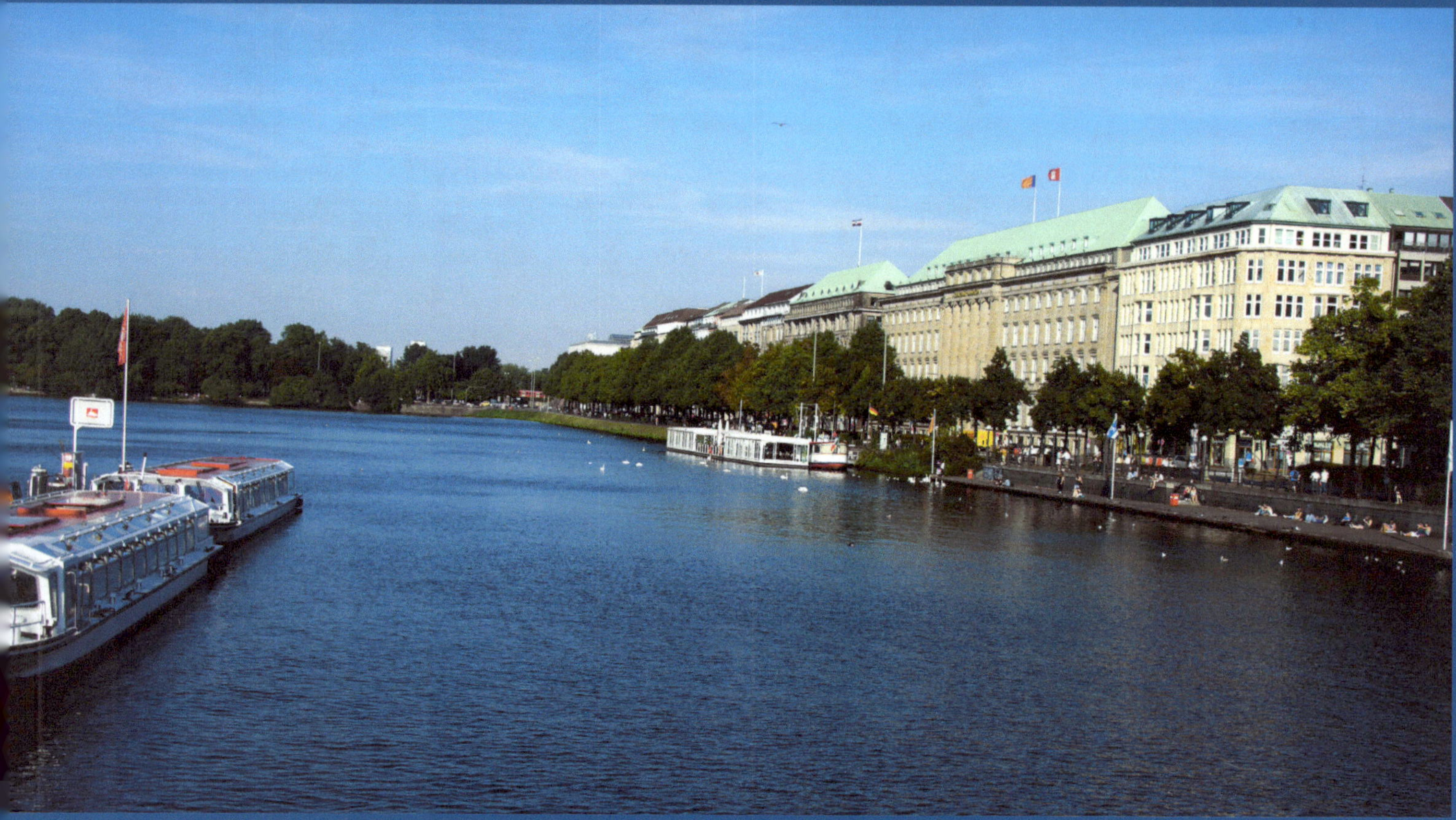

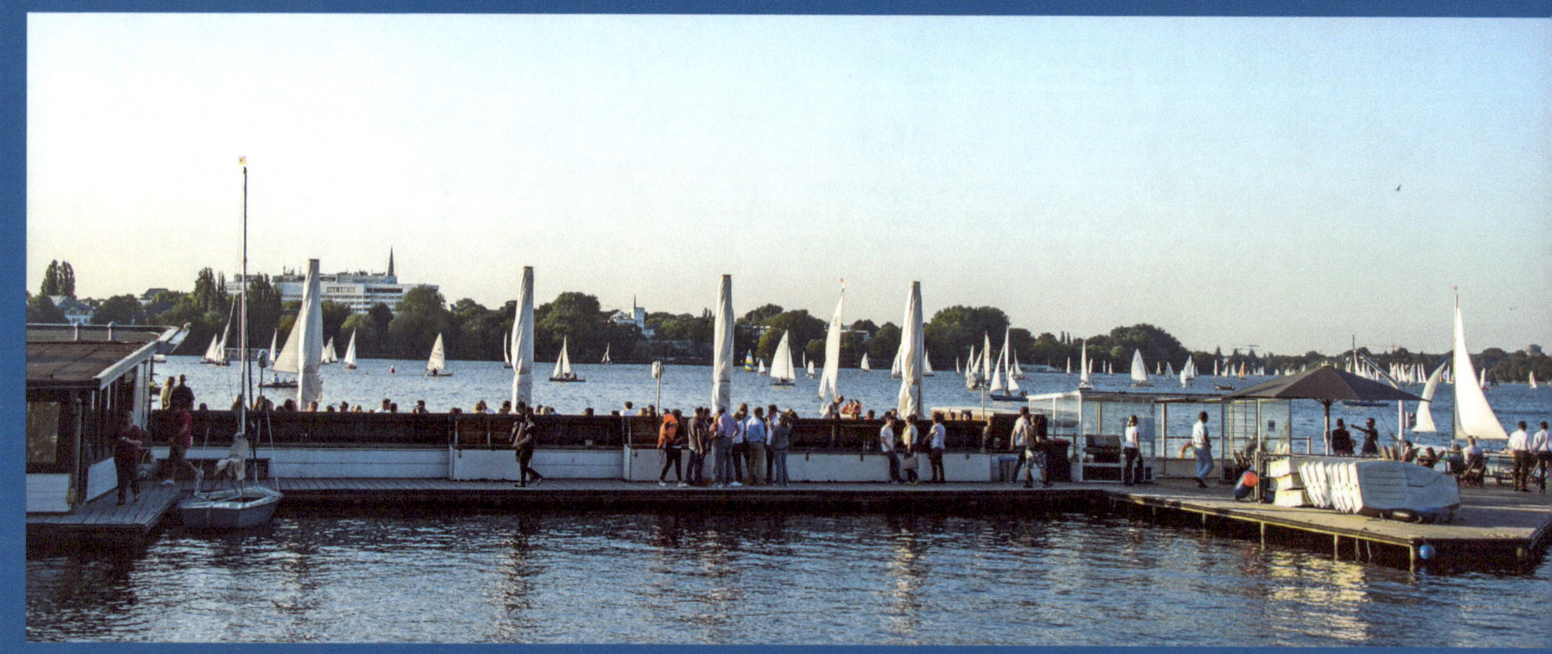

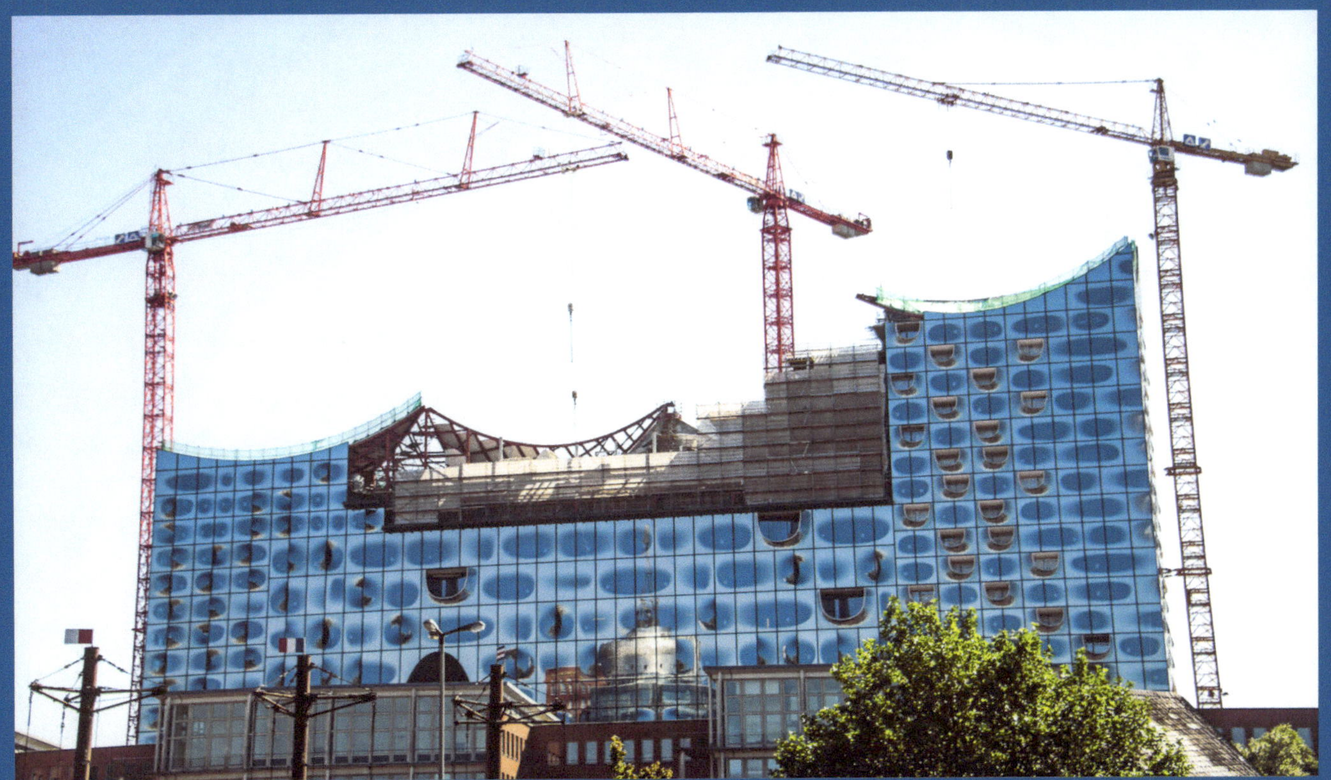

Of the three independent German Hanse atic Leagye cities, Hamburg is the largest. When I lived there from 1993 till 2002, I had a flat near the Hagenbeck Zoo. Lying in bed at night I could hear the chimps chattering.

I started my German music career with Gerig Music Publishing in Cologne in 1984, but it didn't really take off until I returned there in 1988 after a brief stint in Switzerland and started with Phonogram Records, a subsidiary of PolyGram. By the time I moved to Hamburg in 1993, it had become Mercury Records (it's currently Universal Records, by the way). I became head of promotion, which meant that my department was responsible for the promotion of our contracted domestic and international recording artists in the press, on radio and TV, in the clubs, and when they went on tour.

From 1984 to 1998, I looked after 130 of the world's top artists, including Celine Dion, Elton John, Bon Jovi, Metallica and INXS. In 1998, I left the security of being a salaried employee and branched out on my own as a freelancer TV promoter and German-English translator. The record companies would hire me independently to get TV dates for their artists. It was easy work because I had been doing it for so long.

So when I arrived by train in Hamburg from Berlin, the weather was gorgeous, and it was a delight to sit in the beer gardens on the river banks and reminisce with friends. Then it was time to get out again alone with my camera and re-discover this most beautiful of German cities.

Hamburg has two rivers, the Elbe and the Alster. The latter has two parts separated by a bridge—the regular Aussenalster and the Binnenalster, which is essentially a massive lake. There is also a big area called Hafen City, which is going to be the place to go in Hamburg. You see construction everywhere. Basically, Hamburg is like Berlin, a city where the government is pouring a lot of money into building it up.

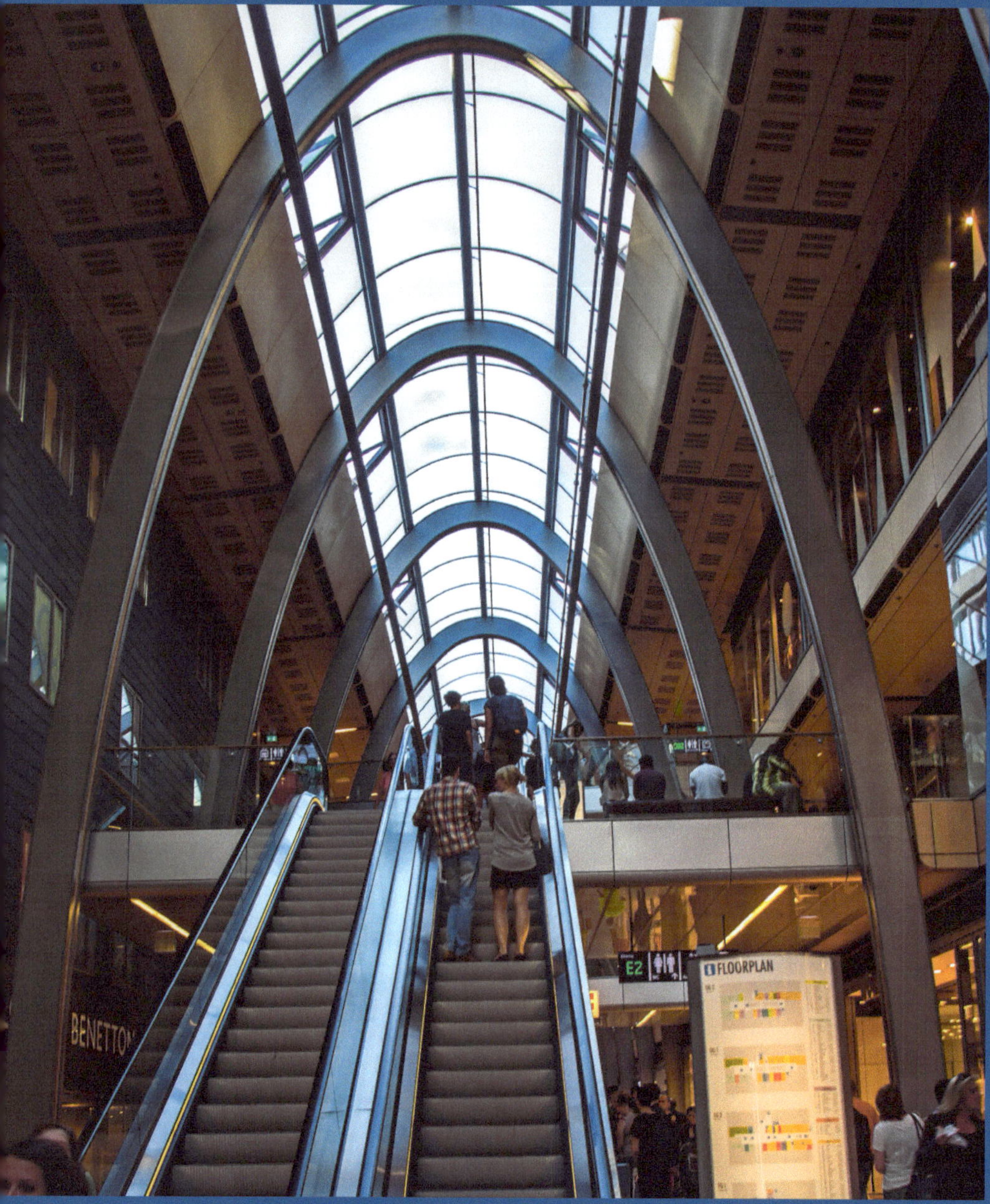

But there are beautiful, older sections, too. This is the Speicherstadt—warehouse city—where Hamburg's old merchants used to sail in with their ships laden with wool, cotton, carpets, herbs and spices, in order to store the cargo and trade freely without having to pay customs. It's the largest warehouse district in the world and a big tourist attraction. There are several museums, including one with a big model railway. Some of the buildings are still used as warehouses, handling one-third of the world's carpet productions along with other goods like cocoa, coffee, tea and electronic equipment.

It was fun to reconnect with my old haunts and discover new ones.

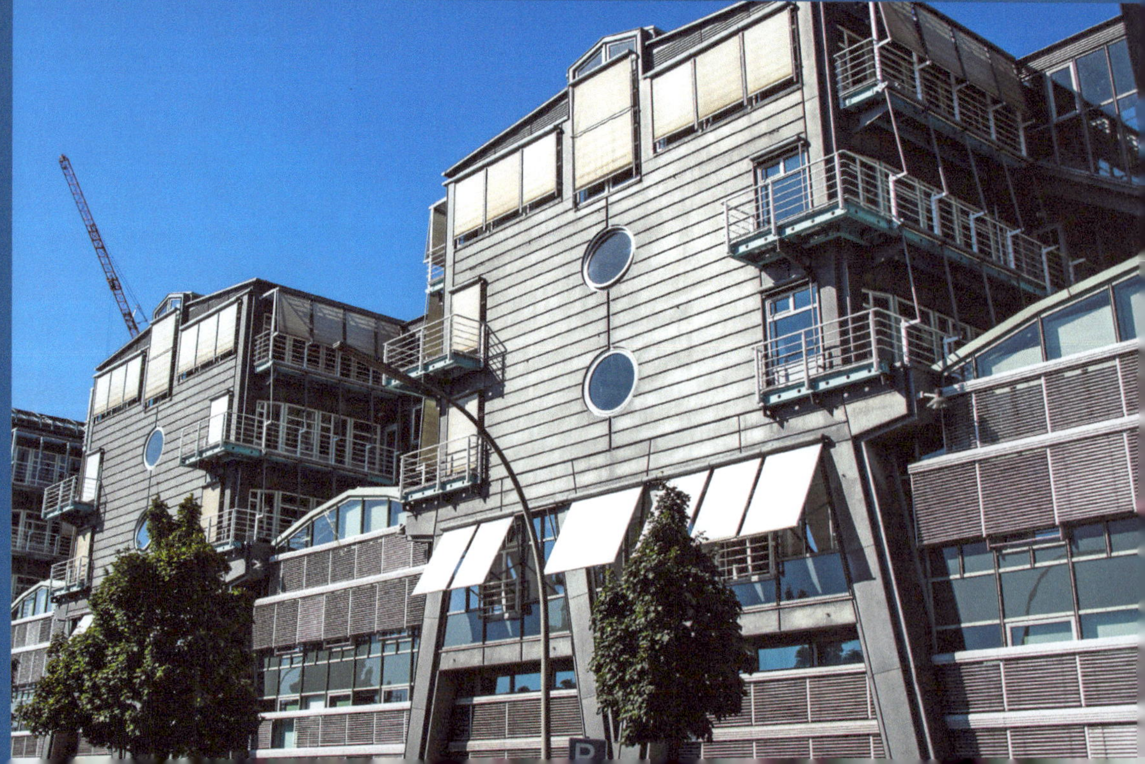

The new arcade on the *Binnenalster* is sleek and ultramodern. I took the picture of the housing complex on the way to the Elbe River because I liked the way the balconies were just hanging off the front.

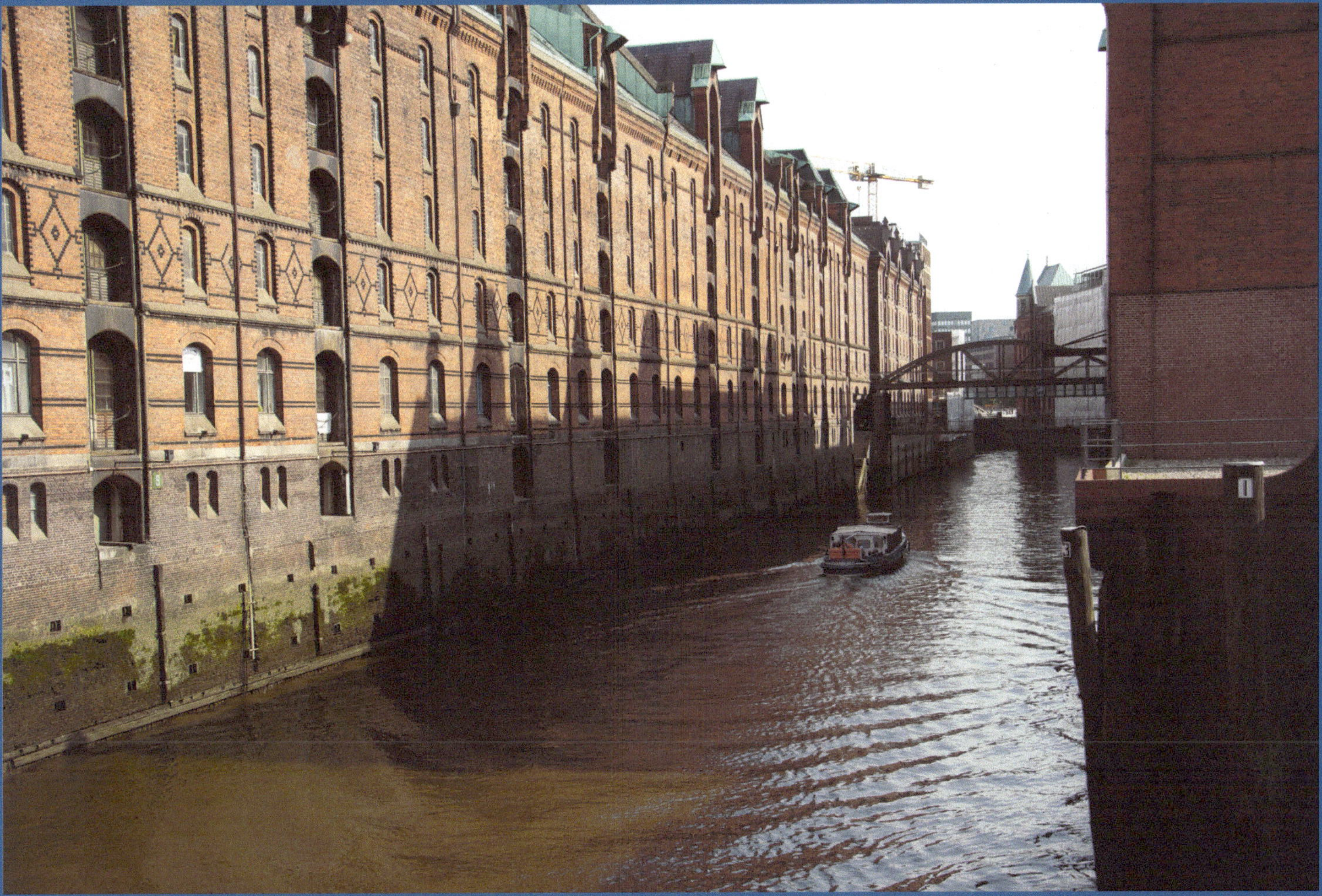

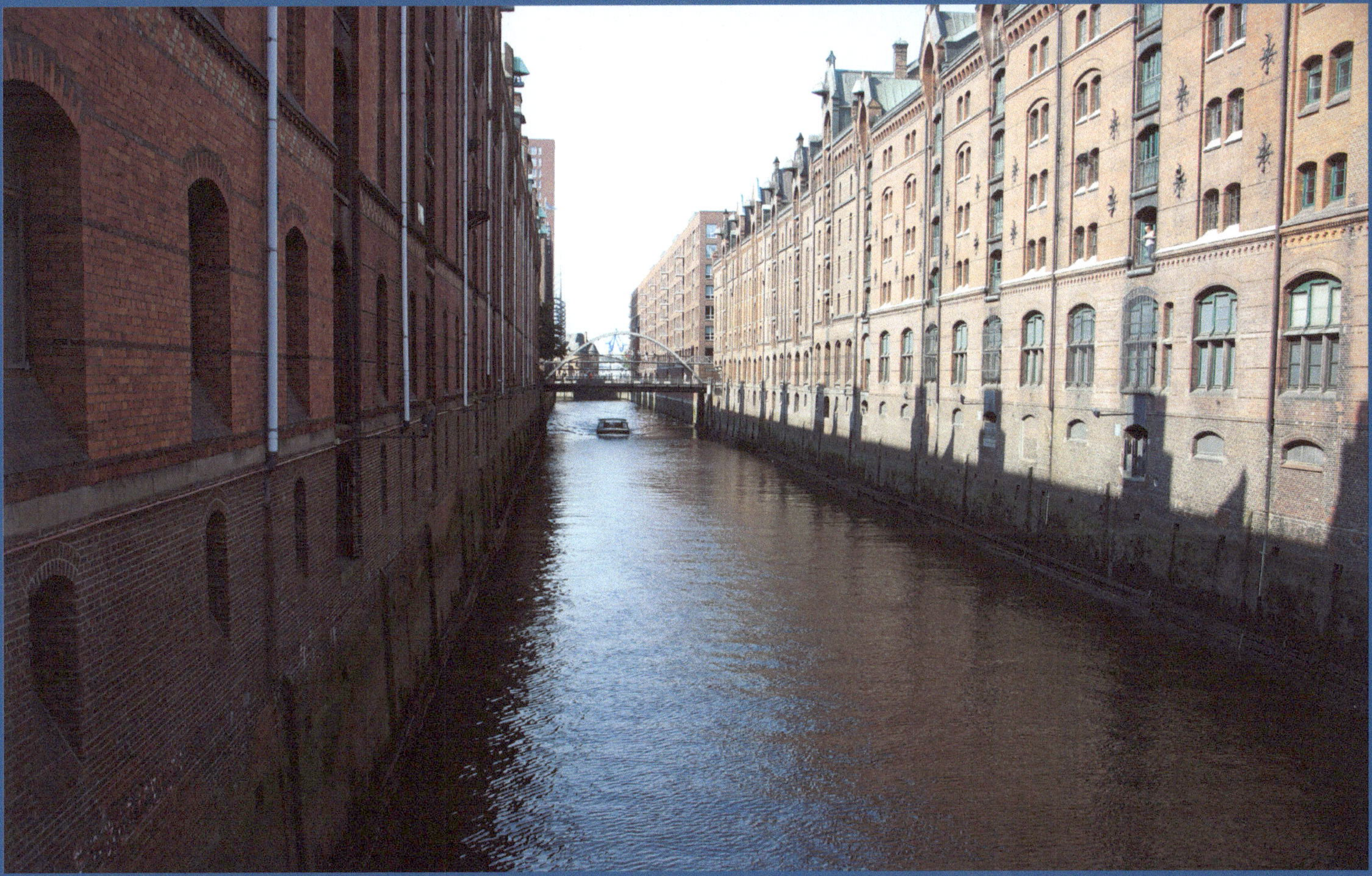

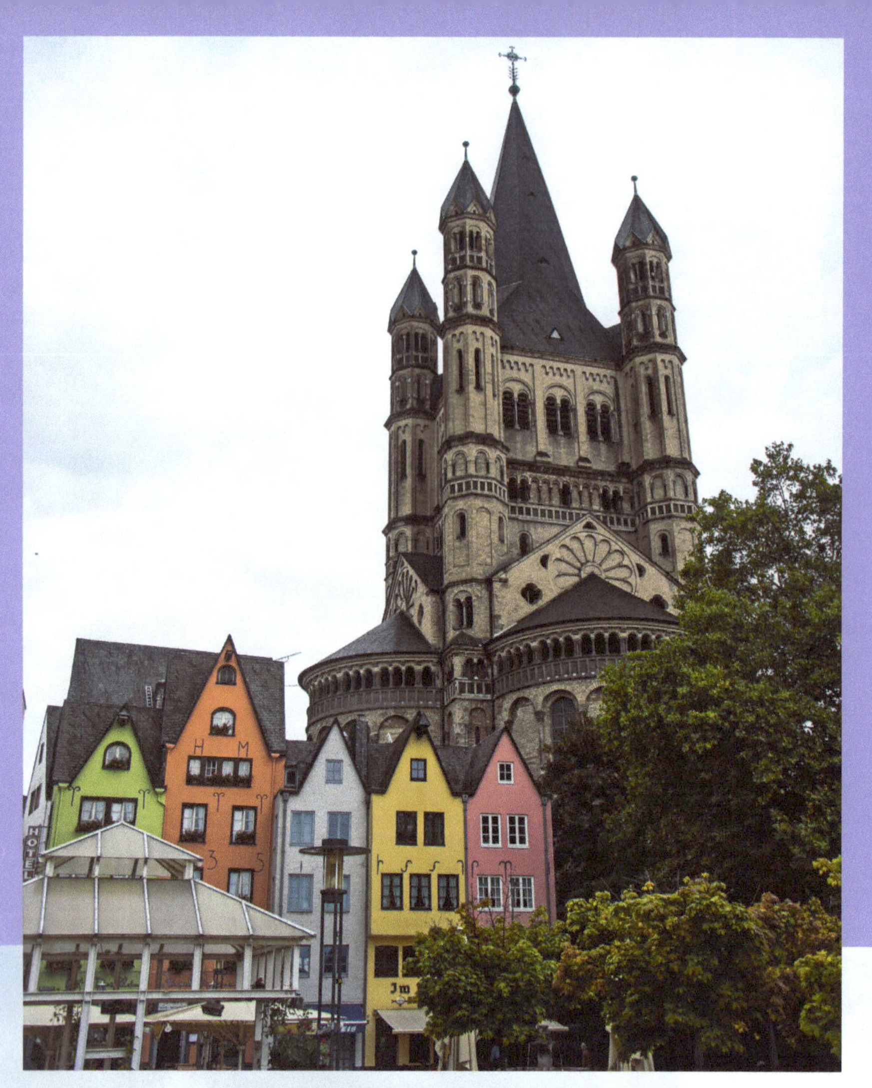

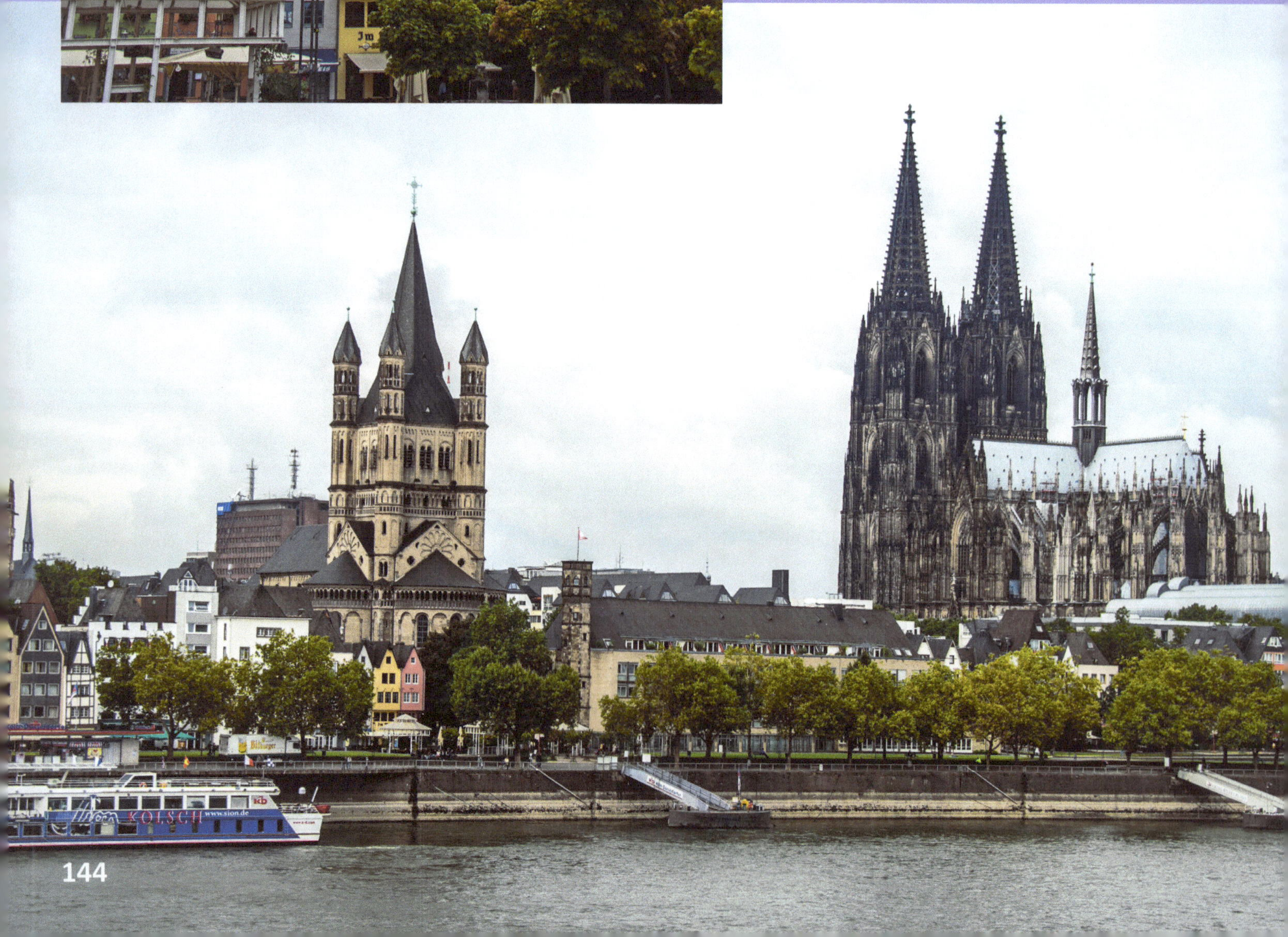

# 21

# COLOGNE

I took the train south from Hamburg to Cologne, which I consider my second home after Sarasota. During the 18 years I lived there I worked at a great job which got me into the German/world music market, and I traveled extensively in continental Europe.

The city, going back to antique Roman times is commercial, cosmopolitan, and it has an energy and vibrancy matched by few other European cities. The people speak a fantastic dialect, which I managed to master, and they know how to have a good time. None of the stereotypes of Germans being stuffy, relentlessly anal and serious-minded apply to Cologne. The annual *Karneval* is a season of festivities, costumes, parades and celebration that is the envy of other German and European cities.

The procession before Lent is incredible. I used to accompany the *Karneval* groups that I looked after back then. It was more grueling than any other job I've ever had because they sometimes play 10 to 15 gigs a day. I included the photo below, which I took in 2011, because I wanted you to get the idea of how wonderfully mad and madcap things can get.

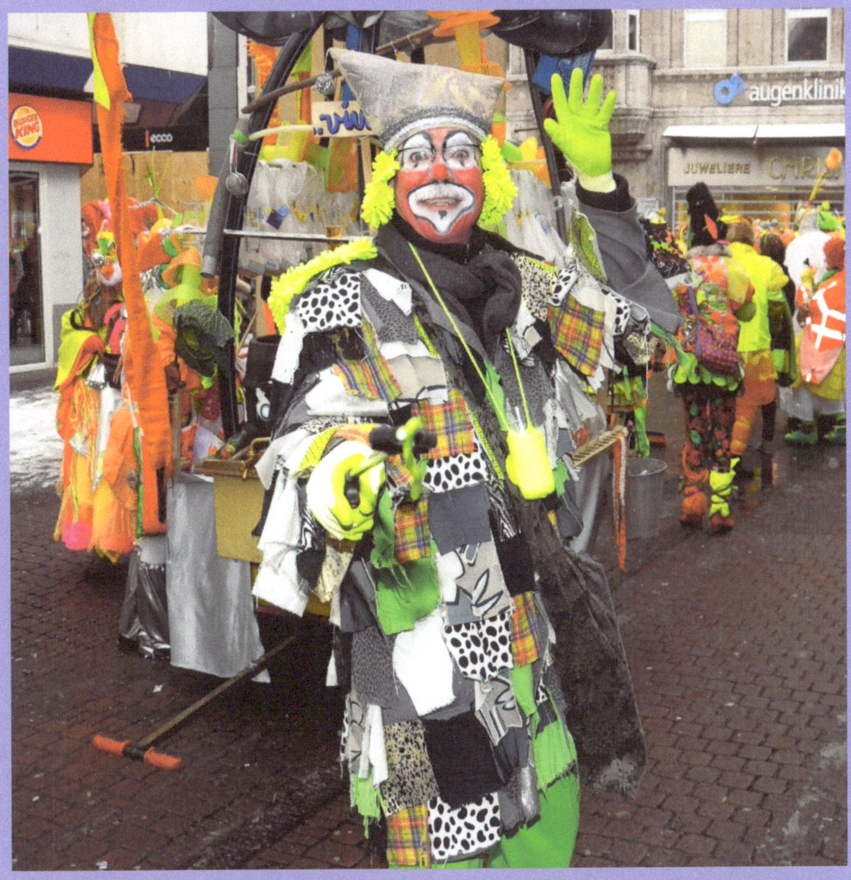

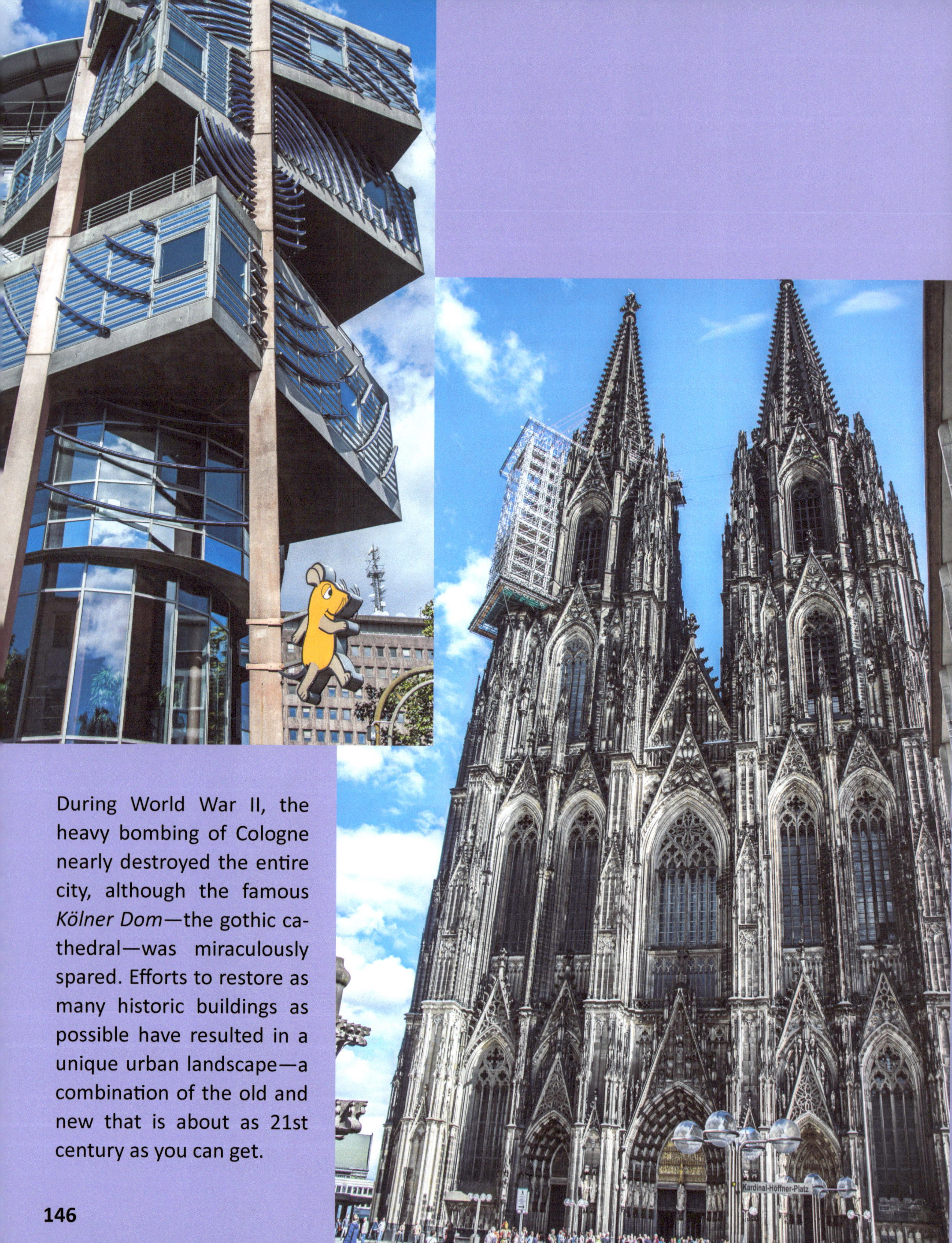


During World War II, the heavy bombing of Cologne nearly destroyed the entire city, although the famous *Kölner Dom*—the gothic cathedral—was miraculously spared. Efforts to restore as many historic buildings as possible have resulted in a unique urban landscape—a combination of the old and new that is about as 21st century as you can get.

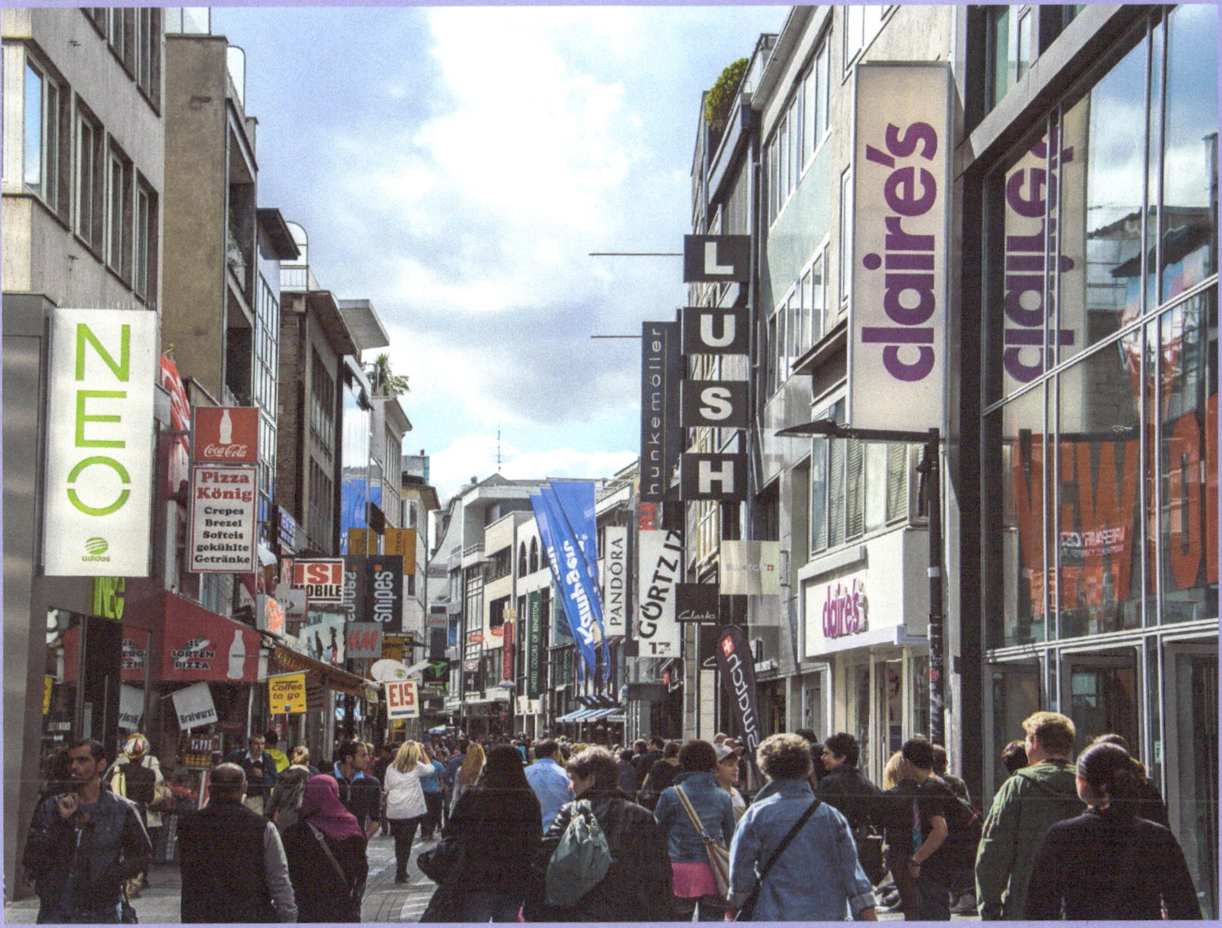

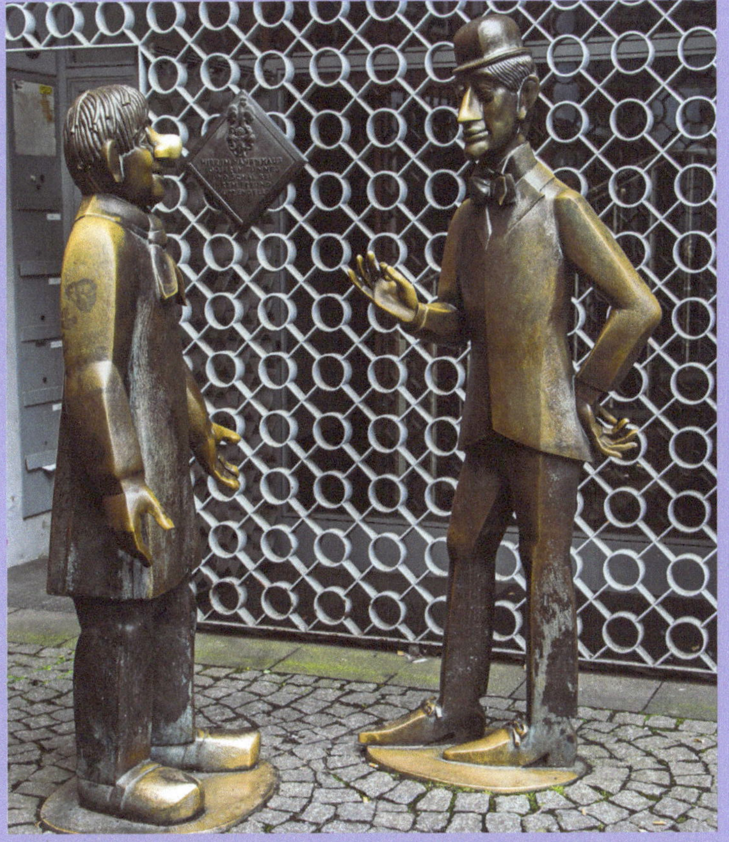

The shopping streets have the same stores as everywhere in Germany, but the *Hohe Strasse* and the *Schildergasse* pedestrian zones have the reputation of commanding the highest commercial rents in Germany.

The statue is of Tünnes and Schäl, two puppets from rival theaters in the 1800s, which have come to represent the culture and humor of the city. Tünnes is a *gemütlich*—laid-back—country rube with more savvy than one would expect from a farmer. Schäl—the name refers to being two-faced and squinty-eyed—is the quintessential city slicker. He is skinnier and wears a tailcoat. The two are featured in countless jokes in Cologne dialect.

# 22
# FRANKFURT

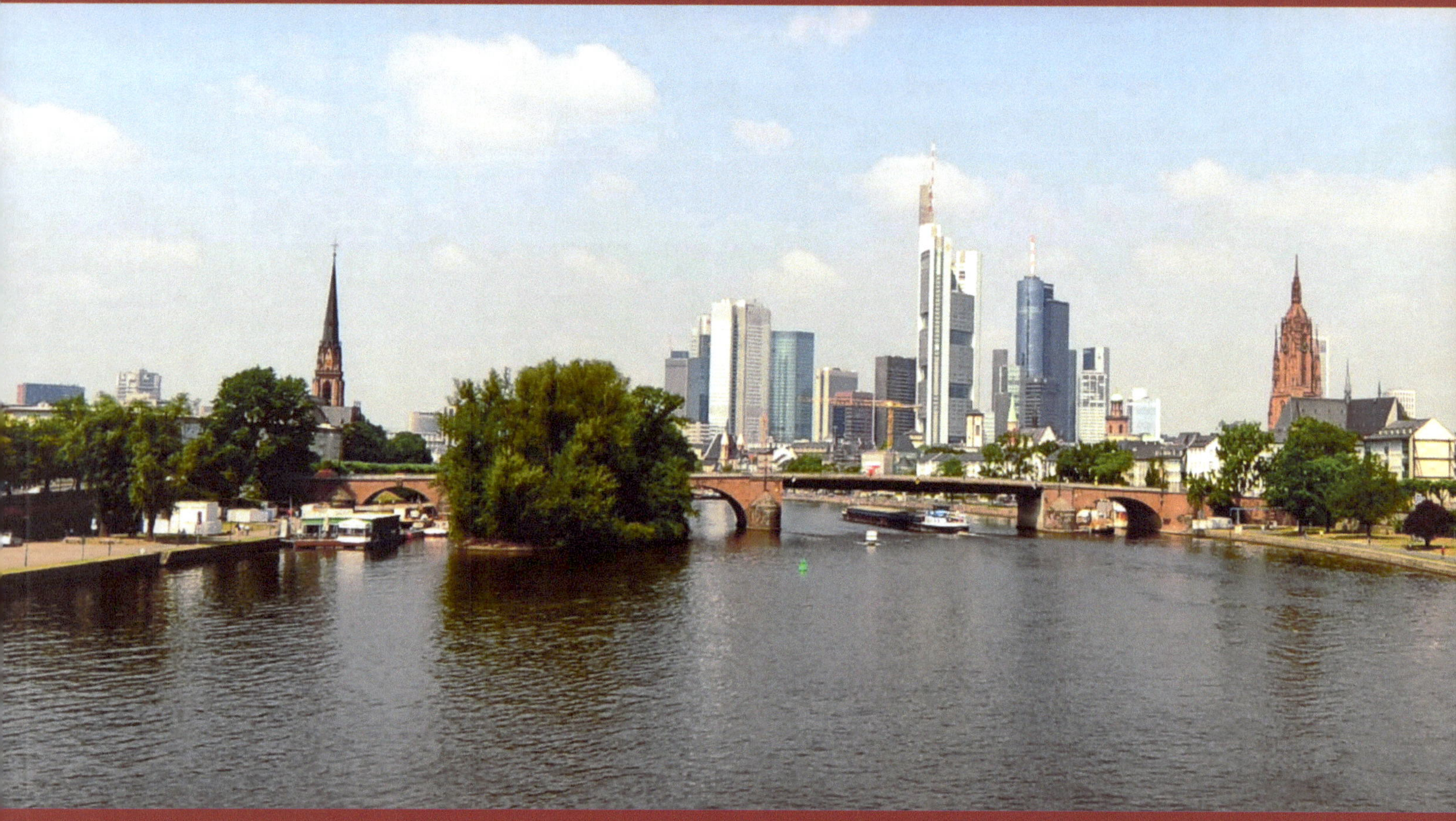

After Cologne I was keen to get back to Sarasota and start earning money again, so I took a train to Frankfurt and spent the night at an airport hotel. As the next day was September 11, one of the busiest airports in the world was remarkably emptied of people. I suppose they were superstitious of that fateful date and preferred not to fly that day.

As a result, there were seats to be had on every plane. On the Lufhansa flight back to Atlanta, I had a whole row of seats to myself, which was fabulous. I was able to stretch out and relax.

I left Europe with mixed feelings. I knew that I'd go back to Hamburg and Berlin. I'm looking forward to seeing Budapest with my wife, Maria. I don't plan to return to any of the other cities except maybe Jerusalem; but I'll return to Cologne, because the minute I set foot in that city, I feel at home.

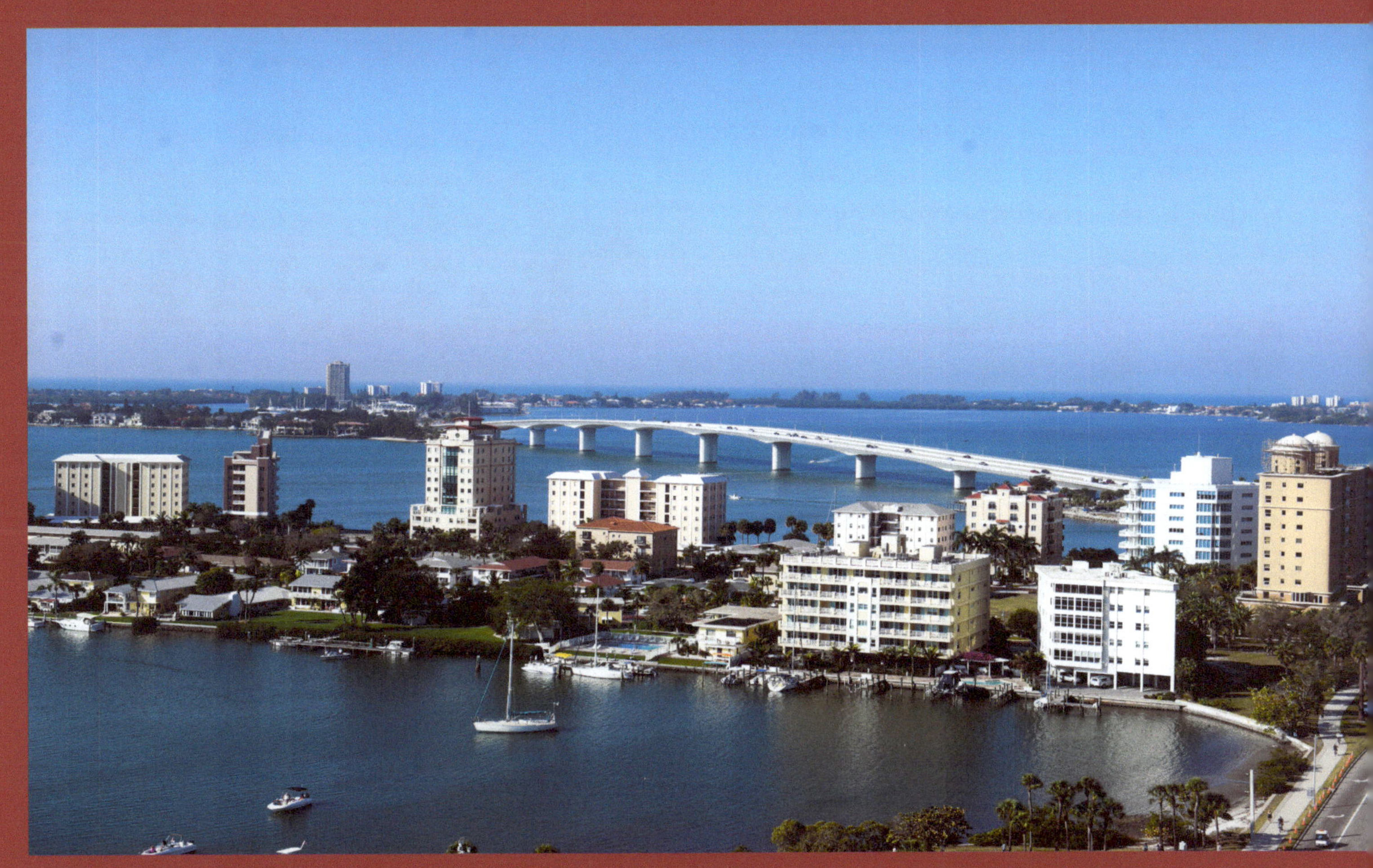

I returned to Sarasota, excited to be back and see Maria, Sam and all of my friends, but also ready to do it again. I decided then and there that I would do a “Walkabout Australia-New Zealand” the following summer. Only this time I ‘d take twice as long.

# Old and New Friends

One of the pleasures of traveling is visiting old friends and making new ones.

I started out in Malta with my brother Andy and sister-in-law Sian at my nephew's wedding.

On Santorini, Vassili and his sister Cassandra at Remezzo Villas became more than hotel proprietors and hosts.

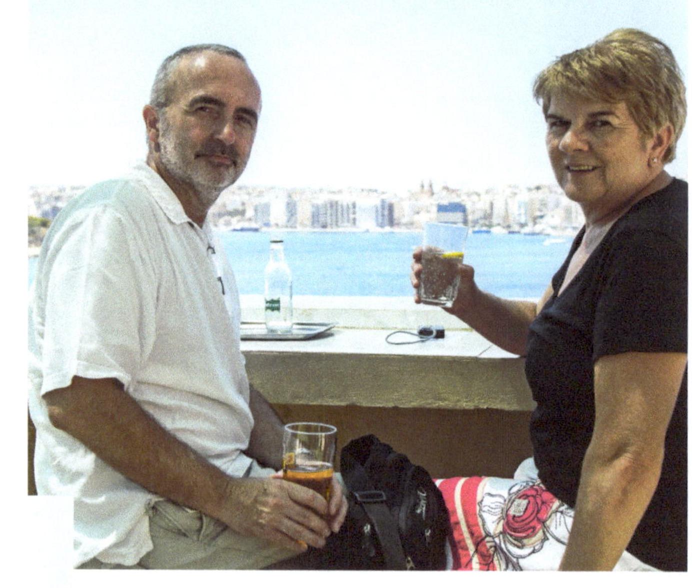

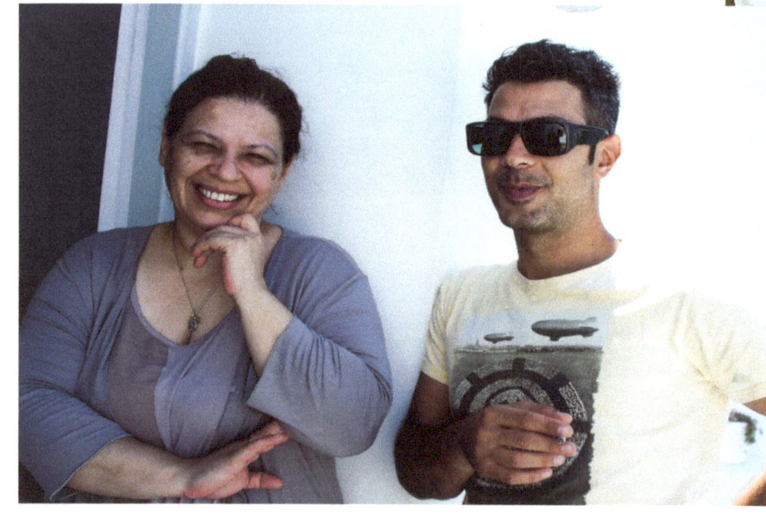

In Berlin I met up with former record-company colleagues Corinna Poeszus (pictured below with her dog Suri), Dagmar Rumpenhorst (with her daughter Rosalia), and Jochen List.

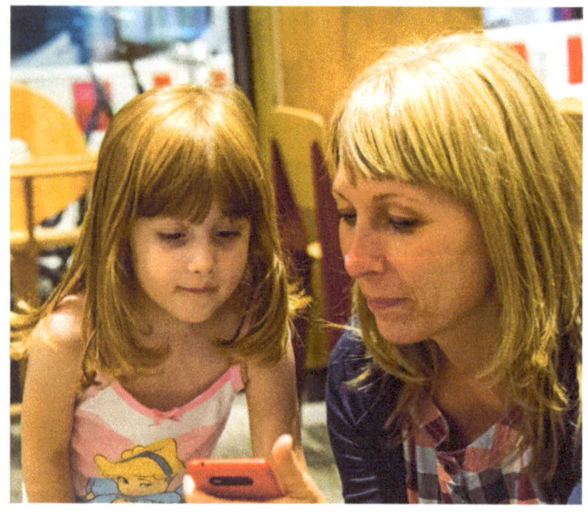

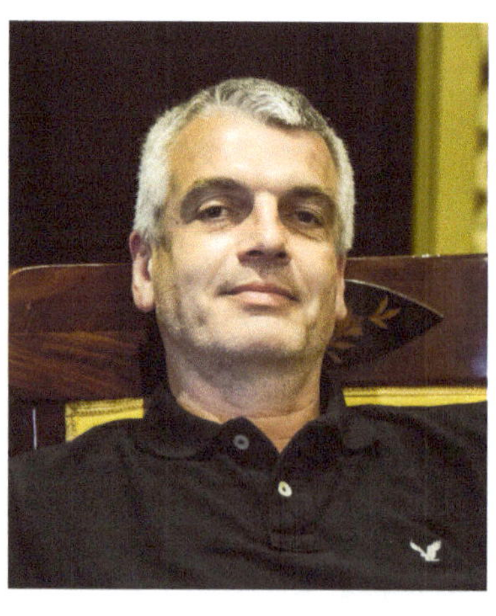

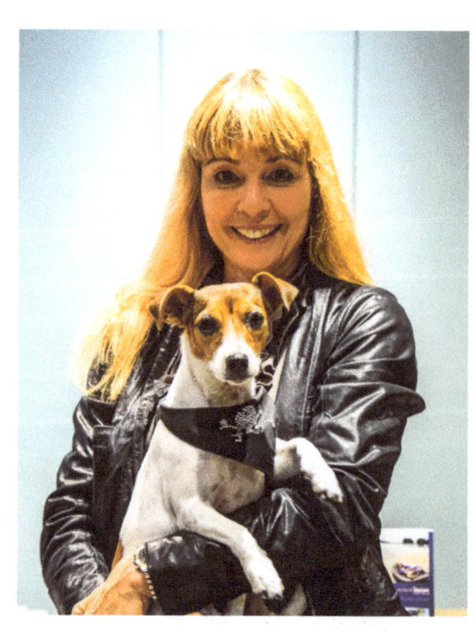

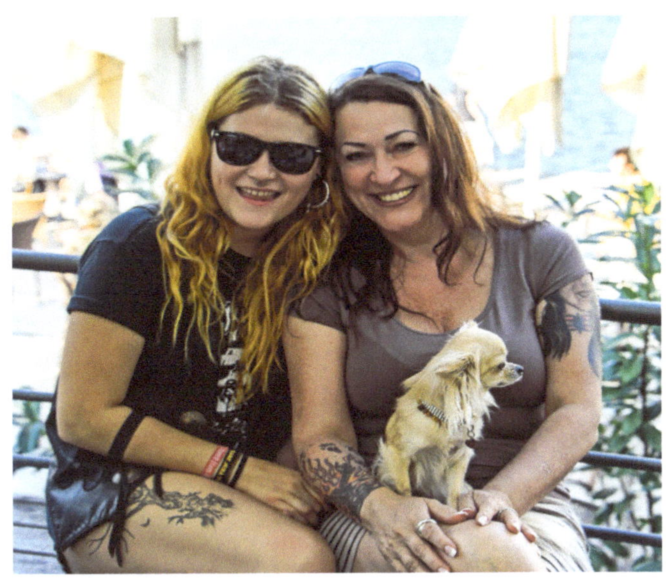

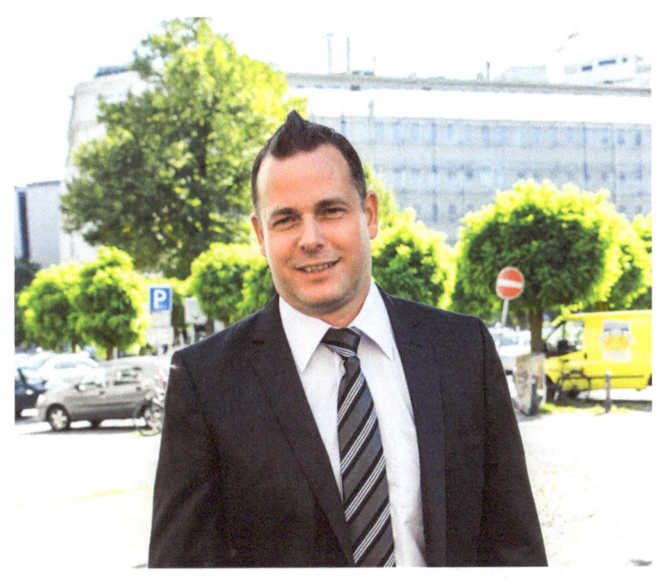

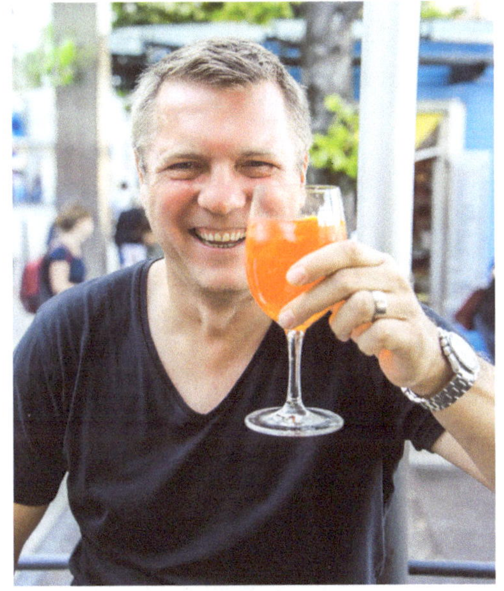

In Hamburg it was a delight to sit in the beer gardens on the river banks and reminisce with friends like my friend and bank-manager Frank Kleinfeld (in suit and tie), Sabina and Joanna Simon (with their dog Peppi), as well as my PolyGram ex-colleague Jens Geisemeyer.

While I was in Cologne, I had a reunion with my friends Gebhard and Helmi Harter and Rudi and Andrea Knelleken in the nearby suburb of Stommeln. I've been friends with Gebhard, Helmi and Rudi since 1979—we were in a *Kegelklub* (skittle club) together for many years. A visit to Cologne wouldn't have been complete without sitting down to dinner of Schnitzel and *Kölsch* beer with them and reminiscing about the "good old days."

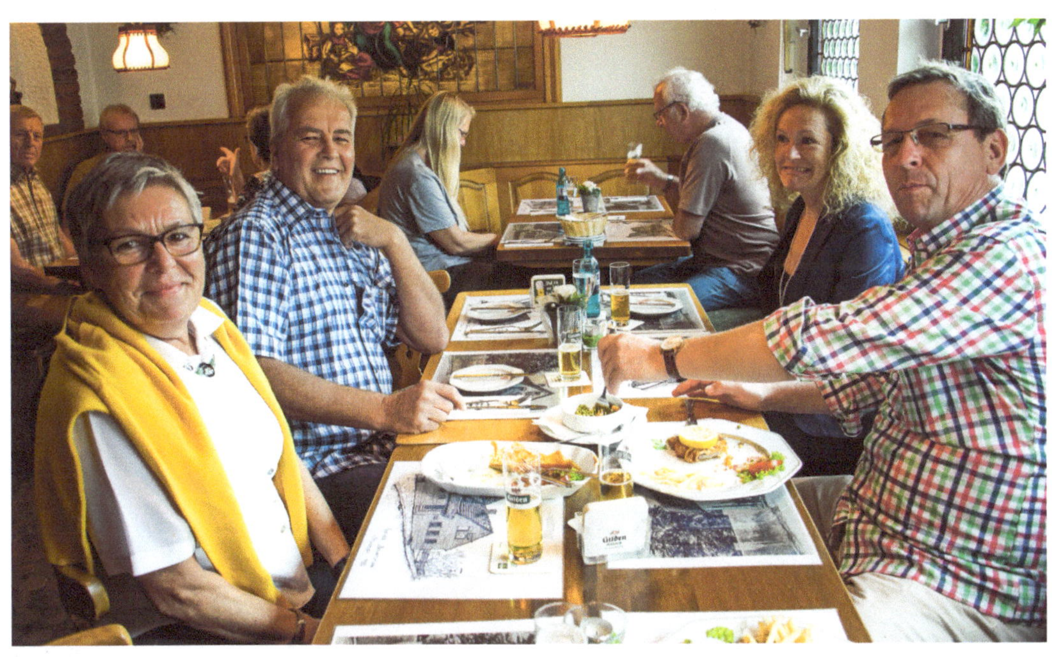

# Acknowledgments

Thanks...

...first and foremost to my wife Maria for her eternal support;

...to Chris Angermann for putting this book together, making sure it contains a good cross-section of photos from every country, and listening to me rattle on about them;

...and to Danielle Beatt for taking care of my dog Sam for two months, certainly no easy task;

...also to the lovely people I met along the way: Piotr P., Sabina & Joanna S., Jens G., Ute D., Wojtek M., Corinna P., Sharon P., Dagmar R., Gebhart & Helmi H., and Jochen L;

...for their endearing comments and enthusiasm, in no particular order: Toni B., Jennifer M., Jennifer S. and Jennifer G., Anny S., Fran S., Dan H., Phil K. & Dennis S., Deb K., Janice L., Mary L., Gila M., Georgia G., Winifried S., Catherine M., Erin M., Sammy L., Roger C., Tracey M., Betsy M., Carolyn M., Kim A., Jeanette L., Jo R., Veronica B., Veronica M., Rick H., Molly S., Kim M., Sheri N., Bern W., Virginia C., Ruth L., Kelly D., Darci J., Tina B., Sean M., Annette D., Diana C., Diana B., June L. and Ed A., Denise M. & Linda P., Jaime & Julie DiD., Phil & Linda DeN., Valerie P., Wendy D.C., LeeAnne M., Cheryl M., Suzette J., Janice I. & Agnes R., Barbara B., Joan G., Terri K., Wendy F., Lisa B., Renee H., Rebecca B. & Renee P., Rosenda C., Sally S., Linda L., Dalia K., Maurice R., Susan B., Jay & Patty J., Jeanie G., Mollie N., Margaret W., Flora M., Phil C., Margery L., Sharon B.F., Diana P.A., J.P.K. & Karen T, Steve S., Pedro & Dolly R., Nik & Erendira W., Christopher B., Jeffrey & Virginia O., Teri D., Michael & Terri K., Jake J., Diana C., Marcia D., Richard and Michael S.

I know I did the trip by myself, but I left a lot of lovely people here at home who awoke every day to guess my next destination and, as they put it, "live vicariously through my travels" via Facebook. Their comments and critiques became my daily invaluable traveling companions, and although there were periods when I didn't speak to anyone on the road, my Facebook friends were always there for me at the end of my iPhone and laptop.

And so it is to them that I dedicate this book—all 5,000 of them—for staying the course from Malta to Frankfurt; and for their daily comments, most especially to Marilyn Billib, Lynne Carpenter, Tammy Halstead, Anna Kearns, Vivian Kouvant, Vivienne Porterfield and Deborah Wynkoop.

# Final Tally

Number of days on walkabout: 53
Miles traveled: 18,000

Number of countries visited: 15
Number of countries I'd go back to: 11
Number of countries I never want to see again: 4
Number of cities visited: 22

Number of hotels: 20

Number of cameras: 1
(Nikon D4 with an AF-S Nikkor 28-300mm 1:3.5-5.6G ED VR lens)

Number of photos taken: No idea, but not that many—quality, not quantity...

Number of beers drunk: No idea, but too many—quantity, not quality...

Pairs of shoes worn: 1
Insoles purchased: 2
Pairs of socks purchased and thrown away: 15
Underwear purchased and thrown away: 1—just kidding! Or am I?...

Number of flights: 12
Number of ferries: 3
Number of buses (between cities): 5
Number of trains: 5

# Postscript

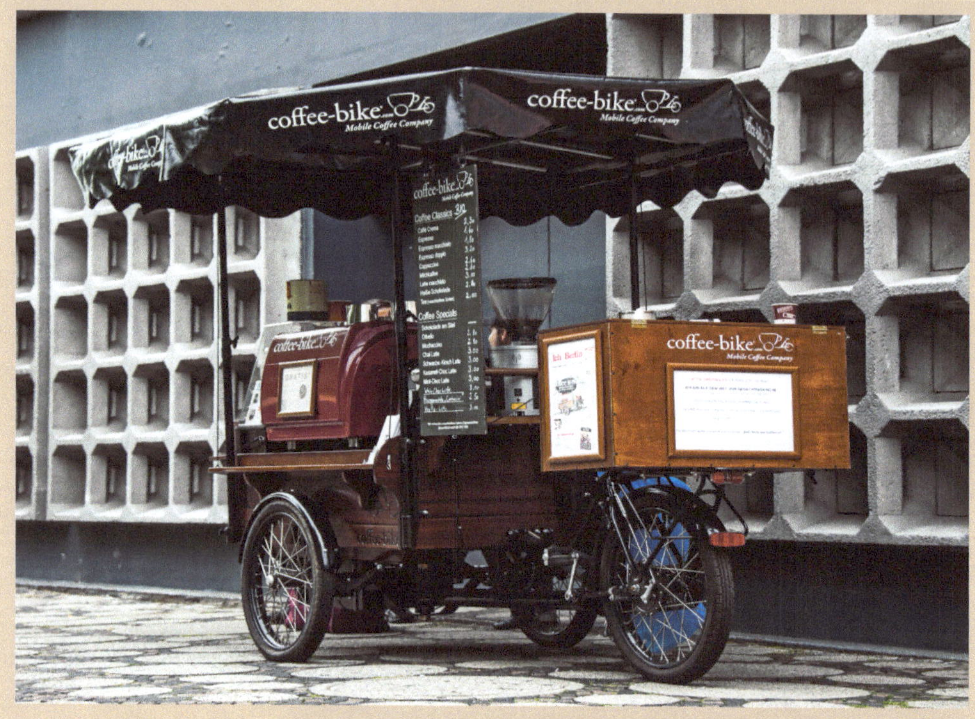


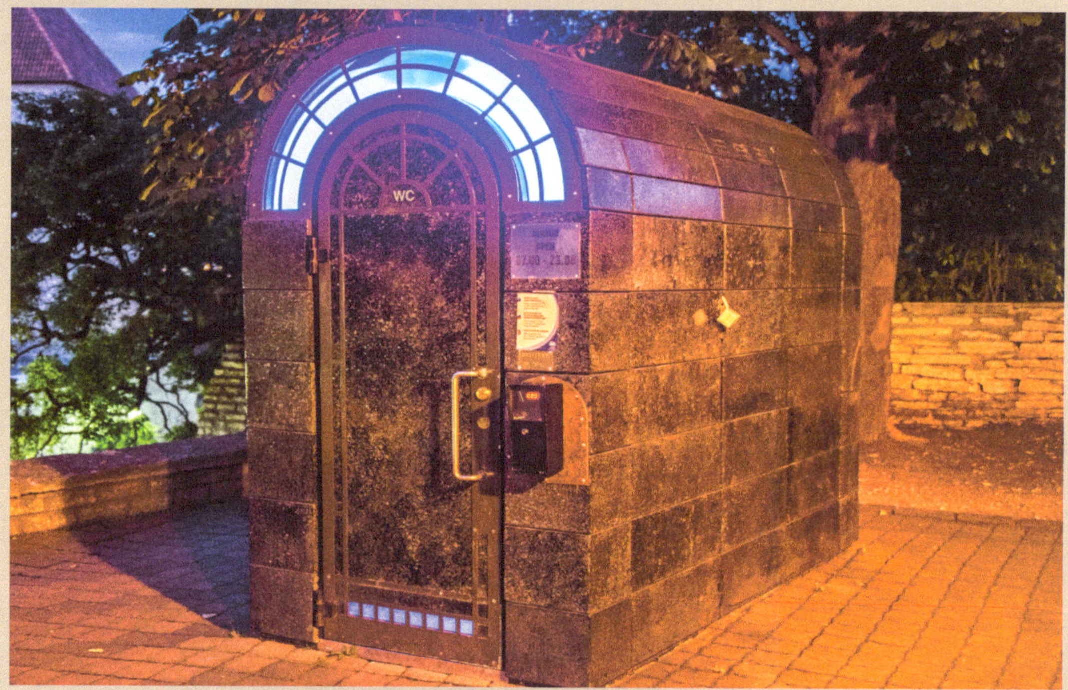


Two travel necessities:

1. Coffee (Berlin)
2. Public toilets (Tallinn)

www.ingramcontent.com/pod-product-compliance
Lightning Source LLC
LaVergne TN
LVHW070123110826
845147LV00002B/175

*9781938842214*